Devils and Realist
vol. 2

story by **Madoka Takadono**
art by **Utako Yukihiro**

Cast of Characters

William

A brilliant realist from a famous noble family. As the descendent of King Solomon, he is an Elector with the authority to choose the representative king of Hell.

Kevin

William's capable butler. He has served generations of the Twining family, and manages all of William's affairs.

Dantalion

Seventy-first Pillar of Hell who commands its leading thirty-six armies. He is Grand Duke of the Underworld and a candidate to represent the king.

Sytry

Twelfth Pillar and Viscount of Hell who leads sixty armies. Sytry is Prince of Hell and a candidate to represent the king.

Isaac

William's classmate who is obsessed with supernatural phenomena.

The Story Thus Far

The once-rich William is penniless after the failure of his uncle's business when the demon Dantalion appears before him. Dantalion demands that William, the Elector, choose him as king in exchange for tuition and living expenses. Next, a second candidate for king shows up in the form of Sytry. Complete realist that he is, William refuses to acknowledge the world of demons and vows to have nothing to do with either of them. They insist that they will stay in the human world until a representative king has been selected and, in the meantime, plan to enjoy life while masquerading as students.

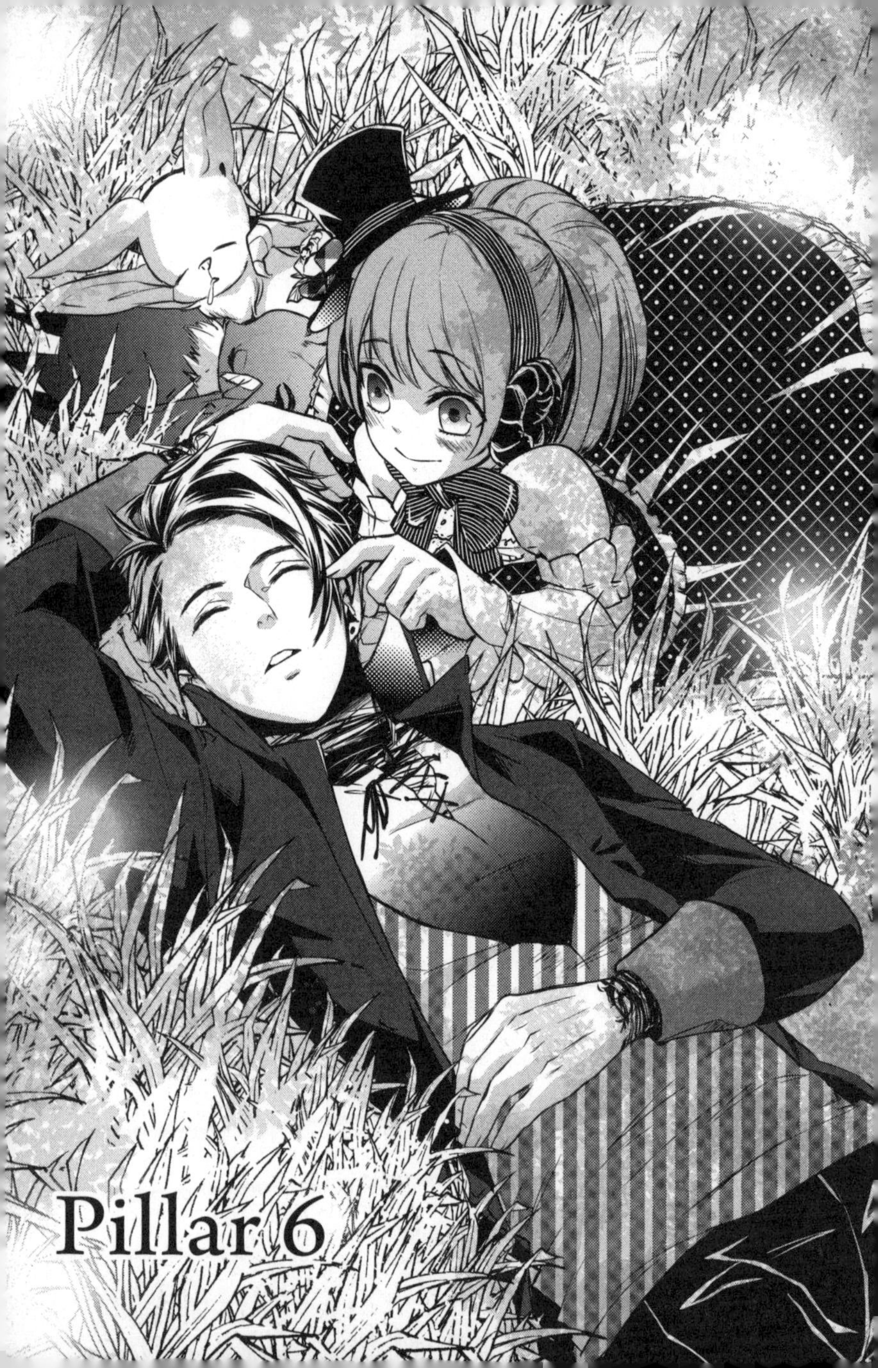
Pillar 6

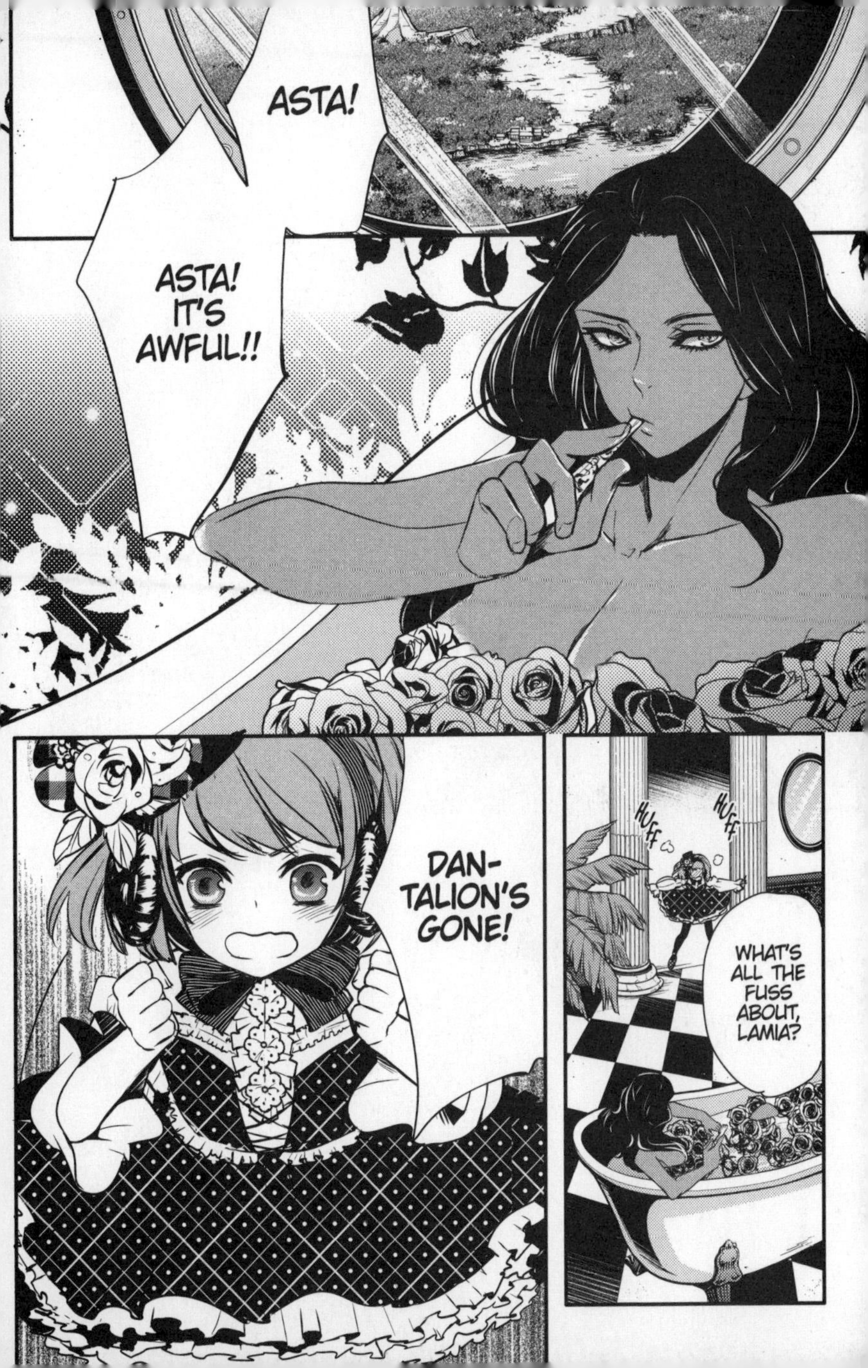
ASTA!
ASTA! IT'S AWFUL!!
HUFF
HUFF
WHAT'S ALL THE FUSS ABOUT, LAMIA?
DAN-TALION'S GONE!

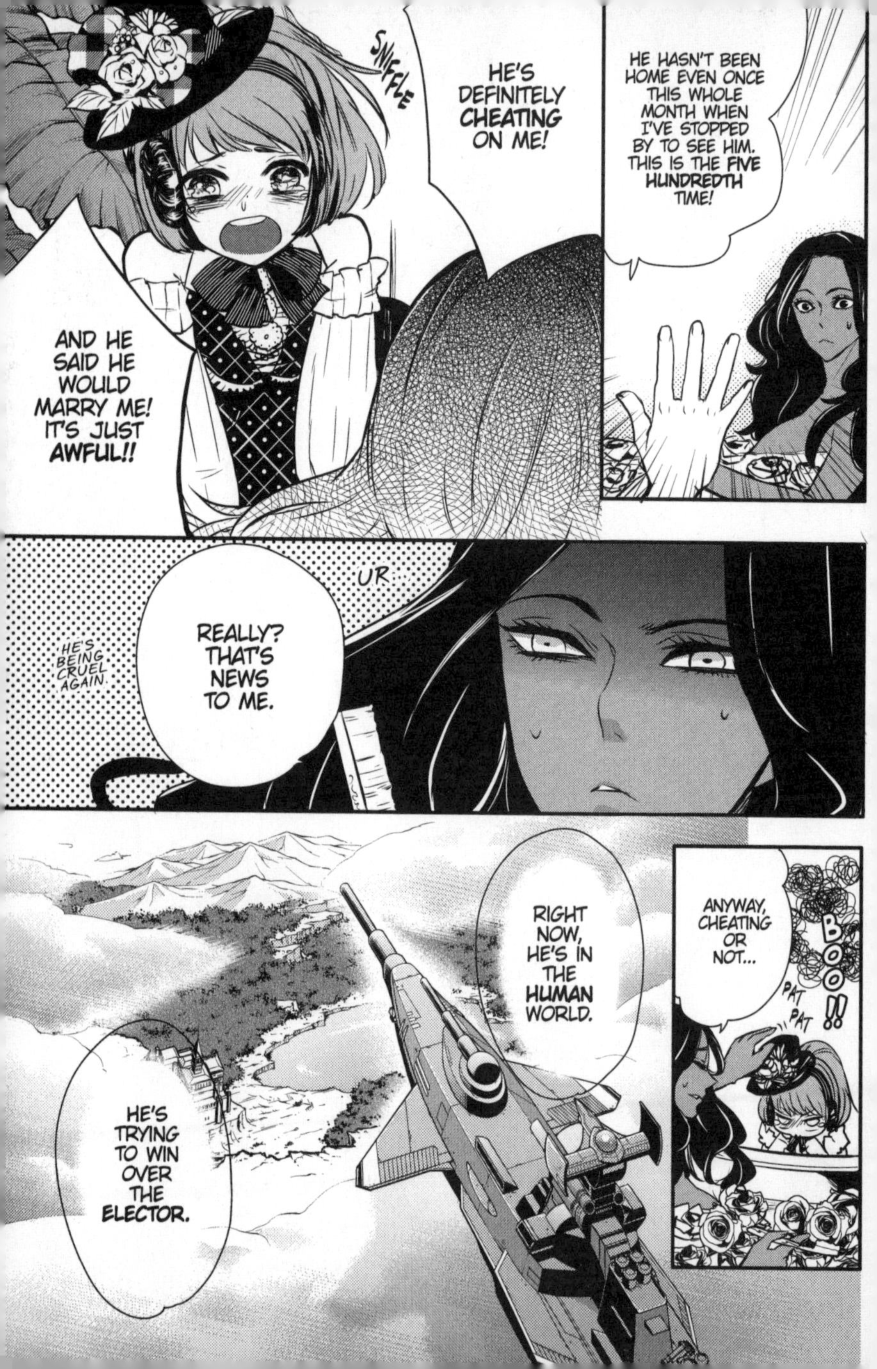
HE HASN'T BEEN HOME EVEN ONCE THIS WHOLE MONTH WHEN I'VE STOPPED BY TO SEE HIM. THIS IS THE FIVE HUNDREDTH TIME!
SNIFFLE
HE'S DEFINITELY CHEATING ON ME!
AND HE SAID HE WOULD MARRY ME! IT'S JUST AWFUL!!
UR...
REALLY? THAT'S NEWS TO ME.
HE'S BEING CRUEL AGAIN.
ANYWAY, CHEATING OR NOT...
BOOO!!
PAT PAT
RIGHT NOW, HE'S IN THE HUMAN WORLD.
HE'S TRYING TO WIN OVER THE ELECTOR.

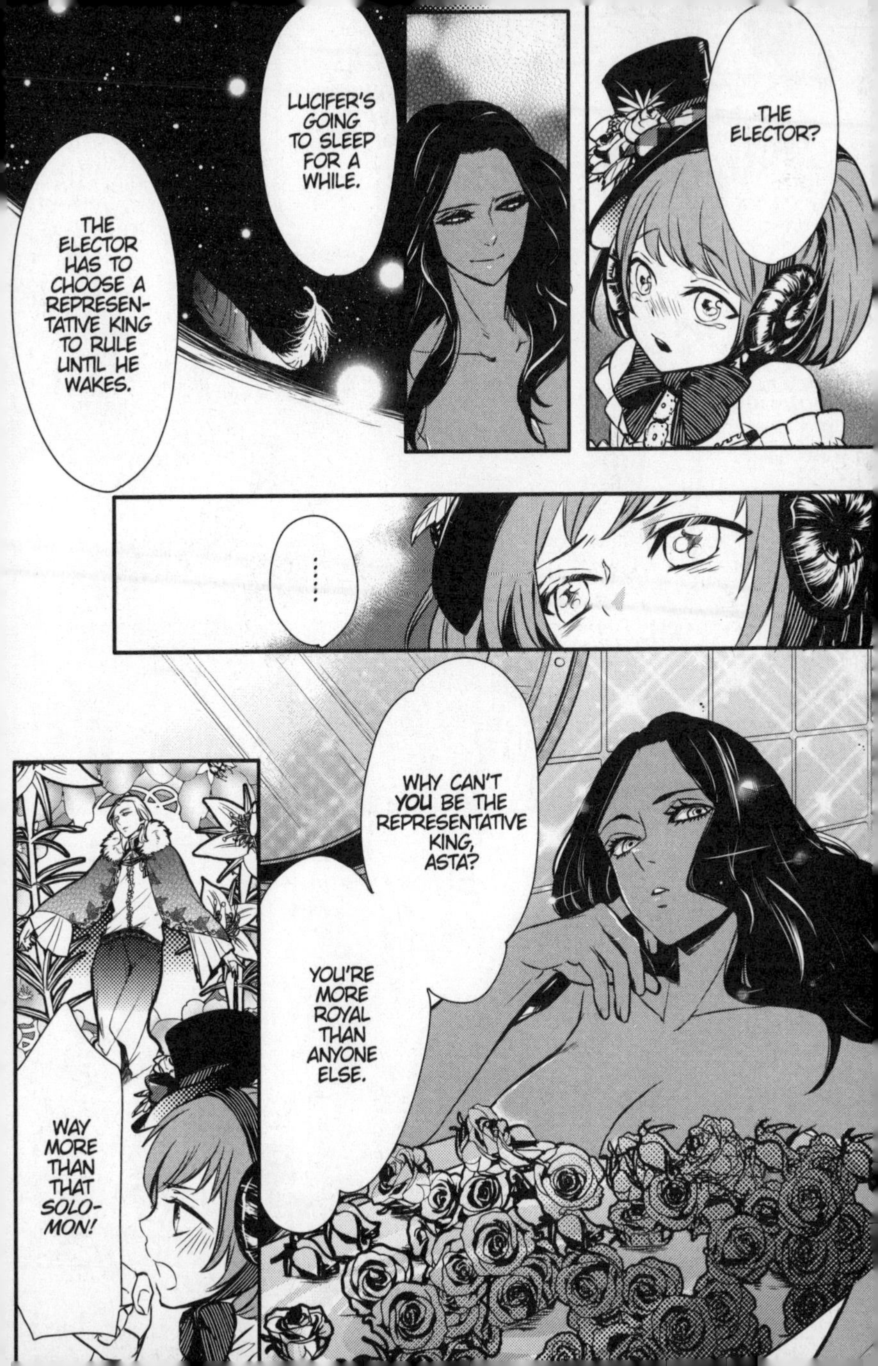
THE ELECTOR?
LUCIFER'S GOING TO SLEEP FOR A WHILE.
THE ELECTOR HAS TO CHOOSE A REPRESENTATIVE KING TO RULE UNTIL HE WAKES.
......
WHY CAN'T YOU BE THE REPRESENTATIVE KING, ASTA?
YOU'RE MORE ROYAL THAN ANYONE ELSE.
WAY MORE THAN THAT SOLOMON!

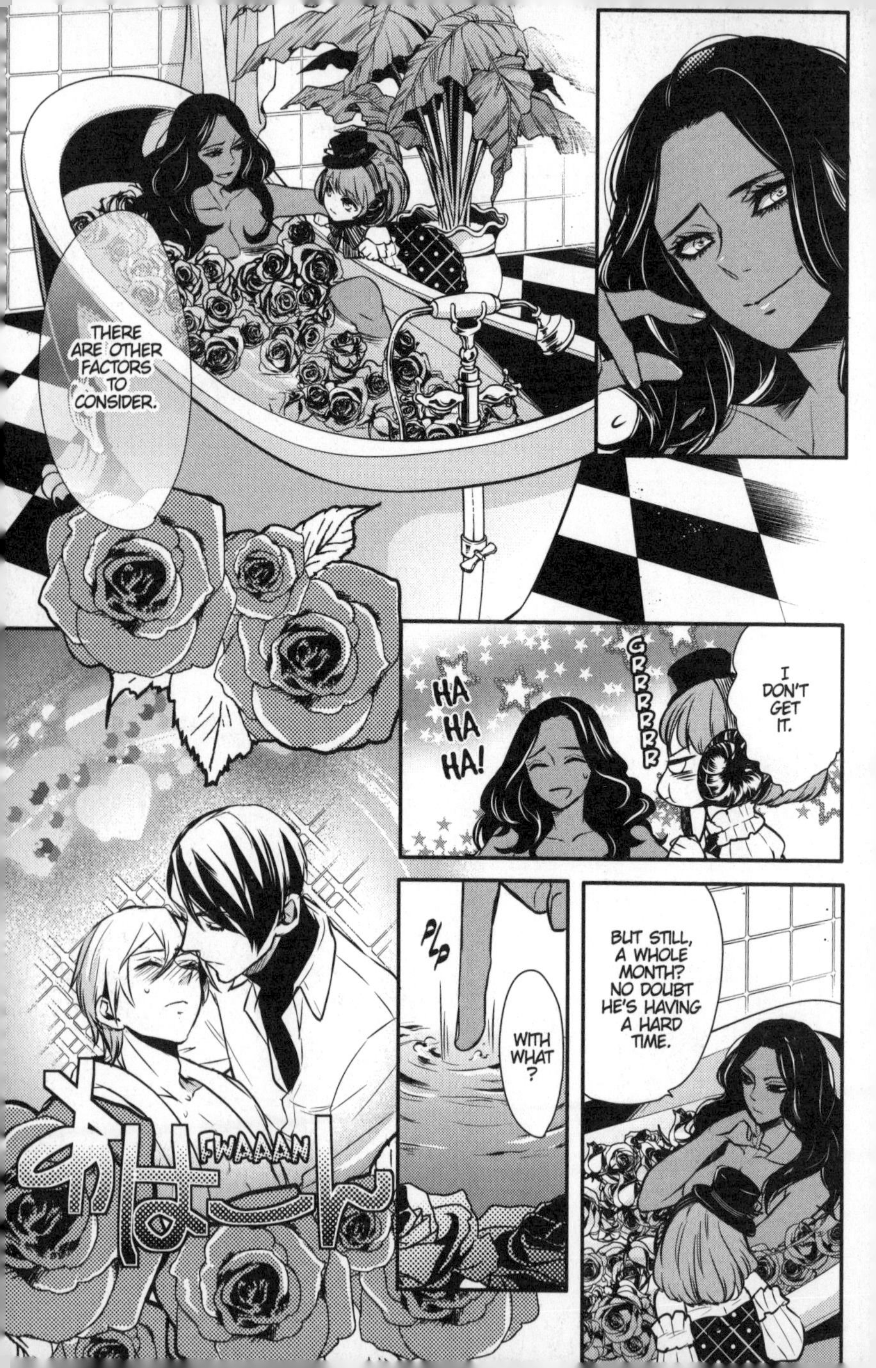
THERE ARE OTHER FACTORS TO CONSIDER.
I DON'T GET IT.
GRRRRRR
HA HA HA!
BUT STILL, A WHOLE MONTH? NO DOUBT HE'S HAVING A HARD TIME.
PLP
WITH WHAT?
FWAAAN

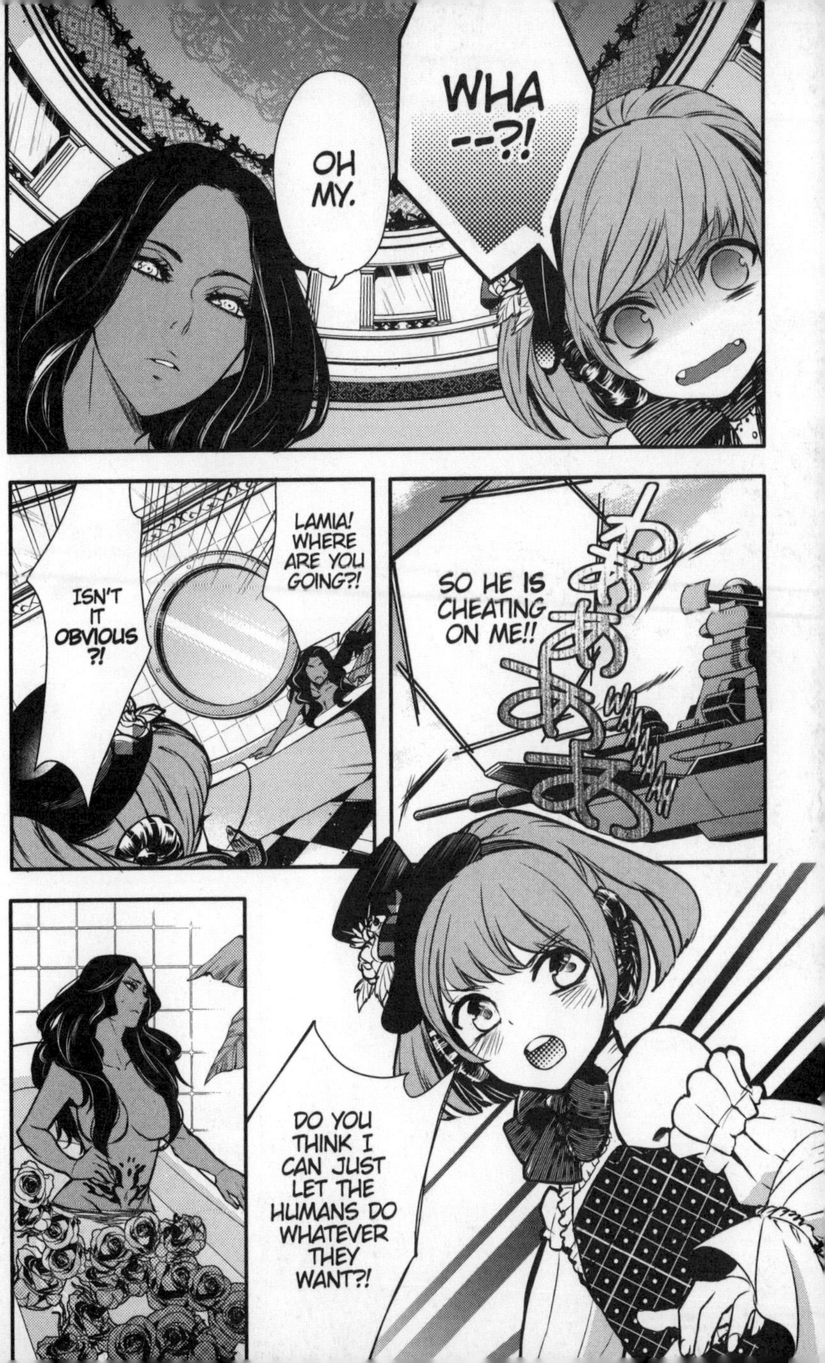
WHA--?!
OH MY.
SO HE IS CHEATING ON ME!!
わああああ
WAAAAAH
LAMIA! WHERE ARE YOU GOING?!
ISN'T IT OBVIOUS?!
DO YOU THINK I CAN JUST LET THE HUMANS DO WHATEVER THEY WANT?!

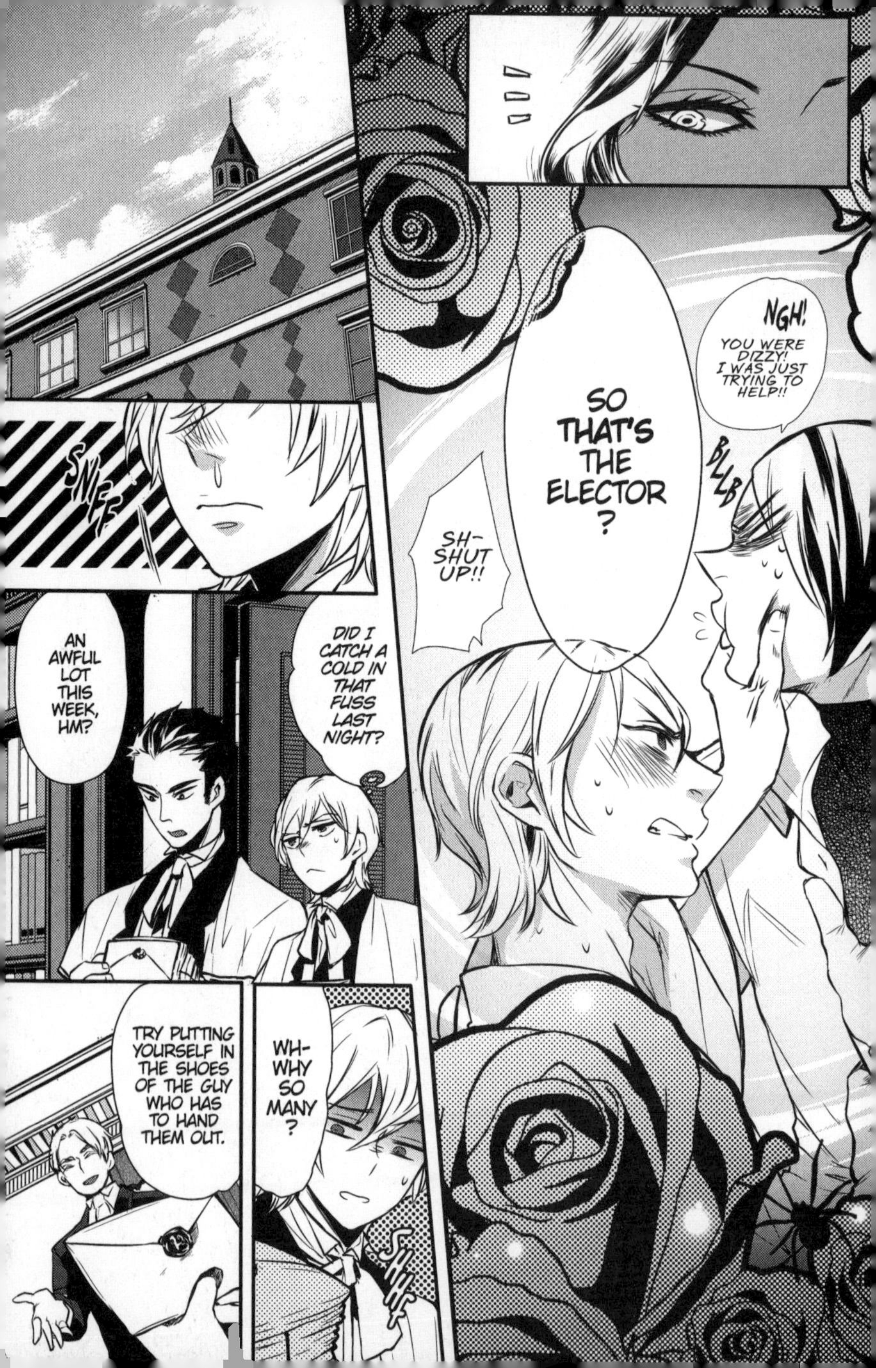
NGH! YOU WERE DIZZY! I WAS JUST TRYING TO HELP!!
BLLB
SO THAT'S THE ELECTOR?
SH- SHUT UP!!
SNIFF
DID I CATCH A COLD IN THAT FUSS LAST NIGHT?
AN AWFUL LOT THIS WEEK, HM?
WH- WHY SO MANY?
TRY PUTTING YOURSELF IN THE SHOES OF THE GUY WHO HAS TO HAND THEM OUT.

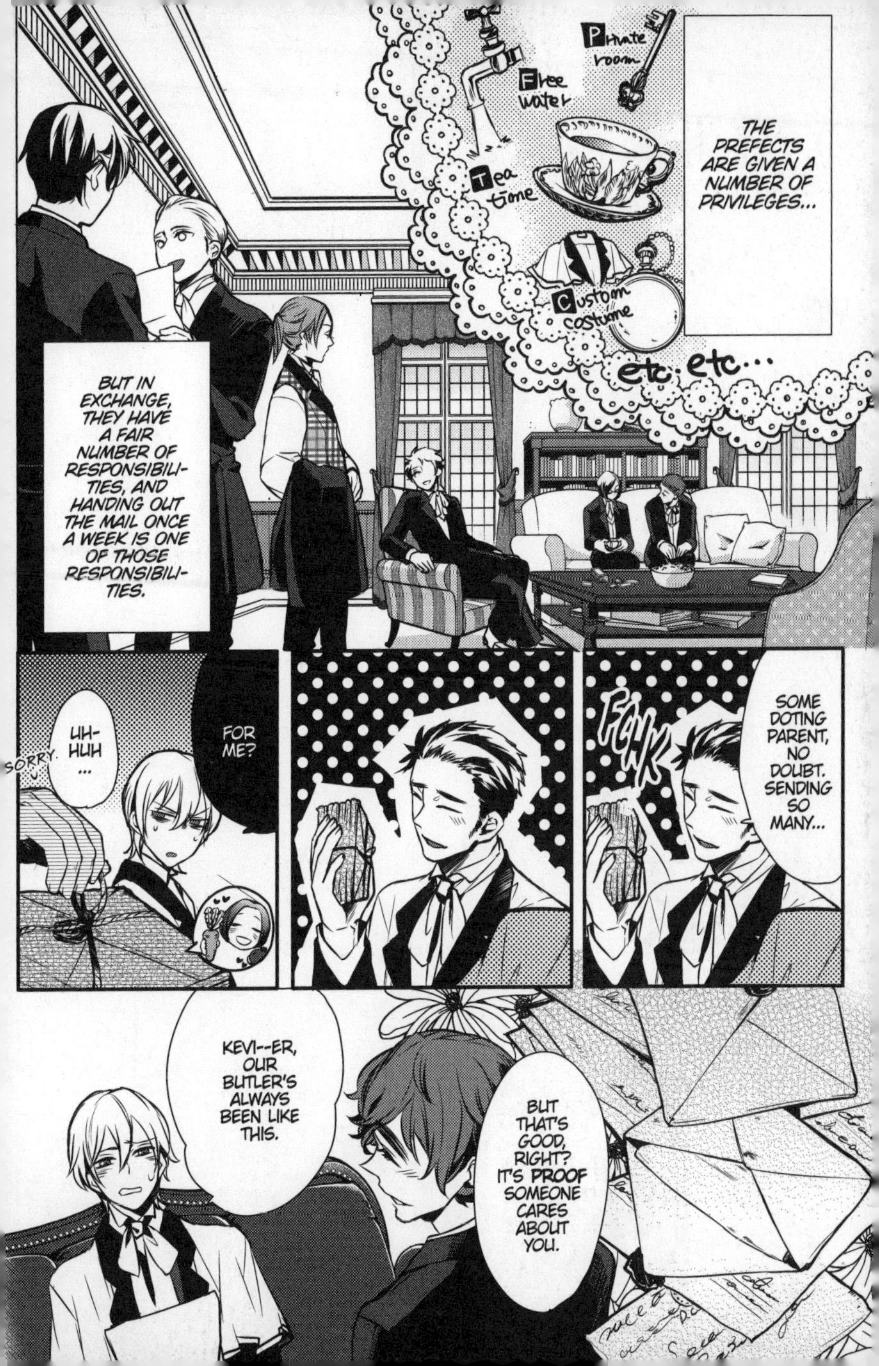
THE PREFECTS ARE GIVEN A NUMBER OF PRIVILEGES...
Private room
Free water
Tea time
Custom costume
etc. etc...
BUT IN EXCHANGE, THEY HAVE A FAIR NUMBER OF RESPONSIBILITIES, AND HANDING OUT THE MAIL ONCE A WEEK IS ONE OF THOSE RESPONSIBILITIES.
SOME DOTING PARENT, NO DOUBT. SENDING SO MANY...
FOR ME?
UH-HUH ...
SORRY.
KEVI--ER, OUR BUTLER'S ALWAYS BEEN LIKE THIS.
BUT THAT'S GOOD, RIGHT? IT'S PROOF SOMEONE CARES ABOUT YOU.

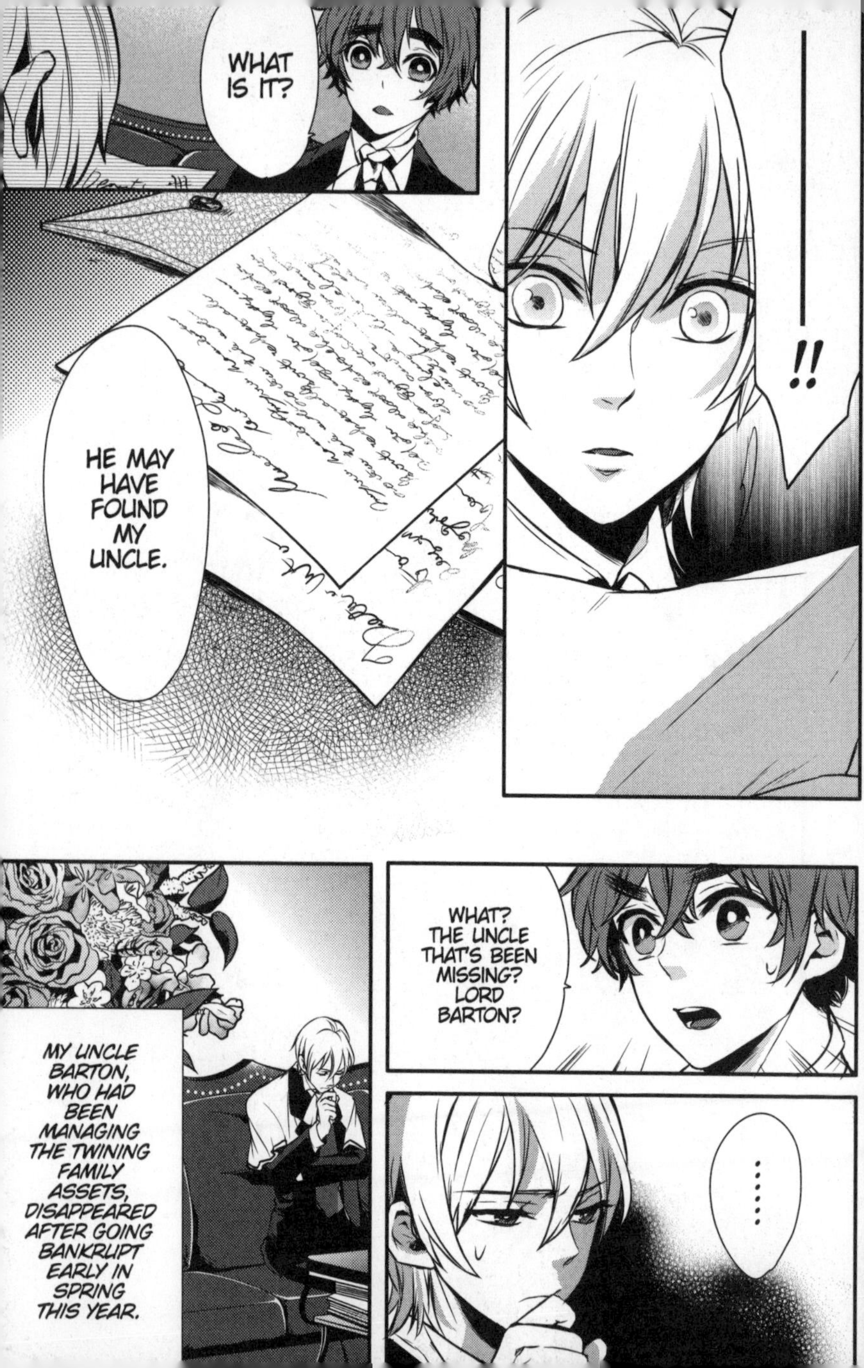
——!!
WHAT IS IT?
HE MAY HAVE FOUND MY UNCLE.
WHAT? THE UNCLE THAT'S BEEN MISSING? LORD BARTON?
......
MY UNCLE BARTON, WHO HAD BEEN MANAGING THE TWINING FAMILY ASSETS, DISAPPEARED AFTER GOING BANKRUPT EARLY IN SPRING THIS YEAR.

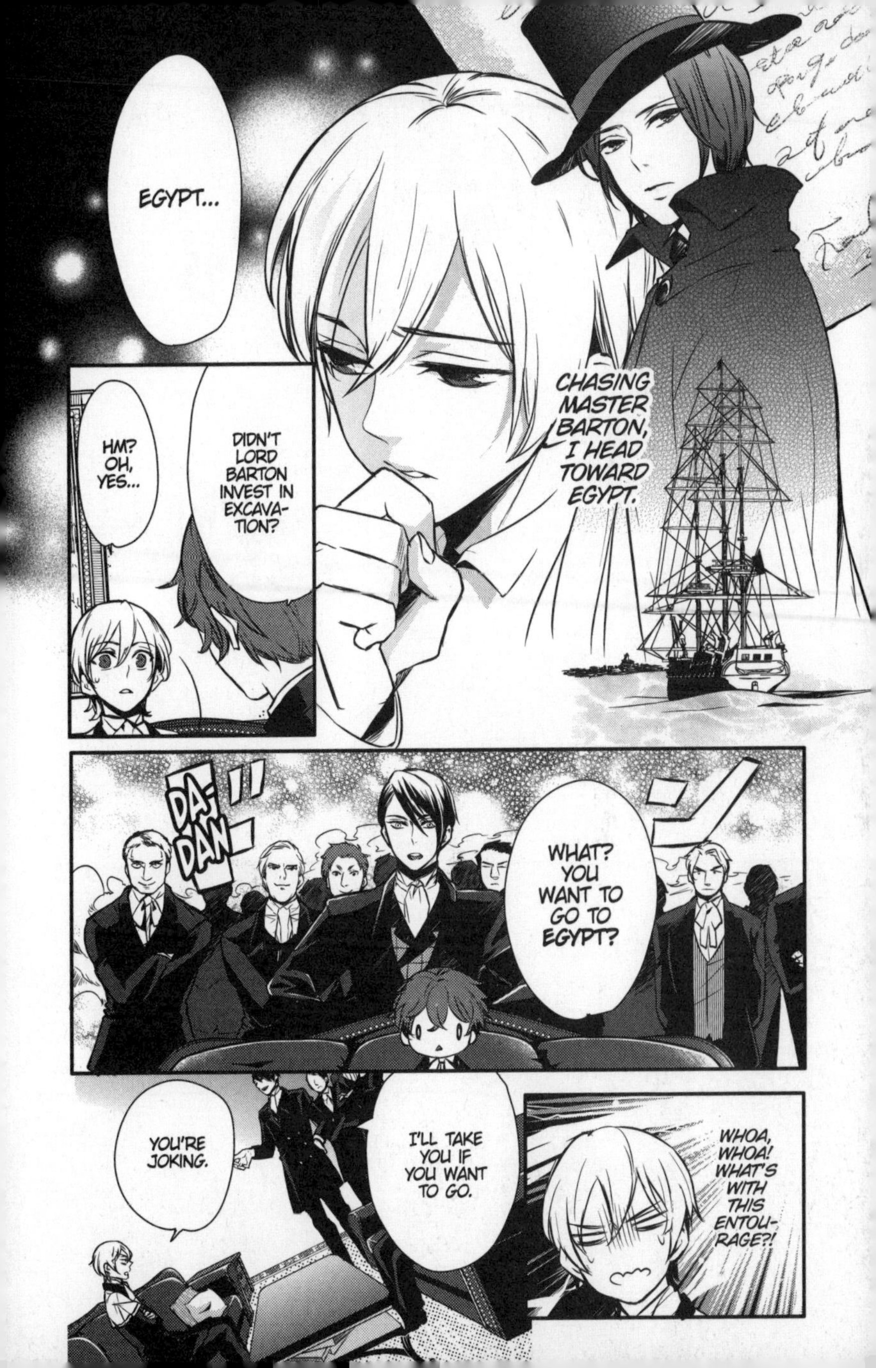
EGYPT...
DIDN'T LORD BARTON INVEST IN EXCAVATION?
HM? OH, YES...
CHASING MASTER BARTON, I HEAD TOWARD EGYPT.
WHAT? YOU WANT TO GO TO EGYPT?
DA-DAN
WHOA, WHOA! WHAT'S WITH THIS ENTOURAGE?!
I'LL TAKE YOU IF YOU WANT TO GO.
YOU'RE JOKING.

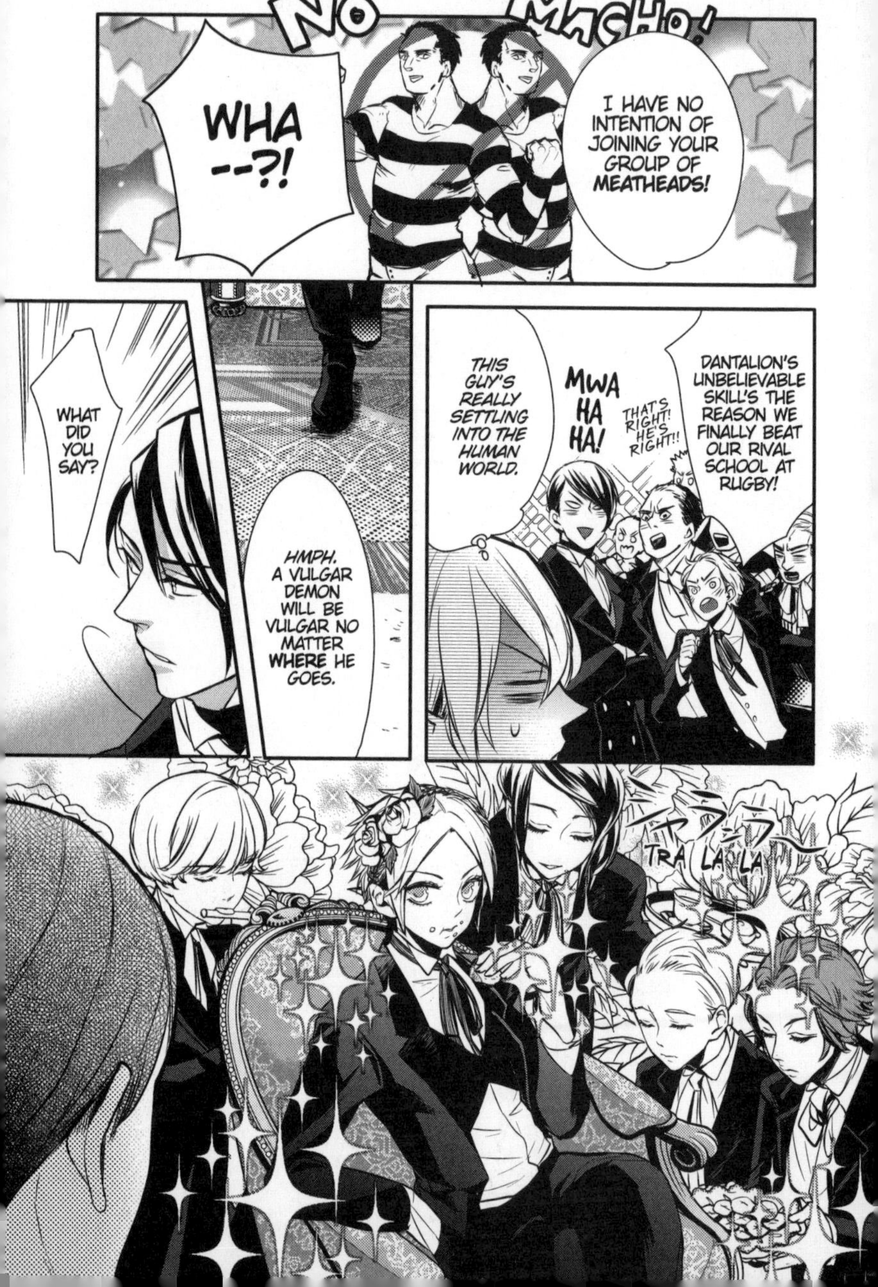
NO MACHO!
I HAVE NO INTENTION OF JOINING YOUR GROUP OF MEATHEADS!
WHA --?!
DANTALION'S UNBELIEVABLE SKILL'S THE REASON WE FINALLY BEAT OUR RIVAL SCHOOL AT RUGBY!
THAT'S RIGHT! HE'S RIGHT!!
MWA HA HA!
THIS GUY'S REALLY SETTLING INTO THE HUMAN WORLD.
HMPH. A VULGAR DEMON WILL BE VULGAR NO MATTER WHERE HE GOES.
WHAT DID YOU SAY?
TRA LA LA

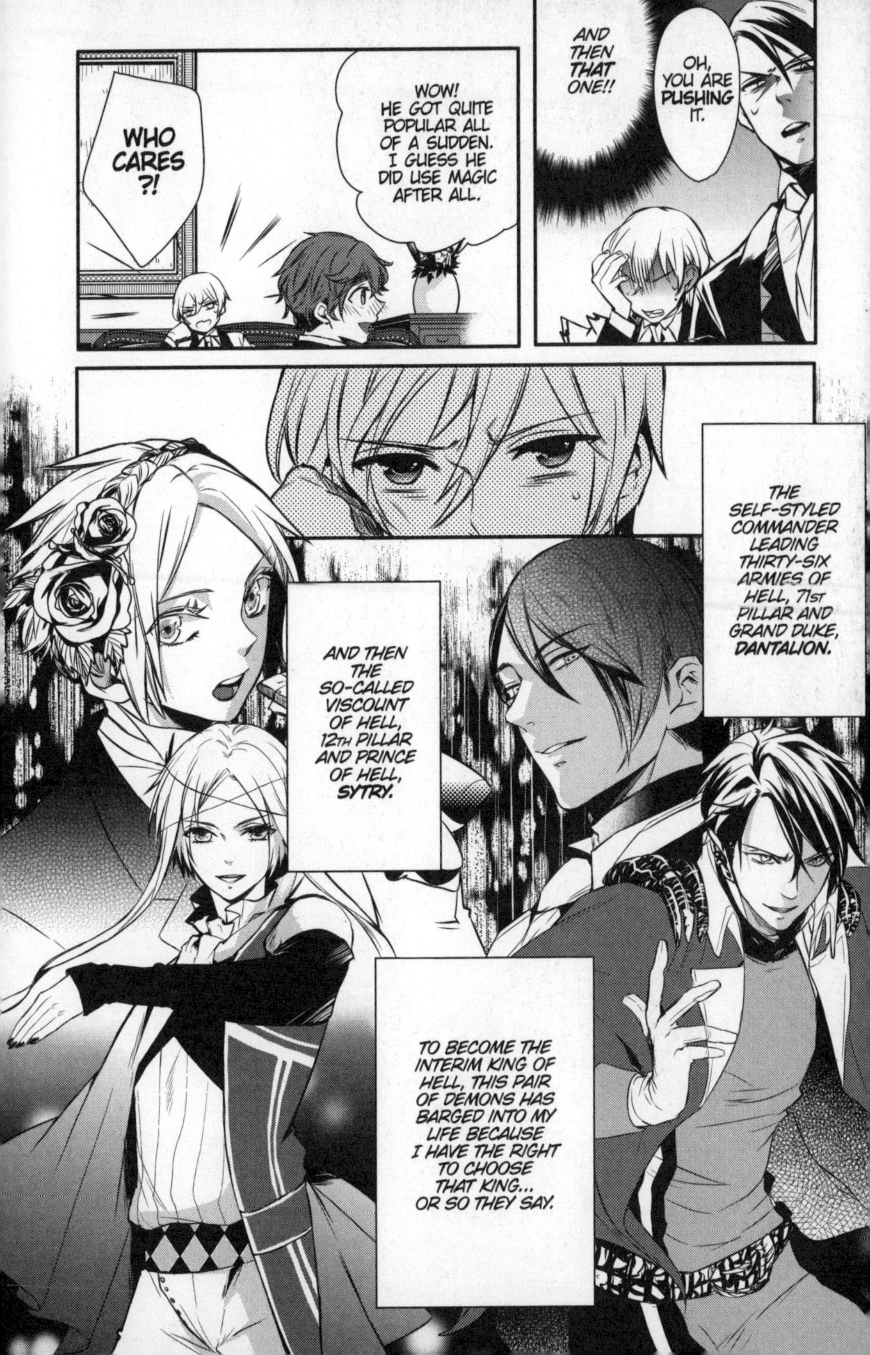
OH, YOU ARE PUSHING IT.
AND THEN THAT ONE!!
WOW! HE GOT QUITE POPULAR ALL OF A SUDDEN. I GUESS HE DID USE MAGIC AFTER ALL.
WHO CARES?!
THE SELF-STYLED COMMANDER LEADING THIRTY-SIX ARMIES OF HELL, 71ST PILLAR AND GRAND DUKE, DANTALION.
AND THEN THE SO-CALLED VISCOUNT OF HELL, 12TH PILLAR AND PRINCE OF HELL, SYTRY.
TO BECOME THE INTERIM KING OF HELL, THIS PAIR OF DEMONS HAS BARGED INTO MY LIFE BECAUSE I HAVE THE RIGHT TO CHOOSE THAT KING... OR SO THEY SAY.

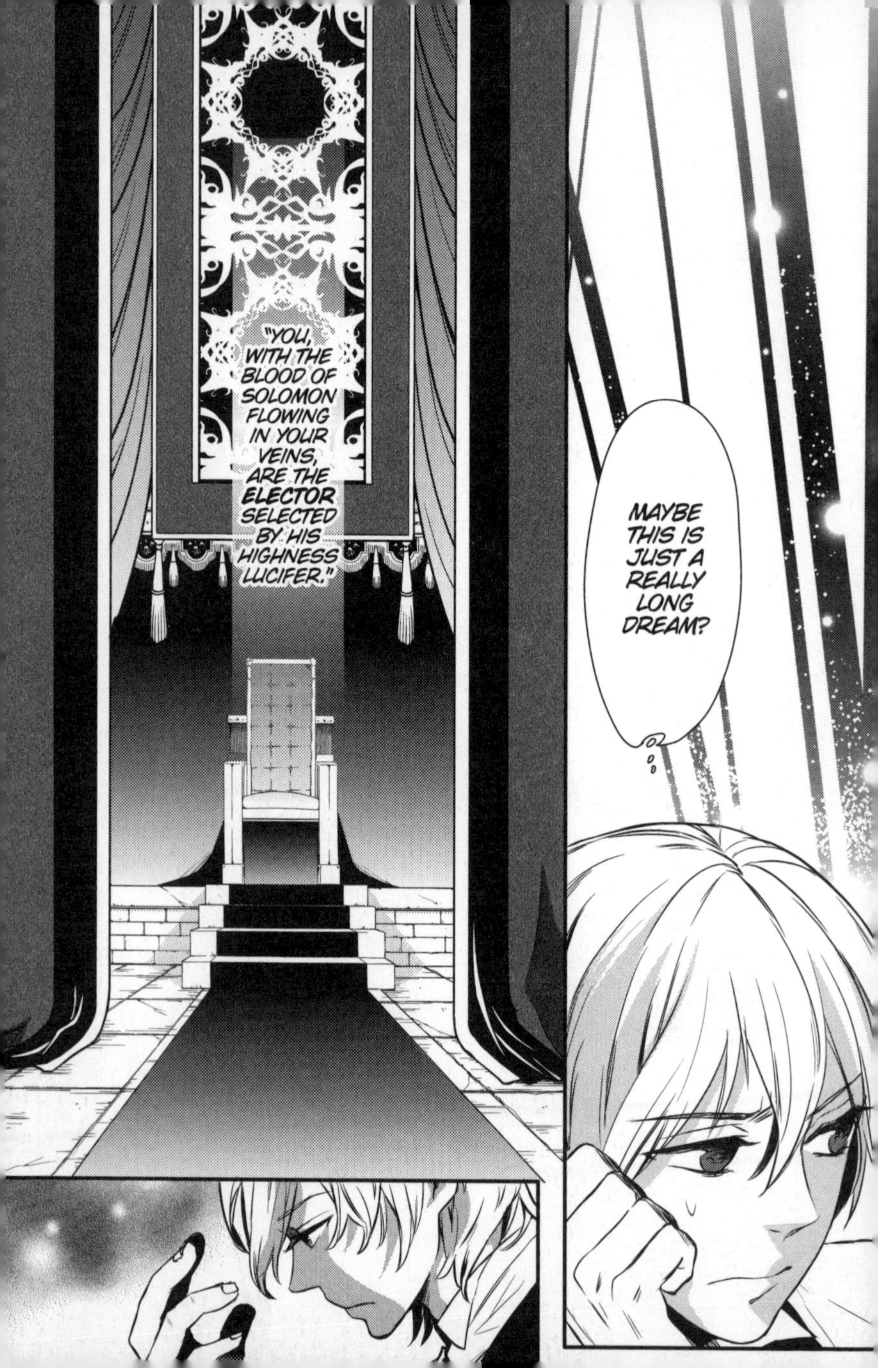
MAYBE THIS IS JUST A REALLY LONG DREAM?
"YOU, WITH THE BLOOD OF SOLOMON FLOWING IN YOUR VEINS, ARE THE ELECTOR SELECTED BY HIS HIGHNESS LUCIFER."

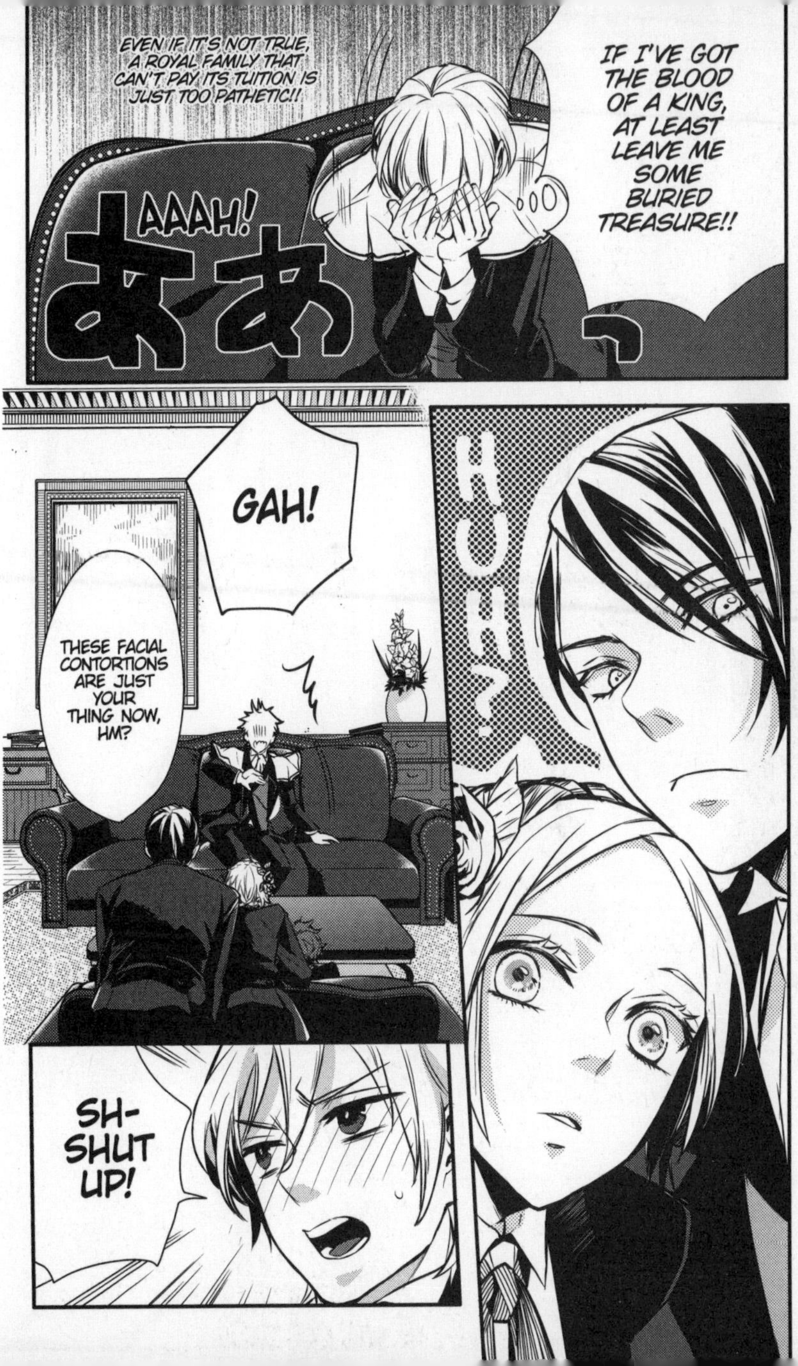
IF I'VE GOT THE BLOOD OF A KING, AT LEAST LEAVE ME SOME BURIED TREASURE!!
EVEN IF IT'S NOT TRUE, A ROYAL FAMILY THAT CAN'T PAY ITS TUITION IS JUST TOO PATHETIC!!
AAAH!
ああっ
HUH?
GAH!
THESE FACIAL CONTORTIONS ARE JUST YOUR THING NOW, HM?
SH-SHUT UP!

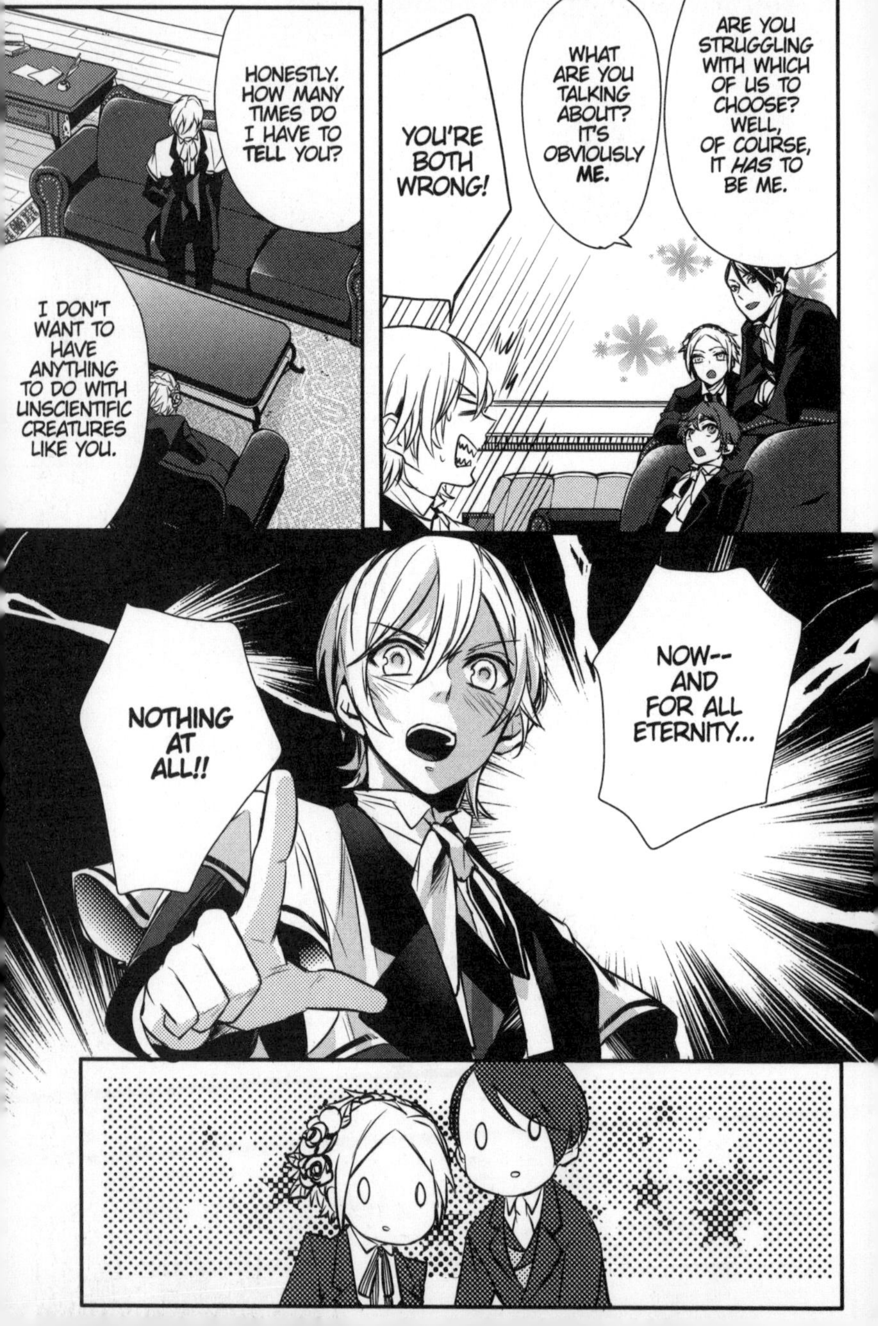
ARE YOU STRUGGLING WITH WHICH OF US TO CHOOSE? WELL, OF COURSE, IT *HAS* TO BE ME.
WHAT ARE YOU TALKING ABOUT? IT'S OBVIOUSLY ME.
YOU'RE BOTH WRONG!
HONESTLY. HOW MANY TIMES DO I HAVE TO TELL YOU?
I DON'T WANT TO HAVE ANYTHING TO DO WITH UNSCIENTIFIC CREATURES LIKE YOU.
NOW-- AND FOR ALL ETERNITY...
NOTHING AT ALL!!

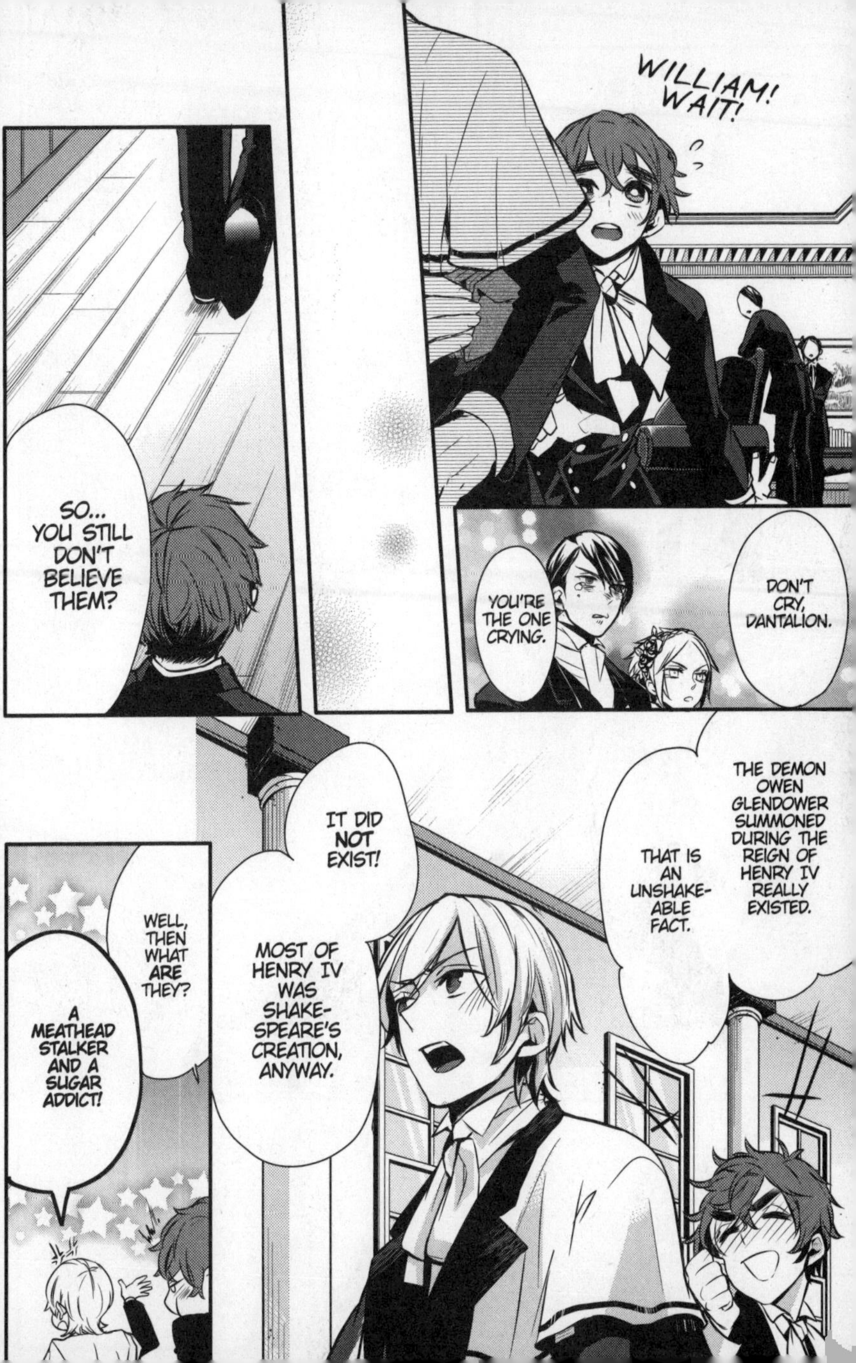
WILLIAM! WAIT!
DON'T CRY, DANTALION.
YOU'RE THE ONE CRYING.
SO... YOU STILL DON'T BELIEVE THEM?
THE DEMON OWEN GLENDOWER SUMMONED DURING THE REIGN OF HENRY IV REALLY EXISTED.
THAT IS AN UNSHAKE-ABLE FACT.
IT DID NOT EXIST!
MOST OF HENRY IV WAS SHAKE-SPEARE'S CREATION, ANYWAY.
WELL, THEN WHAT ARE THEY?
A MEATHEAD STALKER AND A SUGAR ADDICT!

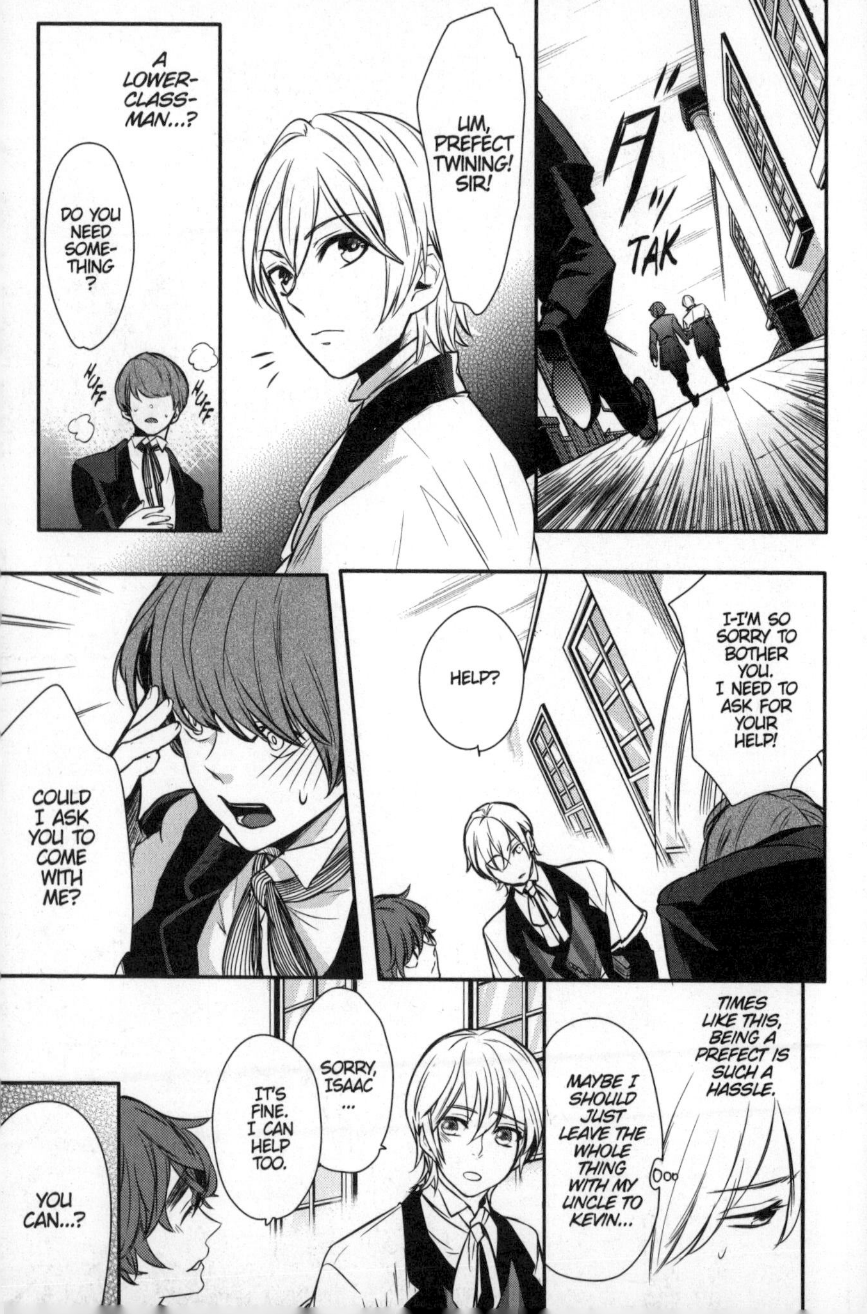
TAK
UM, PREFECT TWINING! SIR!
A LOWER-CLASSMAN...?
DO YOU NEED SOMETHING?
HUFF
HUFF
I-I'M SO SORRY TO BOTHER YOU. I NEED TO ASK FOR YOUR HELP!
HELP?
COULD I ASK YOU TO COME WITH ME?
TIMES LIKE THIS, BEING A PREFECT IS SUCH A HASSLE.
MAYBE I SHOULD JUST LEAVE THE WHOLE THING WITH MY UNCLE TO KEVIN...
SORRY, ISAAC...
IT'S FINE. I CAN HELP TOO.
YOU CAN...?

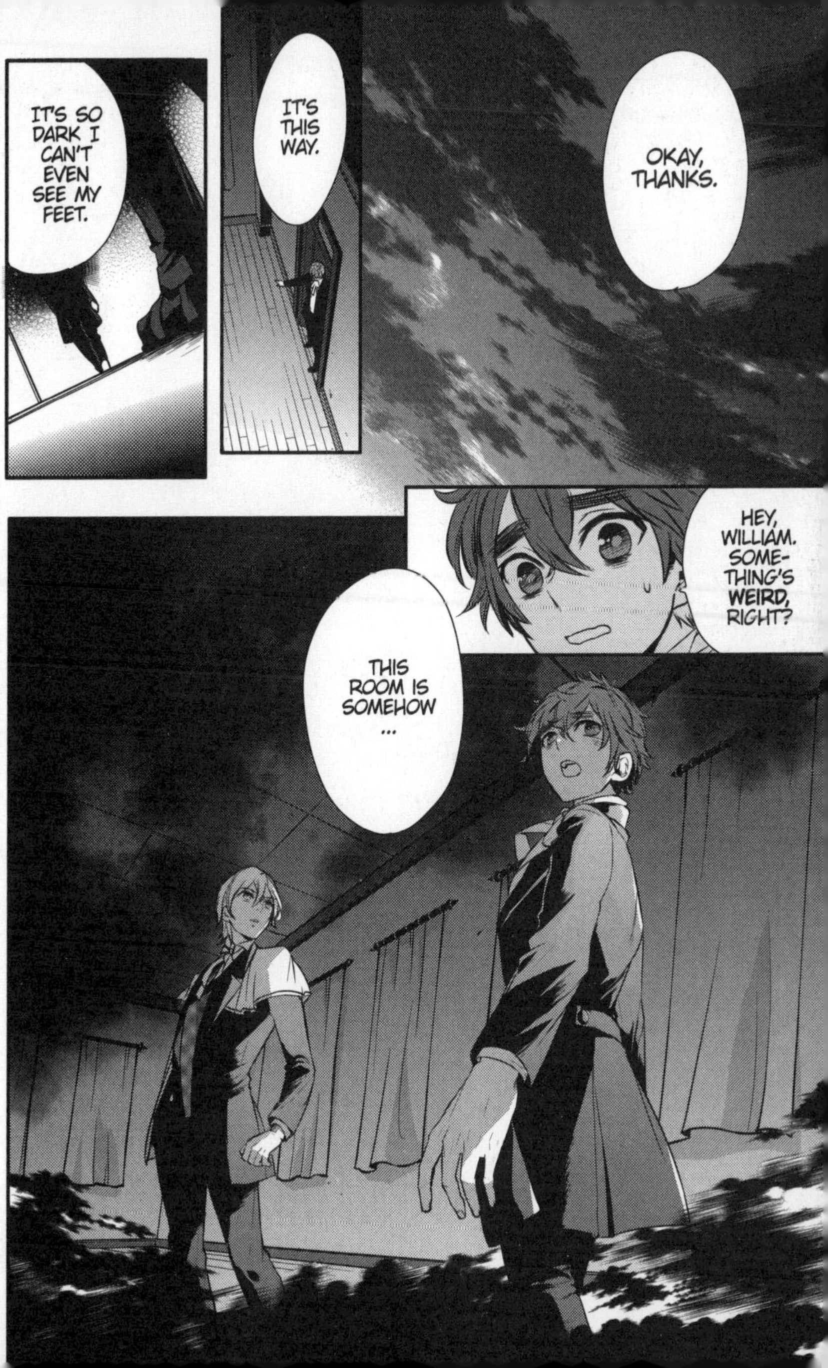
OKAY, THANKS.
IT'S THIS WAY.
IT'S SO DARK I CAN'T EVEN SEE MY FEET.
HEY, WILLIAM. SOME-THING'S WEIRD, RIGHT?
THIS ROOM IS SOMEHOW ...

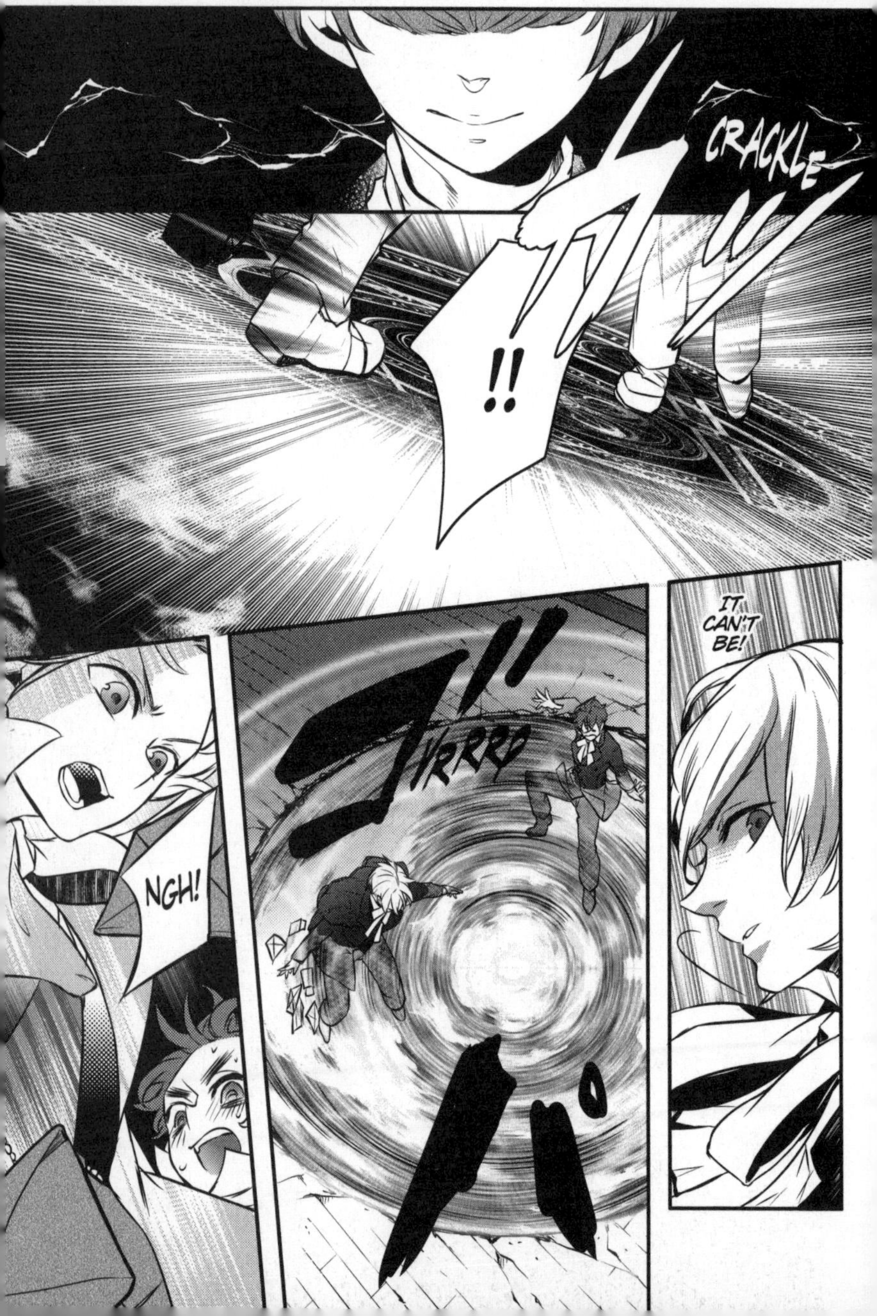
CRACKLE
!!
IT CAN'T BE!
VRRRD
NGH!

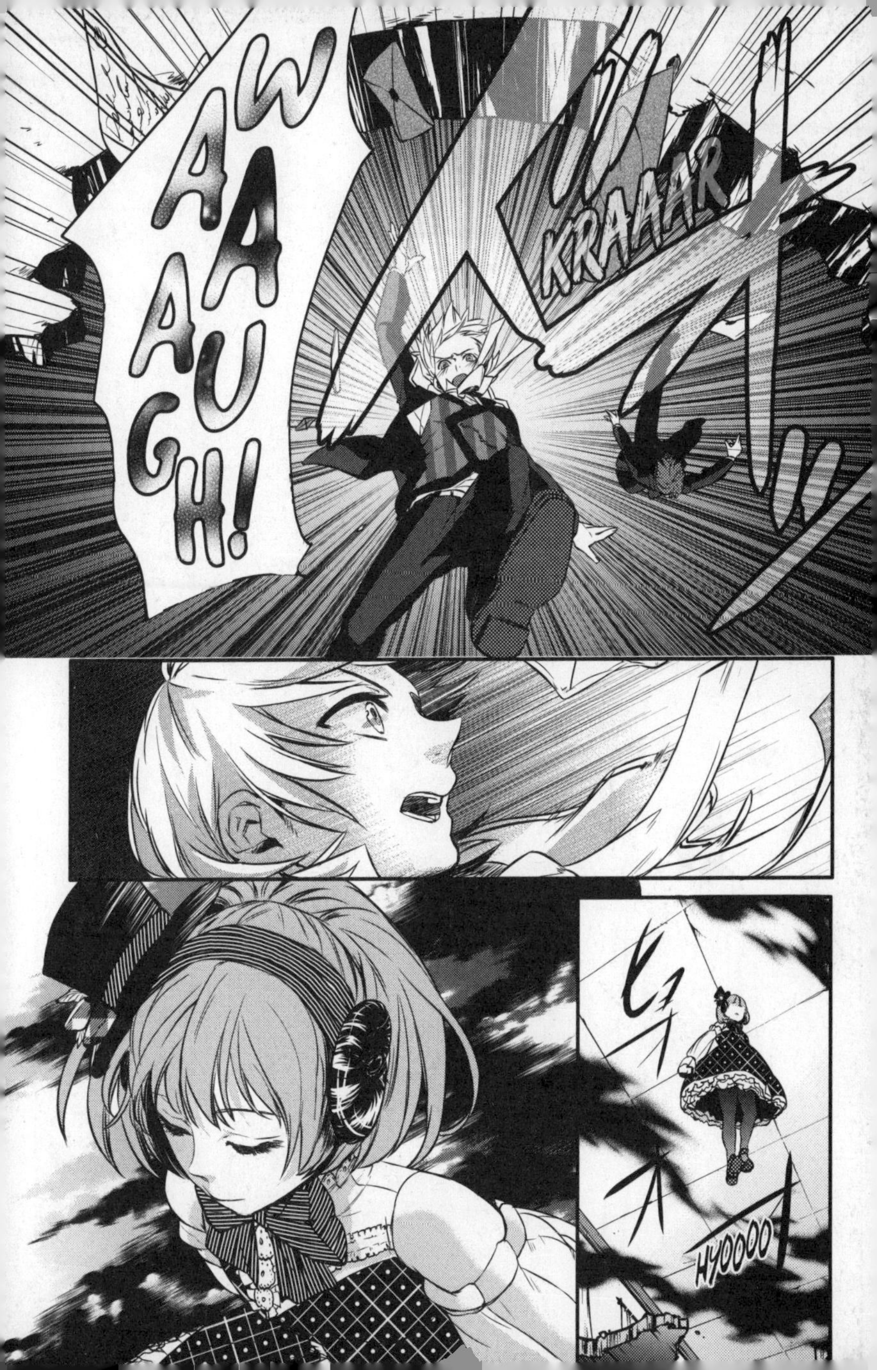
KRAAAR
AWAAAUGH!
HYOOOO

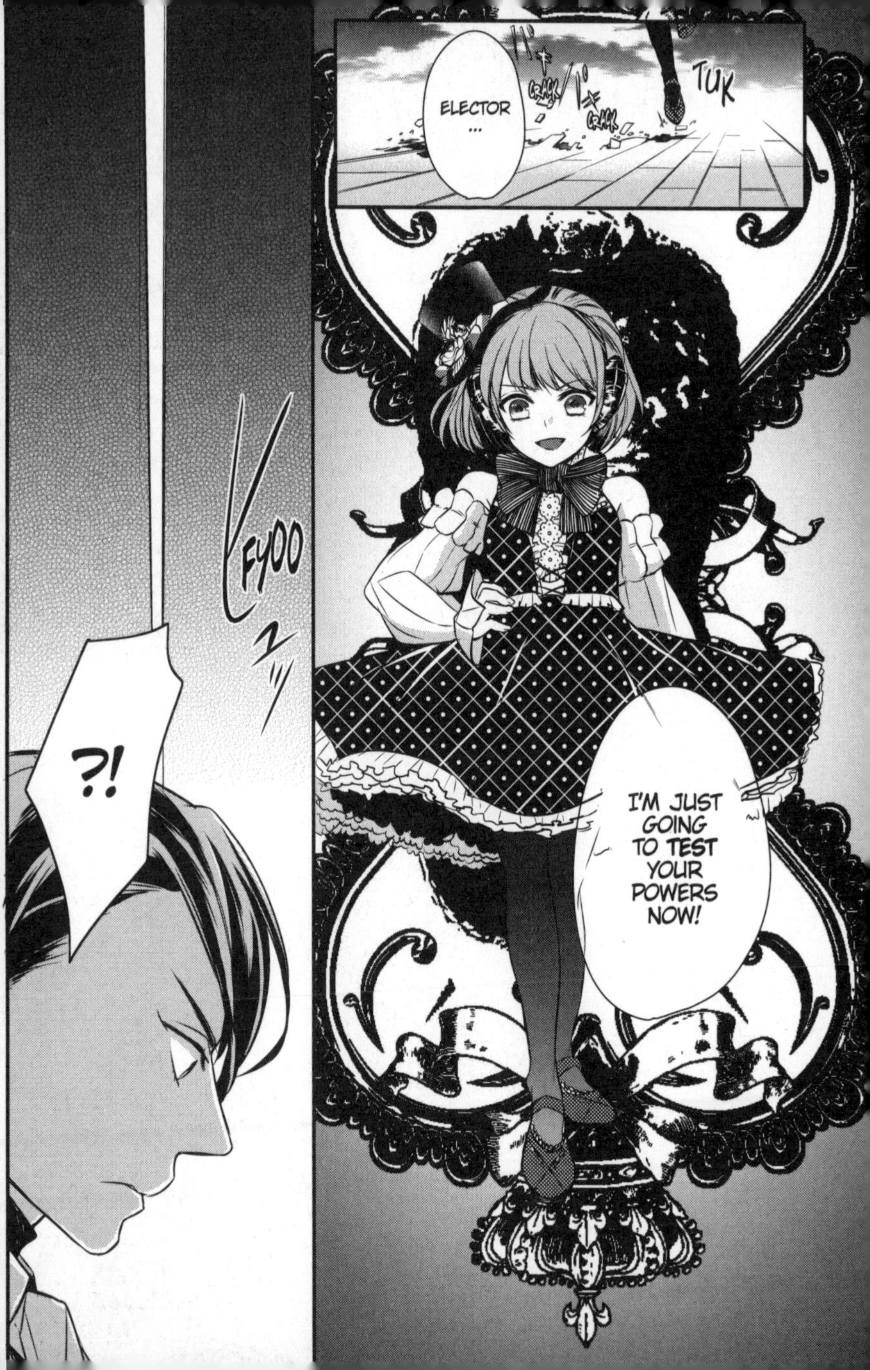
TUK
CRACK
CRACK
ELECTOR ...
I'M JUST GOING TO TEST YOUR POWERS NOW!
FYOO
?!

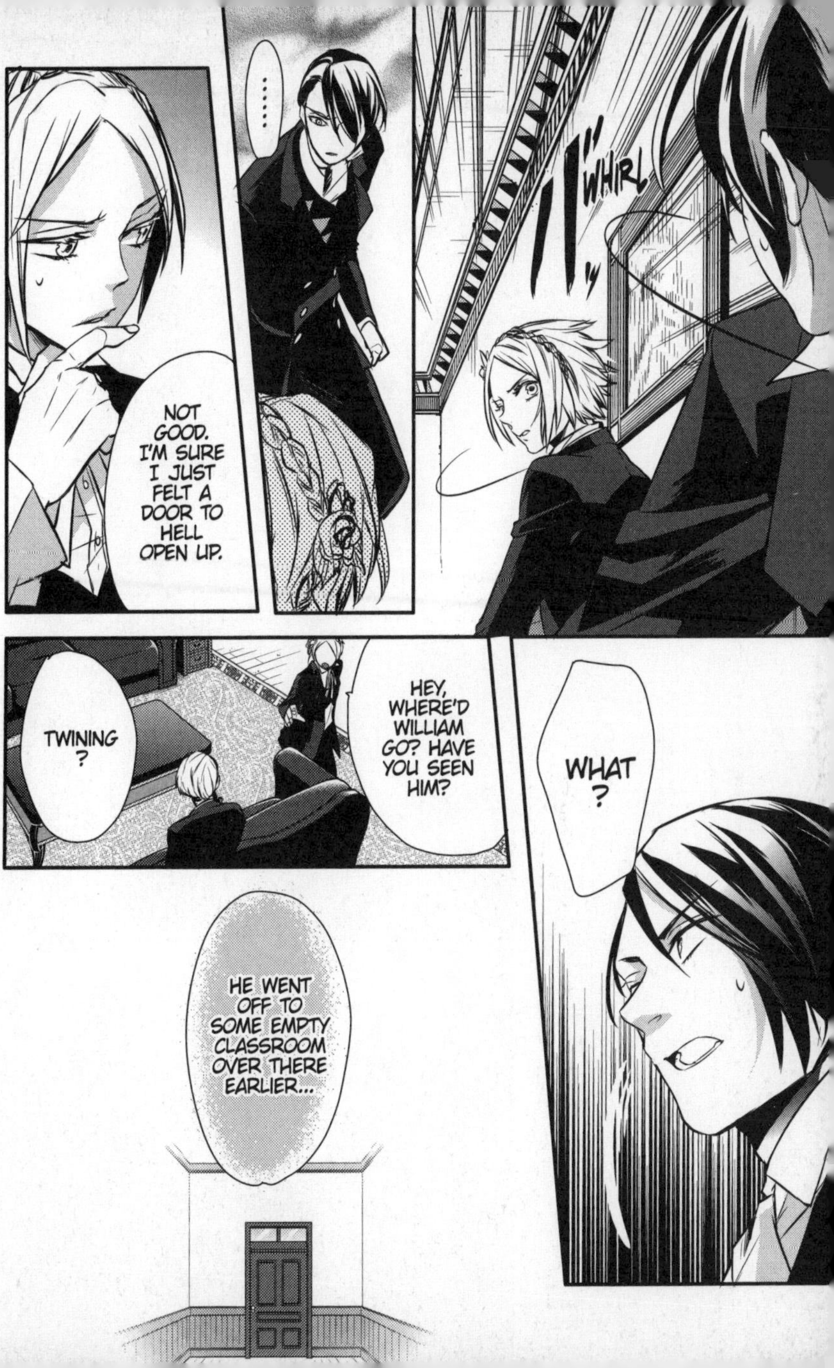
WHIRL
......
NOT GOOD. I'M SURE I JUST FELT A DOOR TO HELL OPEN UP.
WHAT ?
HEY, WHERE'D WILLIAM GO? HAVE YOU SEEN HIM?
TWINING ?
HE WENT OFF TO SOME EMPTY CLASSROOM OVER THERE EARLIER...

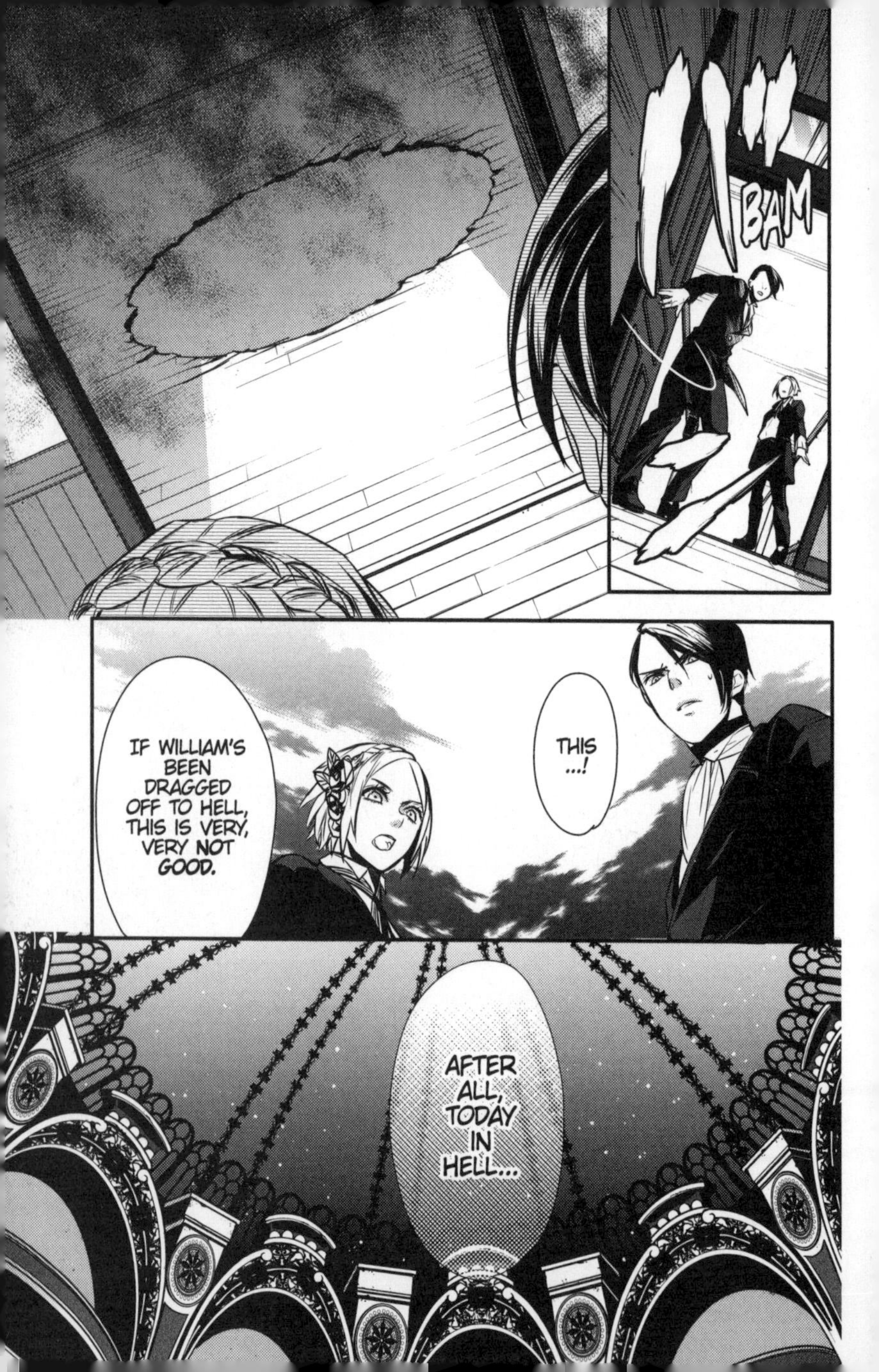
BAM
THIS ...!
IF WILLIAM'S BEEN DRAGGED OFF TO HELL, THIS IS VERY, VERY NOT GOOD.
AFTER ALL, TODAY IN HELL...

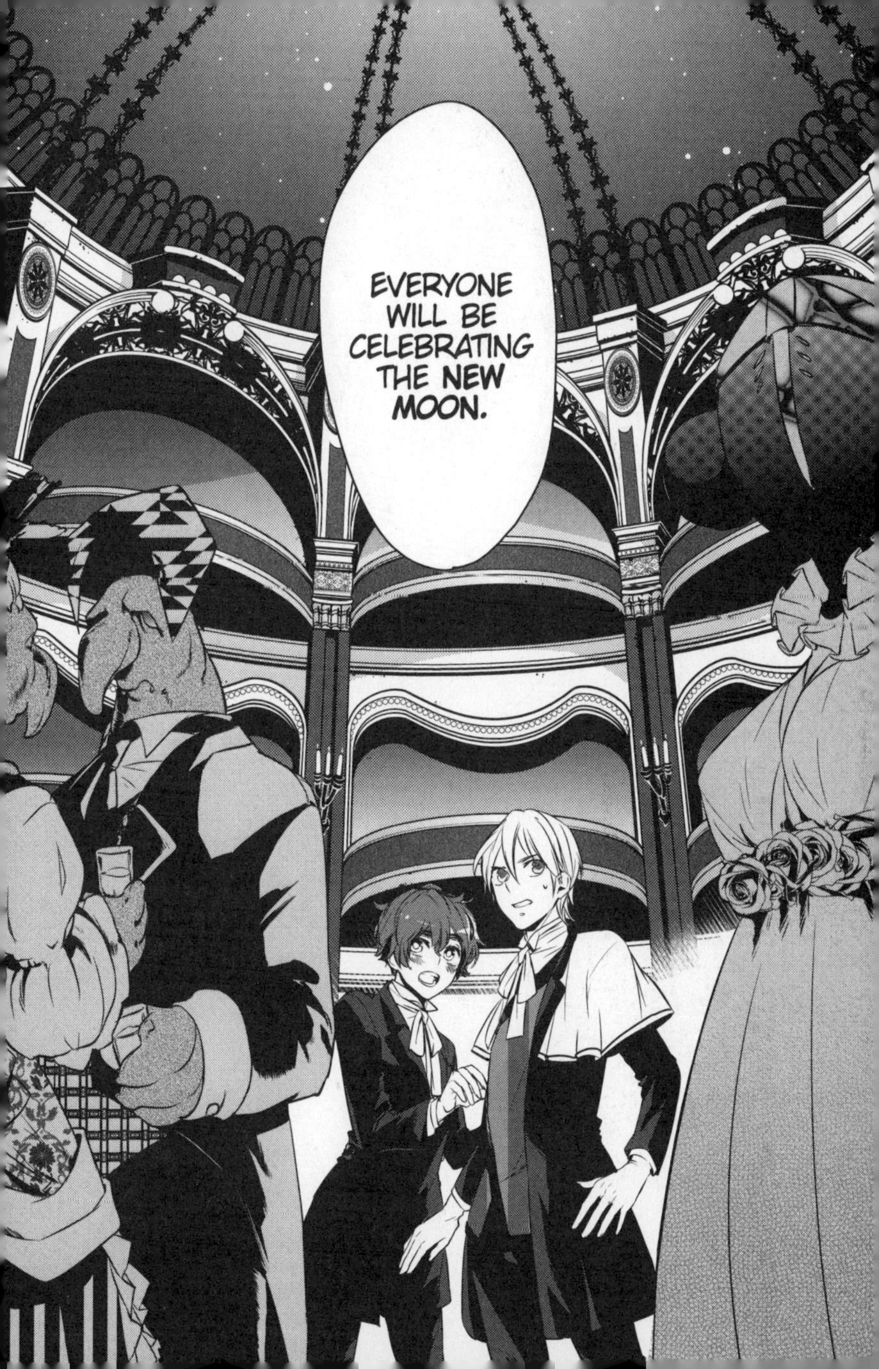
EVERYONE WILL BE CELEBRATING THE NEW MOON.

Pillar 7

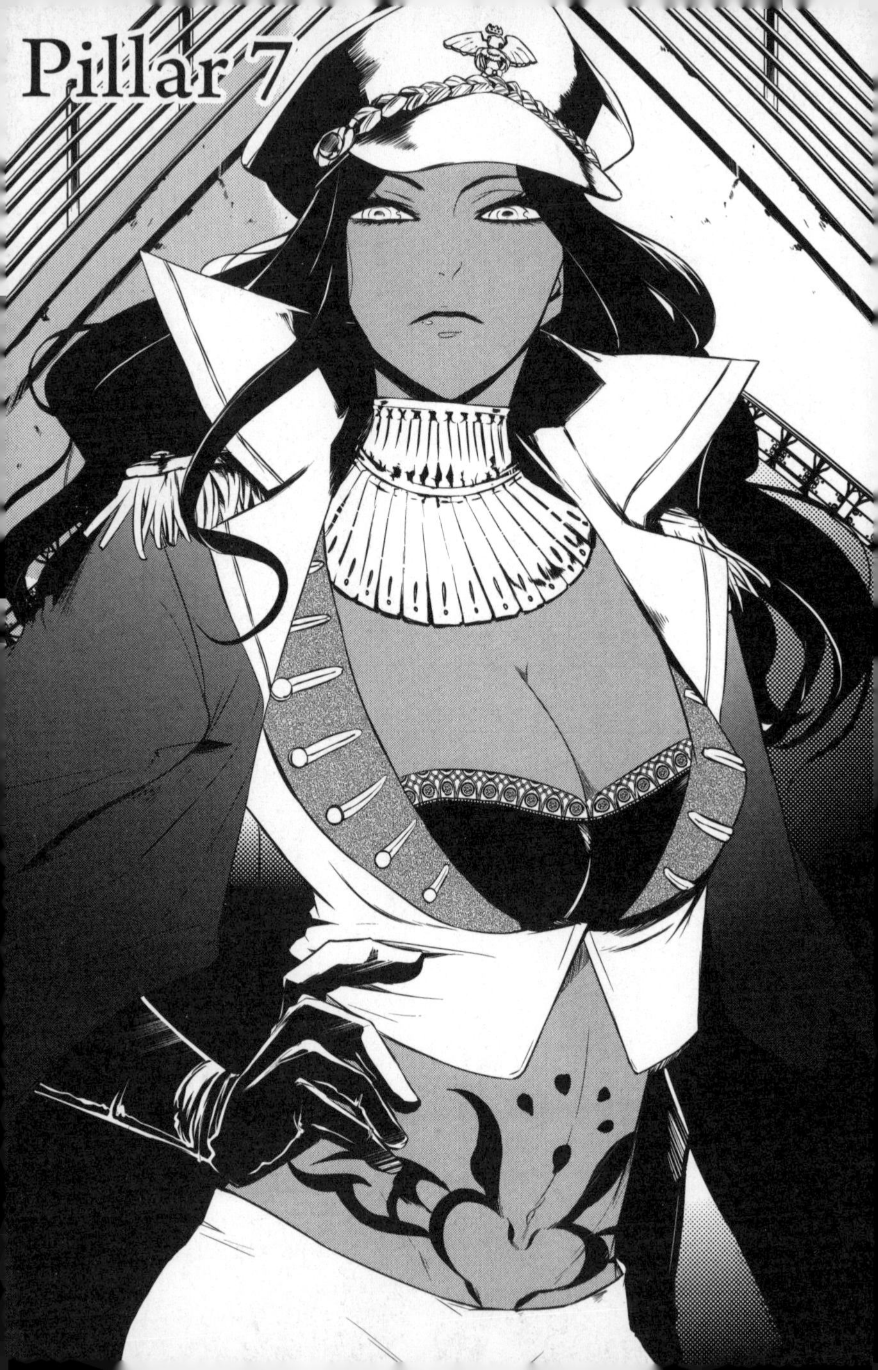

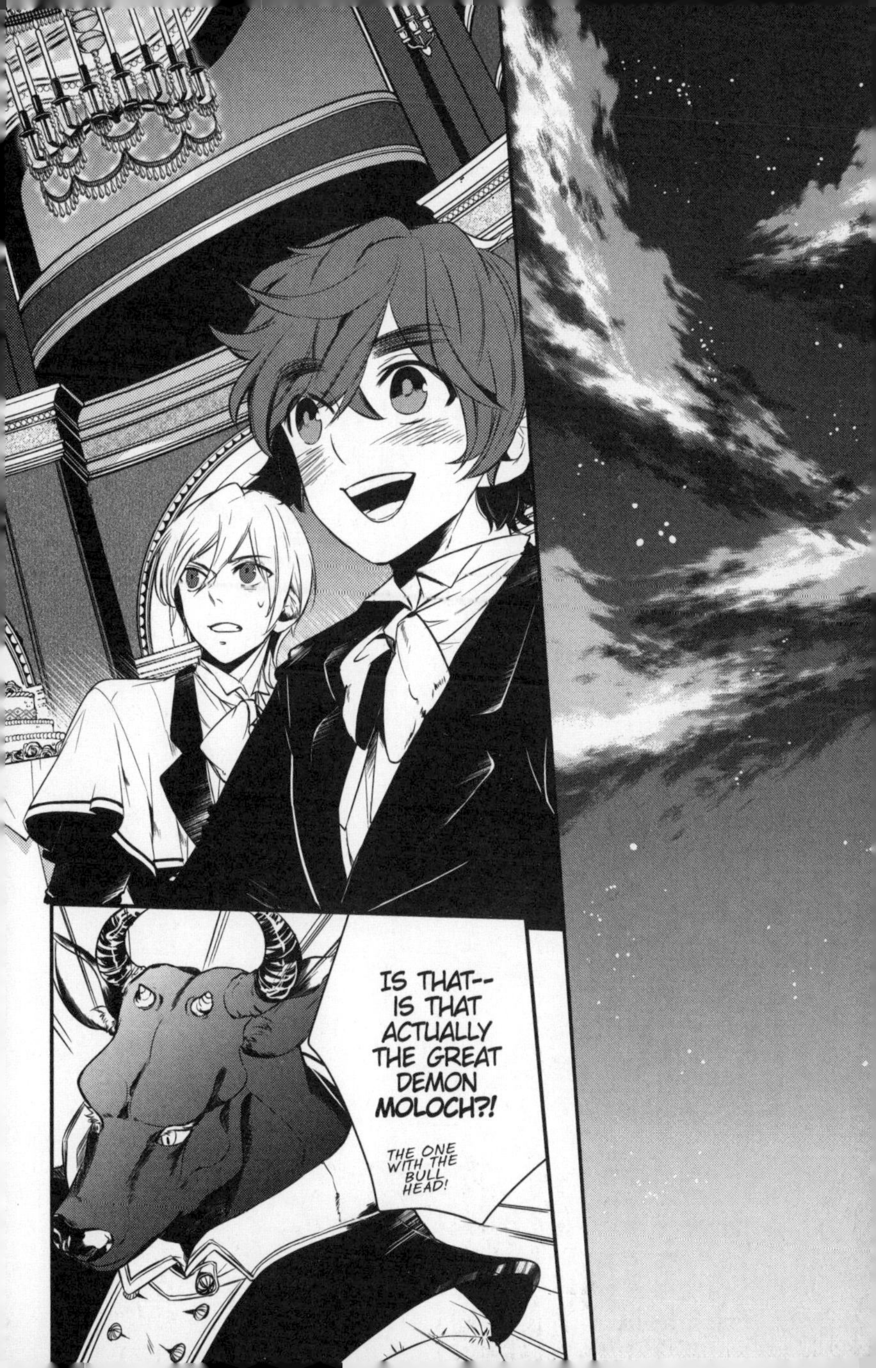
IS THAT-- IS THAT ACTUALLY THE GREAT DEMON MOLOCH?!
THE ONE WITH THE BULL HEAD!

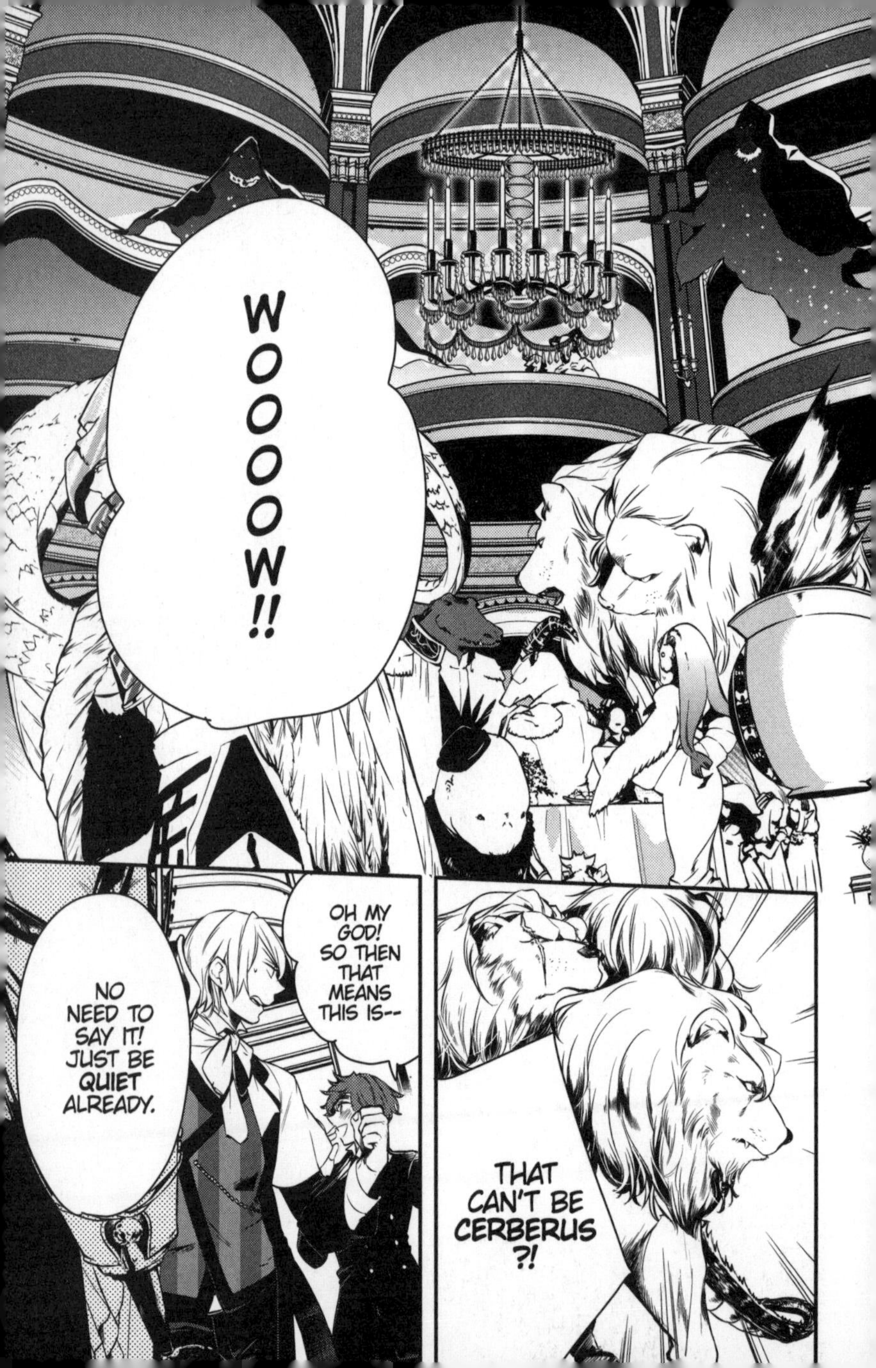
WOOOOOW!!
THAT CAN'T BE CERBERUS ?!
OH MY GOD! SO THEN THAT MEANS THIS IS--
NO NEED TO SAY IT! JUST BE QUIET ALREADY.

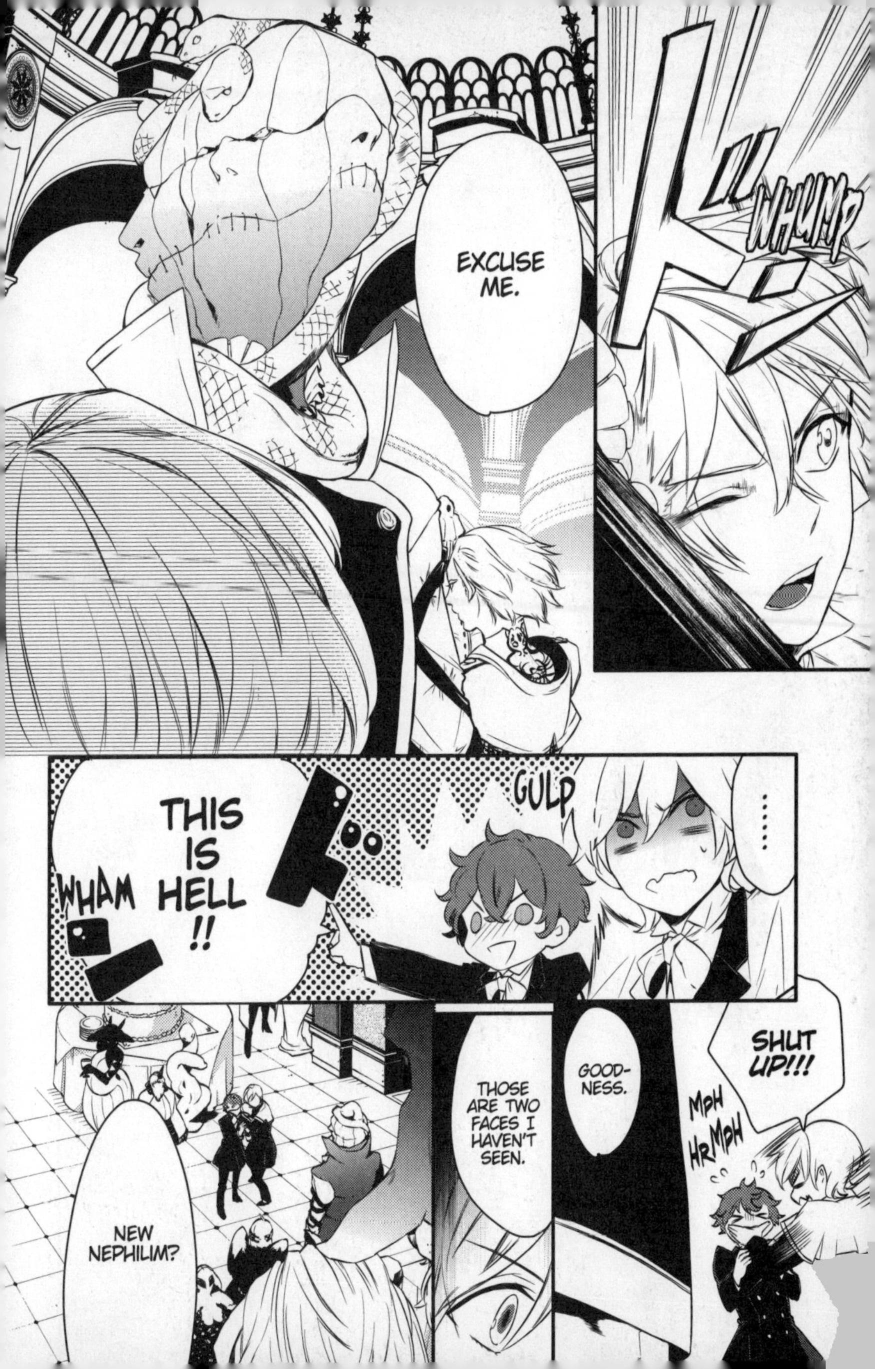
WHUMP
EXCUSE ME.
......
GULP
THIS IS HELL!!
WHAM
SHUT UP!!!
MPH HRMPH
GOOD-NESS.
THOSE ARE TWO FACES I HAVEN'T SEEN.
NEW NEPHILIM?

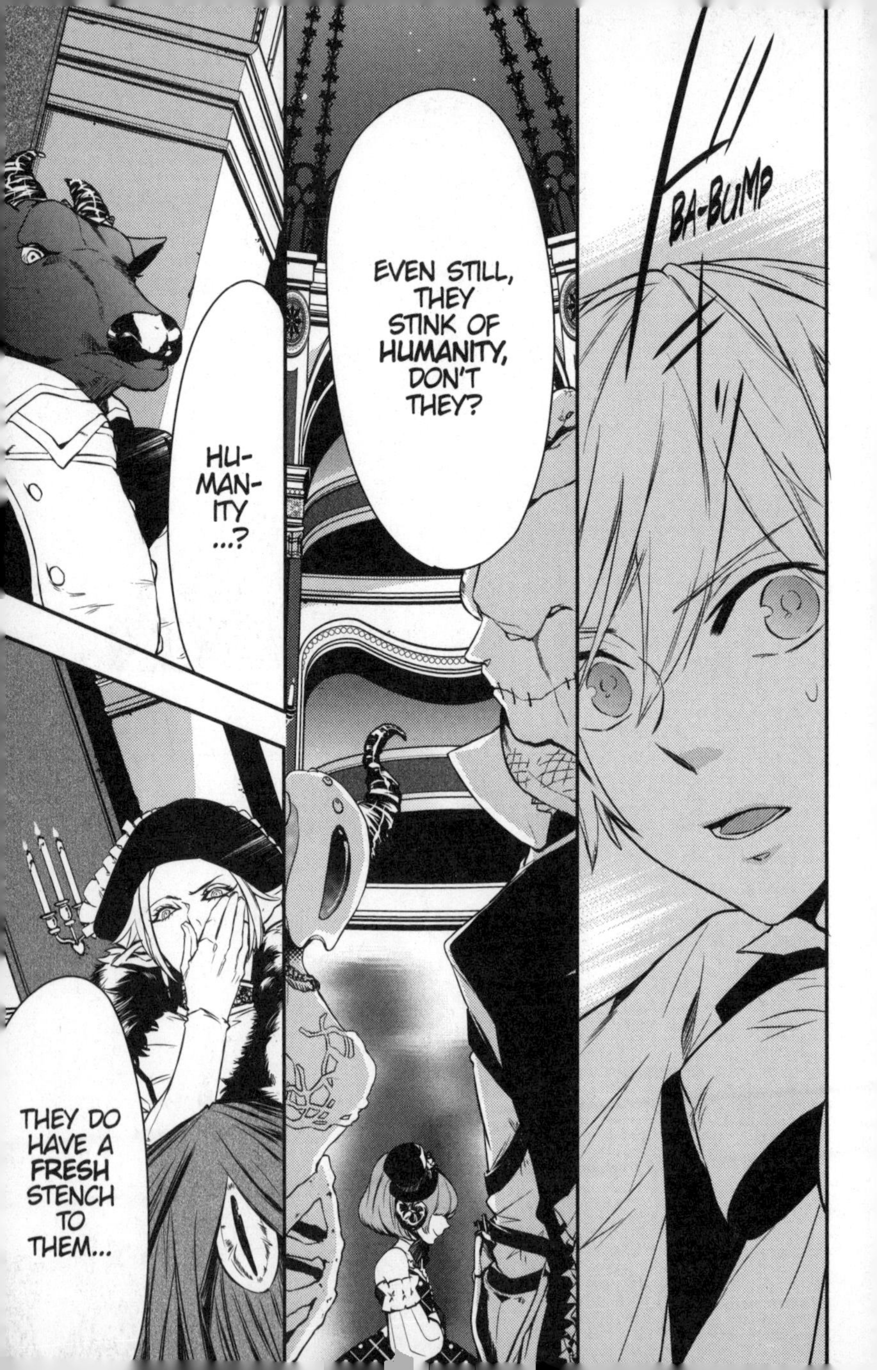
BA-BUMP
EVEN STILL, THEY STINK OF HUMANITY, DON'T THEY?
HU-MAN-ITY ...?
THEY DO HAVE A FRESH STENCH TO THEM...

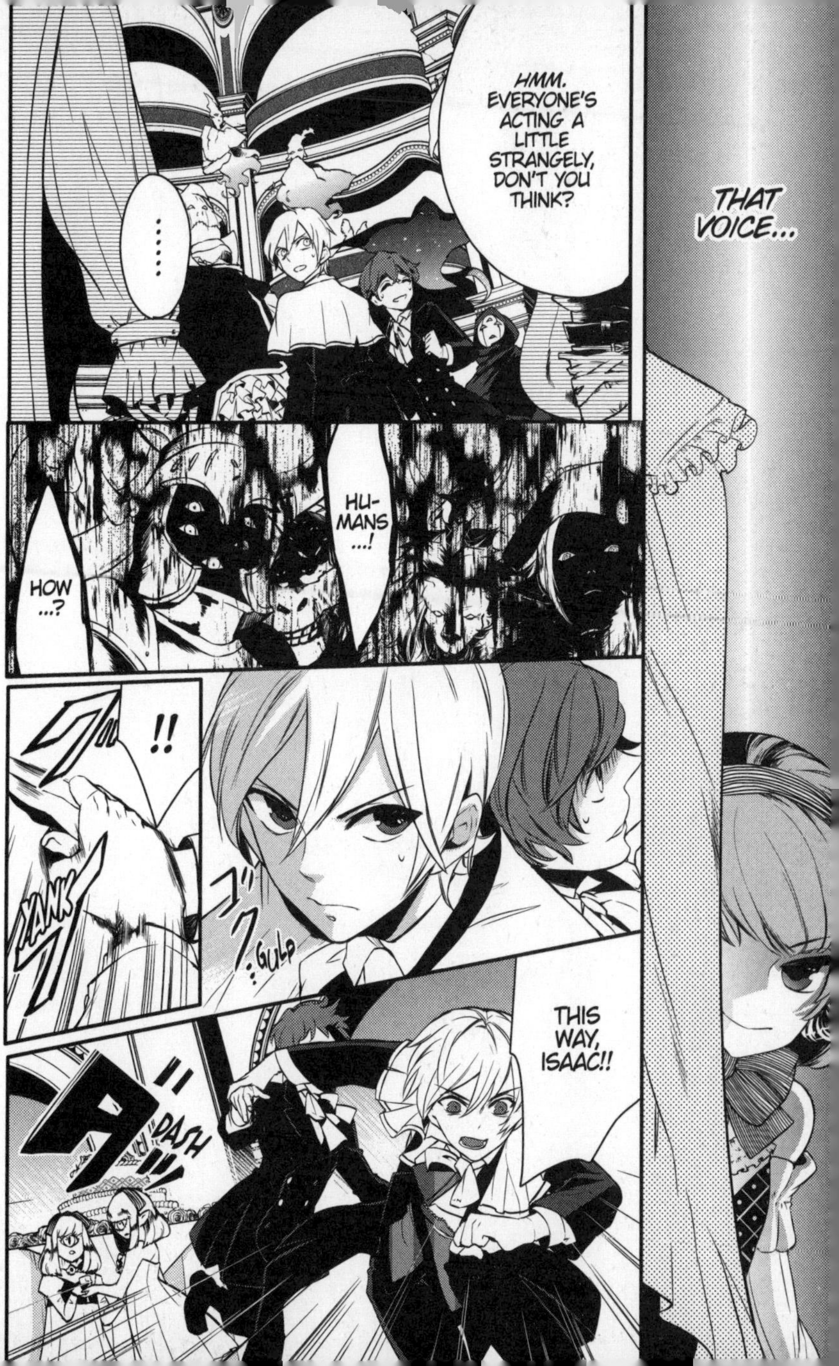
THAT VOICE...
HMM. EVERYONE'S ACTING A LITTLE STRANGELY, DON'T YOU THINK?
......
HU-MANS...!
HOW...?
!!
GULP
YANK
THIS WAY, ISAAC!!
DASH

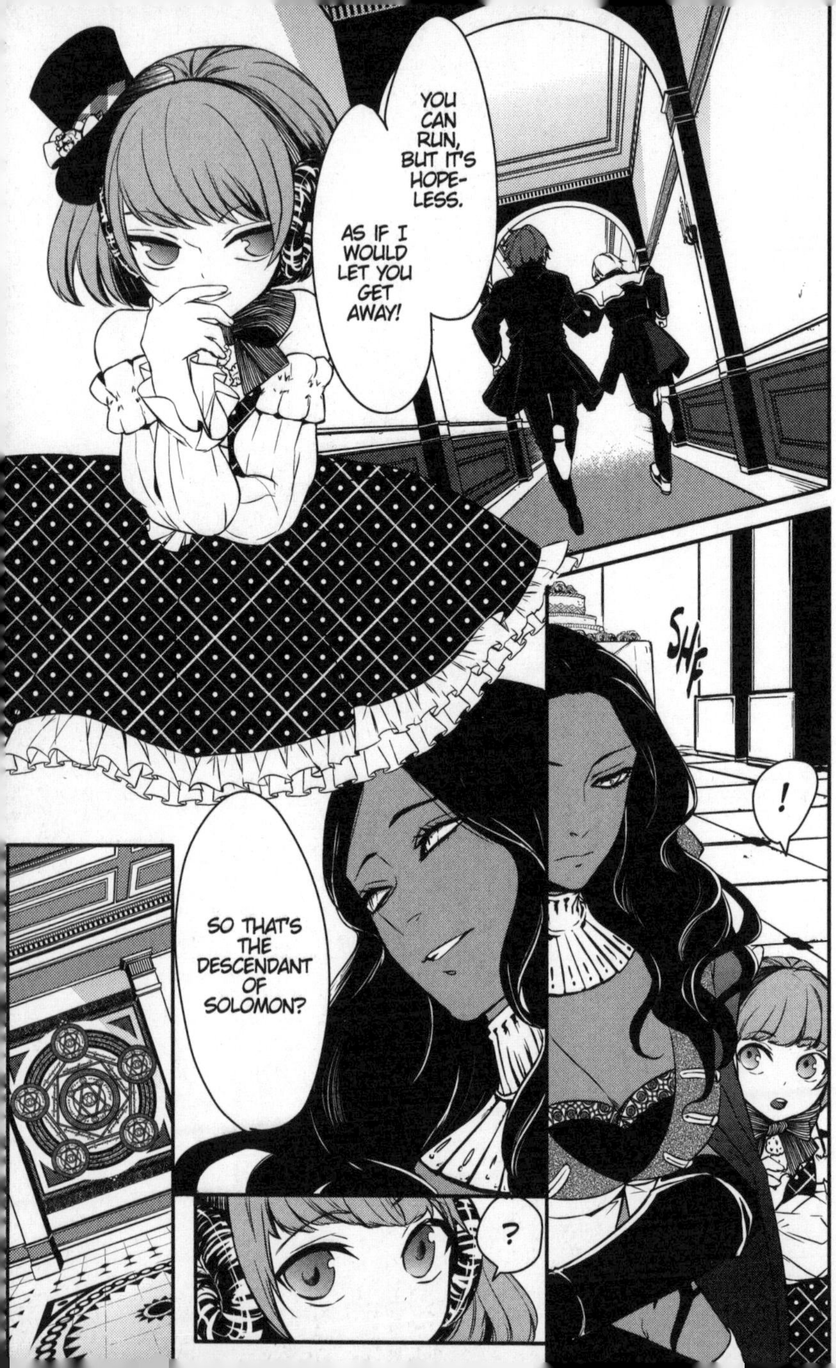
YOU CAN RUN, BUT IT'S HOPE-LESS.
AS IF I WOULD LET YOU GET AWAY!
SHF
!
SO THAT'S THE DESCENDANT OF SOLOMON?
?

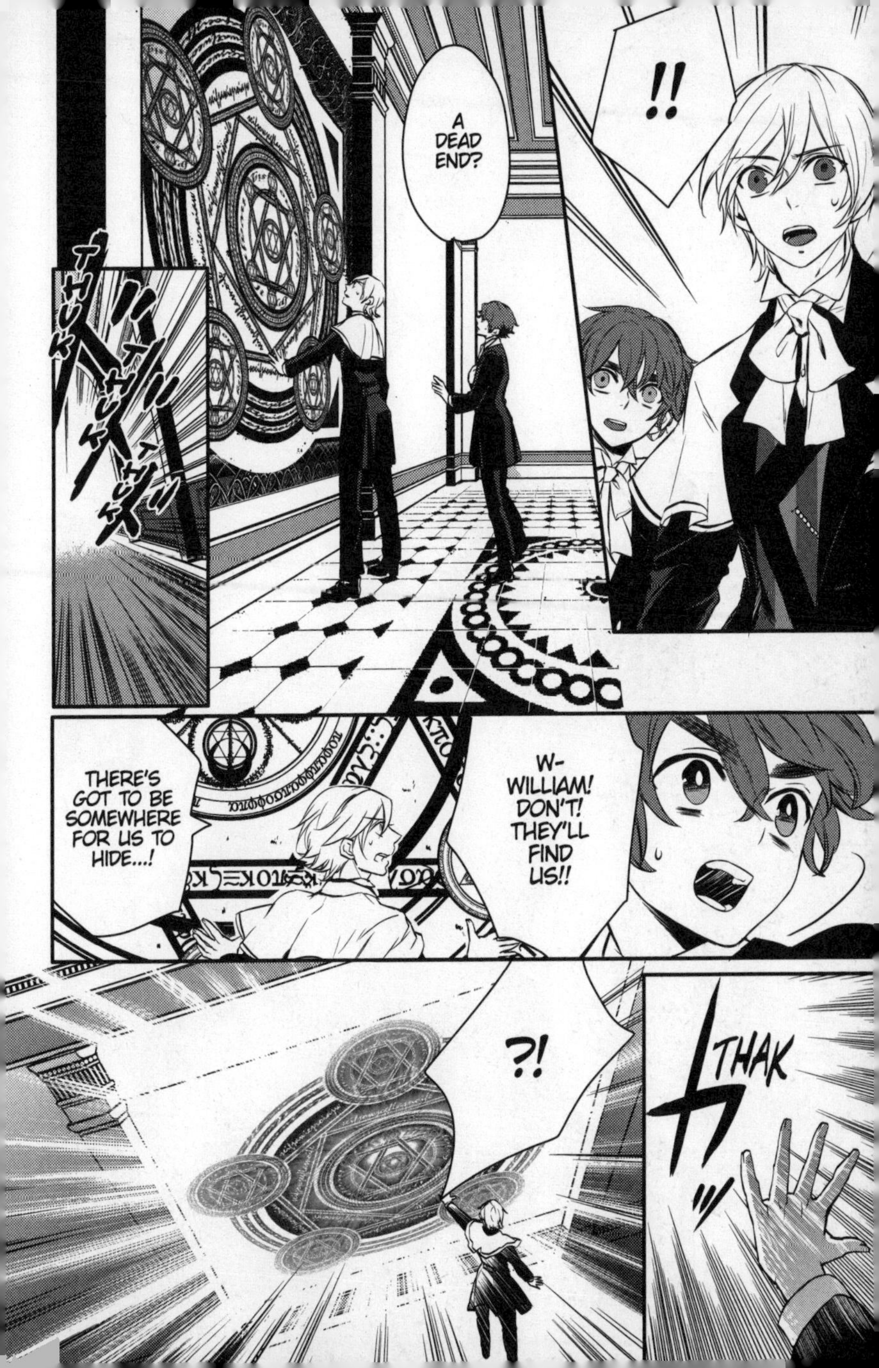
!!
A DEAD END?
W-WILLIAM! DON'T! THEY'LL FIND US!!
THERE'S GOT TO BE SOMEWHERE FOR US TO HIDE...!
THAK
?!

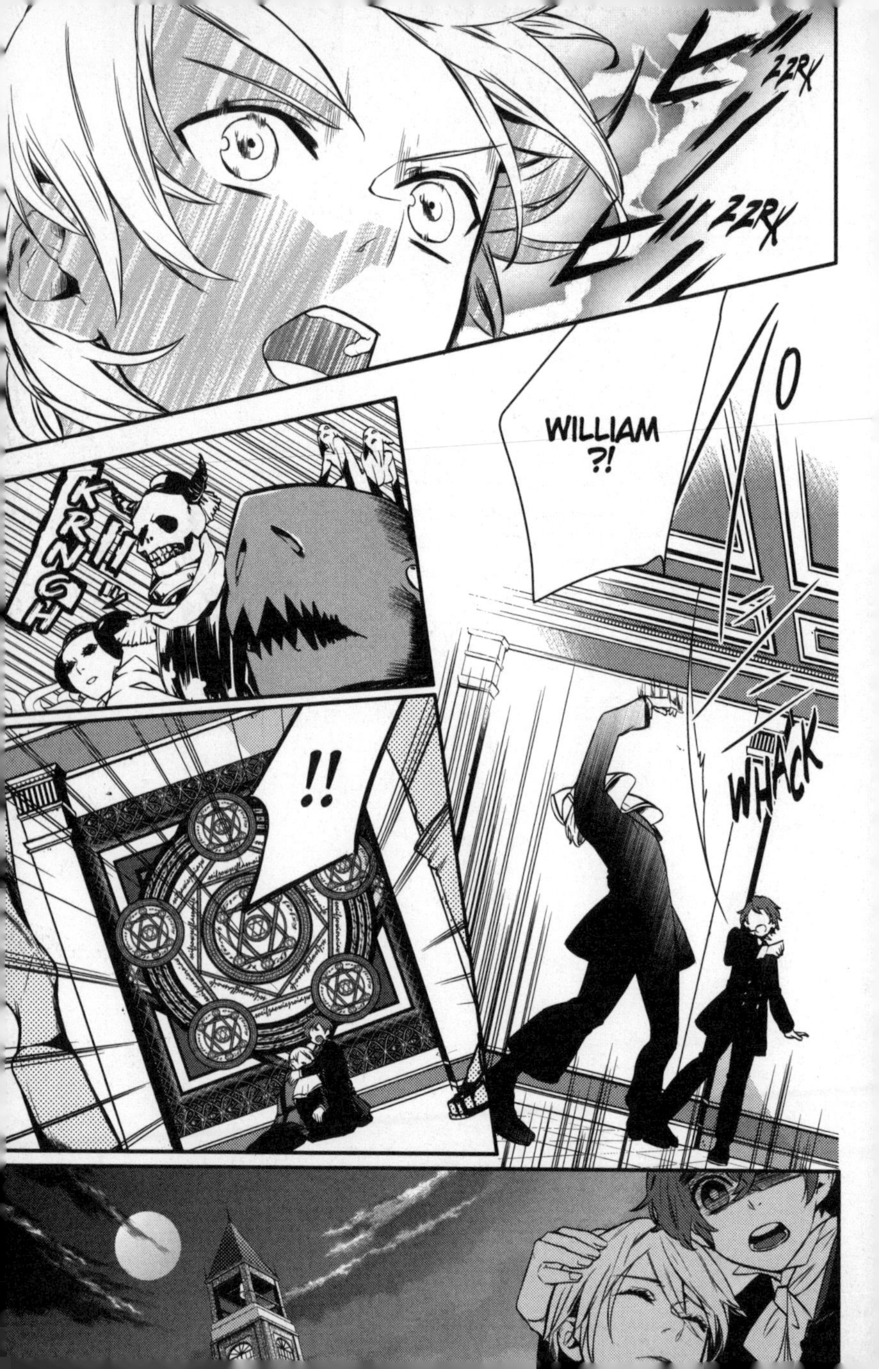
ZZRK
ZZRK
WILLIAM ?!
WHACK
KRNGH
!!

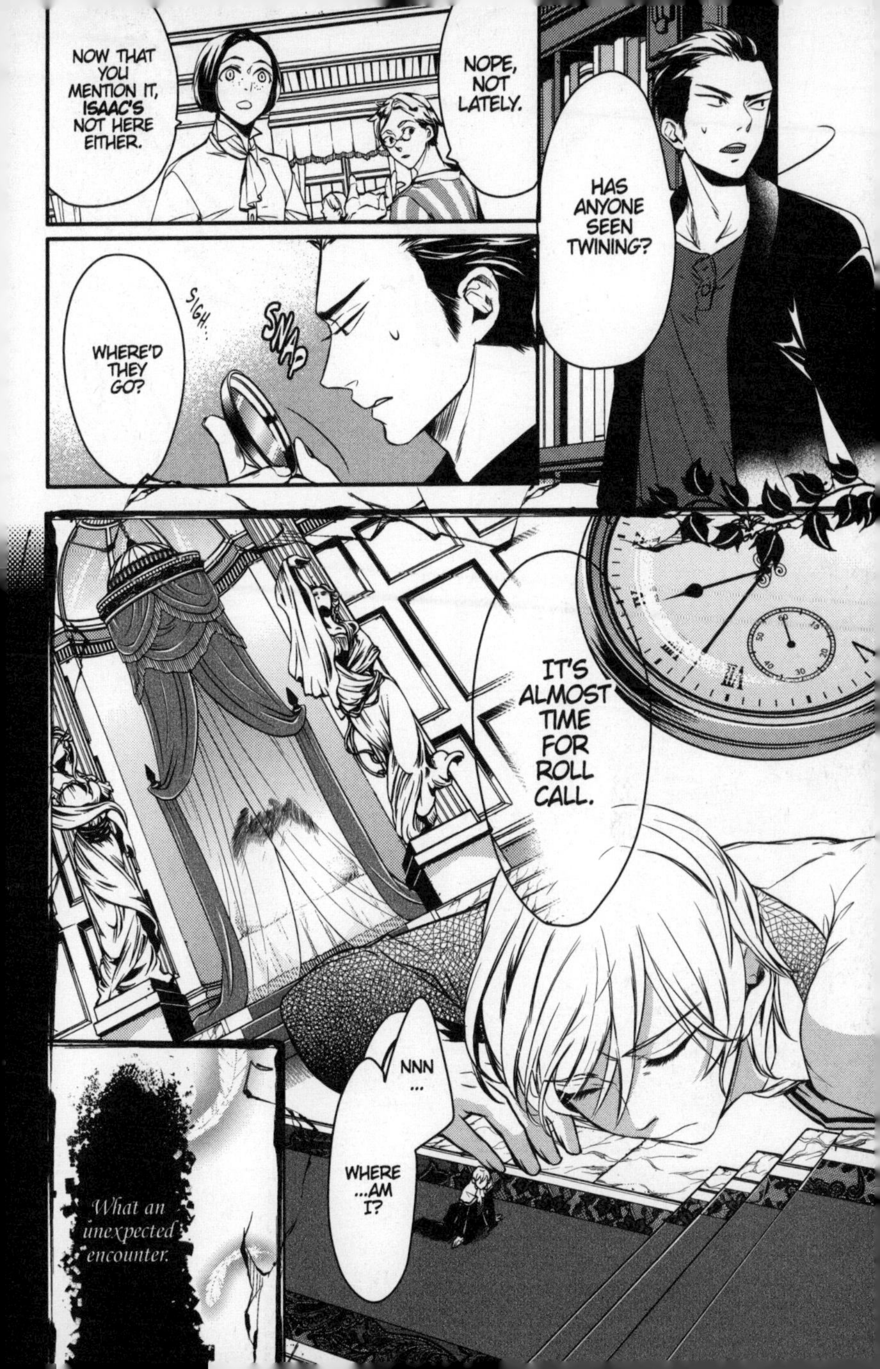
HAS ANYONE SEEN TWINING?
NOPE, NOT LATELY.
NOW THAT YOU MENTION IT, ISAAC'S NOT HERE EITHER.
SNAP
SIGH...
WHERE'D THEY GO?
IT'S ALMOST TIME FOR ROLL CALL.
NNN ...
WHERE ...AM I?
What an unexpected encounter.

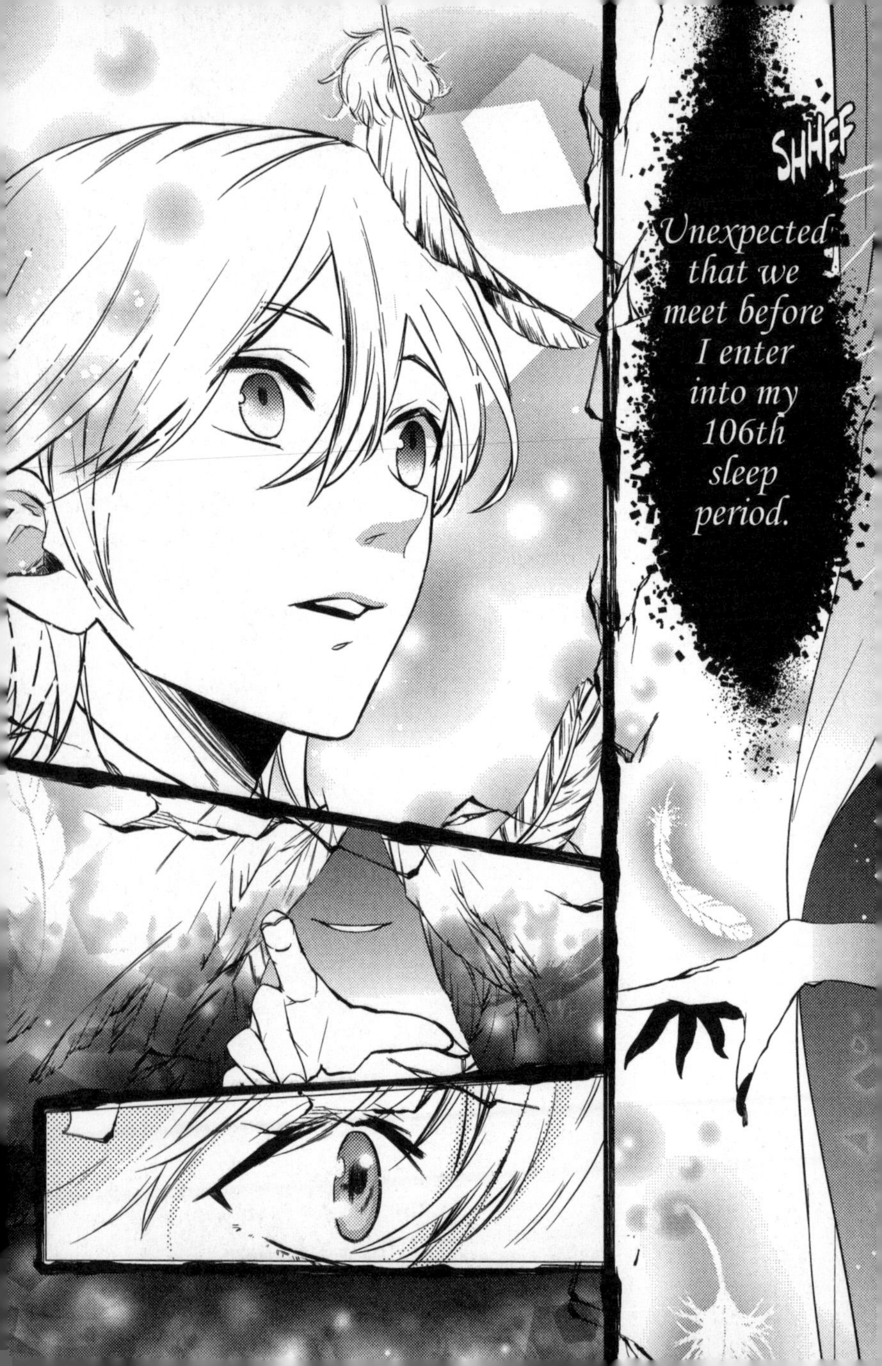
SHHFF
Unexpected that we meet before I enter into my 106th sleep period.

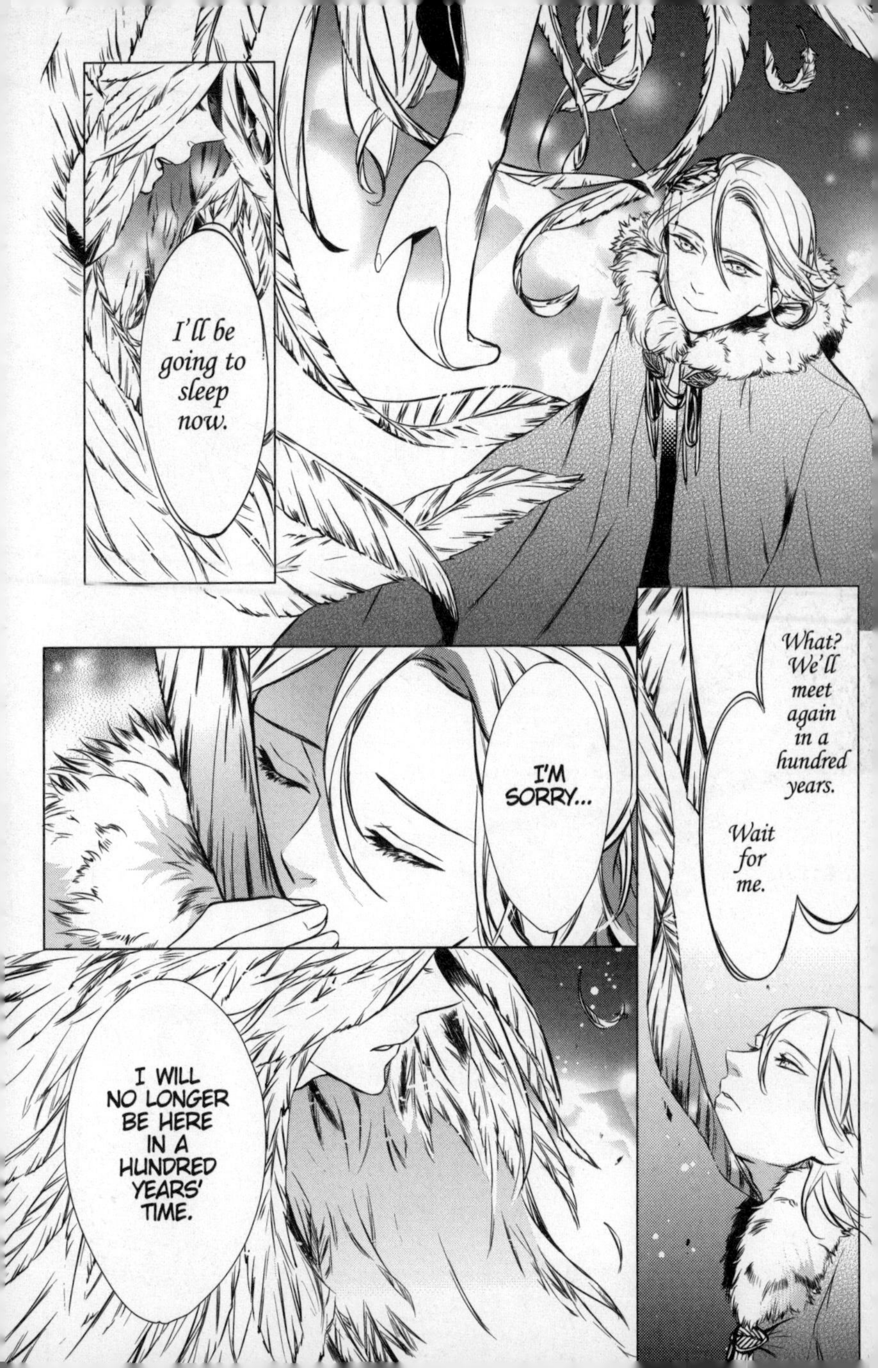
I'll be going to sleep now.
What? We'll meet again in a hundred years.
Wait for me.
I'M SORRY...
I WILL NO LONGER BE HERE IN A HUNDRED YEARS' TIME.

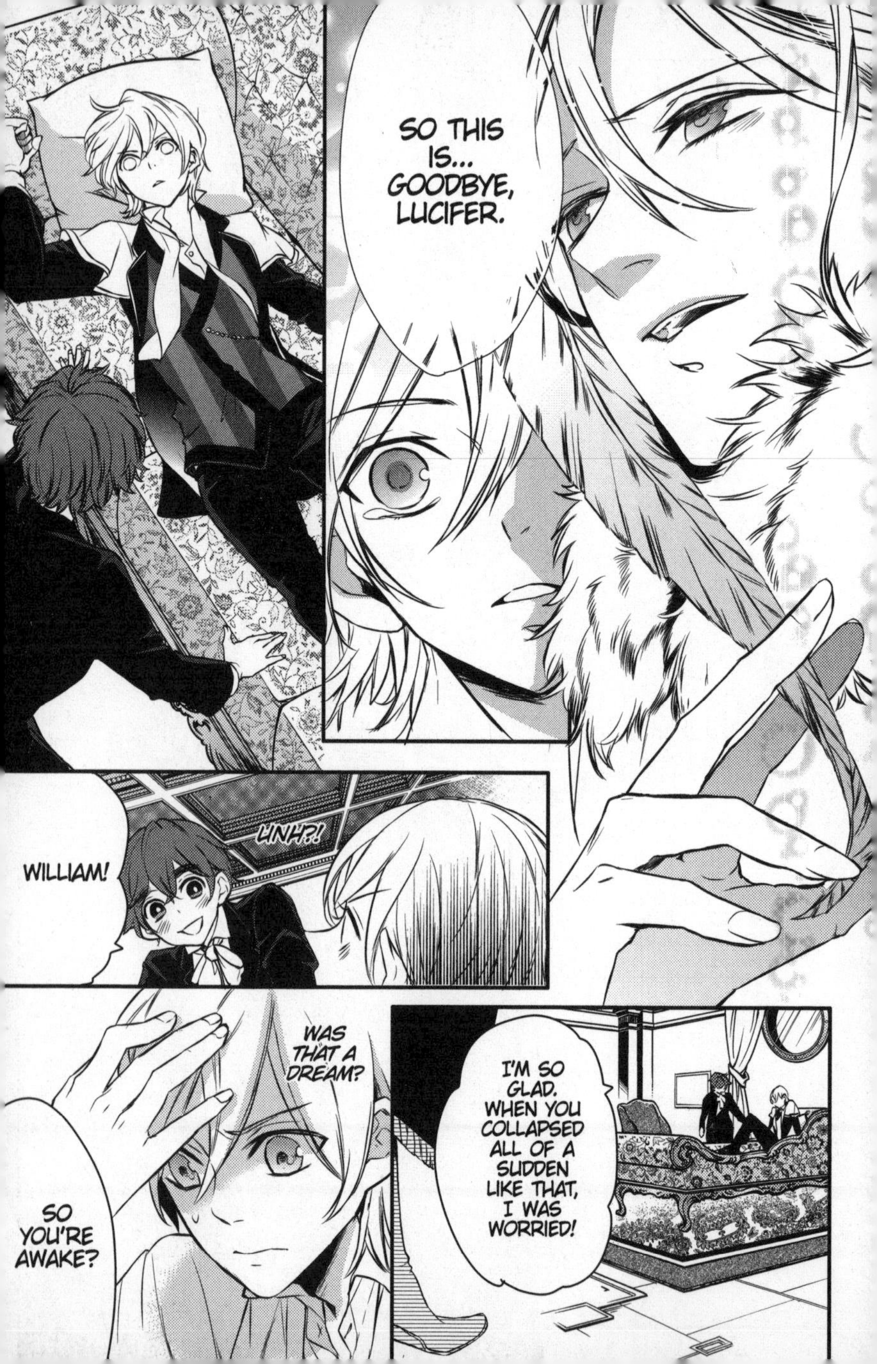
SO THIS IS... GOODBYE, LUCIFER.
UNH?!
WILLIAM!
I'M SO GLAD. WHEN YOU COLLAPSED ALL OF A SUDDEN LIKE THAT, I WAS WORRIED!
WAS THAT A DREAM?
SO YOU'RE AWAKE?

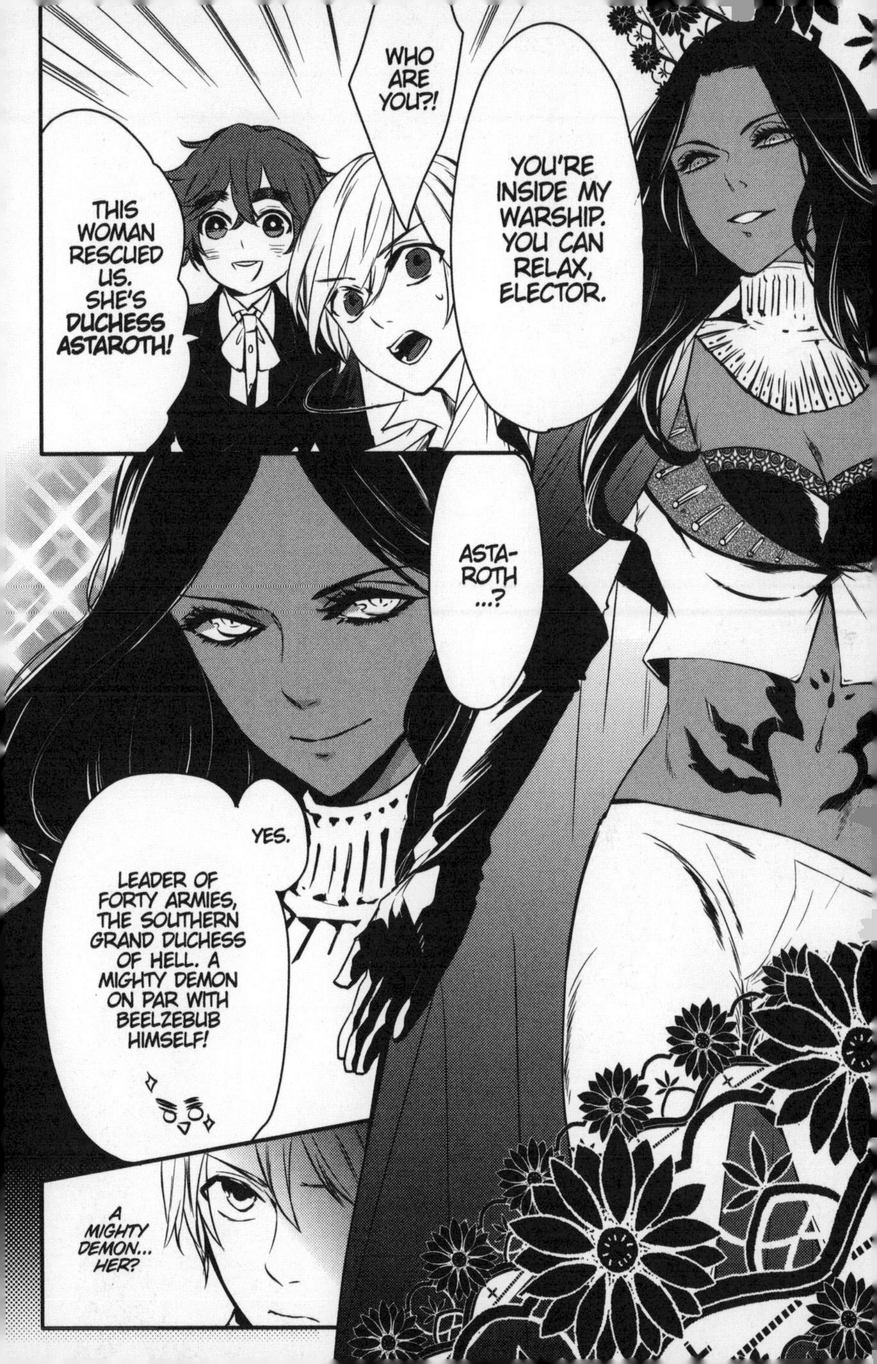
YOU'RE INSIDE MY WARSHIP. YOU CAN RELAX, ELECTOR.
WHO ARE YOU?!
THIS WOMAN RESCUED US. SHE'S DUCHESS ASTAROTH!
ASTA-ROTH ...?
YES.
LEADER OF FORTY ARMIES, THE SOUTHERN GRAND DUCHESS OF HELL. A MIGHTY DEMON ON PAR WITH BEELZEBUB HIMSELF!
A MIGHTY DEMON... HER?

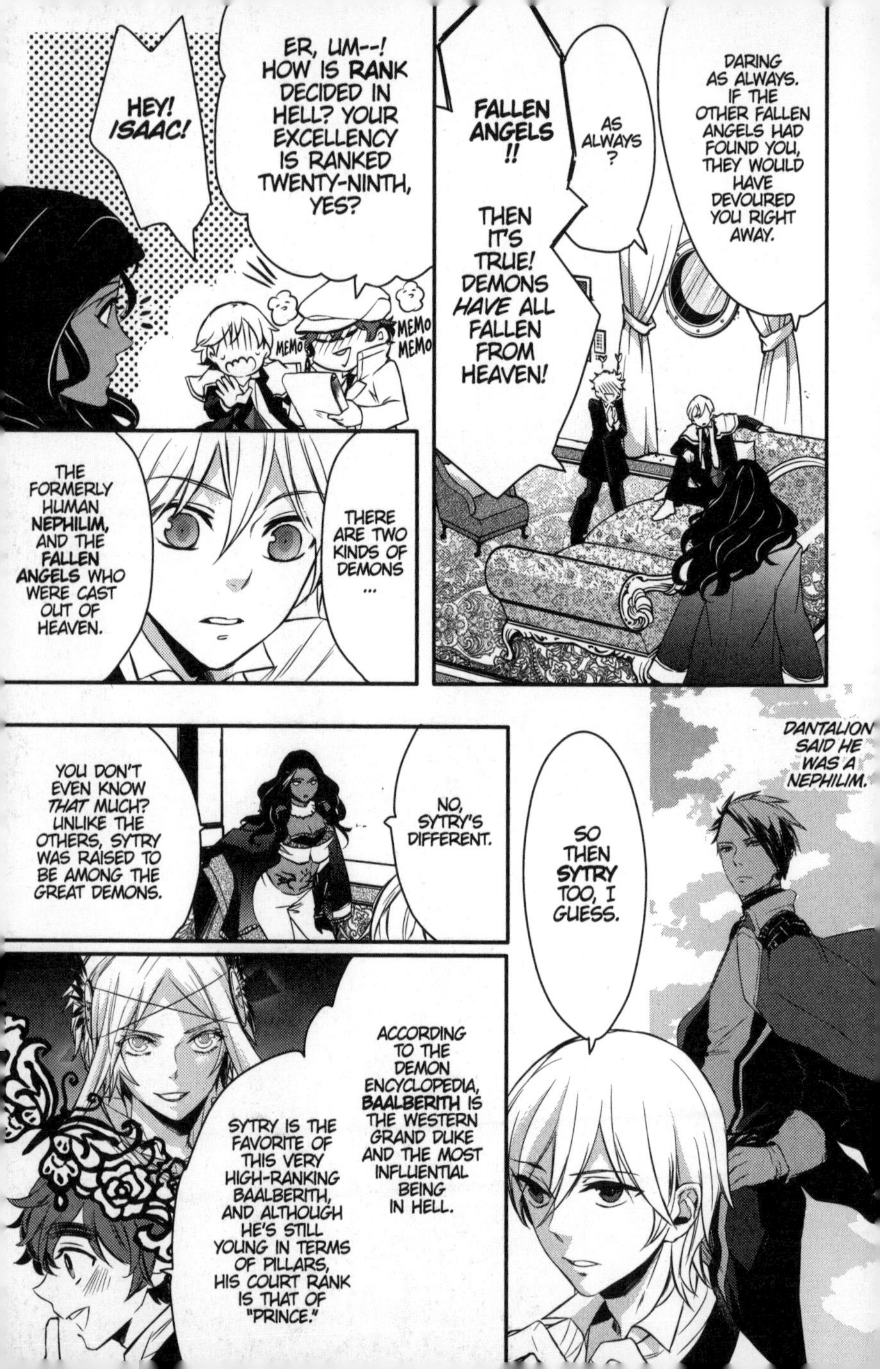
DARING AS ALWAYS. IF THE OTHER FALLEN ANGELS HAD FOUND YOU, THEY WOULD HAVE DEVOURED YOU RIGHT AWAY.
AS ALWAYS?
FALLEN ANGELS!!
THEN IT'S TRUE! DEMONS HAVE ALL FALLEN FROM HEAVEN!
ER, UM--! HOW IS RANK DECIDED IN HELL? YOUR EXCELLENCY IS RANKED TWENTY-NINTH, YES?
HEY! ISAAC!
MEMO MEMO
MEMO
THERE ARE TWO KINDS OF DEMONS...
THE FORMERLY HUMAN NEPHILIM, AND THE FALLEN ANGELS WHO WERE CAST OUT OF HEAVEN.
DANTALION SAID HE WAS A NEPHILIM.
SO THEN SYTRY TOO, I GUESS.
NO, SYTRY'S DIFFERENT.
YOU DON'T EVEN KNOW THAT MUCH? UNLIKE THE OTHERS, SYTRY WAS RAISED TO BE AMONG THE GREAT DEMONS.
ACCORDING TO THE DEMON ENCYCLOPEDIA, BAALBERITH IS THE WESTERN GRAND DUKE AND THE MOST INFLUENTIAL BEING IN HELL.
SYTRY IS THE FAVORITE OF THIS VERY HIGH-RANKING BAALBERITH, AND ALTHOUGH HE'S STILL YOUNG IN TERMS OF PILLARS, HIS COURT RANK IS THAT OF "PRINCE."

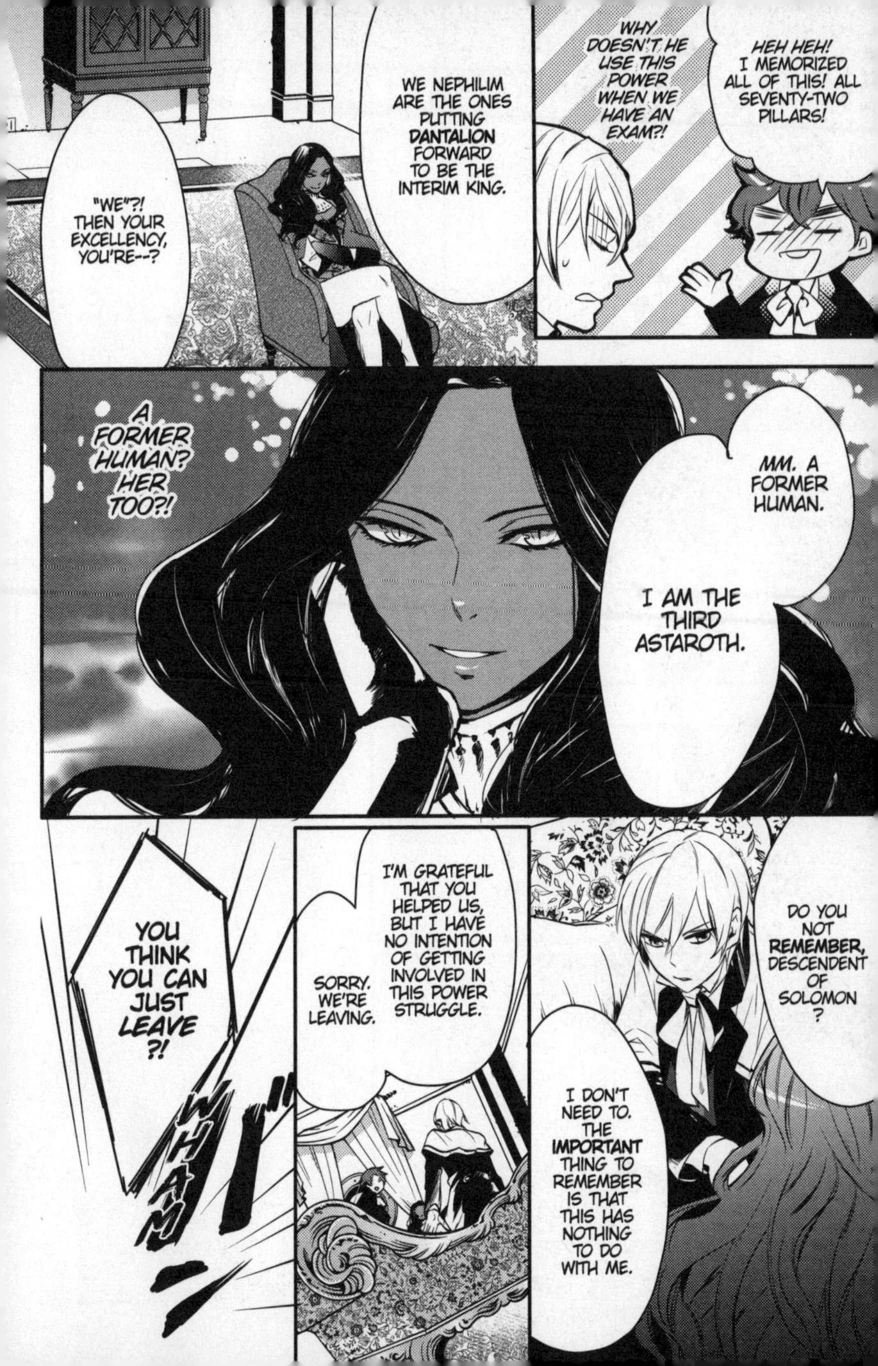
HEH HEH! I MEMORIZED ALL OF THIS! ALL SEVENTY-TWO PILLARS!
WHY DOESN'T HE USE THIS POWER WHEN WE HAVE AN EXAM?!
WE NEPHILIM ARE THE ONES PUTTING **DANTALION** FORWARD TO BE THE INTERIM KING.
"WE"?! THEN YOUR EXCELLENCY, YOU'RE--?
MM. A FORMER HUMAN.
I AM THE THIRD ASTAROTH.
A FORMER HUMAN? HER TOO?!
DO YOU NOT **REMEMBER,** DESCENDENT OF SOLOMON?
I DON'T NEED TO. THE **IMPORTANT** THING TO REMEMBER IS THAT THIS HAS NOTHING TO DO WITH ME.
I'M GRATEFUL THAT YOU HELPED US, BUT I HAVE NO INTENTION OF GETTING INVOLVED IN THIS POWER STRUGGLE.
SORRY. WE'RE LEAVING.
YOU THINK YOU CAN JUST ***LEAVE*** ?!
WHAM

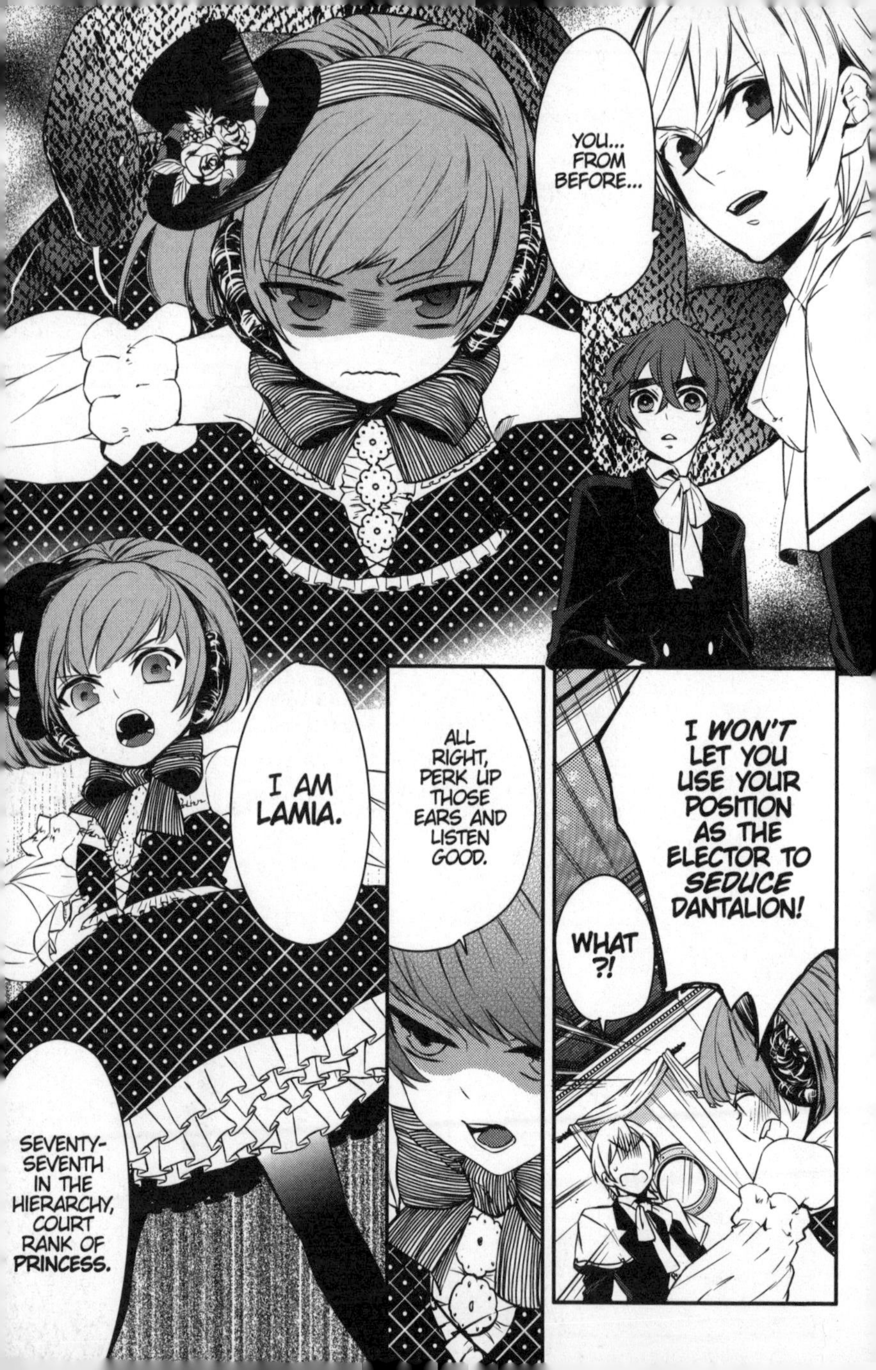
YOU... FROM BEFORE...
I *WON'T* LET YOU USE YOUR POSITION AS THE ELECTOR TO *SEDUCE* DANTALION!
WHAT?!
ALL RIGHT, PERK UP THOSE EARS AND LISTEN GOOD.
I AM LAMIA.
SEVENTY-SEVENTH IN THE HIERARCHY, COURT RANK OF PRINCESS.

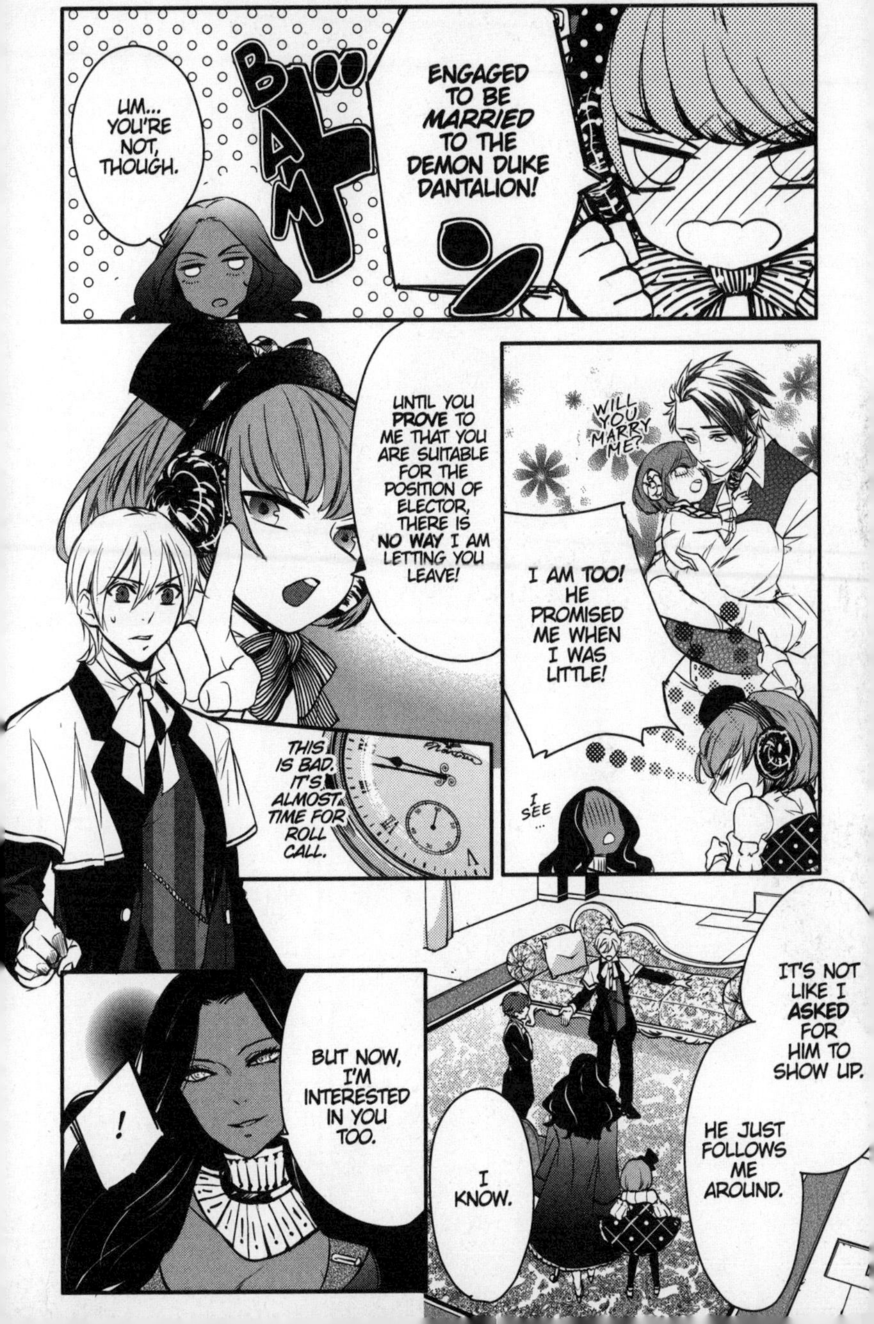
ENGAGED TO BE MARRIED TO THE DEMON DUKE DANTALION!
BLAM
UM... YOU'RE NOT, THOUGH.
WILL YOU MARRY ME?
I AM TOO! HE PROMISED ME WHEN I WAS LITTLE!
I SEE...
UNTIL YOU PROVE TO ME THAT YOU ARE SUITABLE FOR THE POSITION OF ELECTOR, THERE IS NO WAY I AM LETTING YOU LEAVE!
THIS IS BAD. IT'S ALMOST TIME FOR ROLL CALL.
IT'S NOT LIKE I ASKED FOR HIM TO SHOW UP.
HE JUST FOLLOWS ME AROUND.
I KNOW.
BUT NOW, I'M INTERESTED IN YOU TOO.
!

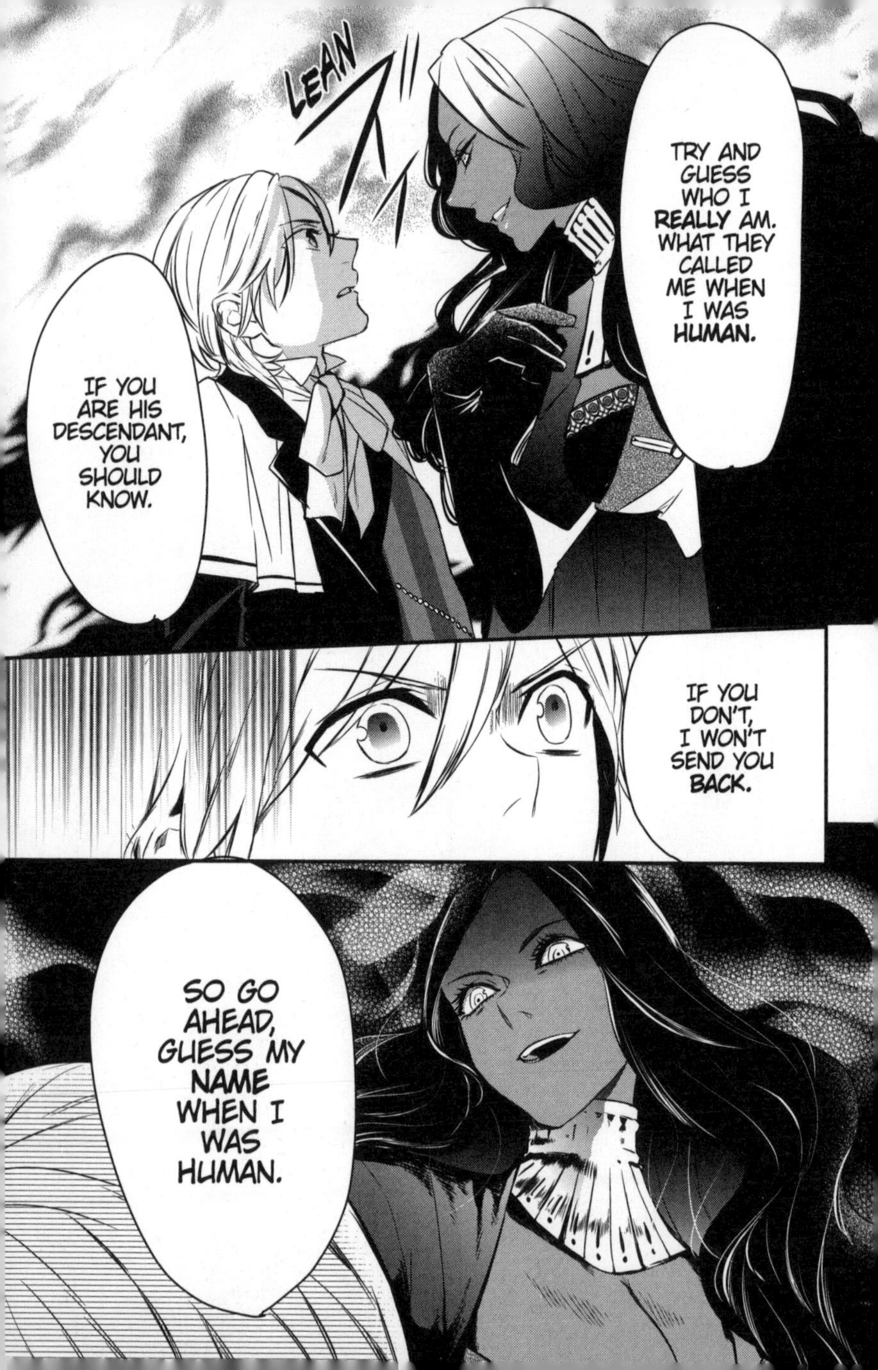
TRY AND GUESS WHO I REALLY AM. WHAT THEY CALLED ME WHEN I WAS HUMAN.
LEAN
IF YOU ARE HIS DESCENDANT, YOU SHOULD KNOW.
IF YOU DON'T, I WON'T SEND YOU BACK.
SO GO AHEAD, GUESS MY NAME WHEN I WAS HUMAN.

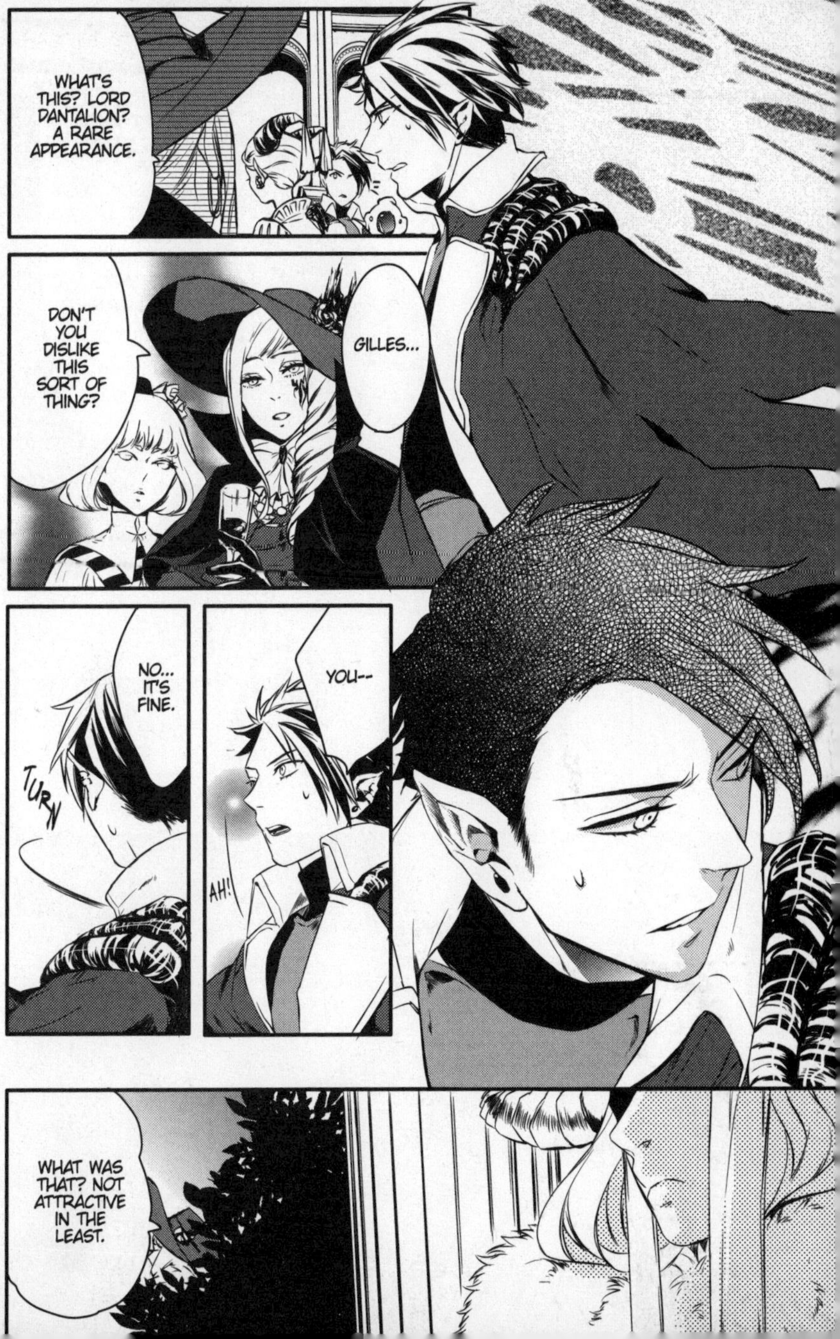
WHAT'S THIS? LORD DANTALION? A RARE APPEARANCE.
GILLES...
DON'T YOU DISLIKE THIS SORT OF THING?
YOU--
AH!
NO... IT'S FINE.
TURN
WHAT WAS THAT? NOT ATTRACTIVE IN THE LEAST.

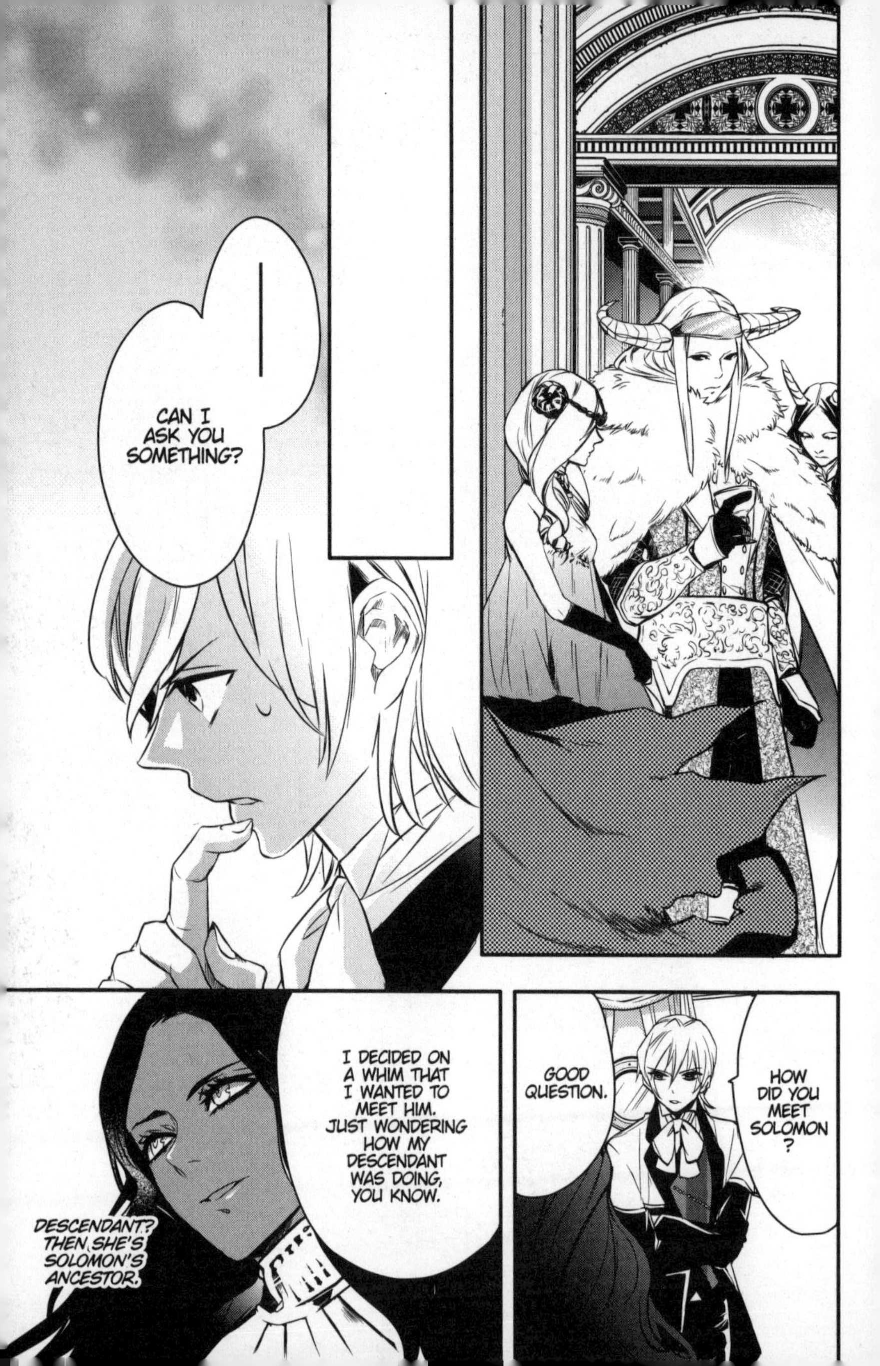
CAN I ASK YOU SOMETHING?
HOW DID YOU MEET SOLOMON?
GOOD QUESTION.
I DECIDED ON A WHIM THAT I WANTED TO MEET HIM. JUST WONDERING HOW MY DESCENDANT WAS DOING, YOU KNOW.
DESCENDANT? THEN SHE'S SOLOMON'S ANCESTOR.

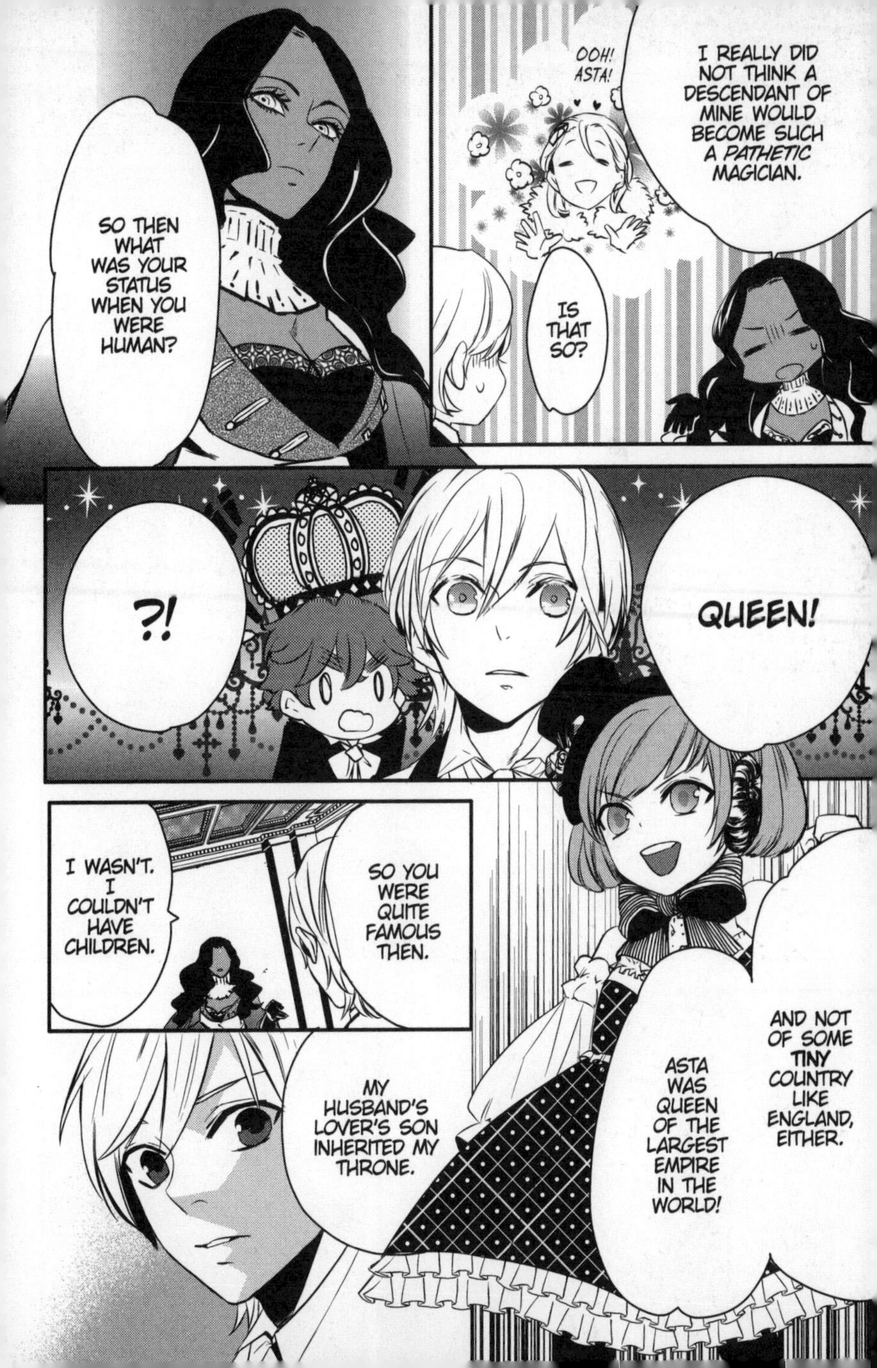
I REALLY DID NOT THINK A DESCENDANT OF MINE WOULD BECOME SUCH A *PATHETIC* MAGICIAN.
OOH! ASTA!
IS THAT SO?
SO THEN WHAT WAS YOUR STATUS WHEN YOU WERE HUMAN?
QUEEN!
?!
AND NOT OF SOME TINY COUNTRY LIKE ENGLAND, EITHER.
ASTA WAS QUEEN OF THE LARGEST EMPIRE IN THE WORLD!
SO YOU WERE QUITE FAMOUS THEN.
I WASN'T. I COULDN'T HAVE CHILDREN.
MY HUSBAND'S LOVER'S SON INHERITED MY THRONE.

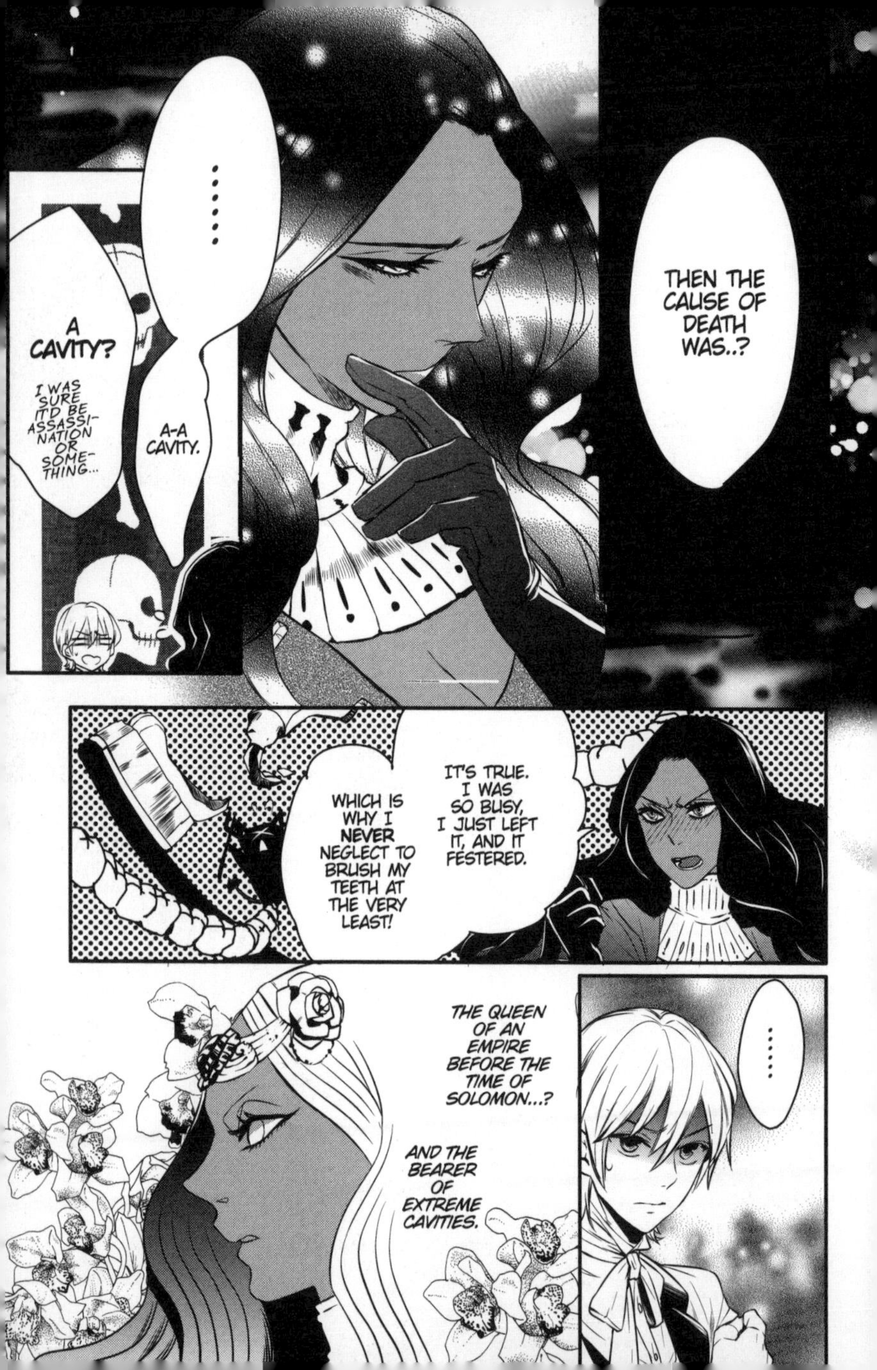
THEN THE CAUSE OF DEATH WAS..?
......
A-A CAVITY.
A CAVITY?
I WAS SURE IT'D BE ASSASSINATION OR SOMETHING...
IT'S TRUE. I WAS SO BUSY, I JUST LEFT IT, AND IT FESTERED.
WHICH IS WHY I **NEVER** NEGLECT TO BRUSH MY TEETH AT THE VERY LEAST!
......
THE QUEEN OF AN EMPIRE BEFORE THE TIME OF SOLOMON...?
AND THE BEARER OF EXTREME CAVITIES.

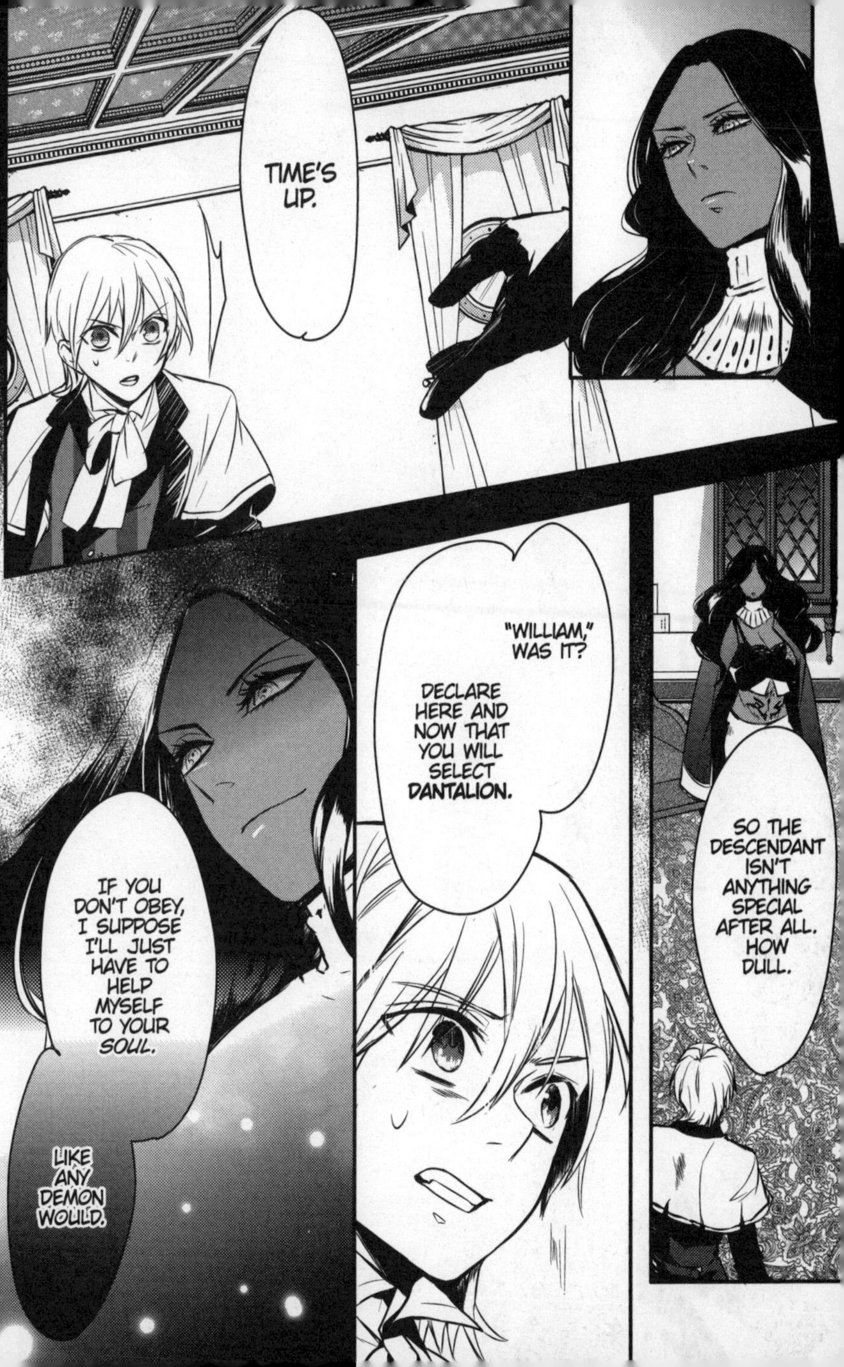
TIME'S UP.
SO THE DESCENDANT ISN'T ANYTHING SPECIAL AFTER ALL. HOW DULL.
"WILLIAM," WAS IT?
DECLARE HERE AND NOW THAT YOU WILL SELECT DANTALION.
IF YOU DON'T OBEY, I SUPPOSE I'LL JUST HAVE TO HELP MYSELF TO YOUR SOUL.
LIKE ANY DEMON WOULD.

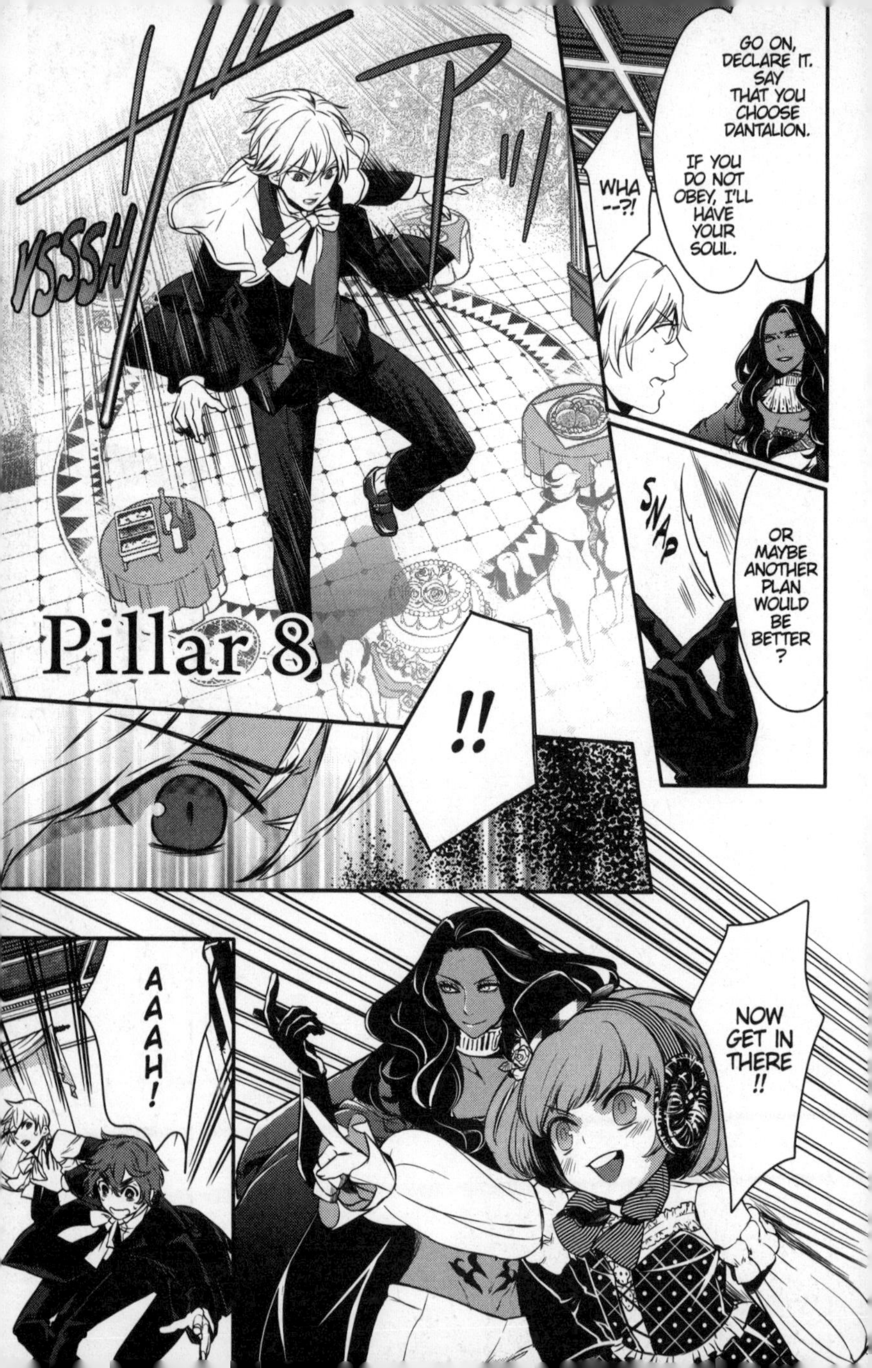
GO ON, DECLARE IT. SAY THAT YOU CHOOSE DANTALION.
IF YOU DO NOT OBEY, I'LL HAVE YOUR SOUL.
WHA--?!
SNAP
OR MAYBE ANOTHER PLAN WOULD BE BETTER?
VSSSH
Pillar 8
!!
NOW GET IN THERE!!
AAAAH!

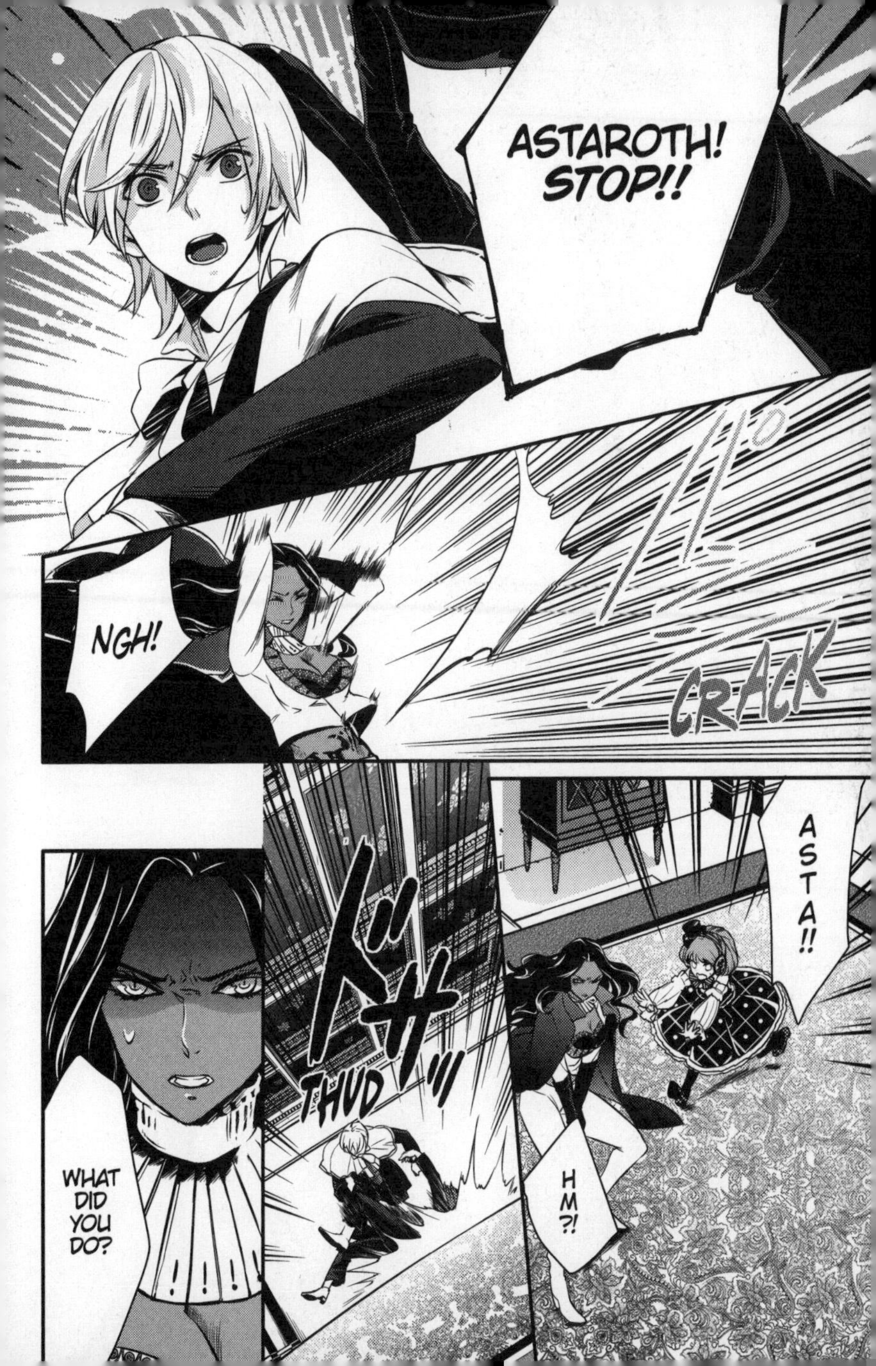
ASTAROTH! STOP!!
CRACK
NGH!
ASTA!!
HM?!
THUD
WHAT DID YOU DO?

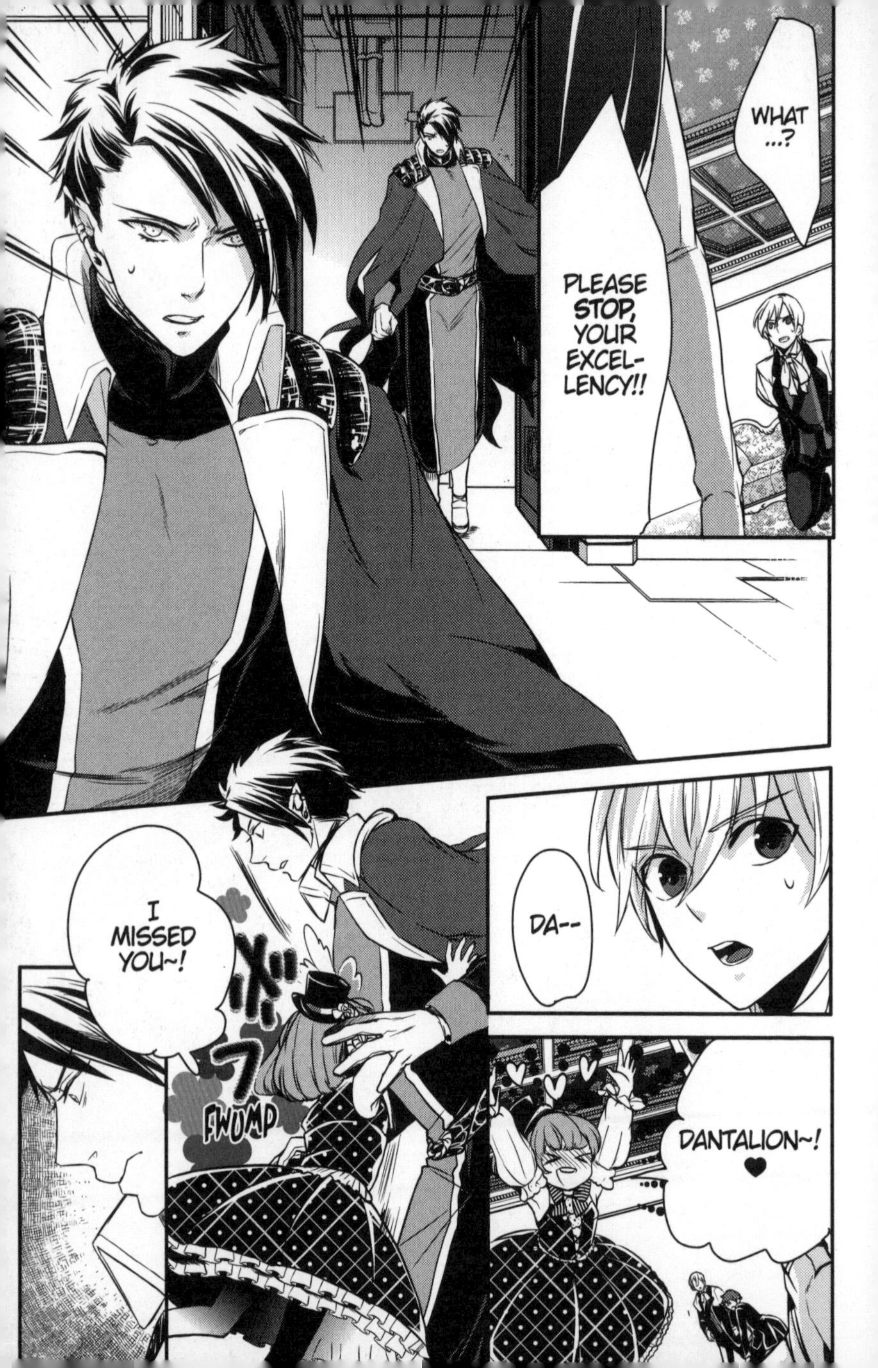
WHAT ...?
PLEASE STOP, YOUR EXCEL-LENCY!!
DA--
DANTALION~!
I MISSED YOU~!
FWUMP

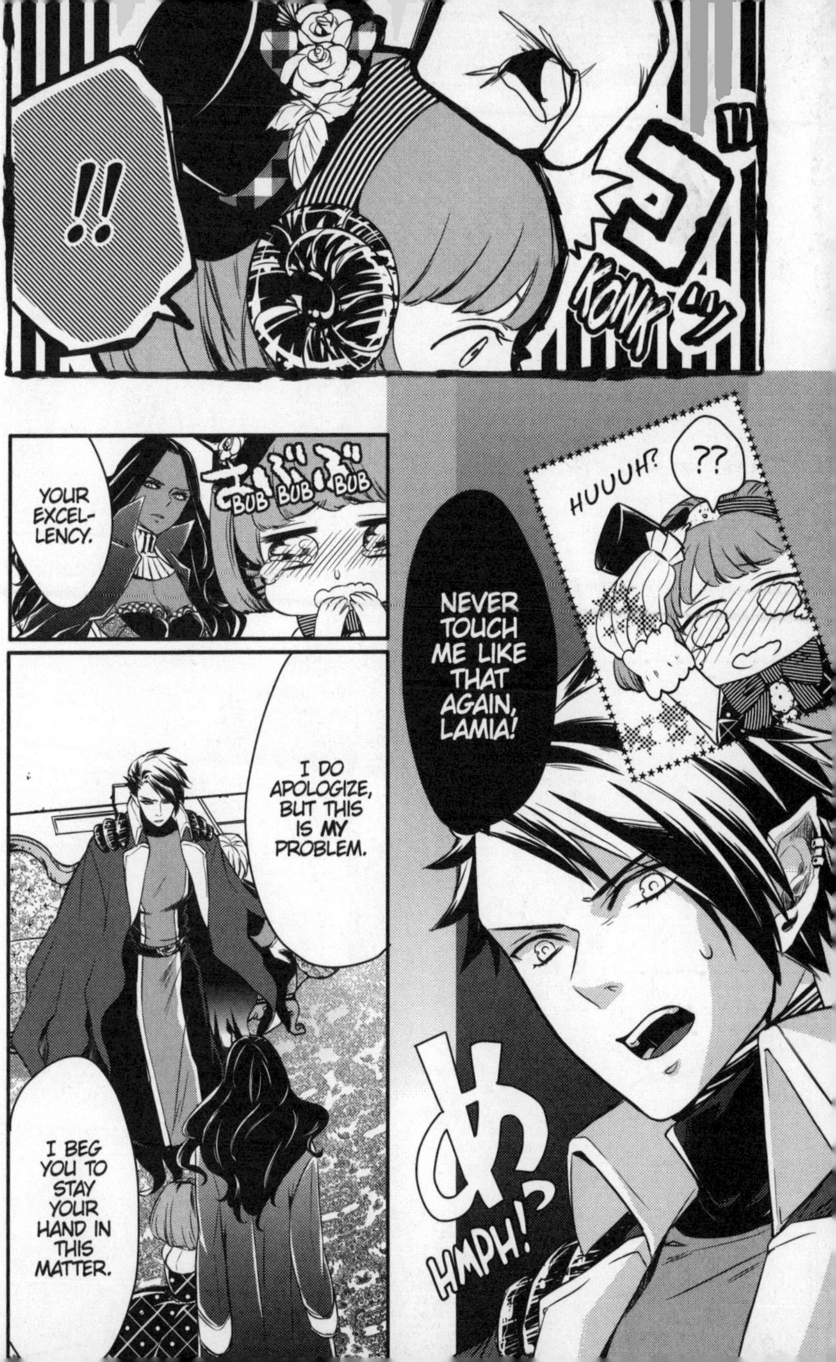
!!
KONK
HUUUH?
??
NEVER TOUCH ME LIKE THAT AGAIN, LAMIA!
HMPH!
BUB BUB BUB
YOUR EXCEL-LENCY.
I DO APOLOGIZE, BUT THIS IS MY PROBLEM.
I BEG YOU TO STAY YOUR HAND IN THIS MATTER.

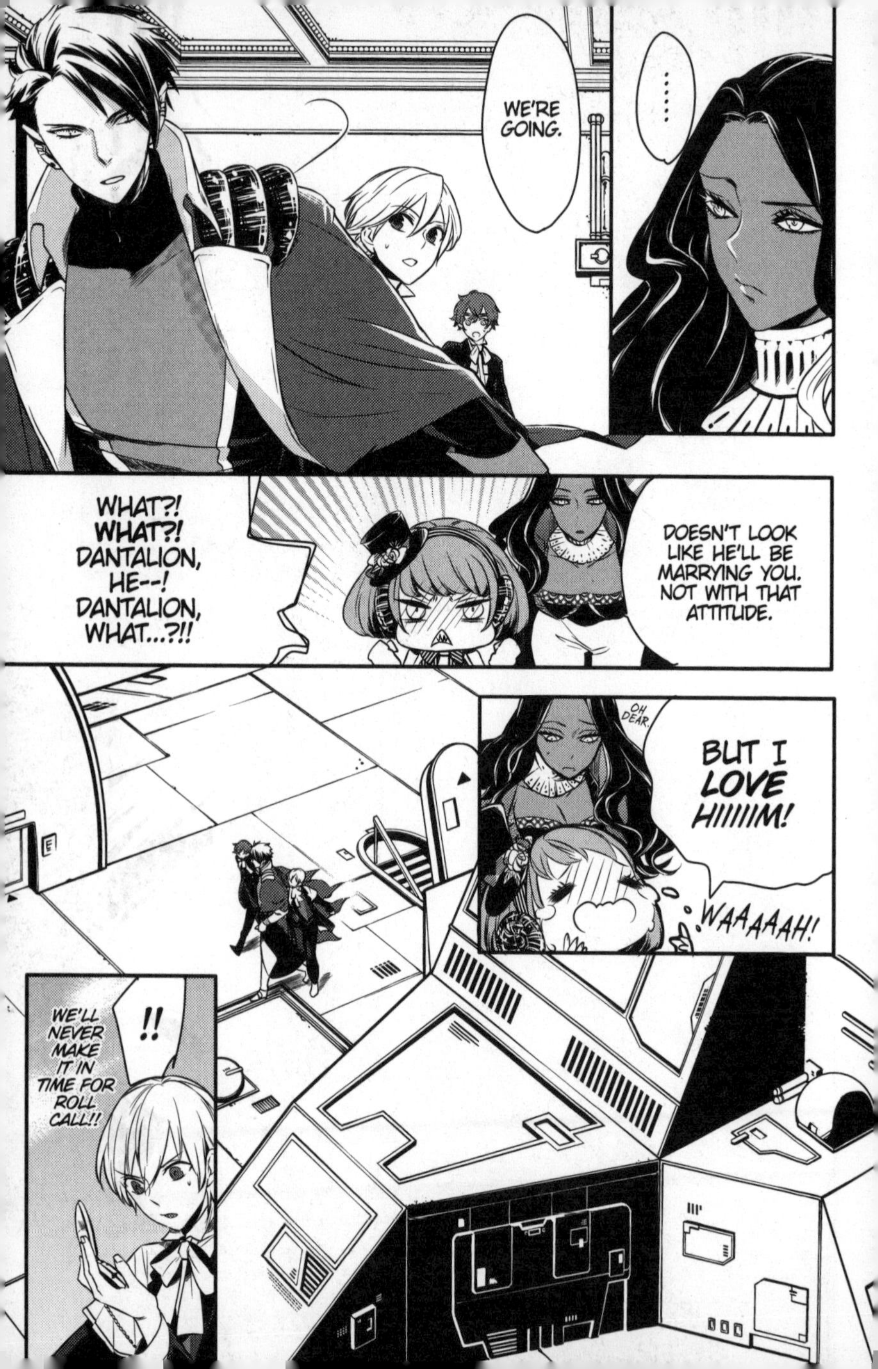
......
WE'RE GOING.
DOESN'T LOOK LIKE HE'LL BE MARRYING YOU. NOT WITH THAT ATTITUDE.
WHAT?! WHAT?! DANTALION, HE--! DANTALION, WHAT...?!!
OH DEAR.
BUT I LOVE HIIIIIM!
WAAAAAH!
!!
WE'LL NEVER MAKE IT IN TIME FOR ROLL CALL!!

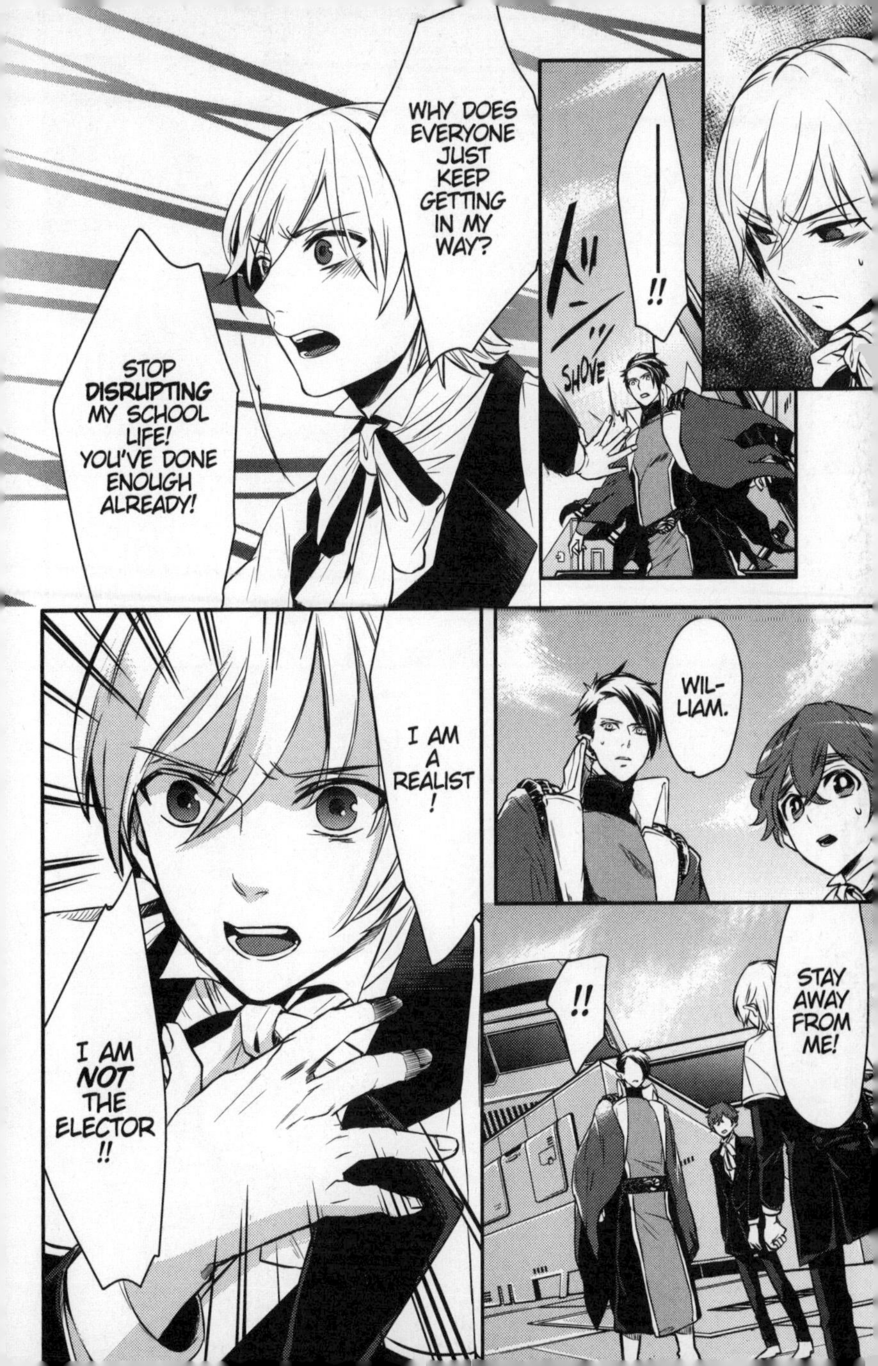
!!
SHOVE
WHY DOES EVERYONE JUST KEEP GETTING IN MY WAY?
STOP DISRUPTING MY SCHOOL LIFE! YOU'VE DONE ENOUGH ALREADY!
WIL-LIAM.
STAY AWAY FROM ME!
!!
I AM A REALIST!
I AM *NOT* THE ELECTOR!!

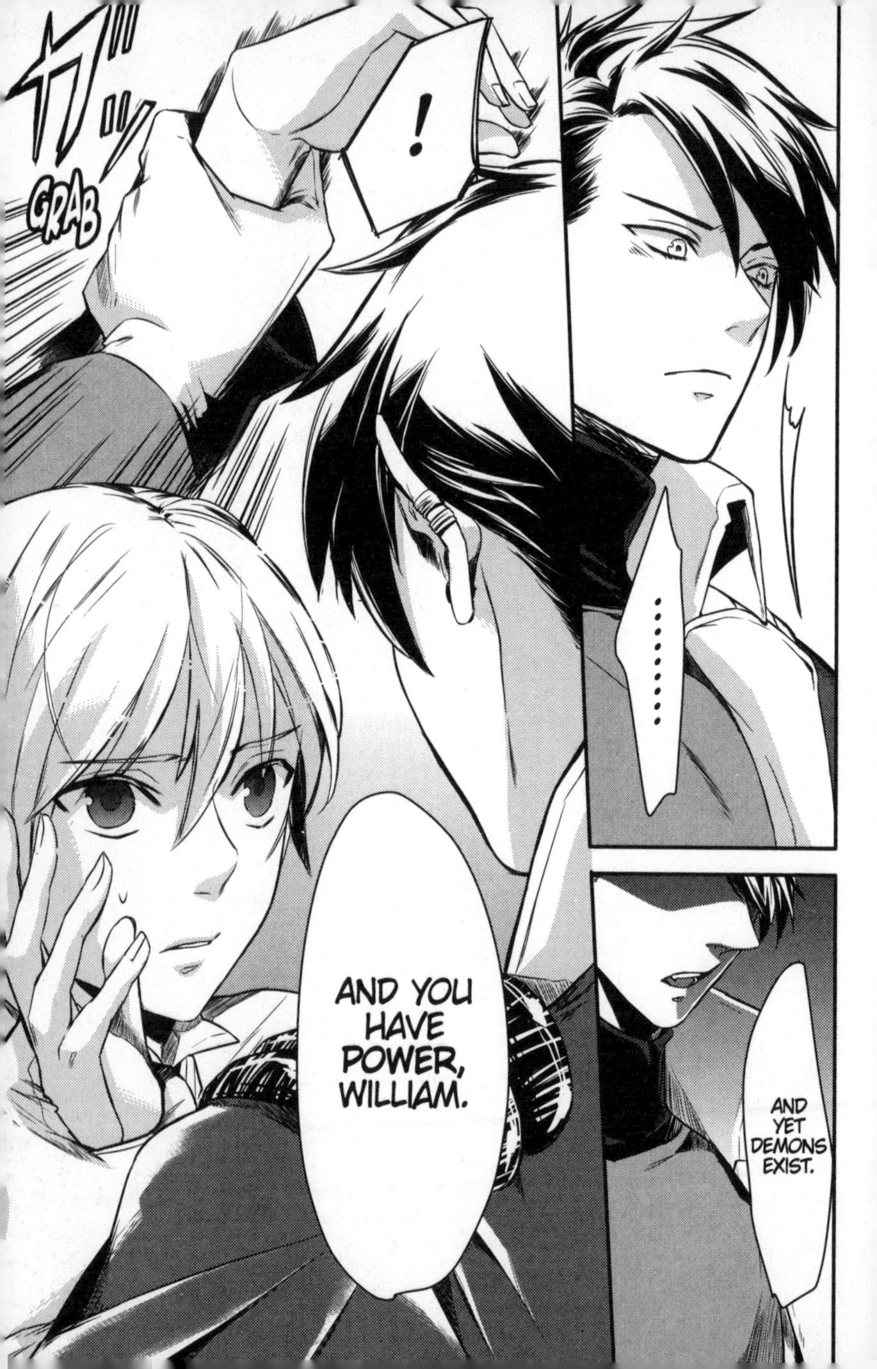

......
AND YET DEMONS EXIST.
!
ガッ
GRAB
AND YOU HAVE POWER, WILLIAM.

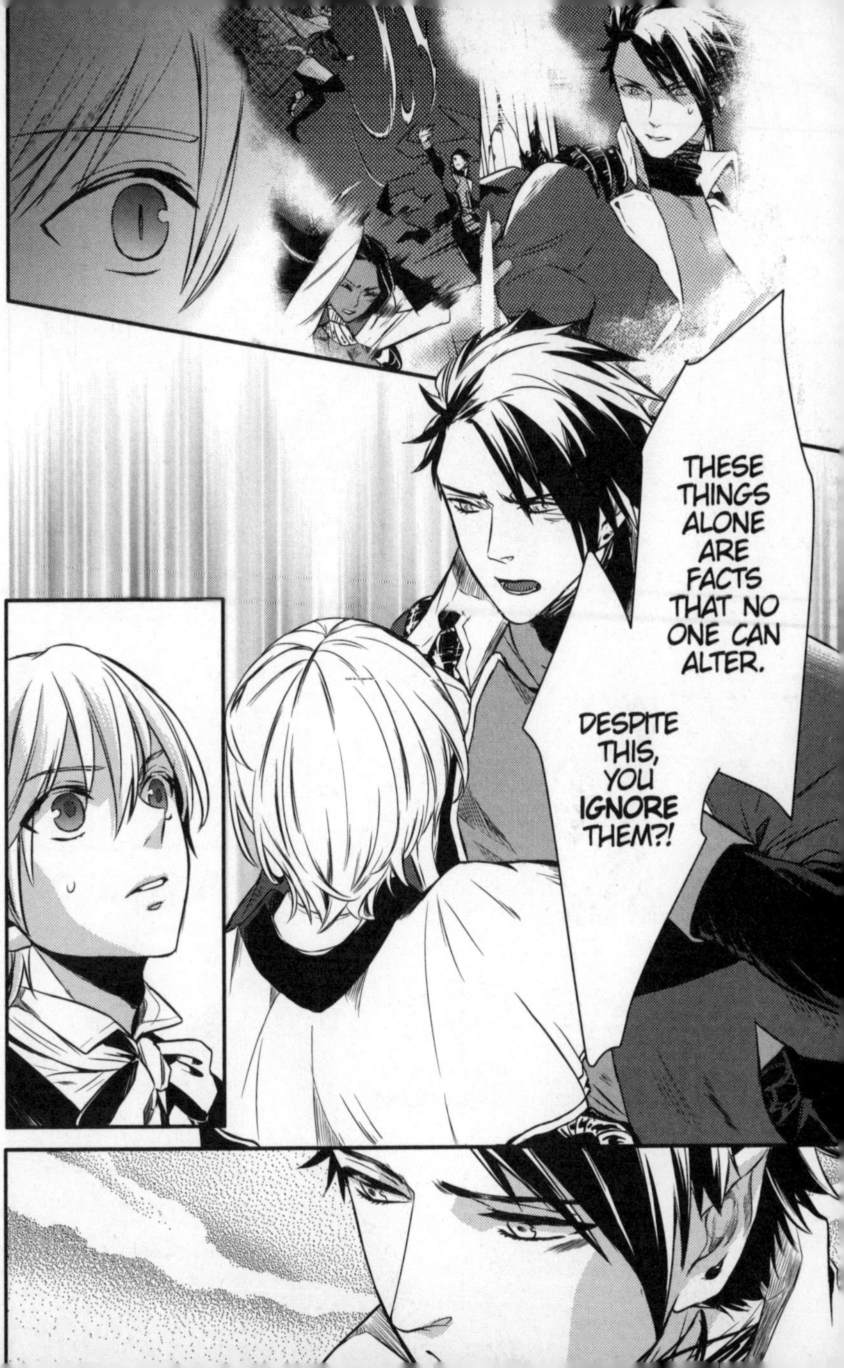
THESE THINGS ALONE ARE FACTS THAT NO ONE CAN ALTER.
DESPITE THIS, YOU IGNORE THEM?!

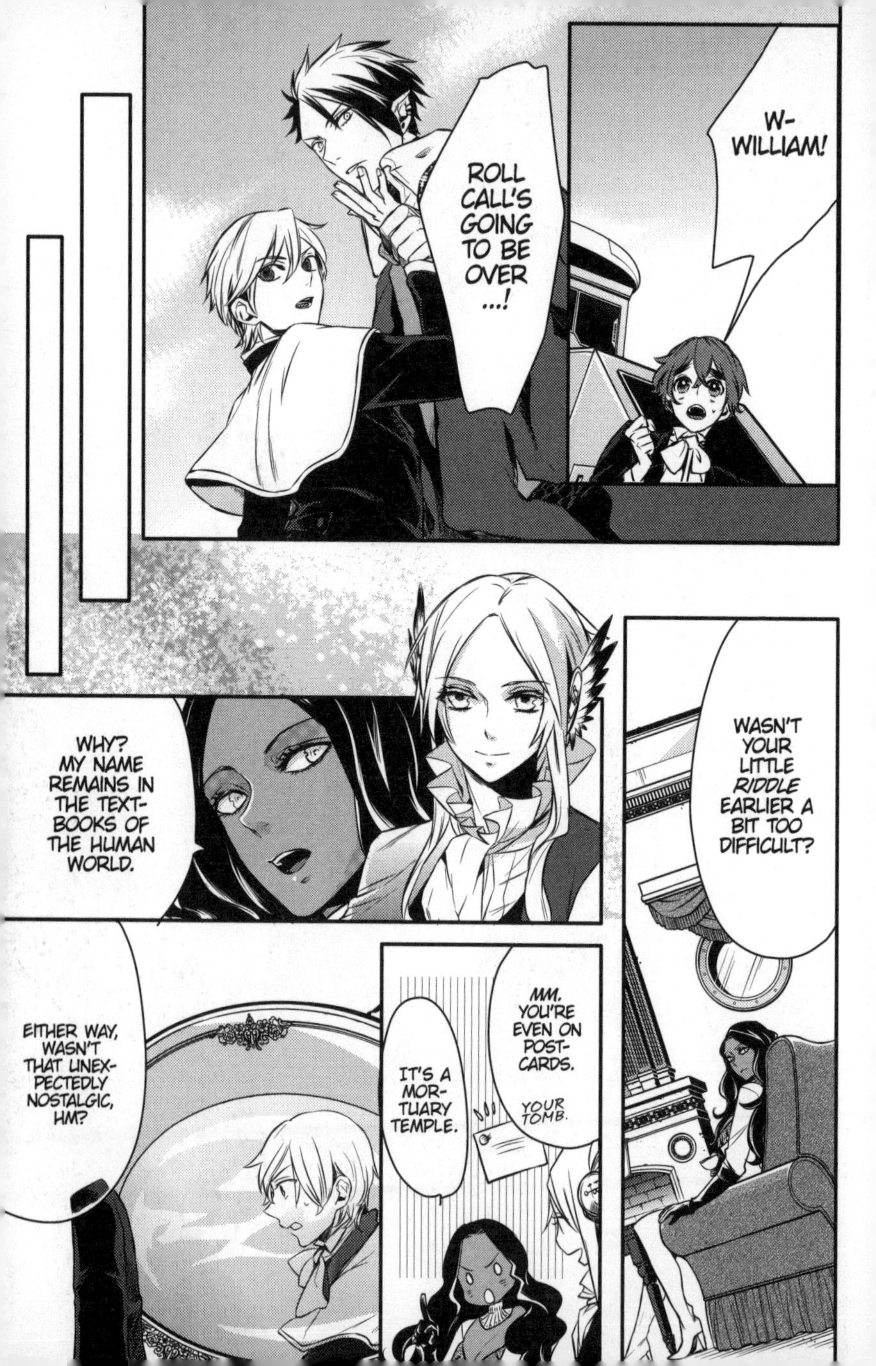
W-WILLIAM!
ROLL CALL'S GOING TO BE OVER ...!
WASN'T YOUR LITTLE *RIDDLE* EARLIER A BIT TOO DIFFICULT?
WHY? MY NAME REMAINS IN THE TEXTBOOKS OF THE HUMAN WORLD.
MM. YOU'RE EVEN ON POSTCARDS.
YOUR TOMB.
IT'S A MORTUARY TEMPLE.
EITHER WAY, WASN'T THAT UNEXPECTEDLY NOSTALGIC, HM?

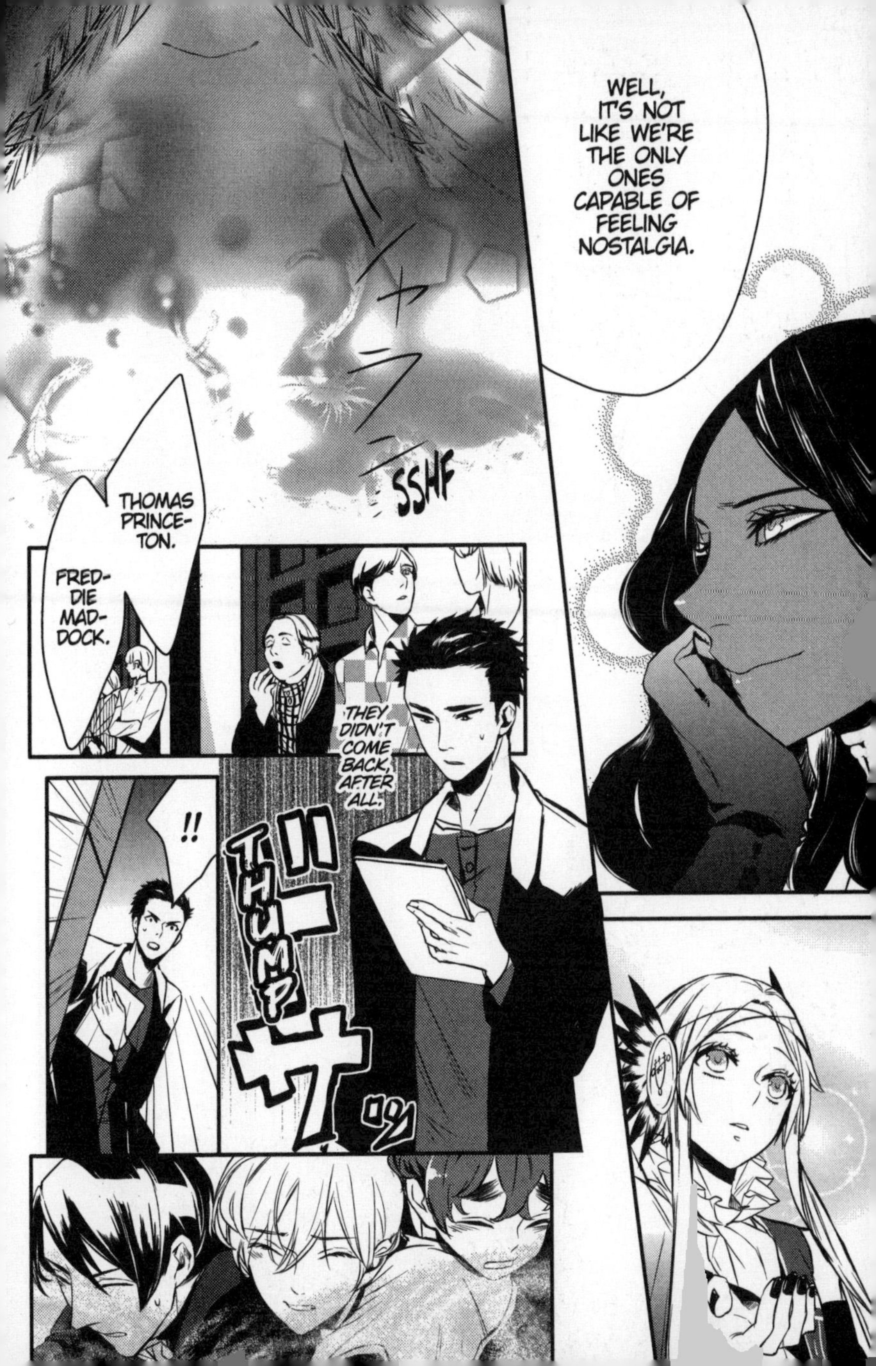
WELL, IT'S NOT LIKE WE'RE THE ONLY ONES CAPABLE OF FEELING NOSTALGIA.
SSHF
THOMAS PRINCE-TON.
FRED-DIE MAD-DOCK.
THEY DIDN'T COME BACK, AFTER ALL.
THUMP
!!

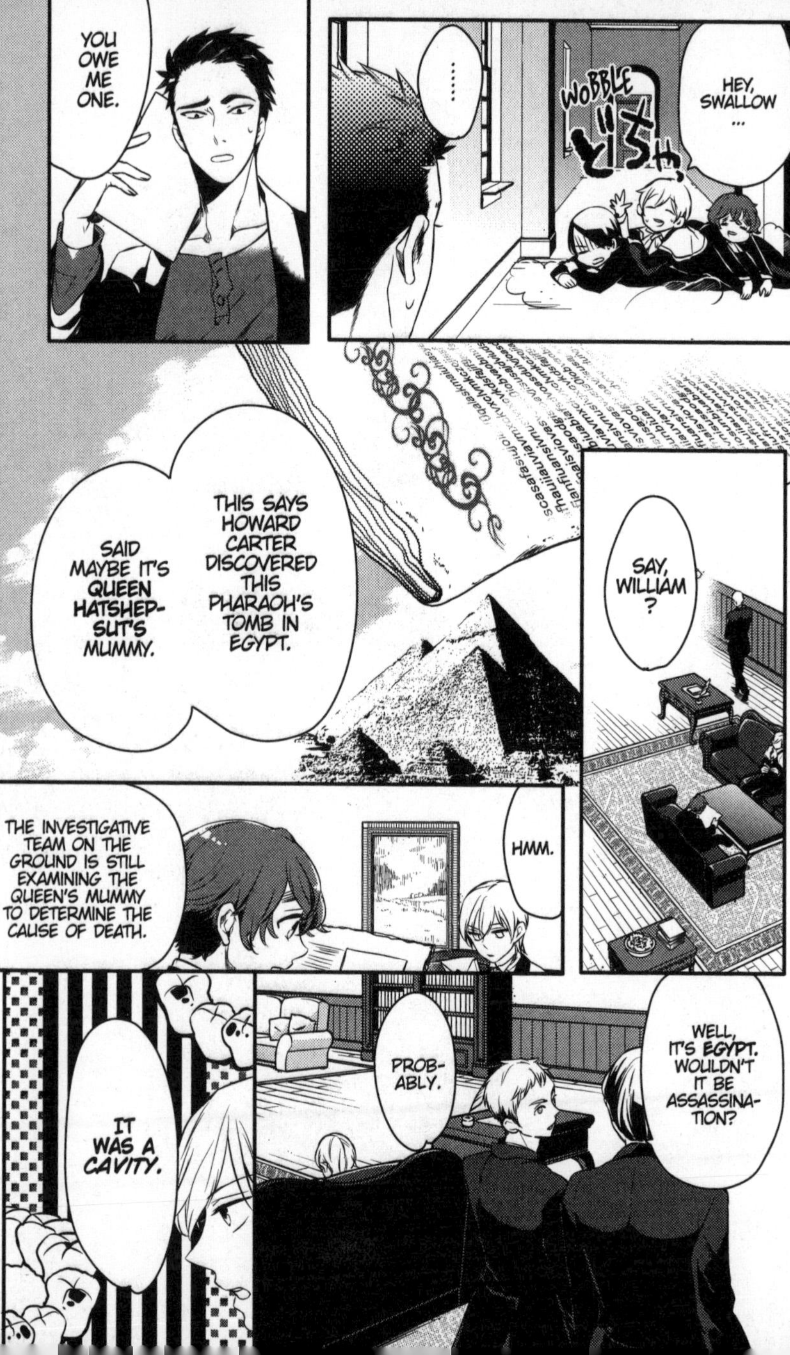
HEY, SWALLOW ...
WOBBLE
......
YOU OWE ME ONE.
SAY, WILLIAM?
THIS SAYS HOWARD CARTER DISCOVERED THIS PHARAOH'S TOMB IN EGYPT.
SAID MAYBE IT'S QUEEN HATSHEPSUT'S MUMMY.
HMM.
THE INVESTIGATIVE TEAM ON THE GROUND IS STILL EXAMINING THE QUEEN'S MUMMY TO DETERMINE THE CAUSE OF DEATH.
WELL, IT'S EGYPT. WOULDN'T IT BE ASSASSINATION?
PROBABLY.
IT WAS A CAVITY.

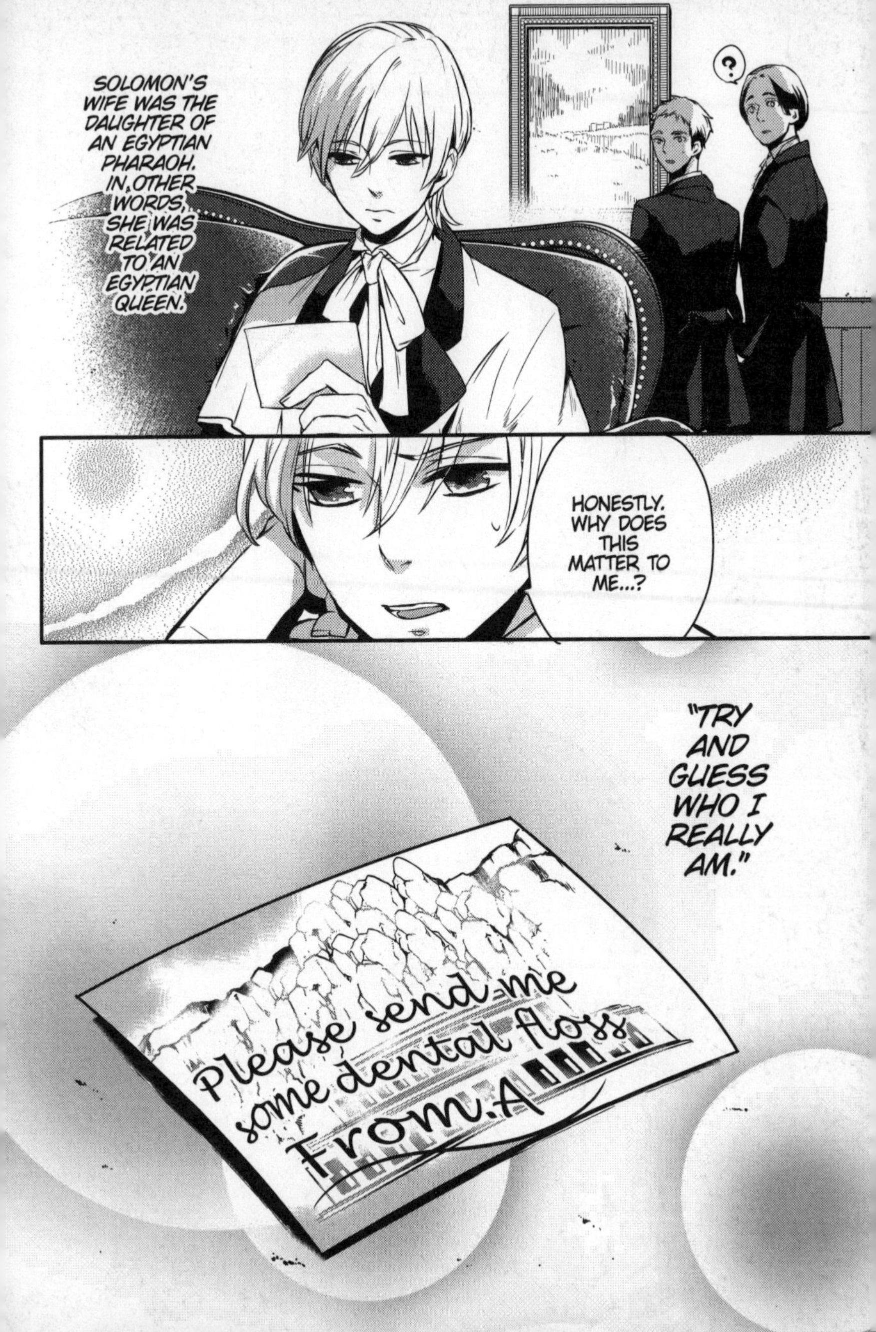
?
SOLOMON'S WIFE WAS THE DAUGHTER OF AN EGYPTIAN PHARAOH. IN OTHER WORDS, SHE WAS RELATED TO AN EGYPTIAN QUEEN.
HONESTLY. WHY DOES THIS MATTER TO ME...?
"TRY AND GUESS WHO I REALLY AM."
Please send me some dental floss
From.A

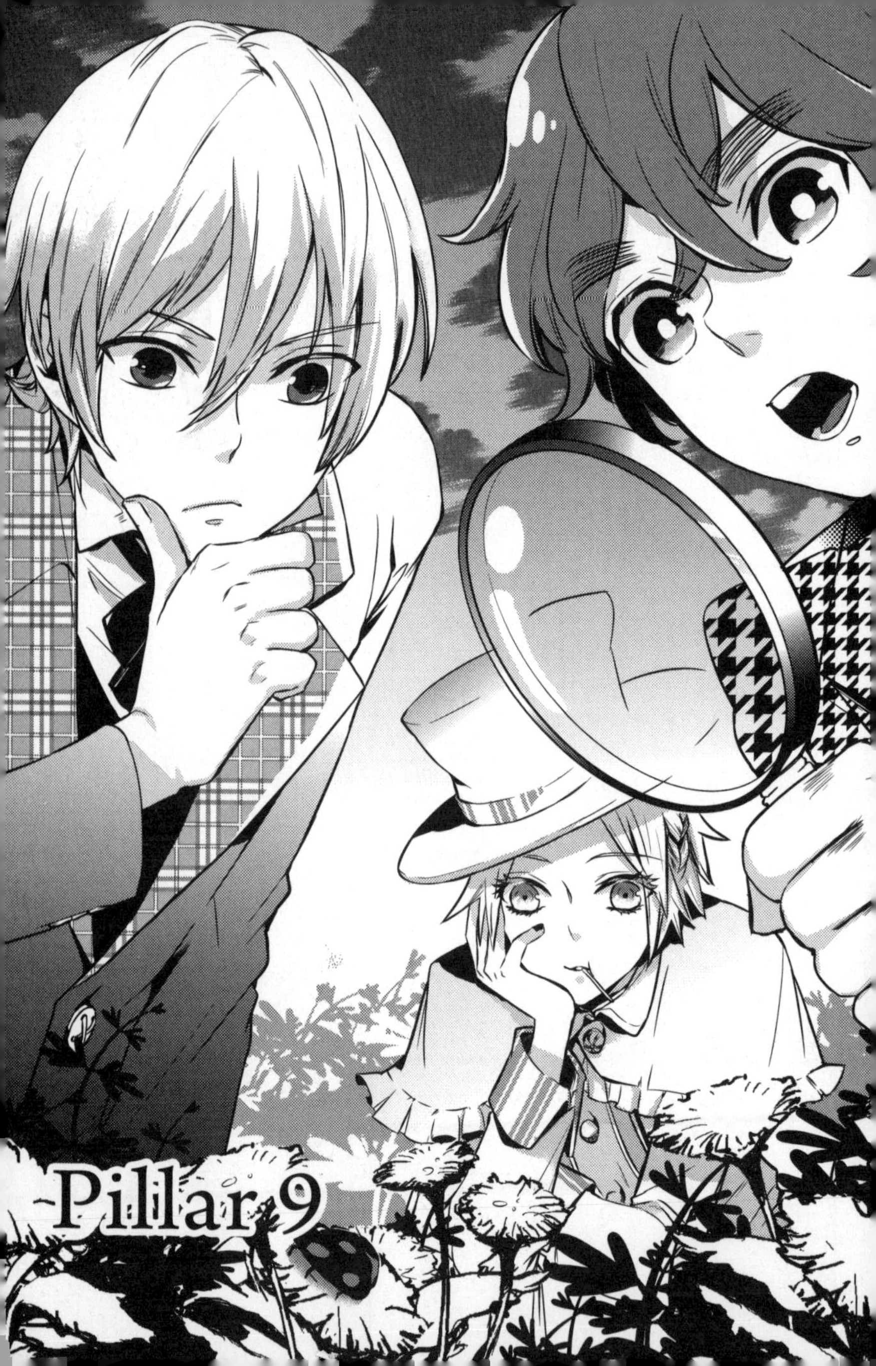
Pillar 9

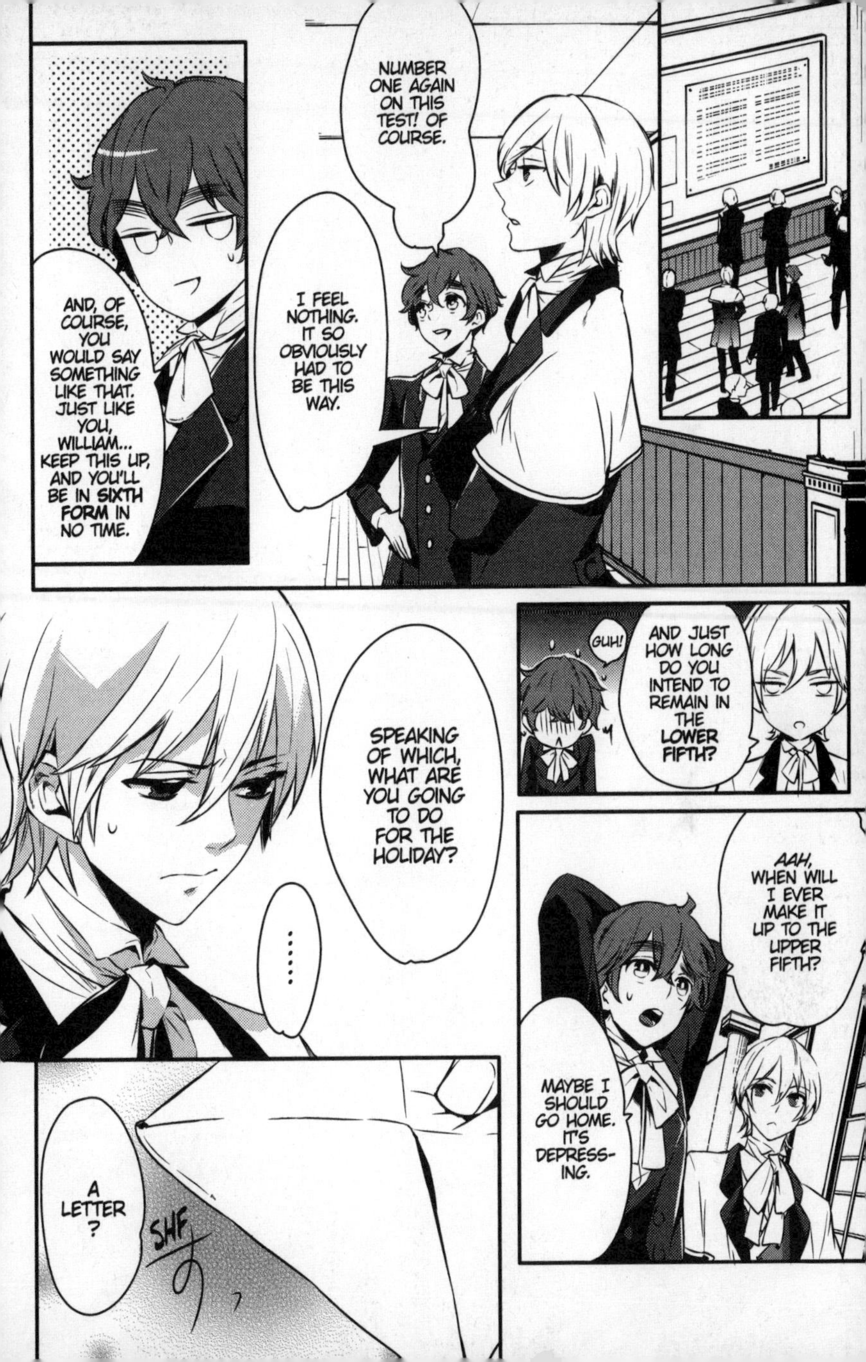
NUMBER ONE AGAIN ON THIS TEST! OF COURSE.
I FEEL NOTHING. IT SO OBVIOUSLY HAD TO BE THIS WAY.
AND, OF COURSE, YOU WOULD SAY SOMETHING LIKE THAT. JUST LIKE YOU, WILLIAM... KEEP THIS UP, AND YOU'LL BE IN **SIXTH FORM** IN NO TIME.
AND JUST HOW LONG DO YOU INTEND TO REMAIN IN THE **LOWER FIFTH**?
GUH!
AAH, WHEN WILL I EVER MAKE IT UP TO THE UPPER FIFTH?
MAYBE I SHOULD GO HOME. IT'S DEPRESS-ING.
SPEAKING OF WHICH, WHAT ARE YOU GOING TO DO FOR THE HOLIDAY?
......
A LETTER?
SHF

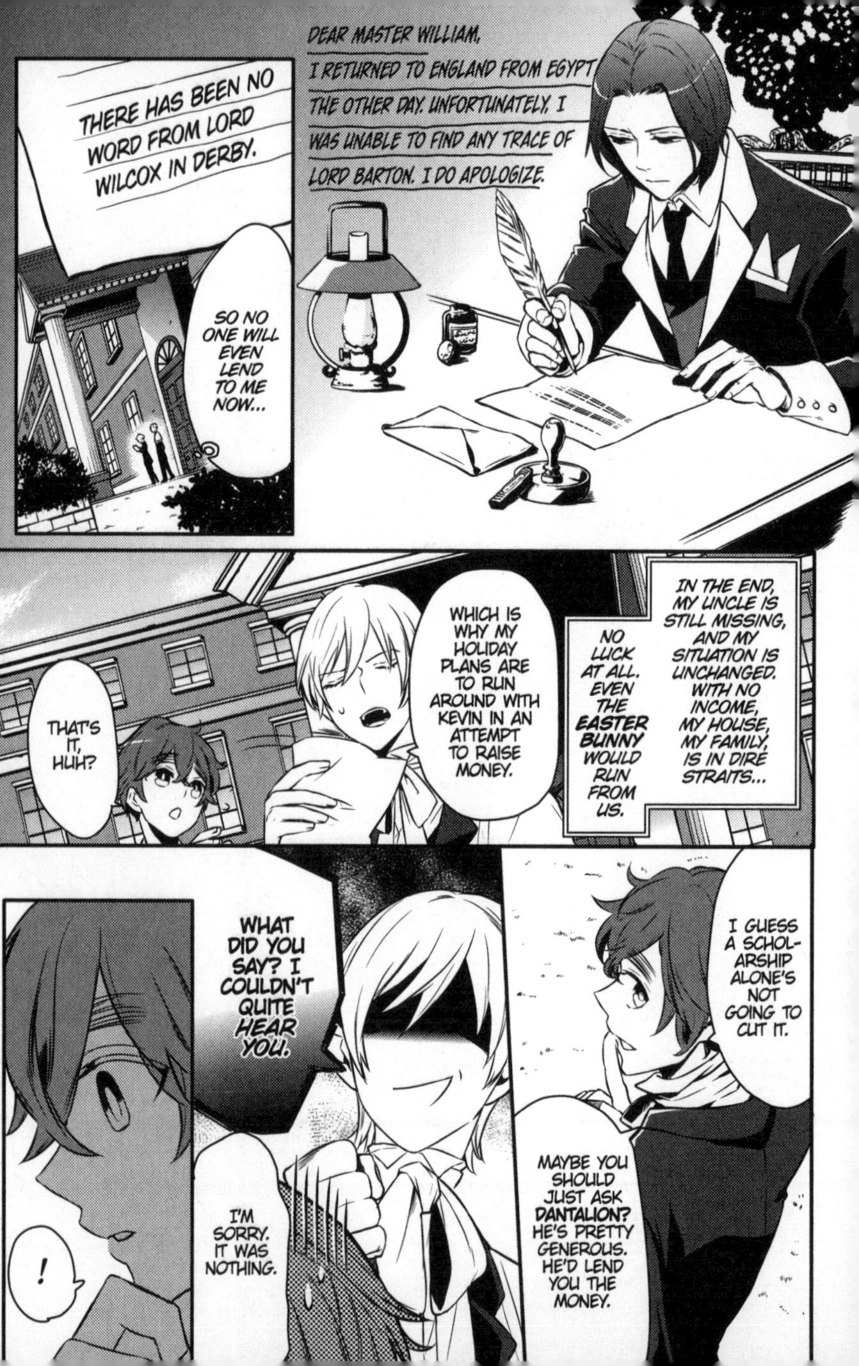
DEAR MASTER WILLIAM,
I RETURNED TO ENGLAND FROM EGYPT THE OTHER DAY. UNFORTUNATELY, I WAS UNABLE TO FIND ANY TRACE OF LORD BARTON. I DO APOLOGIZE.
THERE HAS BEEN NO WORD FROM LORD WILCOX IN DERBY.
SO NO ONE WILL EVEN LEND TO ME NOW...
IN THE END, MY UNCLE IS STILL MISSING, AND MY SITUATION IS UNCHANGED. WITH NO INCOME, MY HOUSE, MY FAMILY, IS IN DIRE STRAITS...
NO LUCK AT ALL. EVEN THE EASTER BUNNY WOULD RUN FROM US.
WHICH IS WHY MY HOLIDAY PLANS ARE TO RUN AROUND WITH KEVIN IN AN ATTEMPT TO RAISE MONEY.
THAT'S IT, HUH?
I GUESS A SCHOL-ARSHIP ALONE'S NOT GOING TO CUT IT.
MAYBE YOU SHOULD JUST ASK DANTALION? HE'S PRETTY GENEROUS. HE'D LEND YOU THE MONEY.
WHAT DID YOU SAY? I COULDN'T QUITE HEAR YOU.
I'M SORRY. IT WAS NOTHING.
!

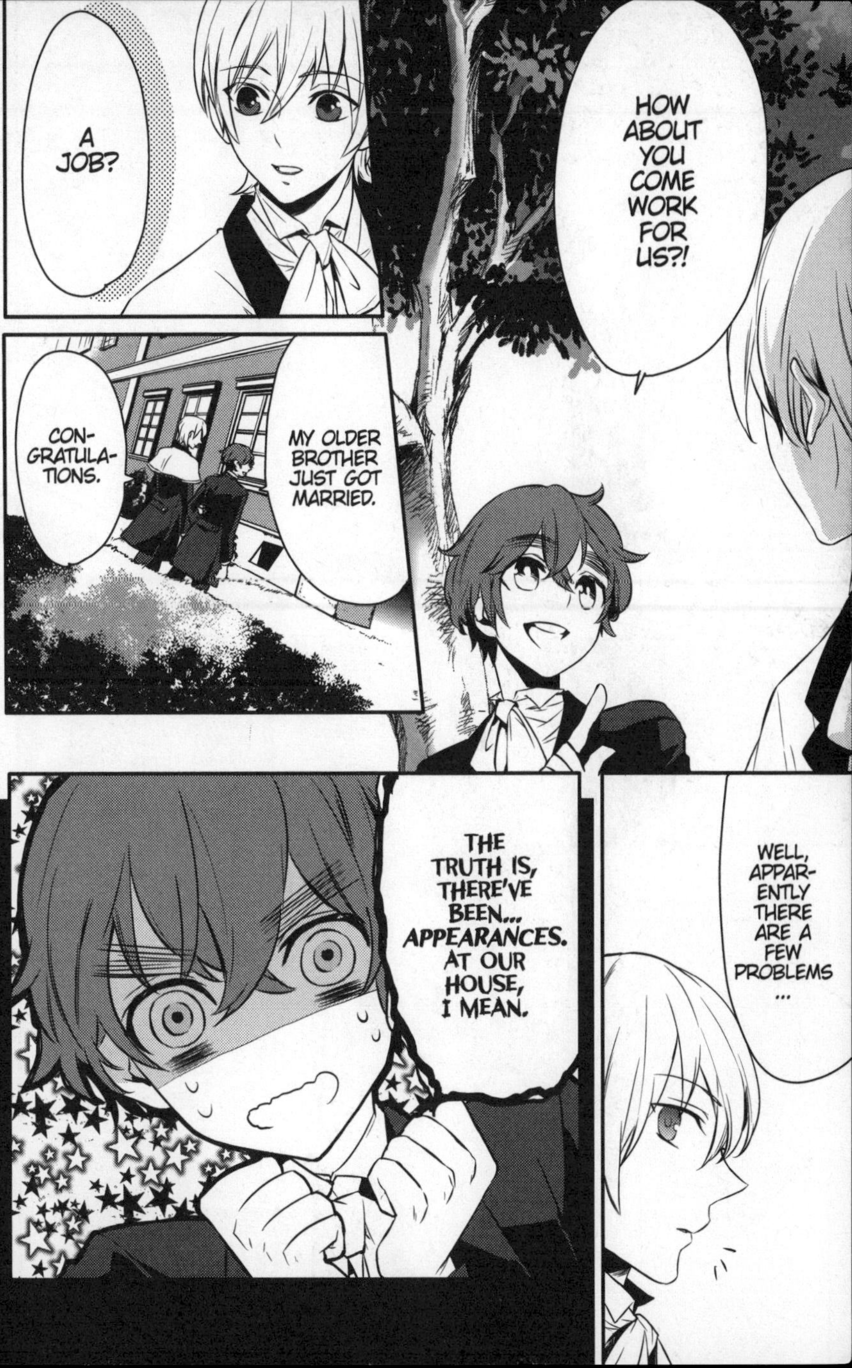
HOW ABOUT YOU COME WORK FOR US?!
A JOB?
MY OLDER BROTHER JUST GOT MARRIED.
CON-GRATULA-TIONS.
WELL, APPAR-ENTLY THERE ARE A FEW PROBLEMS ...
THE TRUTH IS, THERE'VE BEEN... APPEARANCES. AT OUR HOUSE, I MEAN.

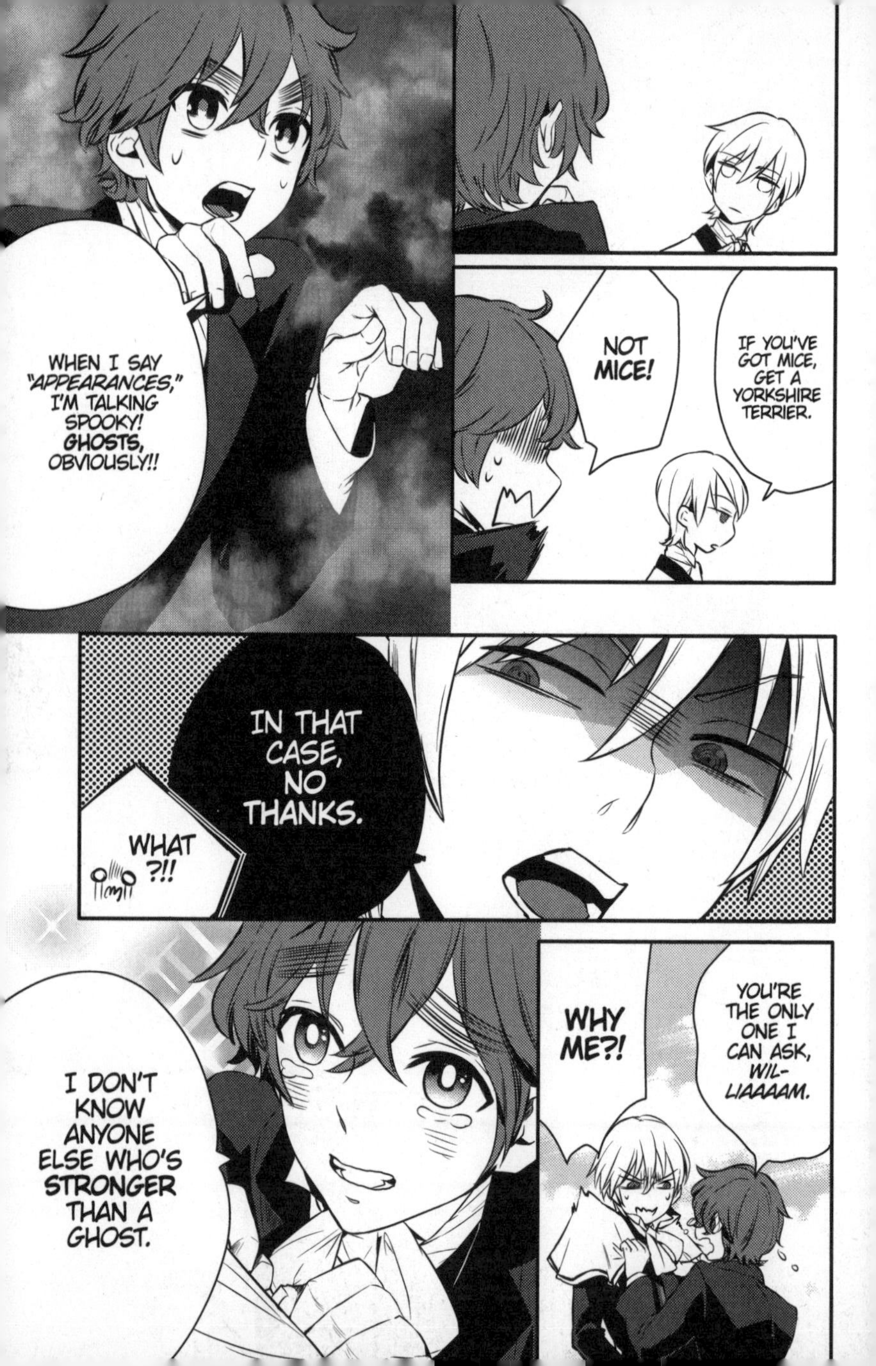
IF YOU'VE GOT MICE, GET A YORKSHIRE TERRIER.
NOT MICE!
WHEN I SAY "APPEARANCES," I'M TALKING SPOOKY! GHOSTS, OBVIOUSLY!!
IN THAT CASE, NO THANKS.
WHAT?!!
YOU'RE THE ONLY ONE I CAN ASK, WIL-LIAAAAM.
WHY ME?!
I DON'T KNOW ANYONE ELSE WHO'S STRONGER THAN A GHOST.

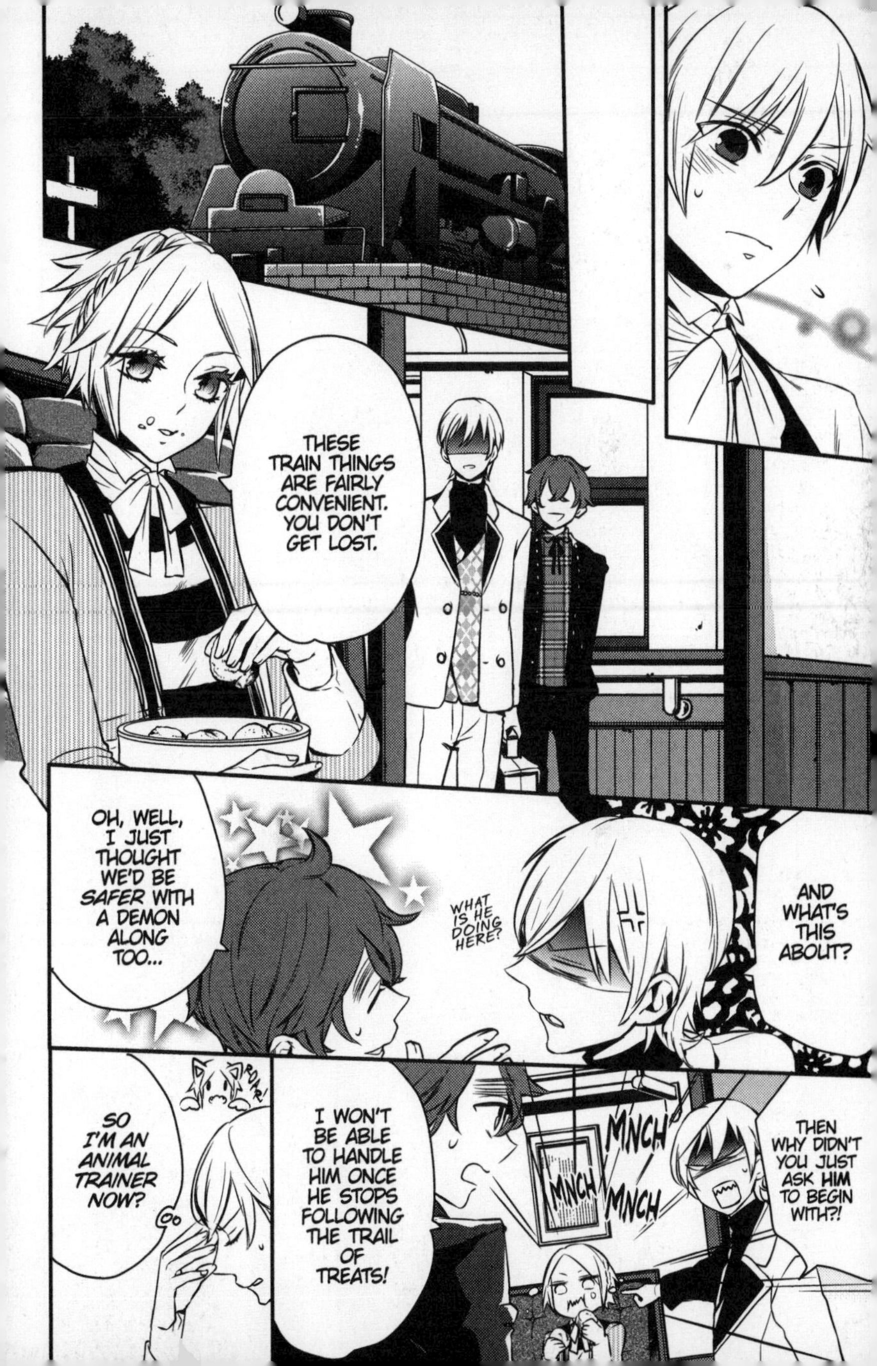
THESE TRAIN THINGS ARE FAIRLY CONVENIENT. YOU DON'T GET LOST.
AND WHAT'S THIS ABOUT?
WHAT IS HE DOING HERE?
OH, WELL, I JUST THOUGHT WE'D BE SAFER WITH A DEMON ALONG TOO...
THEN WHY DIDN'T YOU JUST ASK HIM TO BEGIN WITH?!
MNCH
MNCH
MNCH
I WON'T BE ABLE TO HANDLE HIM ONCE HE STOPS FOLLOWING THE TRAIL OF TREATS!
ROAR!
SO I'M AN ANIMAL TRAINER NOW?

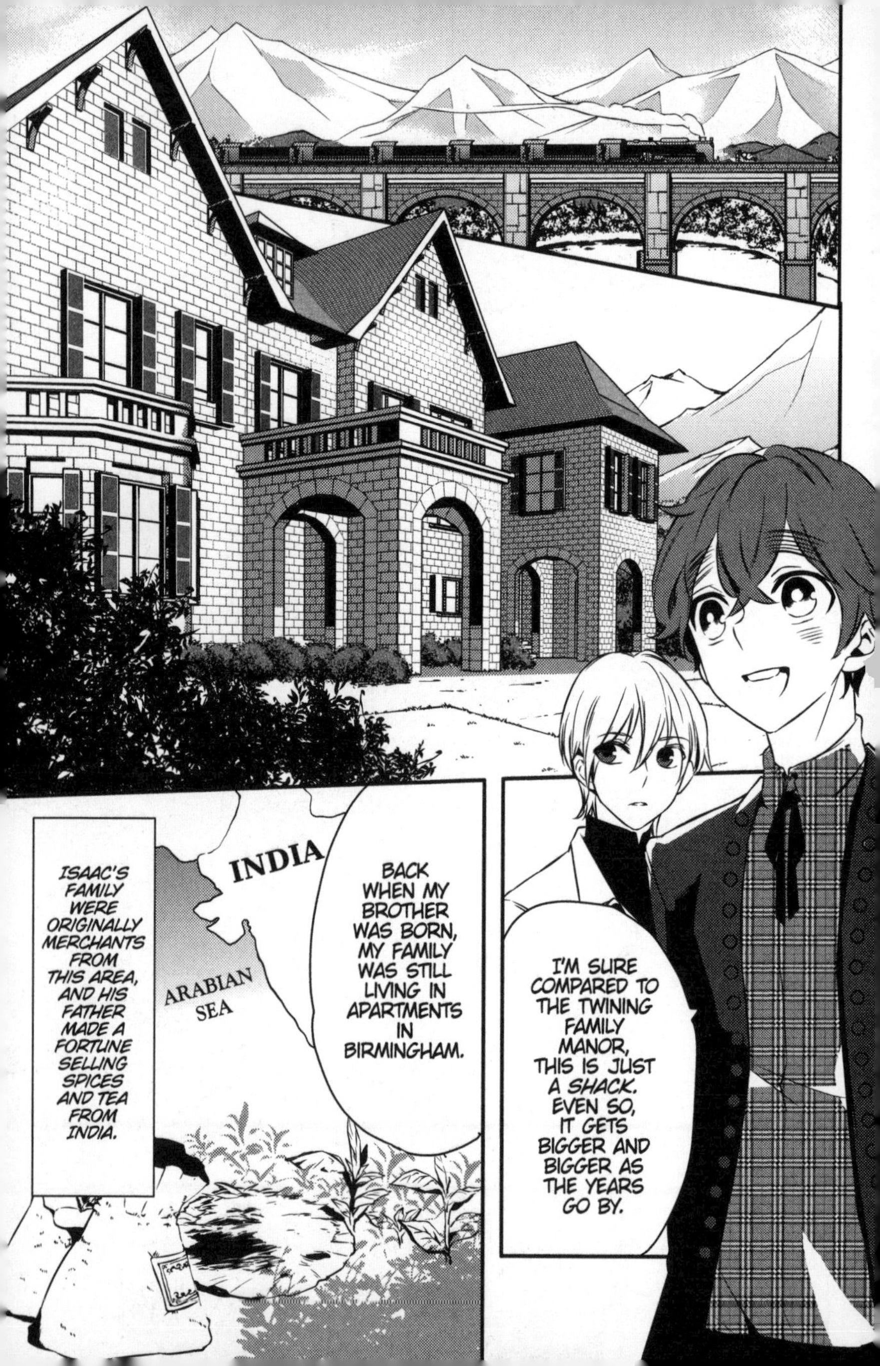
I'M SURE COMPARED TO THE TWINING FAMILY MANOR, THIS IS JUST A *SHACK*. EVEN SO, IT GETS BIGGER AND BIGGER AS THE YEARS GO BY.
BACK WHEN MY BROTHER WAS BORN, MY FAMILY WAS STILL LIVING IN APARTMENTS IN BIRMINGHAM.
INDIA
ARABIAN SEA
ISAAC'S FAMILY WERE ORIGINALLY MERCHANTS FROM THIS AREA, AND HIS FATHER MADE A FORTUNE SELLING SPICES AND TEA FROM INDIA.

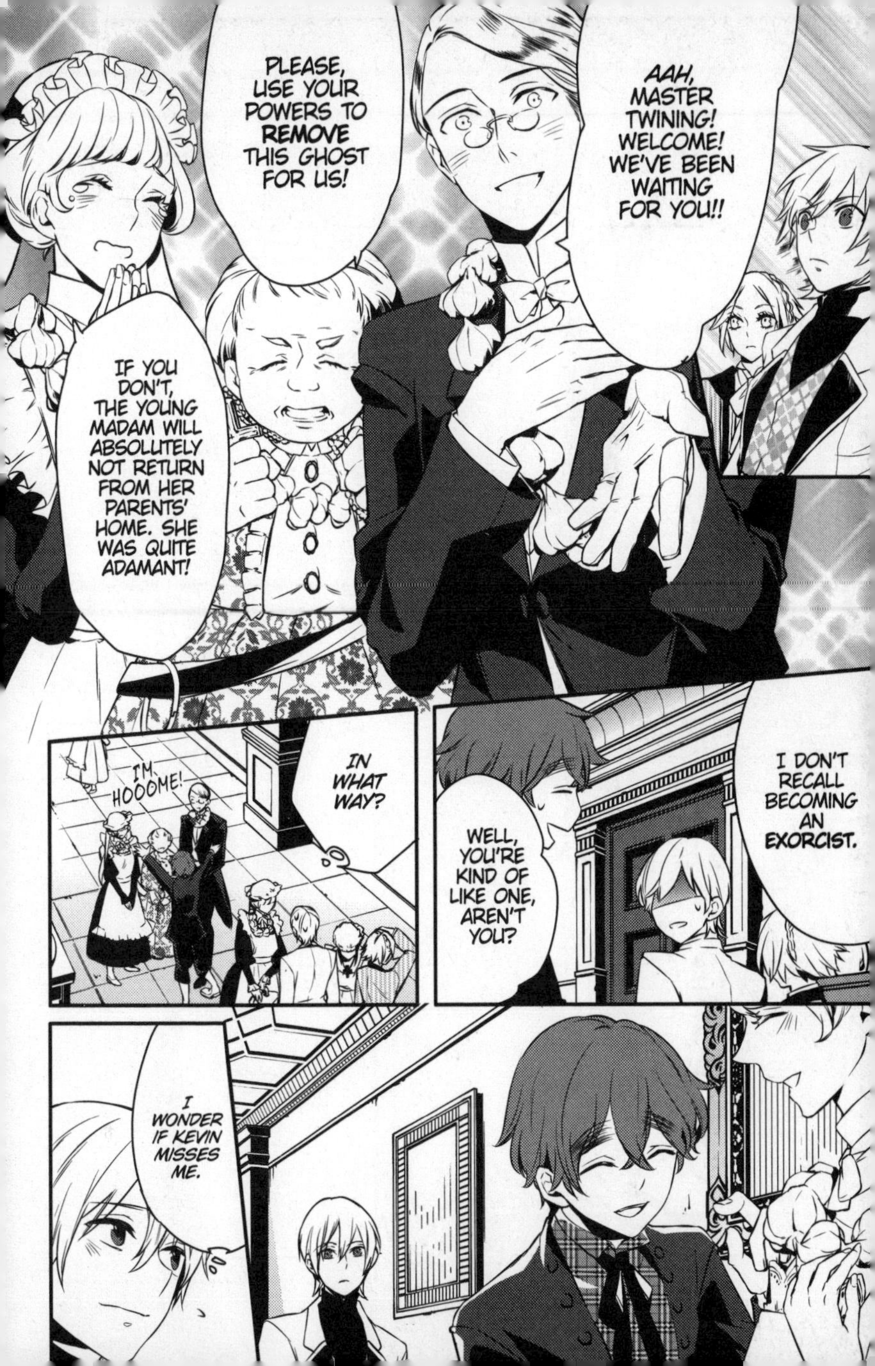
AAH, MASTER TWINING! WELCOME! WE'VE BEEN WAITING FOR YOU!!
PLEASE, USE YOUR POWERS TO REMOVE THIS GHOST FOR US!
IF YOU DON'T, THE YOUNG MADAM WILL ABSOLUTELY NOT RETURN FROM HER PARENTS' HOME. SHE WAS QUITE ADAMANT!
I DON'T RECALL BECOMING AN EXORCIST.
WELL, YOU'RE KIND OF LIKE ONE, AREN'T YOU?
IN WHAT WAY?
I'M HOOOME!
I WONDER IF KEVIN MISSES ME.

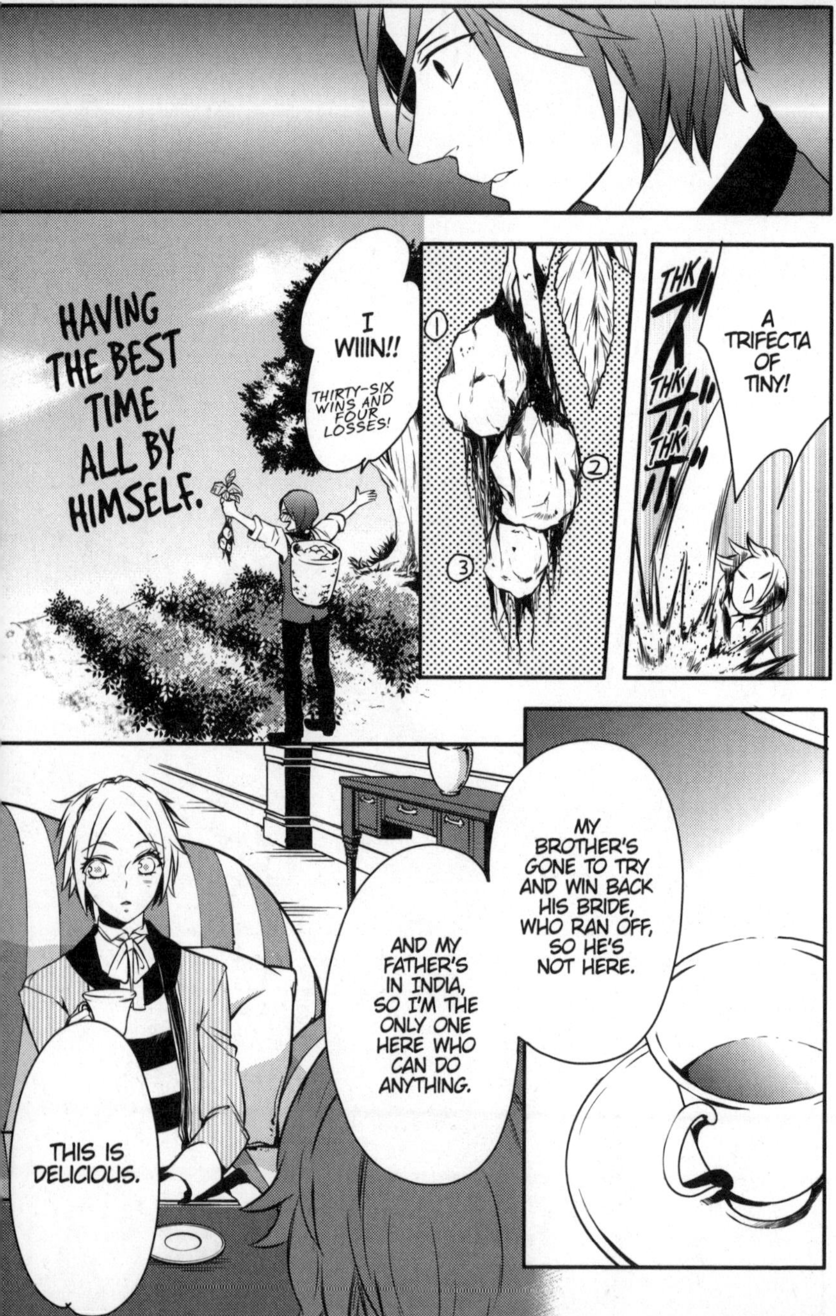
A TRIFECTA OF TINY!
THK
THK
THK
1
2
3
I WIIIN!!
THIRTY-SIX WINS AND FOUR LOSSES!
HAVING THE BEST TIME ALL BY HIMSELF.
MY BROTHER'S GONE TO TRY AND WIN BACK HIS BRIDE, WHO RAN OFF, SO HE'S NOT HERE.
AND MY FATHER'S IN INDIA, SO I'M THE ONLY ONE HERE WHO CAN DO ANYTHING.
THIS IS DELICIOUS.

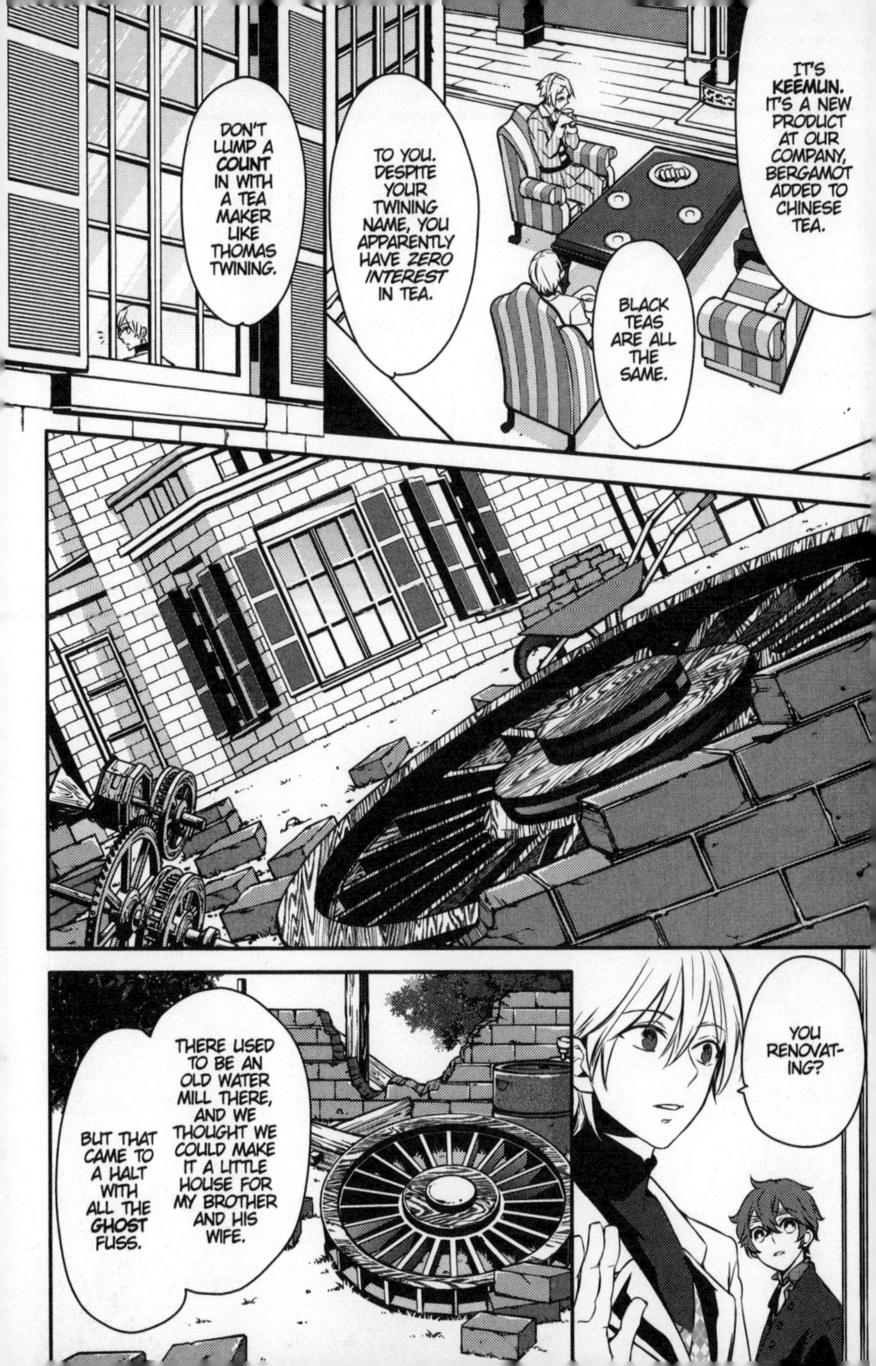
IT'S KEEMUN. IT'S A NEW PRODUCT AT OUR COMPANY, BERGAMOT ADDED TO CHINESE TEA.
BLACK TEAS ARE ALL THE SAME.
TO YOU. DESPITE YOUR TWINING NAME, YOU APPARENTLY HAVE ZERO INTEREST IN TEA.
DON'T LUMP A COUNT IN WITH A TEA MAKER LIKE THOMAS TWINING.
YOU RENOVATING?
THERE USED TO BE AN OLD WATER MILL THERE, AND WE THOUGHT WE COULD MAKE IT A LITTLE HOUSE FOR MY BROTHER AND HIS WIFE.
BUT THAT CAME TO A HALT WITH ALL THE GHOST FUSS.

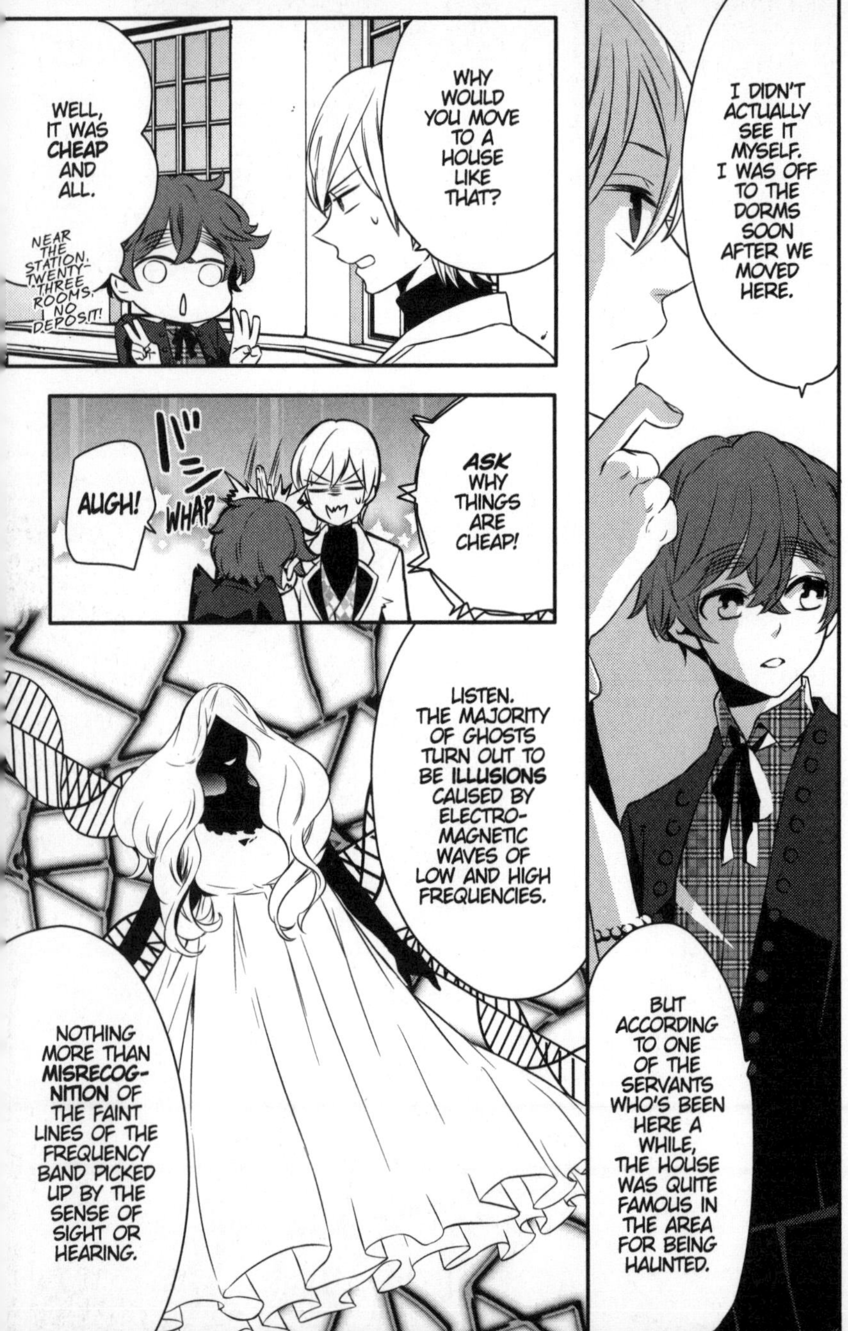
I DIDN'T ACTUALLY SEE IT MYSELF. I WAS OFF TO THE DORMS SOON AFTER WE MOVED HERE.
BUT ACCORDING TO ONE OF THE SERVANTS WHO'S BEEN HERE A WHILE, THE HOUSE WAS QUITE FAMOUS IN THE AREA FOR BEING HAUNTED.
WHY WOULD YOU MOVE TO A HOUSE LIKE THAT?
WELL, IT WAS **CHEAP** AND ALL.
NEAR THE STATION. TWENTY-THREE ROOMS, NO DEPOSIT!
ASK WHY THINGS ARE CHEAP!
WHAP
AUGH!
LISTEN. THE MAJORITY OF GHOSTS TURN OUT TO BE **ILLUSIONS** CAUSED BY ELECTRO-MAGNETIC WAVES OF LOW AND HIGH FREQUENCIES.
NOTHING MORE THAN **MISRECOG-NITION** OF THE FAINT LINES OF THE FREQUENCY BAND PICKED UP BY THE SENSE OF SIGHT OR HEARING.

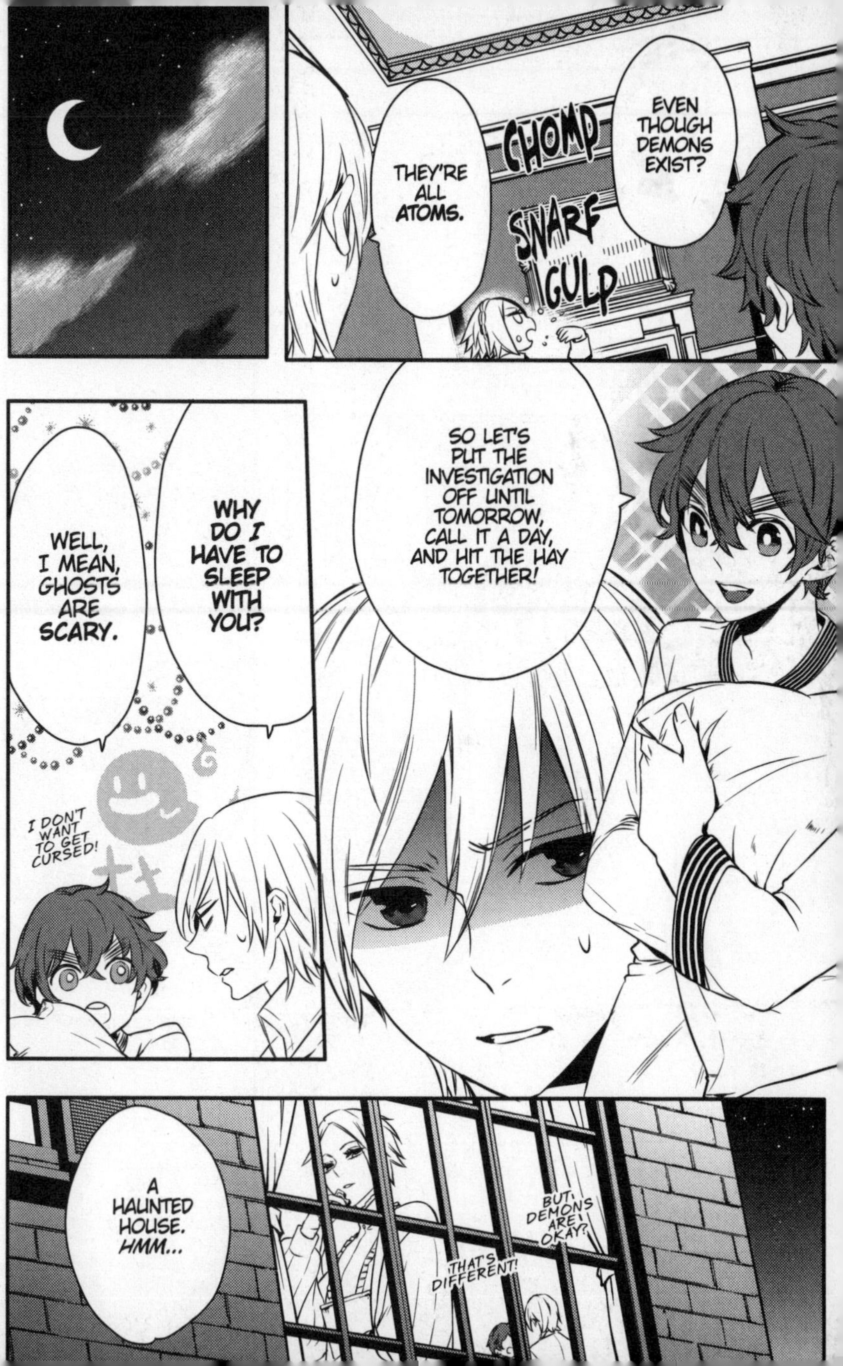
EVEN THOUGH DEMONS EXIST?
CHOMP
SNARF
GULP
THEY'RE ALL ATOMS.
SO LET'S PUT THE INVESTIGATION OFF UNTIL TOMORROW, CALL IT A DAY, AND HIT THE HAY TOGETHER!
WHY DO I HAVE TO SLEEP WITH YOU?
WELL, I MEAN, GHOSTS ARE SCARY.
I DON'T WANT TO GET CURSED!
BUT, DEMONS ARE OKAY?
THAT'S DIFFERENT!
A HAUNTED HOUSE. HMM...

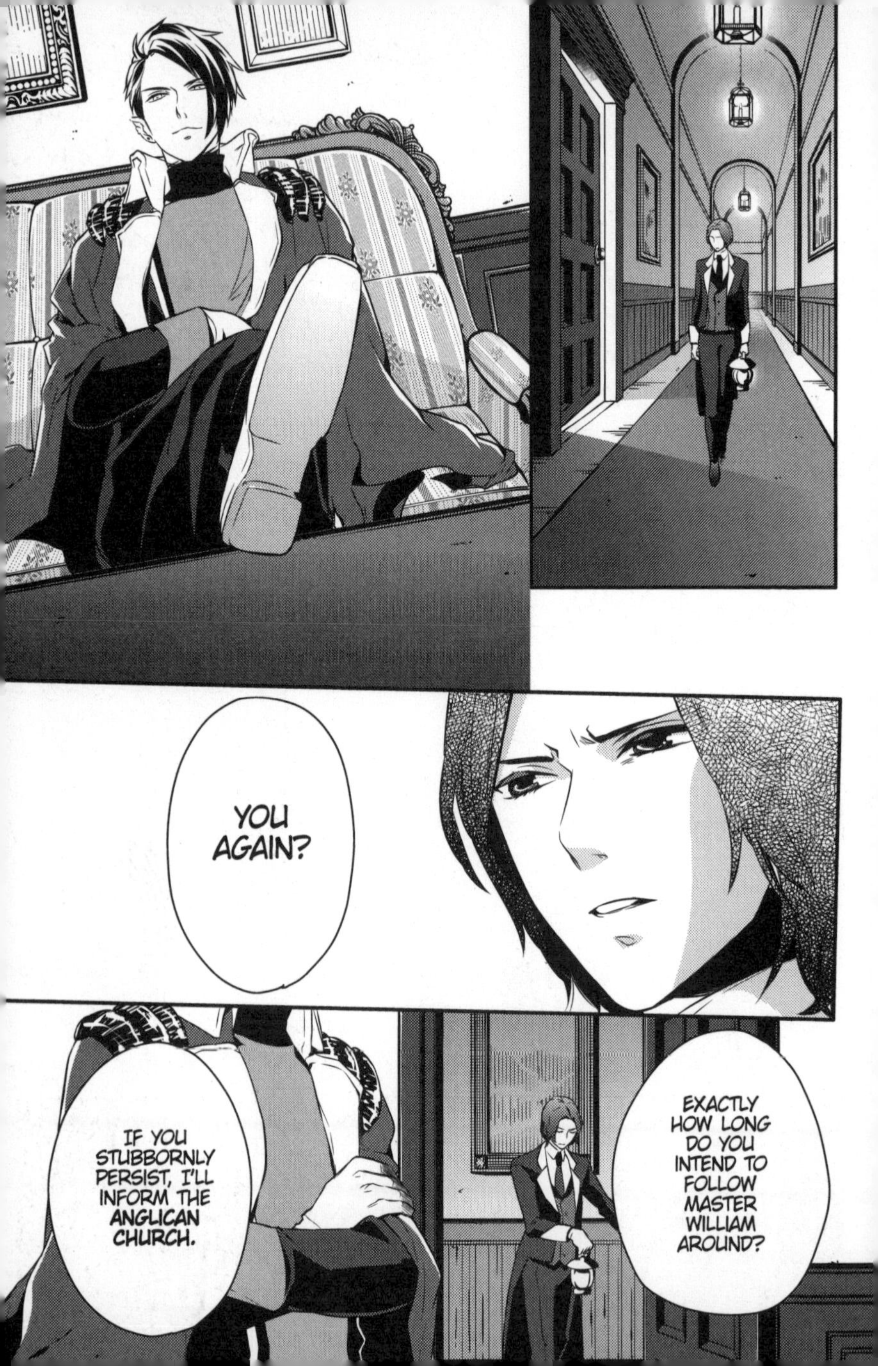
YOU AGAIN?
EXACTLY HOW LONG DO YOU INTEND TO FOLLOW MASTER WILLIAM AROUND?
IF YOU STUBBORNLY PERSIST, I'LL INFORM THE ANGLICAN CHURCH.

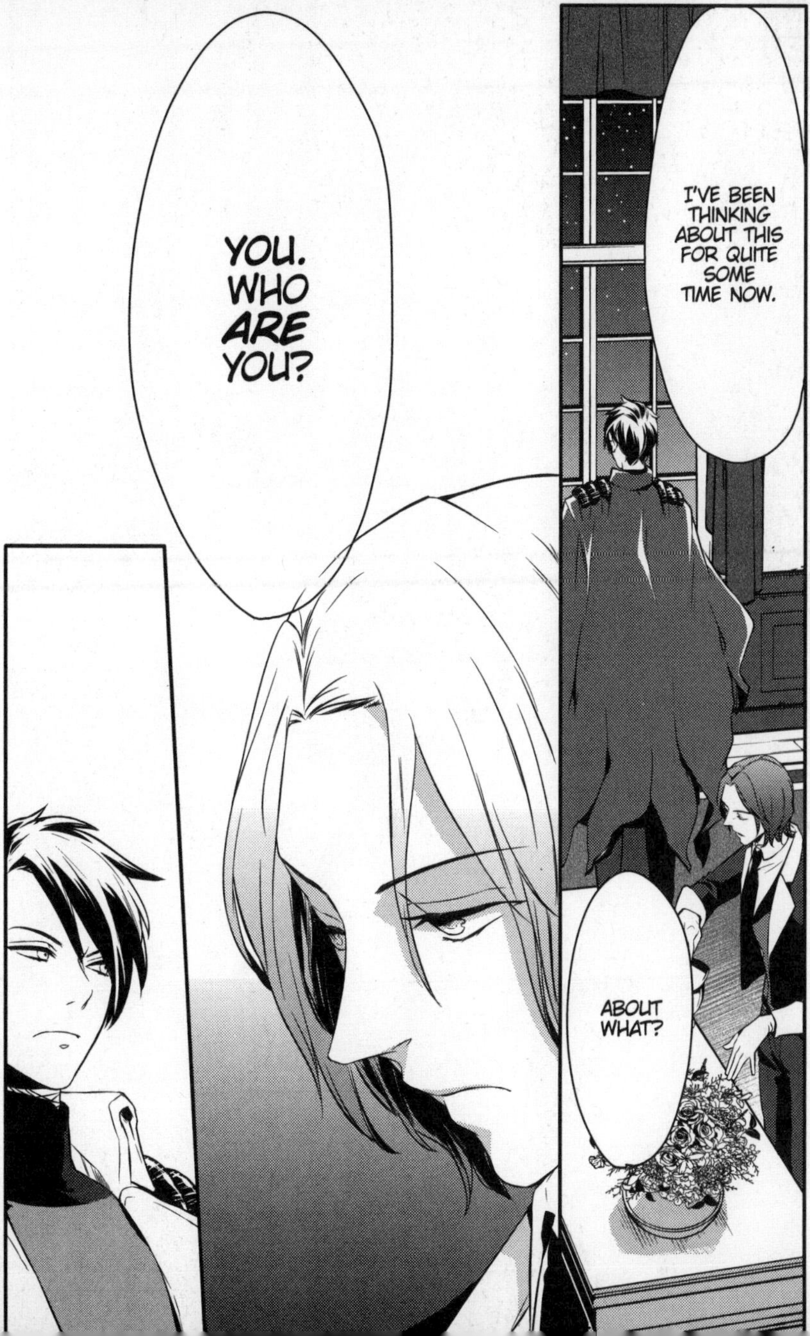
I'VE BEEN THINKING ABOUT THIS FOR QUITE SOME TIME NOW.
ABOUT WHAT?
YOU. WHO ARE YOU?

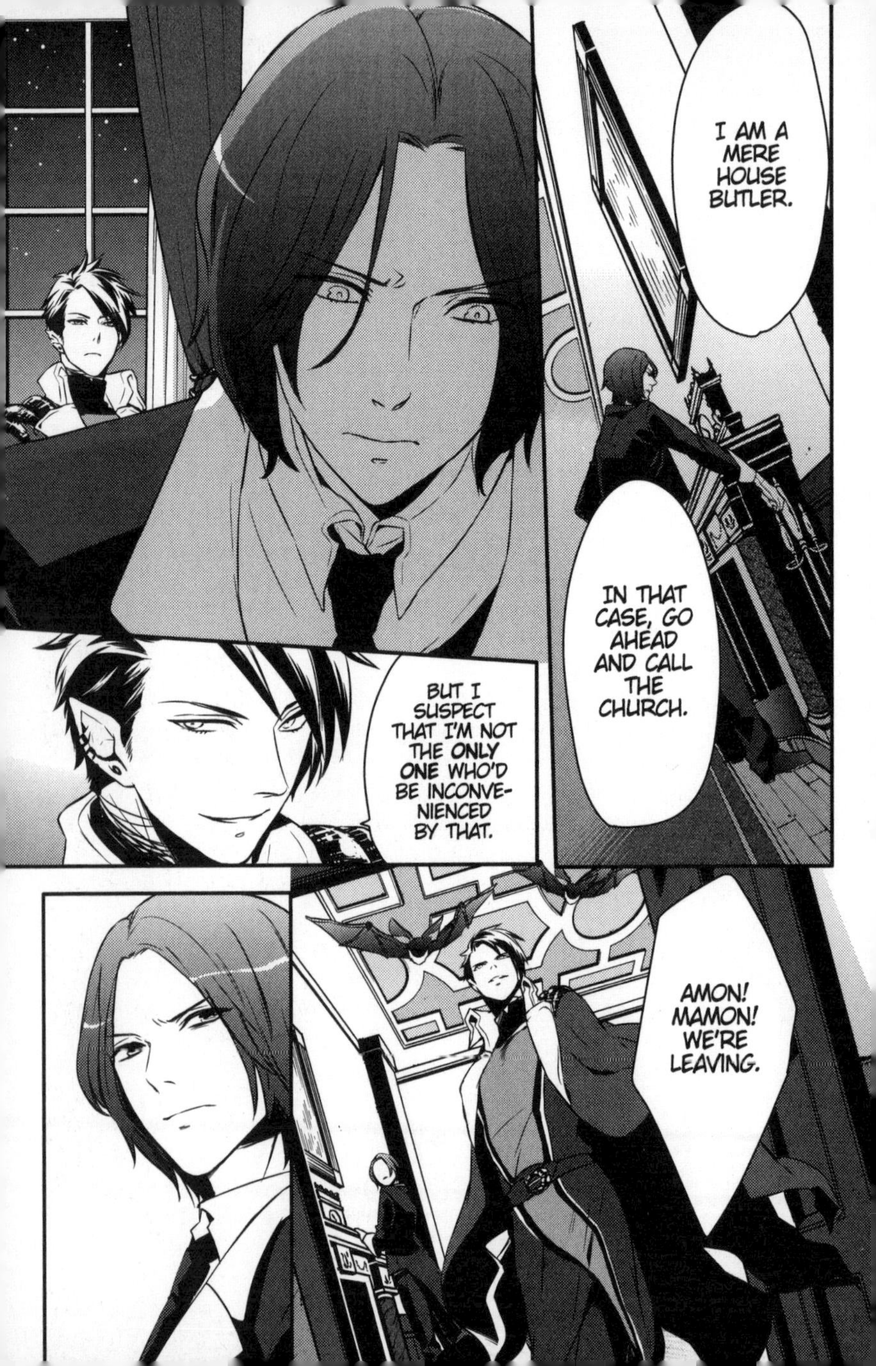
I AM A MERE HOUSE BUTLER.
IN THAT CASE, GO AHEAD AND CALL THE CHURCH.
BUT I SUSPECT THAT I'M NOT THE ONLY ONE WHO'D BE INCONVENIENCED BY THAT.
AMON! MAMON! WE'RE LEAVING.

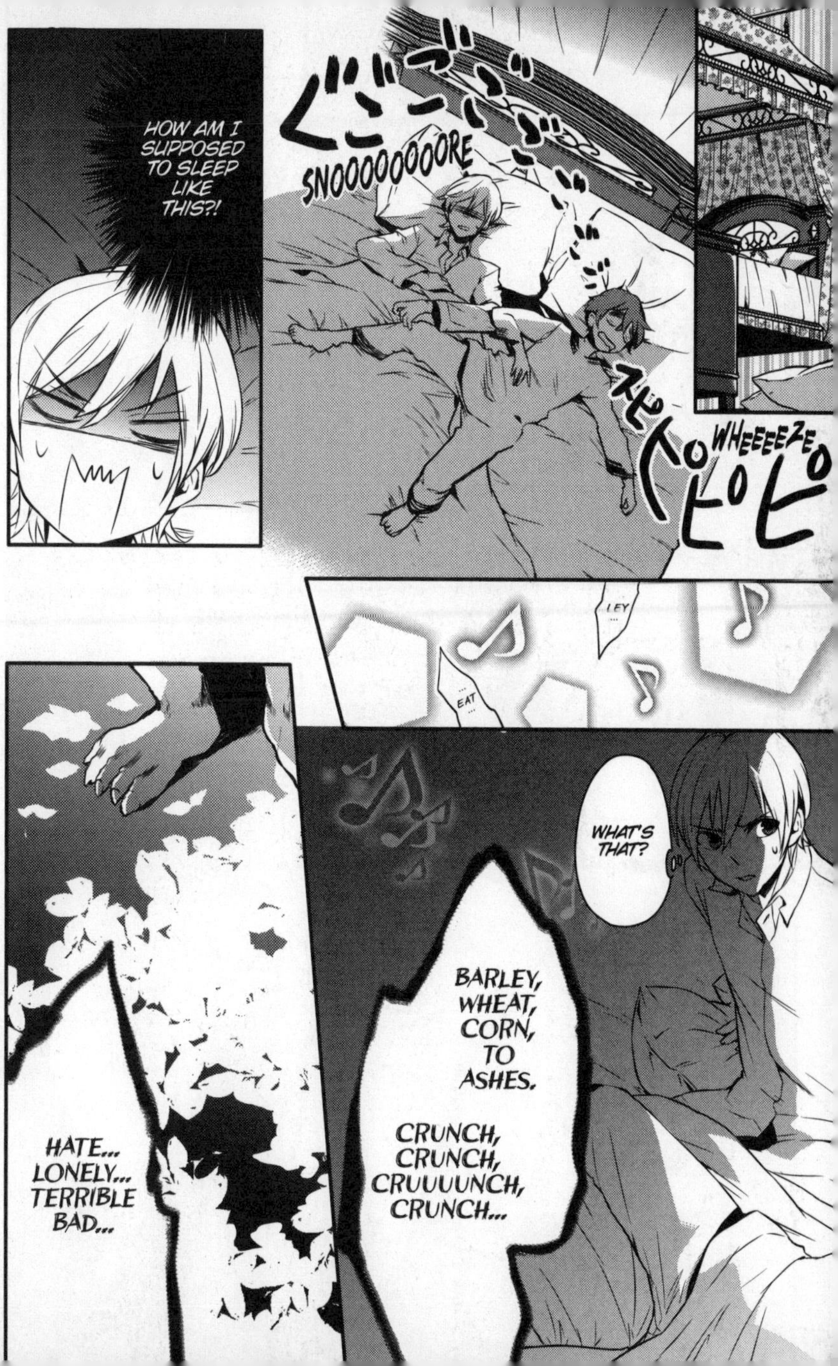
SNOOOOOOOORE
WHEEEEZE
HOW AM I SUPPOSED TO SLEEP LIKE THIS?!
LEY ...
... EAT ...
WHAT'S THAT?
BARLEY, WHEAT, CORN, TO ASHES.
CRUNCH, CRUNCH, CRUUUUNCH, CRUNCH...
HATE... LONELY... TERRIBLE BAD...

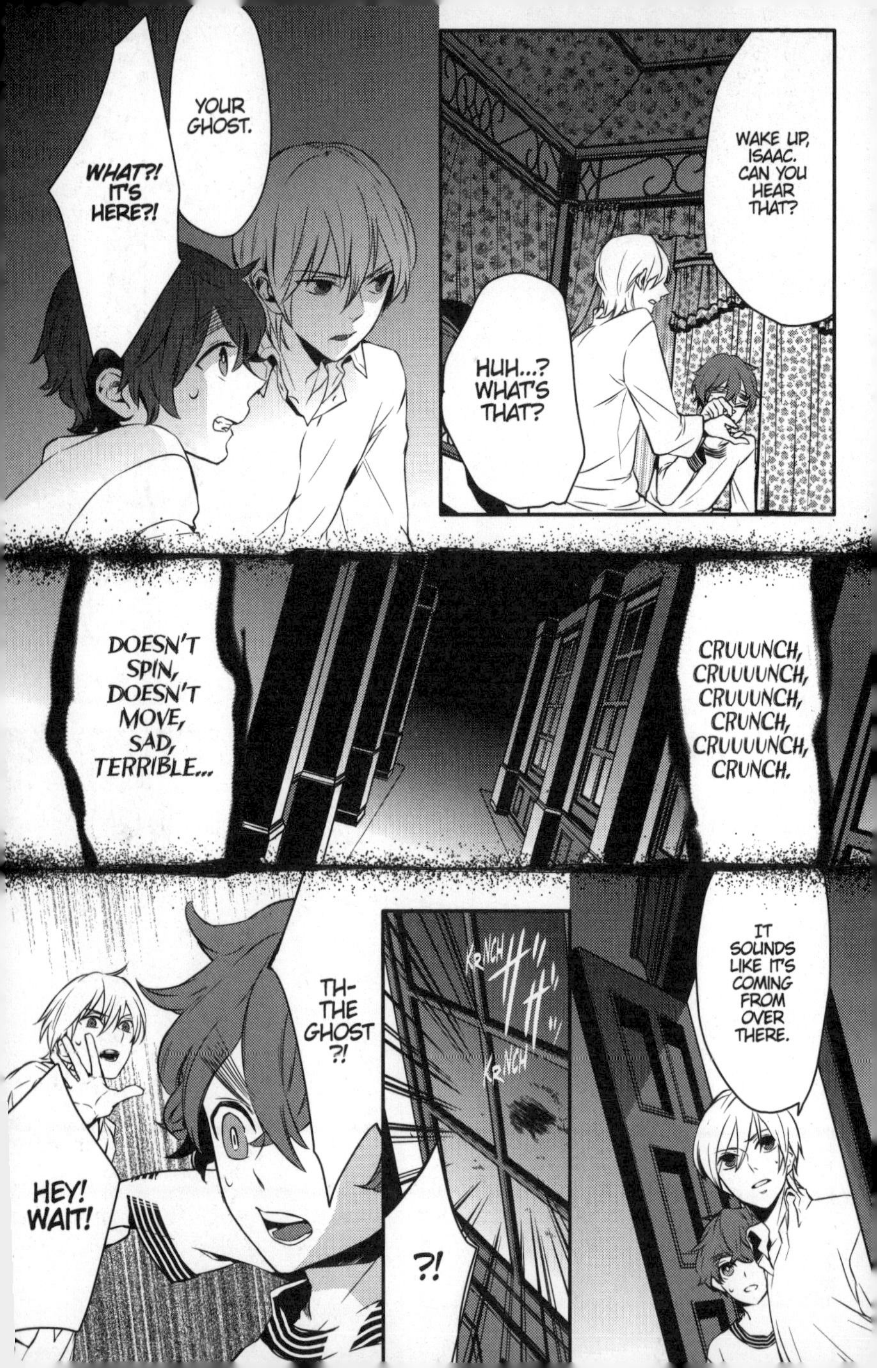
WAKE UP, ISAAC. CAN YOU HEAR THAT?
HUH...? WHAT'S THAT?
YOUR GHOST.
WHAT?! IT'S HERE?!
CRUUUNCH, CRUUUUNCH, CRUUUNCH, CRUNCH, CRUUUUNCH, CRUNCH.
DOESN'T SPIN, DOESN'T MOVE, SAD, TERRIBLE...
IT SOUNDS LIKE IT'S COMING FROM OVER THERE.
KRINCH
KRINCH
?!
TH-THE GHOST?!
HEY! WAIT!

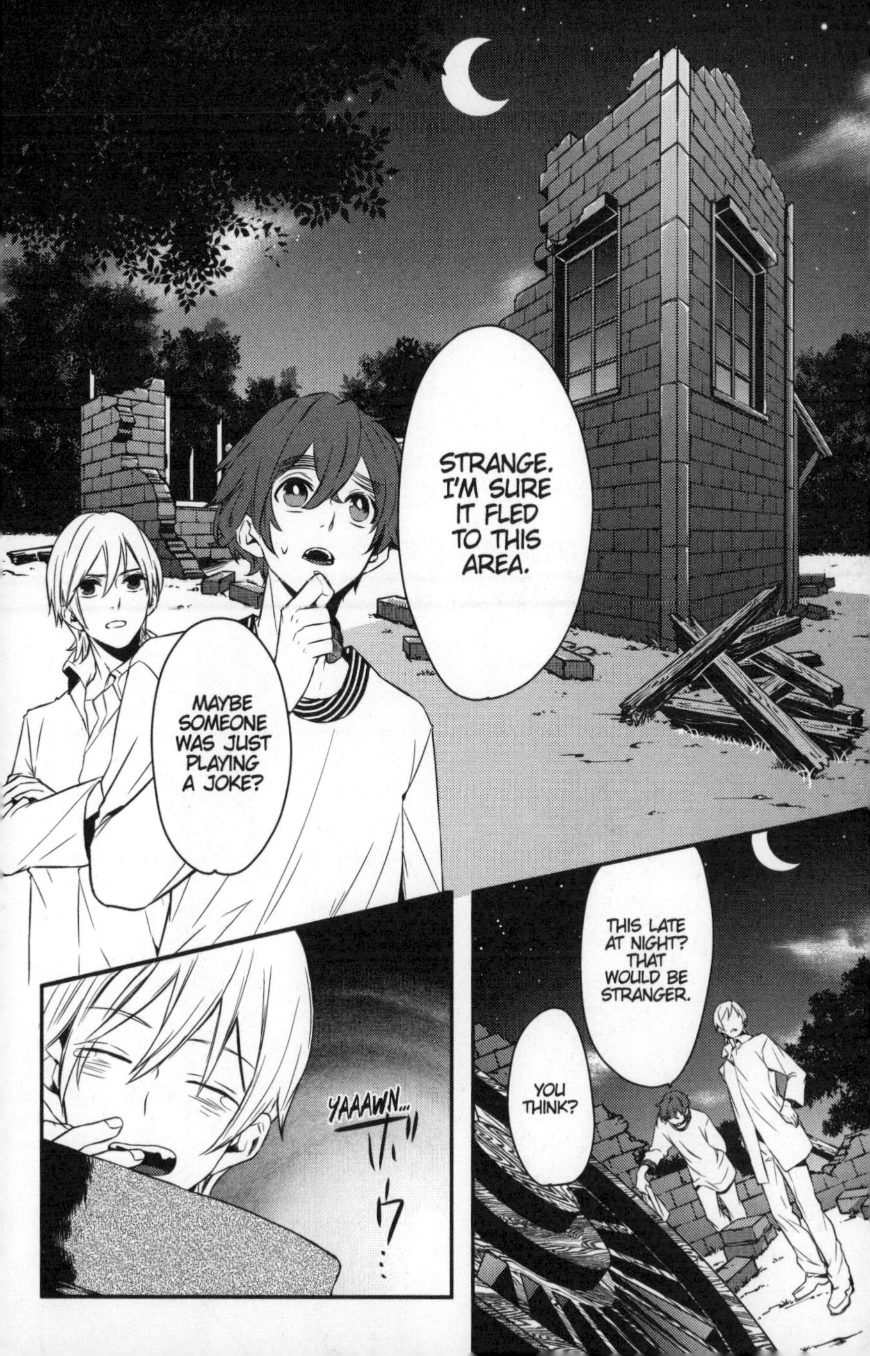
STRANGE. I'M SURE IT FLED TO THIS AREA.
MAYBE SOMEONE WAS JUST PLAYING A JOKE?
THIS LATE AT NIGHT? THAT WOULD BE STRANGER.
YOU THINK?
YAAAWN...

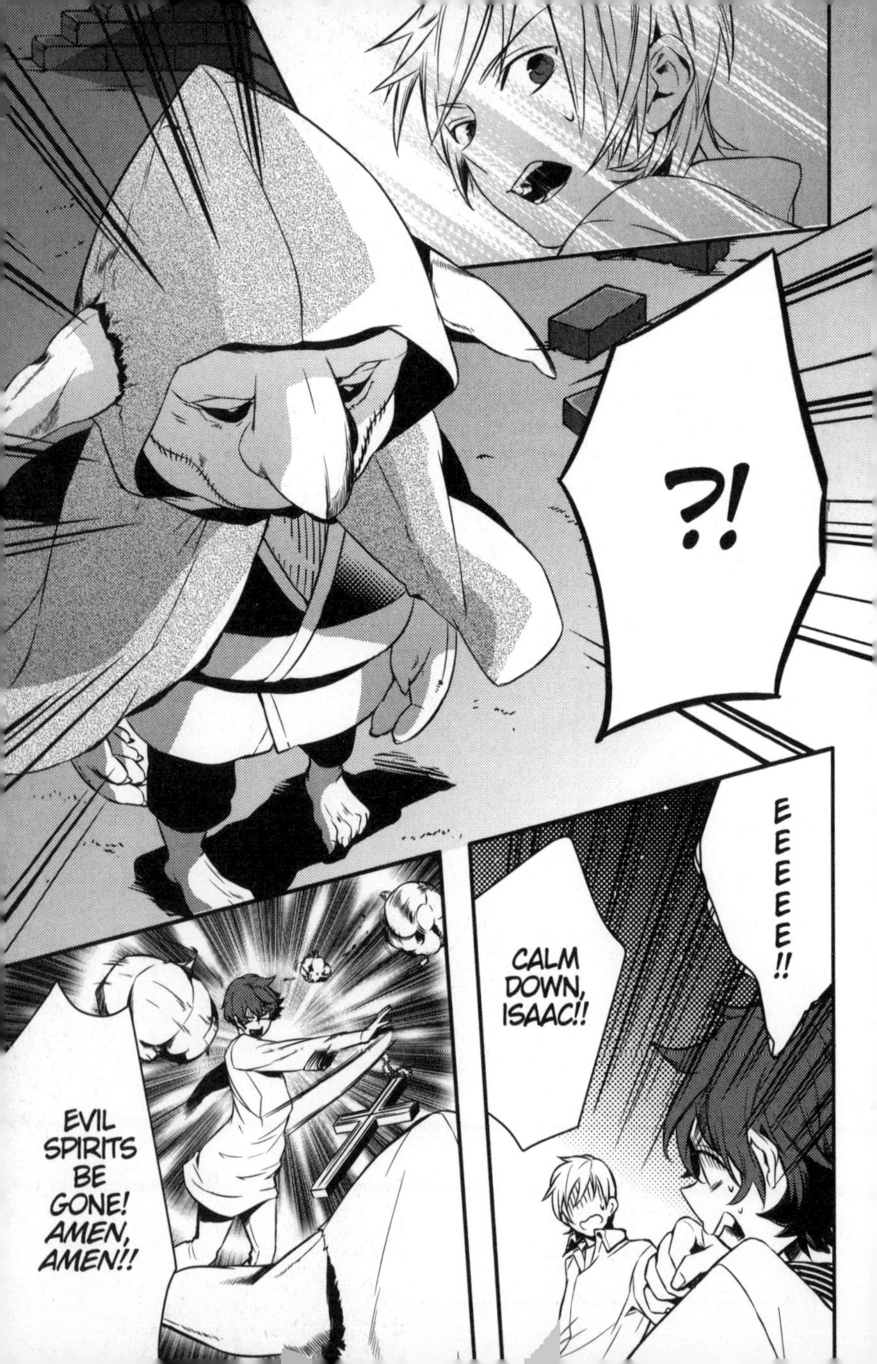
?!
EEEEEE!!
CALM DOWN, ISAAC!!
EVIL SPIRITS BE GONE! AMEN, AMEN!!

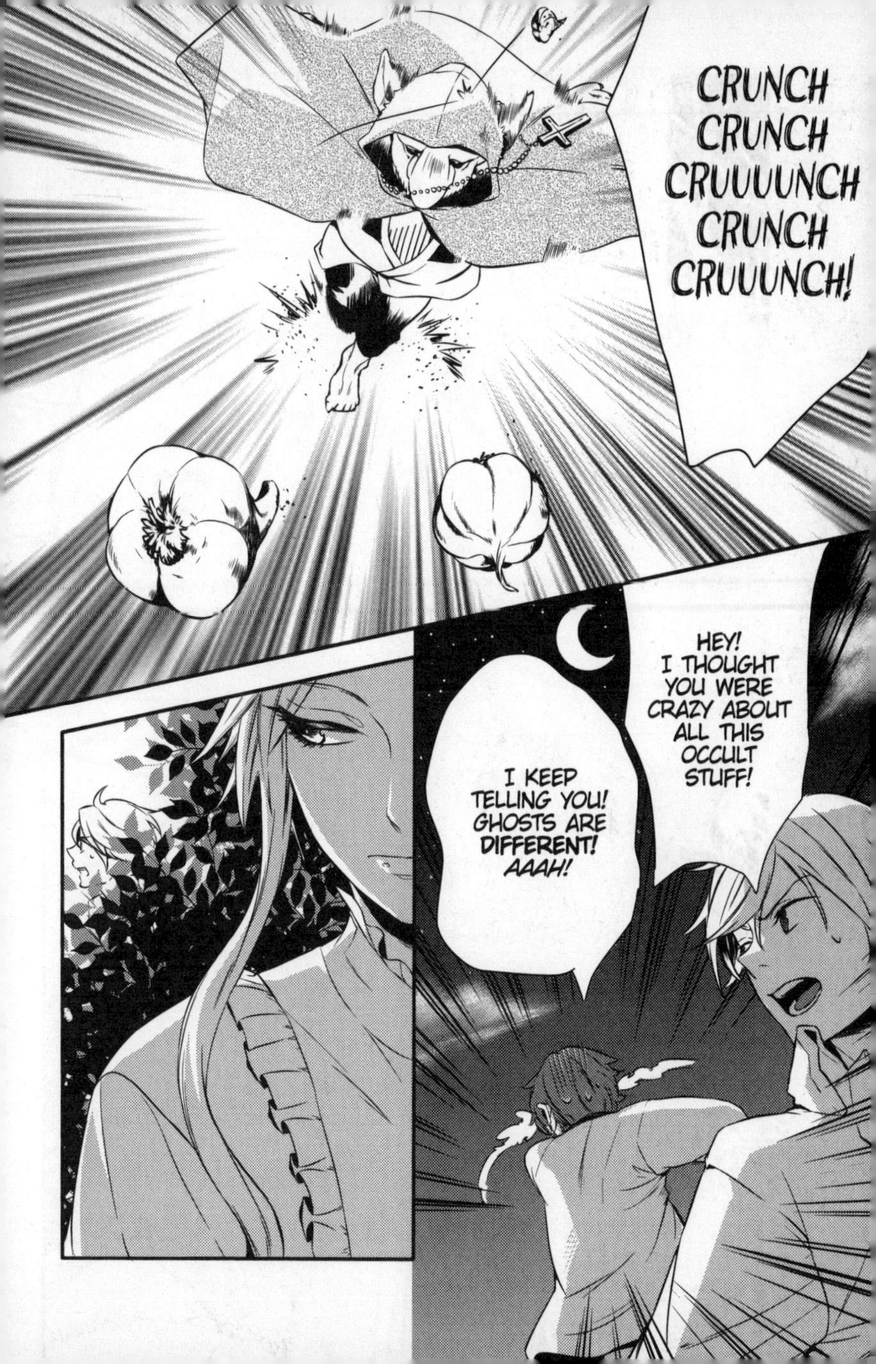
CRUNCH CRUNCH CRUUUUNCH CRUNCH CRUUUNCH!
HEY! I THOUGHT YOU WERE CRAZY ABOUT ALL THIS OCCULT STUFF!
I KEEP TELLING YOU! GHOSTS ARE DIFFERENT! AAAH!

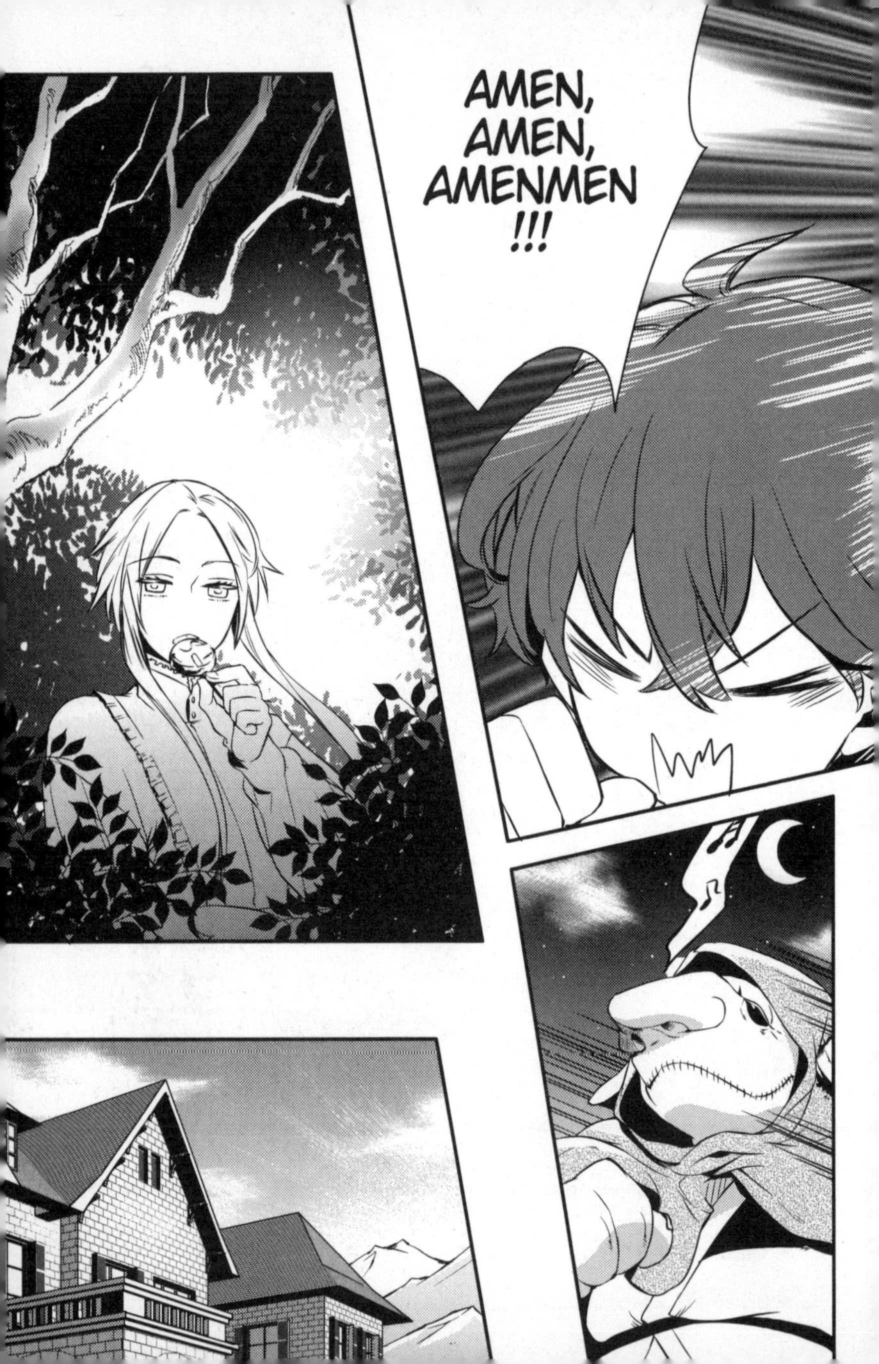
AMEN,
AMEN,
AMENMEN
!!!

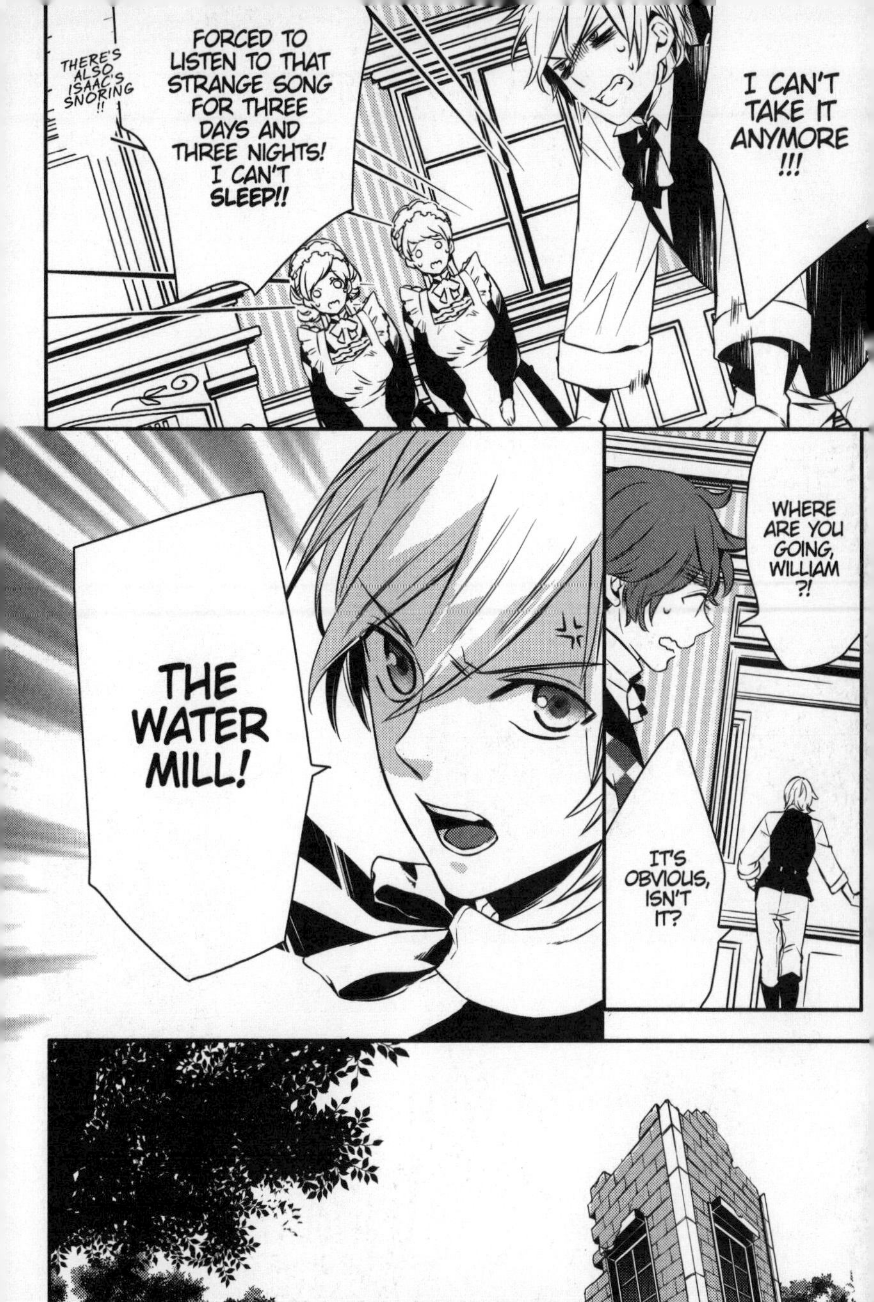
I CAN'T TAKE IT ANYMORE!!!
FORCED TO LISTEN TO THAT STRANGE SONG FOR THREE DAYS AND THREE NIGHTS! I CAN'T SLEEP!!
THERE'S ALSO ISAAC'S SNORING!!
WHERE ARE YOU GOING, WILLIAM?!
IT'S OBVIOUS, ISN'T IT?
THE WATER MILL!

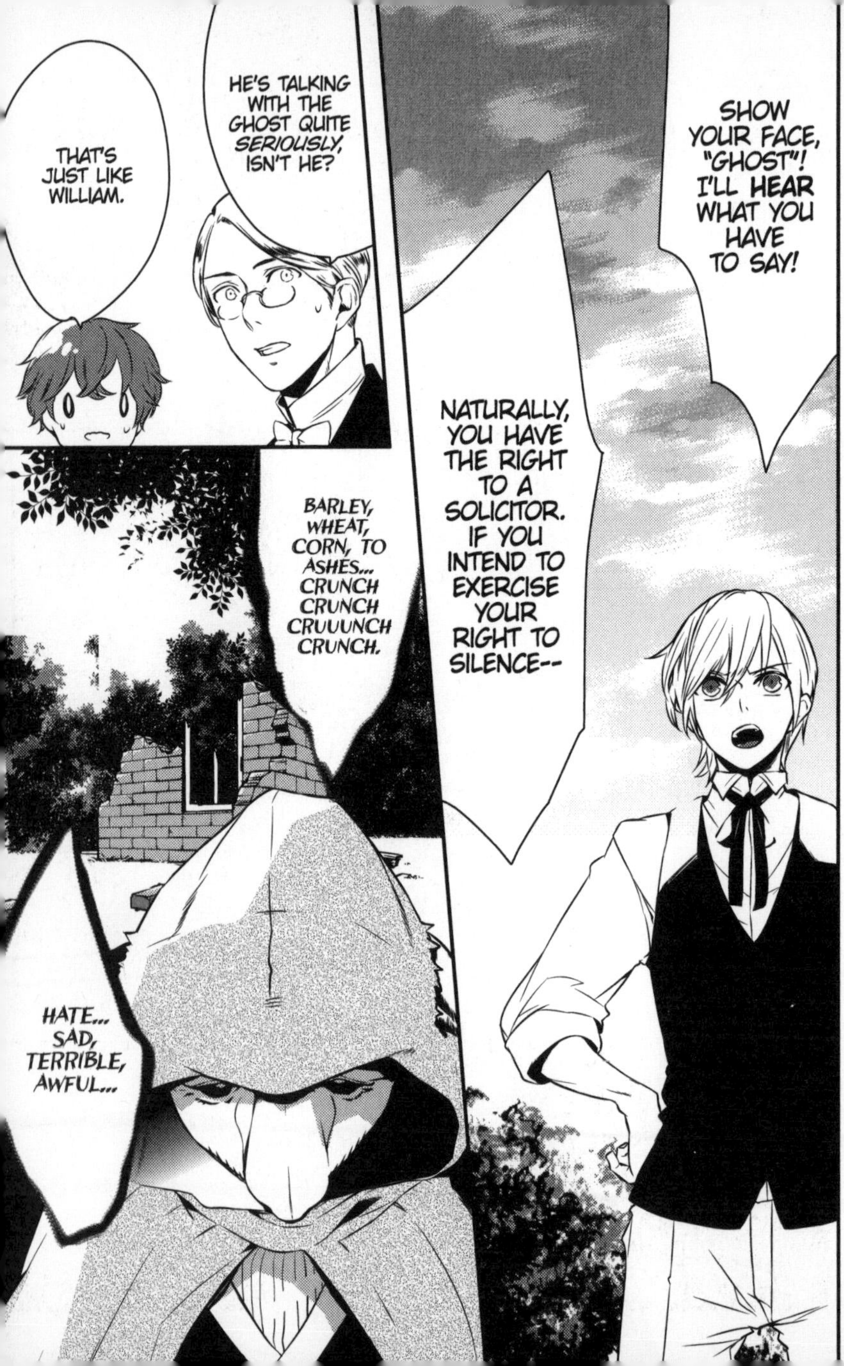
SHOW YOUR FACE, "GHOST"! I'LL HEAR WHAT YOU HAVE TO SAY!
NATURALLY, YOU HAVE THE RIGHT TO A SOLICITOR. IF YOU INTEND TO EXERCISE YOUR RIGHT TO SILENCE--
HE'S TALKING WITH THE GHOST QUITE SERIOUSLY, ISN'T HE?
THAT'S JUST LIKE WILLIAM.
BARLEY, WHEAT, CORN, TO ASHES... CRUNCH CRUNCH CRUUUNCH CRUNCH.
HATE... SAD, TERRIBLE, AWFUL...

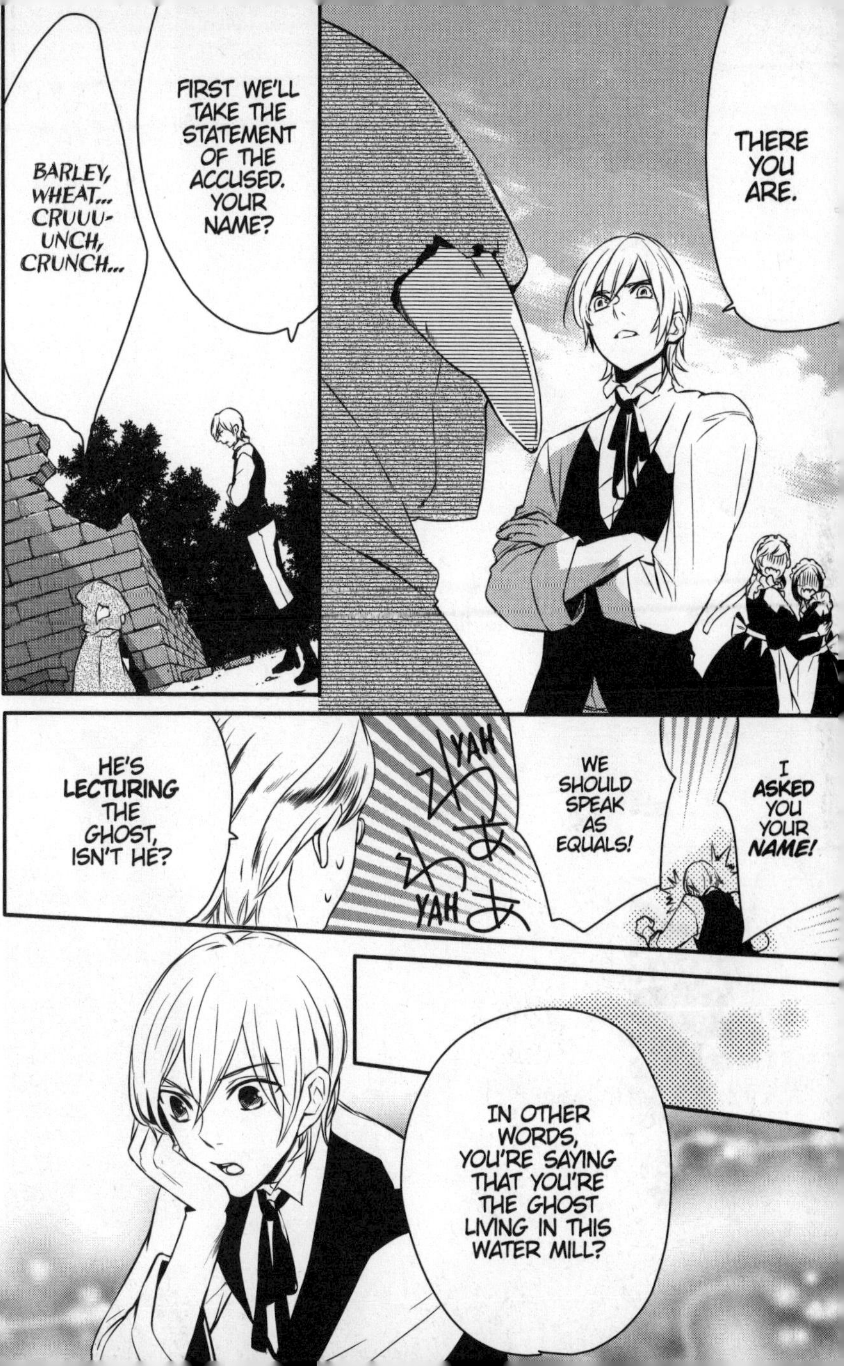
THERE YOU ARE.
FIRST WE'LL TAKE THE STATEMENT OF THE ACCUSED. YOUR NAME?
BARLEY, WHEAT... CRUUU-UNCH, CRUNCH...
I ASKED YOU YOUR *NAME!*
WE SHOULD SPEAK AS EQUALS!
YAH YAH
HE'S LECTURING THE GHOST, ISN'T HE?
IN OTHER WORDS, YOU'RE SAYING THAT YOU'RE THE GHOST LIVING IN THIS WATER MILL?

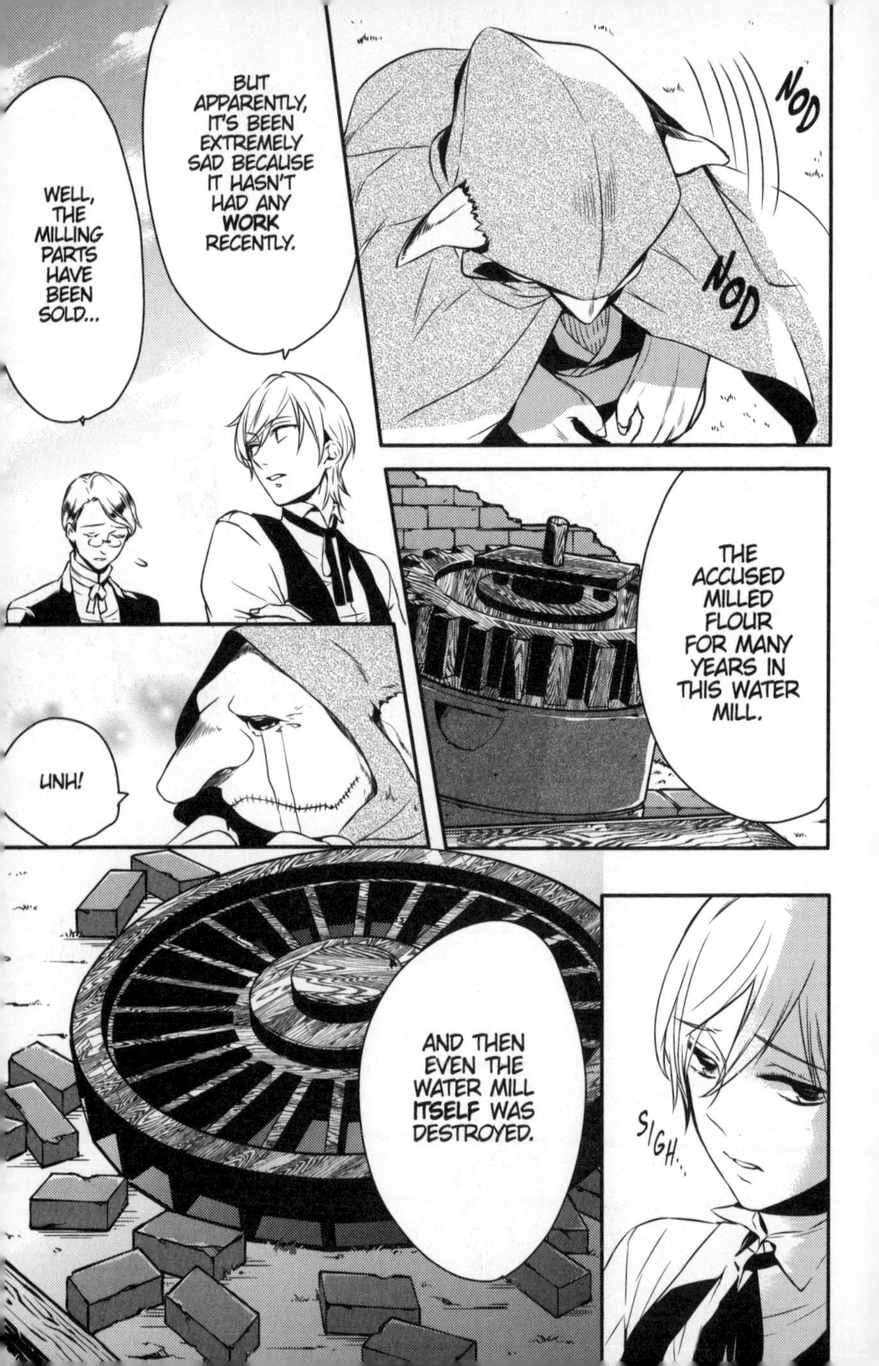
NOD
NOD
BUT APPARENTLY, IT'S BEEN EXTREMELY SAD BECAUSE IT HASN'T HAD ANY **WORK** RECENTLY.
WELL, THE MILLING PARTS HAVE BEEN SOLD...
THE ACCUSED MILLED FLOUR FOR MANY YEARS IN THIS WATER MILL.
UNH!
SIGH...
AND THEN EVEN THE WATER MILL **ITSELF** WAS DESTROYED.

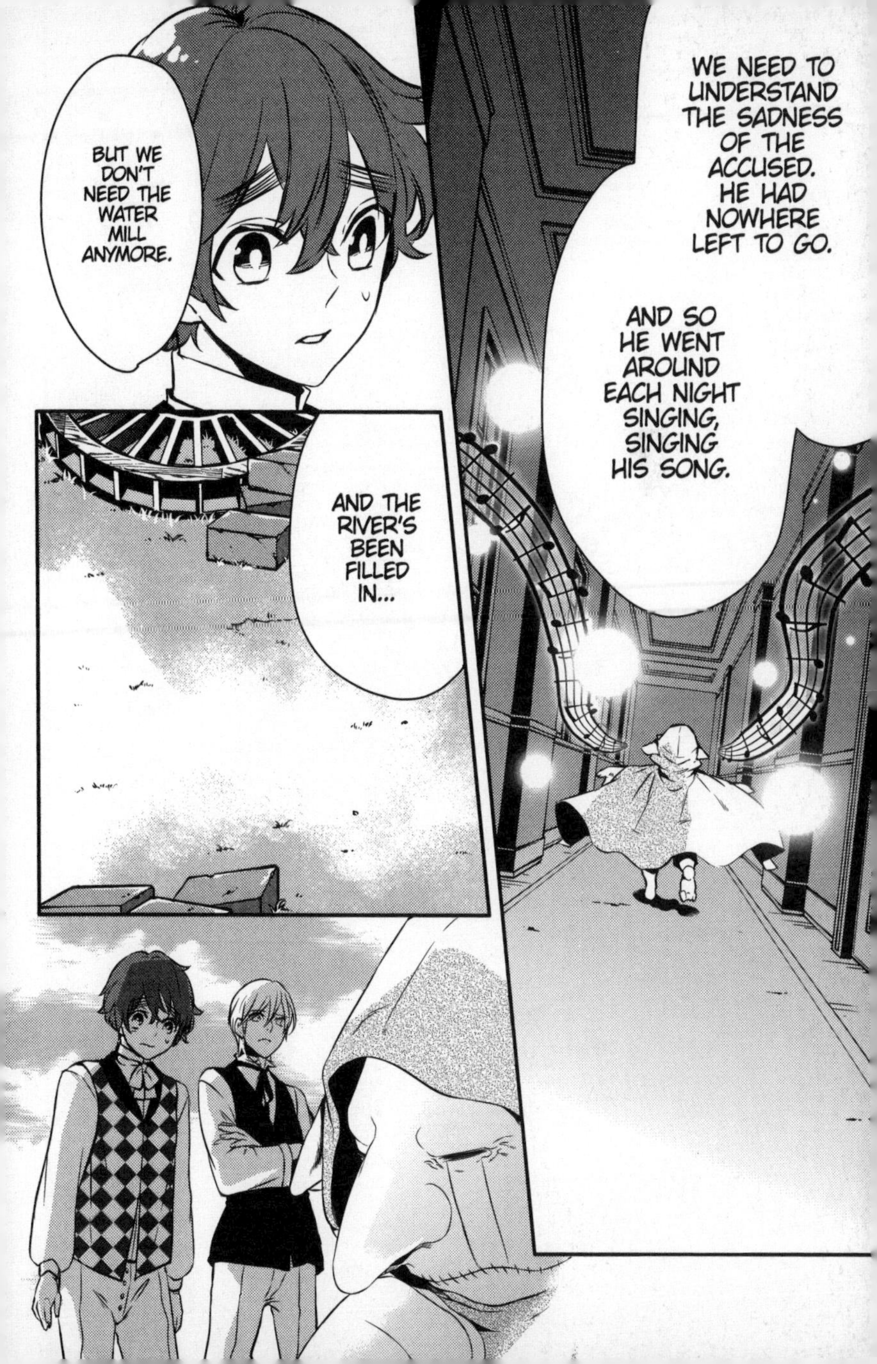
WE NEED TO UNDERSTAND THE SADNESS OF THE ACCUSED. HE HAD NOWHERE LEFT TO GO.
AND SO HE WENT AROUND EACH NIGHT SINGING, SINGING HIS SONG.
BUT WE DON'T NEED THE WATER MILL ANYMORE.
AND THE RIVER'S BEEN FILLED IN...

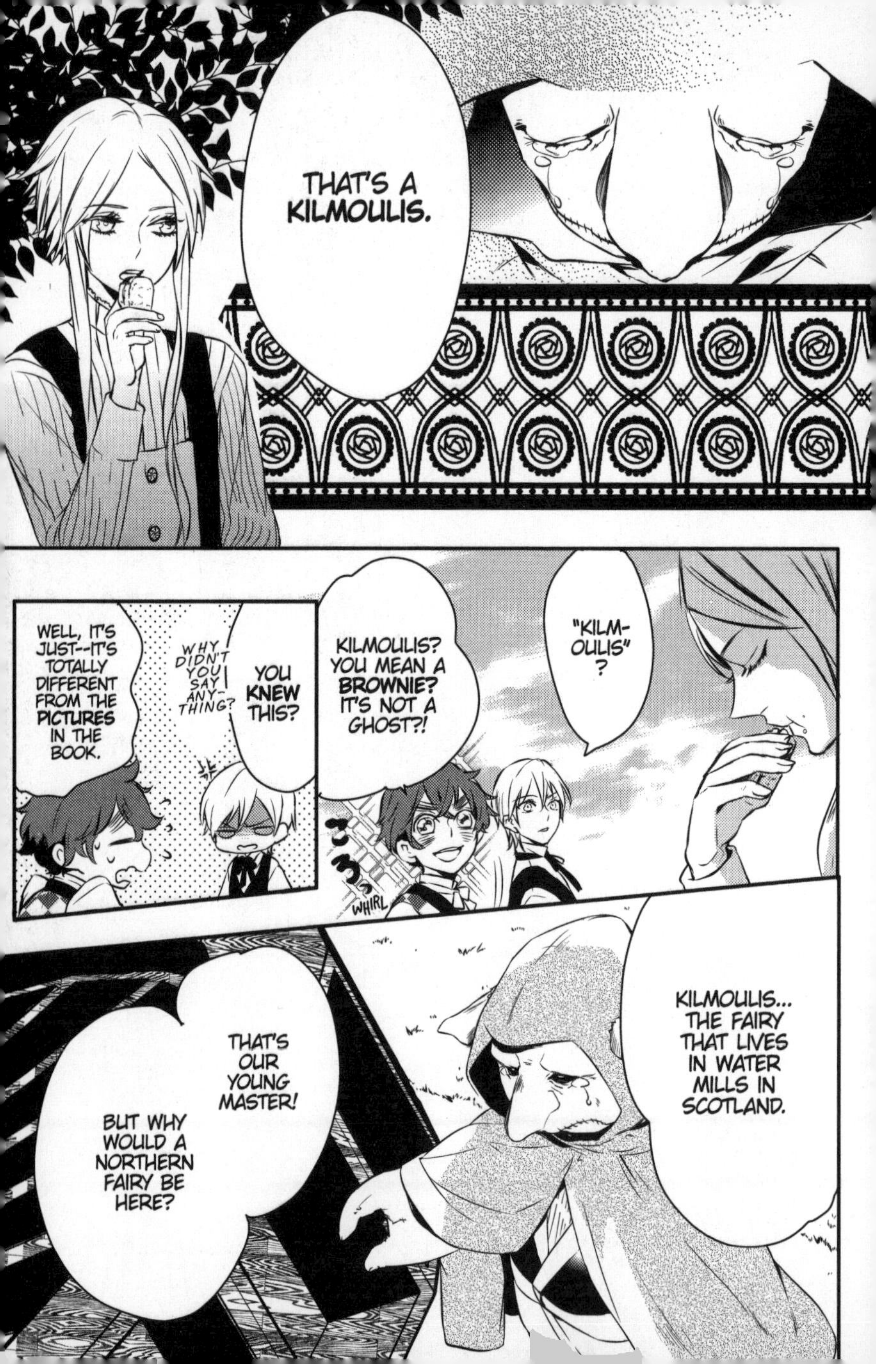
THAT'S A KILMOULIS.
"KILM-OULIS"?
KILMOULIS? YOU MEAN A BROWNIE? IT'S NOT A GHOST?!
WHIRL
YOU KNEW THIS?
WHY DIDN'T YOU SAY ANYTHING?
WELL, IT'S JUST--IT'S TOTALLY DIFFERENT FROM THE PICTURES IN THE BOOK.
KILMOULIS... THE FAIRY THAT LIVES IN WATER MILLS IN SCOTLAND.
THAT'S OUR YOUNG MASTER!
BUT WHY WOULD A NORTHERN FAIRY BE HERE?

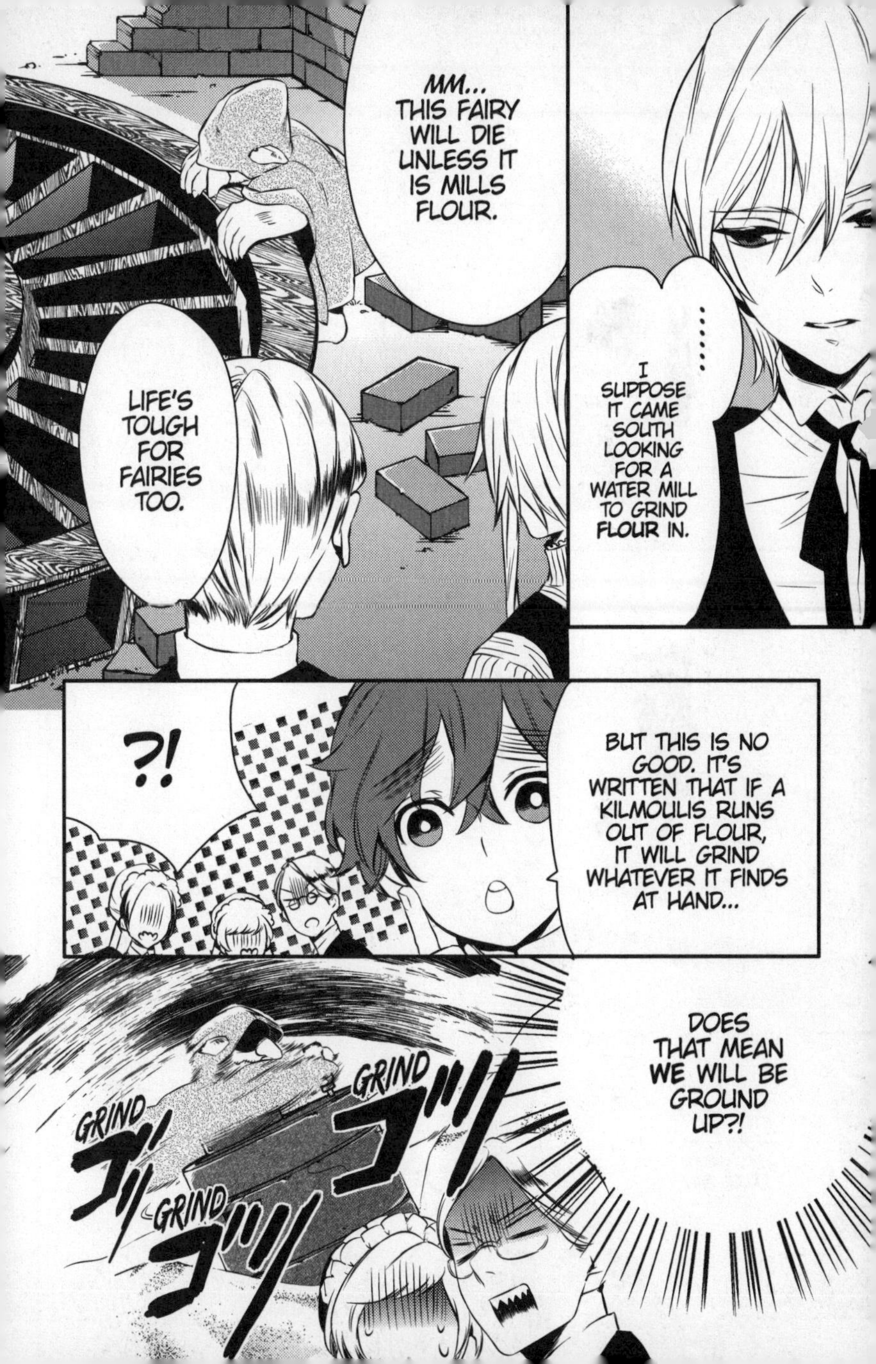
......
I SUPPOSE IT CAME SOUTH LOOKING FOR A WATER MILL TO GRIND FLOUR IN.
MM... THIS FAIRY WILL DIE UNLESS IT IS MILLS FLOUR.
LIFE'S TOUGH FOR FAIRIES TOO.
BUT THIS IS NO GOOD. IT'S WRITTEN THAT IF A KILMOULIS RUNS OUT OF FLOUR, IT WILL GRIND WHATEVER IT FINDS AT HAND...
?!
DOES THAT MEAN WE WILL BE GROUND UP?!
GRIND
GRIND
GRIND

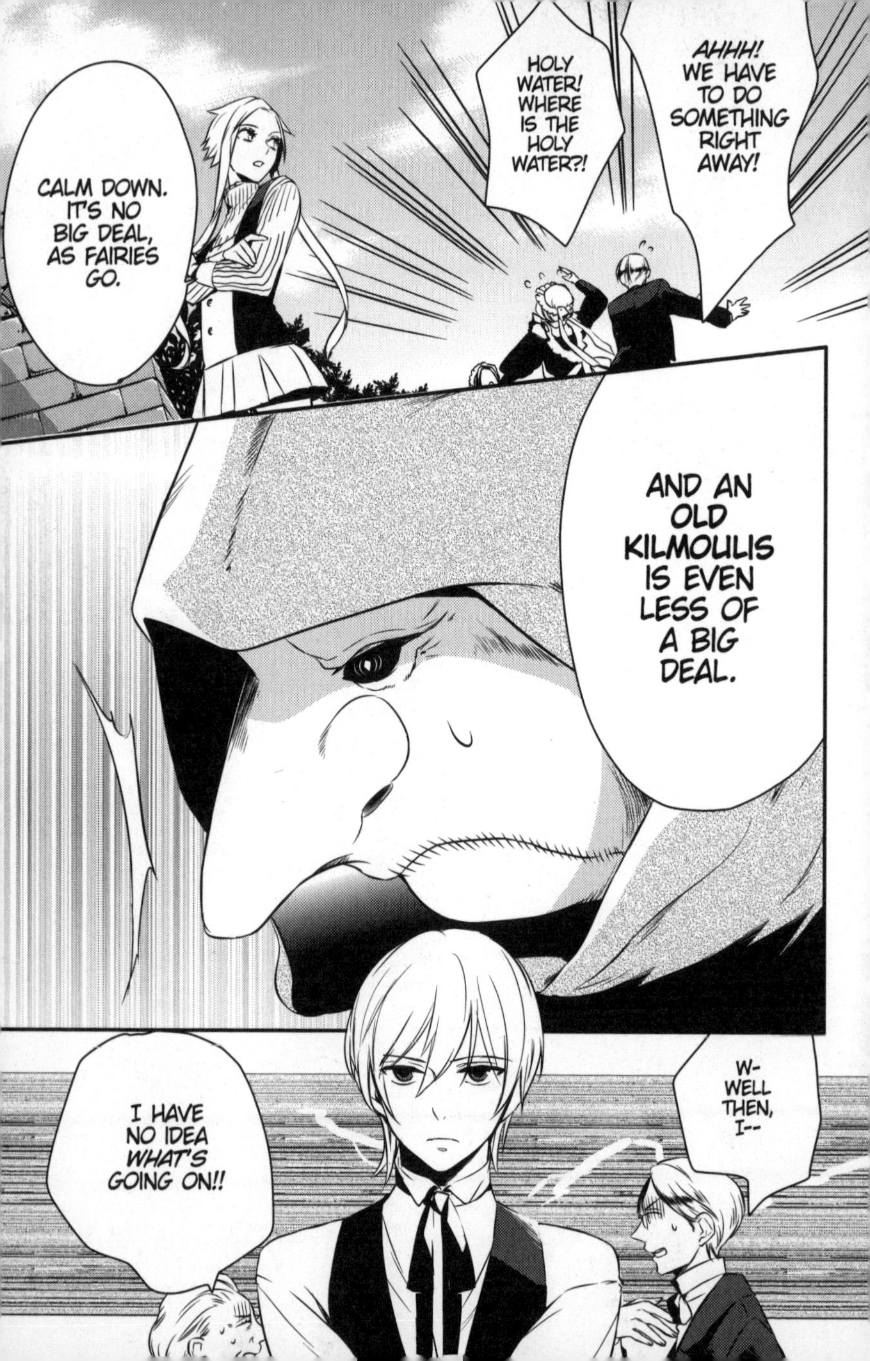
AHHH! WE HAVE TO DO SOMETHING RIGHT AWAY!
HOLY WATER! WHERE IS THE HOLY WATER?!
CALM DOWN. IT'S NO BIG DEAL, AS FAIRIES GO.
AND AN OLD KILMOULIS IS EVEN LESS OF A BIG DEAL.
W-WELL THEN, I--
I HAVE NO IDEA *WHAT'S* GOING ON!!

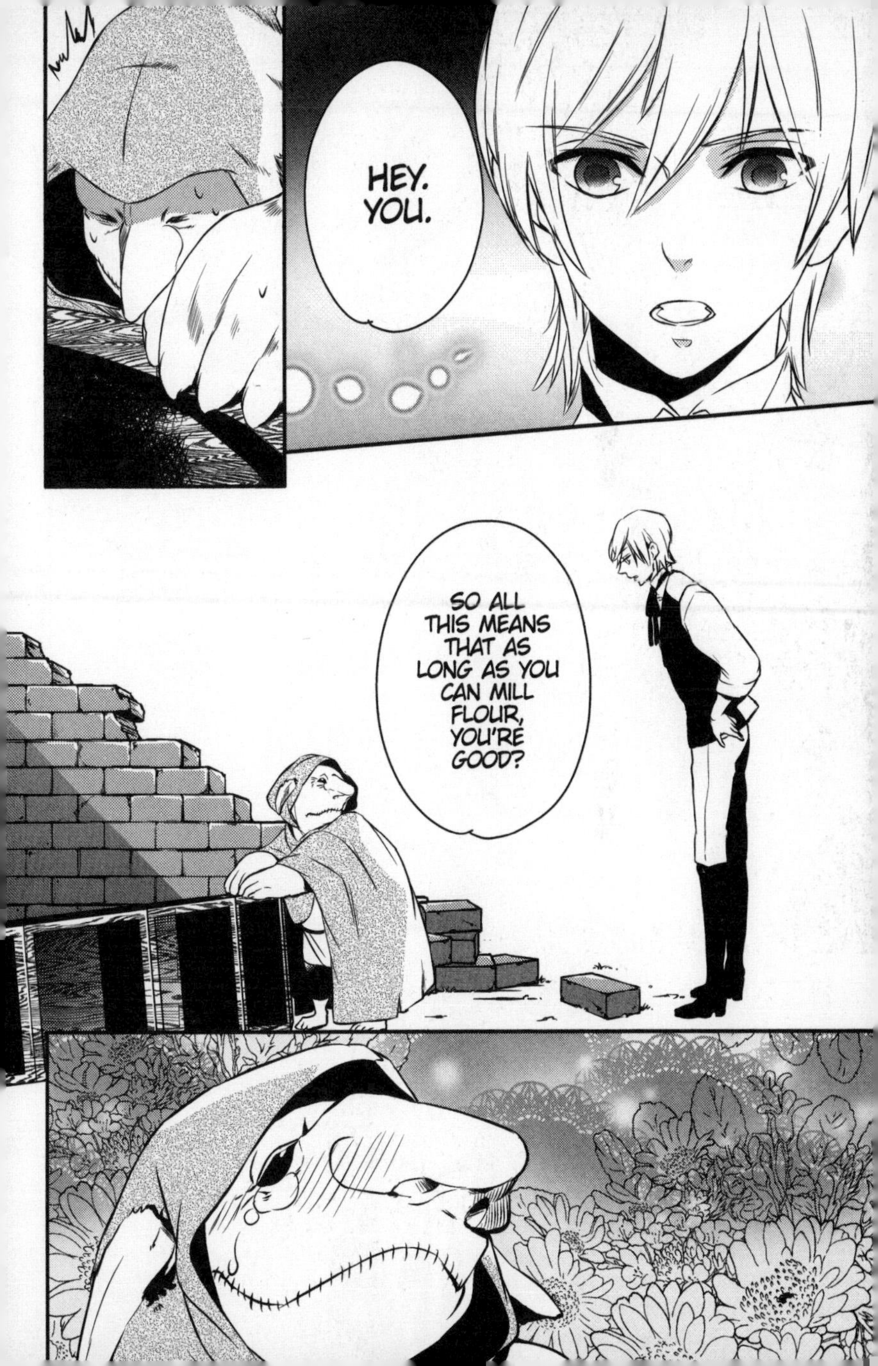
HEY. YOU.
SO ALL THIS MEANS THAT AS LONG AS YOU CAN MILL FLOUR, YOU'RE GOOD?

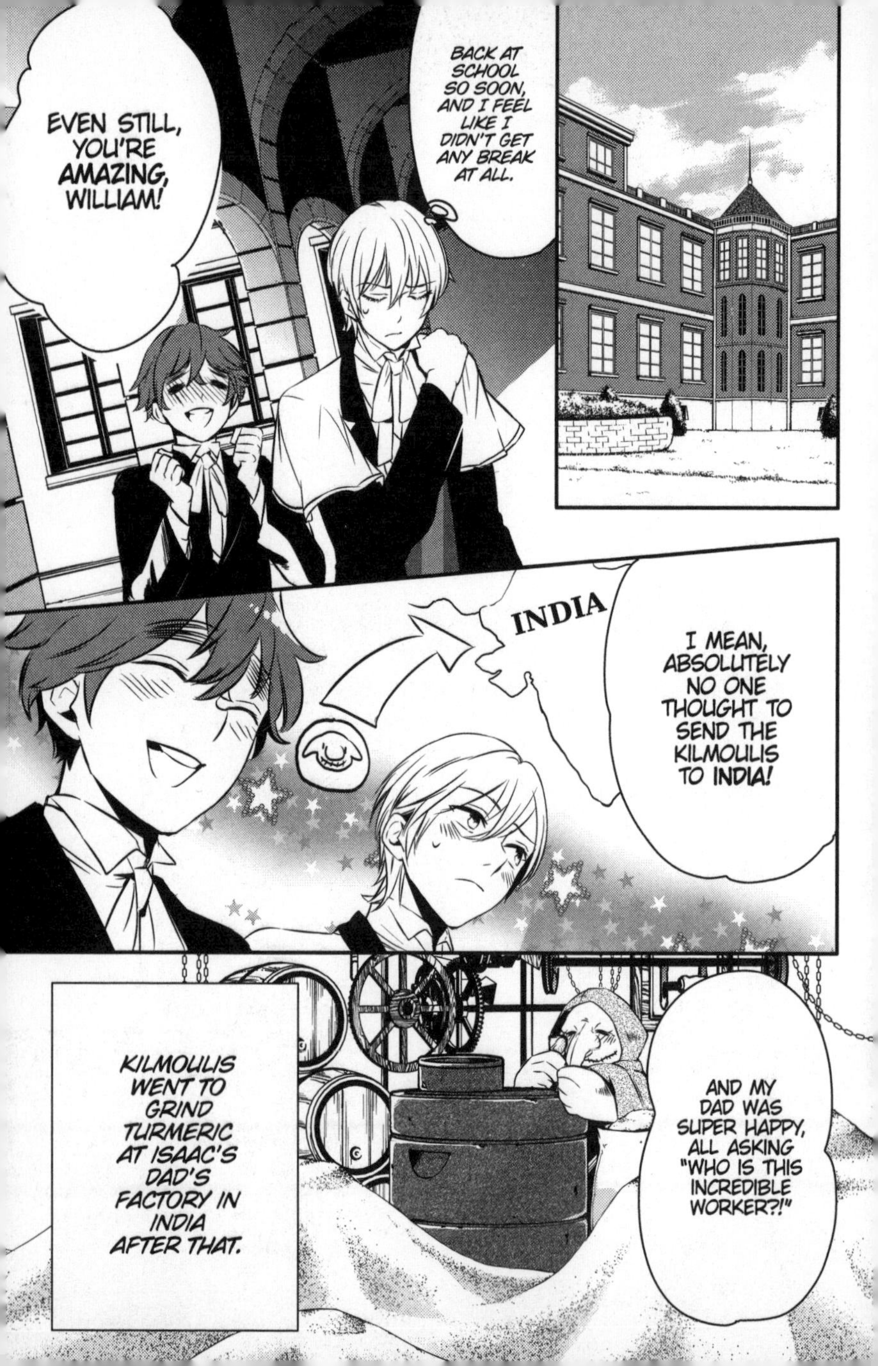
BACK AT SCHOOL SO SOON, AND I FEEL LIKE I DIDN'T GET ANY BREAK AT ALL.
EVEN STILL, YOU'RE AMAZING, WILLIAM!
INDIA
I MEAN, ABSOLUTELY NO ONE THOUGHT TO SEND THE KILMOULIS TO INDIA!
AND MY DAD WAS SUPER HAPPY, ALL ASKING "WHO IS THIS INCREDIBLE WORKER?!"
KILMOULIS WENT TO GRIND TURMERIC AT ISAAC'S DAD'S FACTORY IN INDIA AFTER THAT.

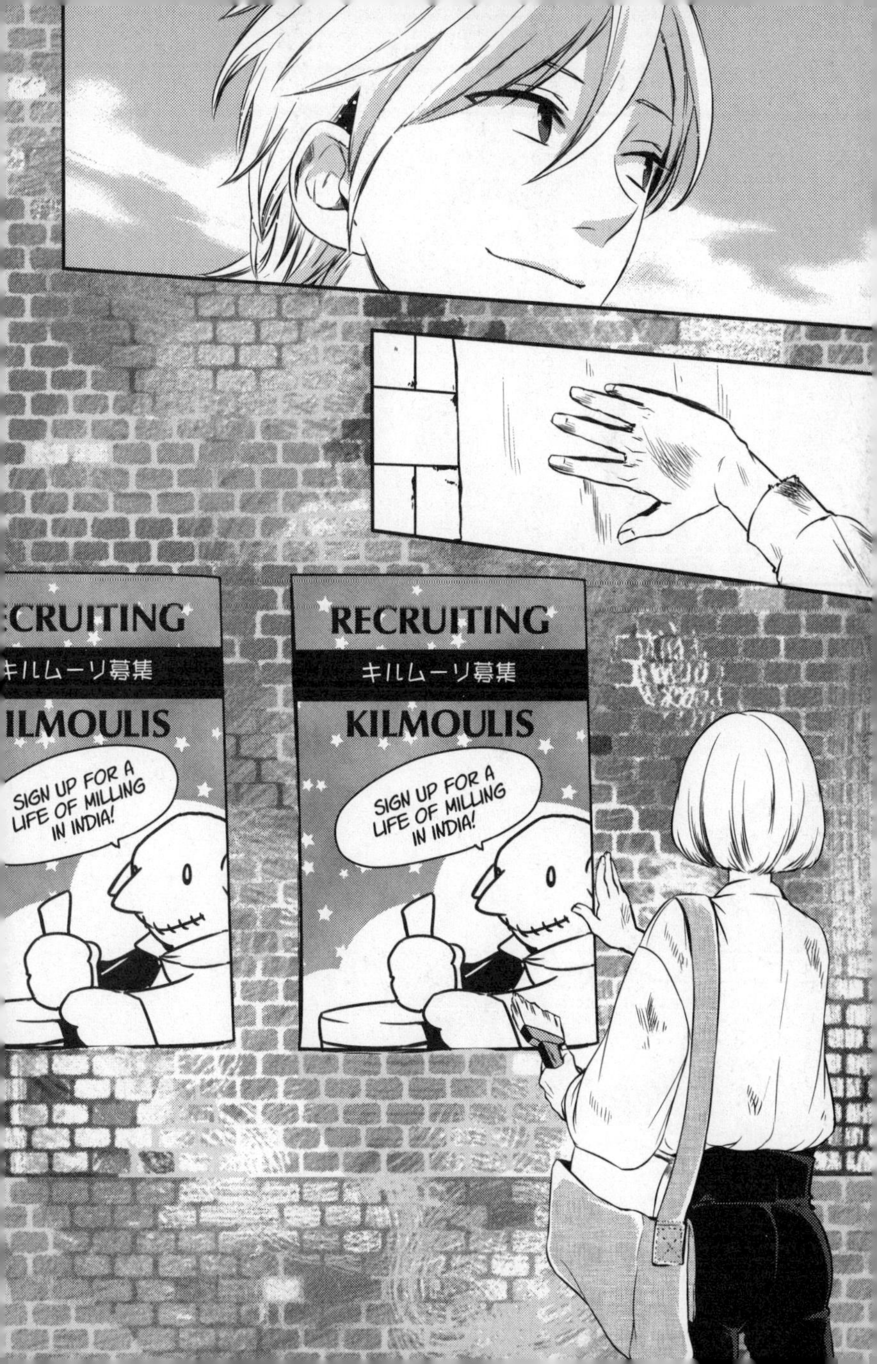
RECRUITING
キルムーリ募集
KILMOULIS
SIGN UP FOR A LIFE OF MILLING IN INDIA!
CRUITING
キルムーリ募集
ILMOULIS
SIGN UP FOR A LIFE OF MILLING IN INDIA!

Pillar 10

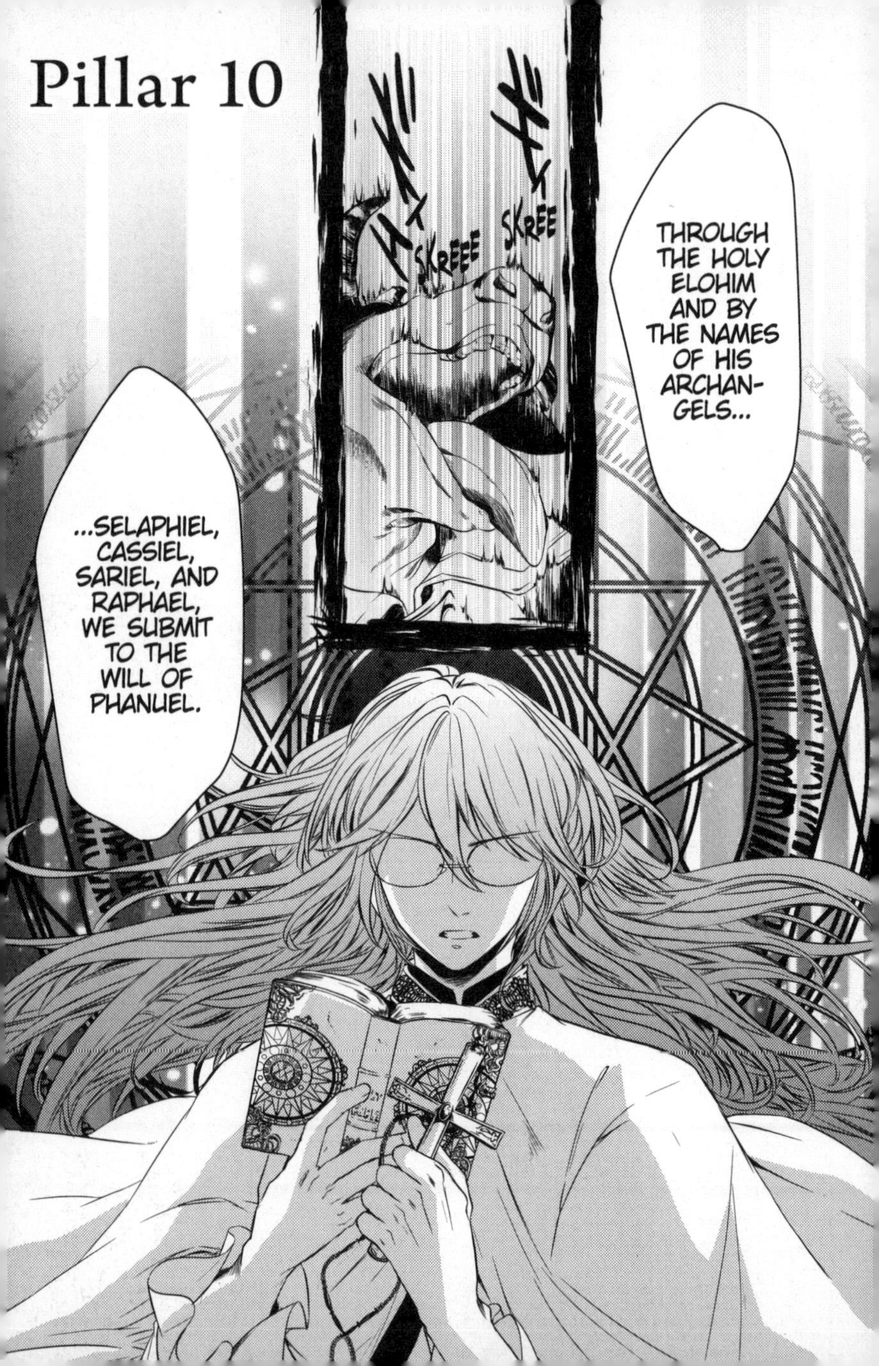
SKREE
SKREEE
THROUGH THE HOLY ELOHIM AND BY THE NAMES OF HIS ARCHANGELS...
...SELAPHIEL, CASSIEL, SARIEL, AND RAPHAEL, WE SUBMIT TO THE WILL OF PHANUEL.

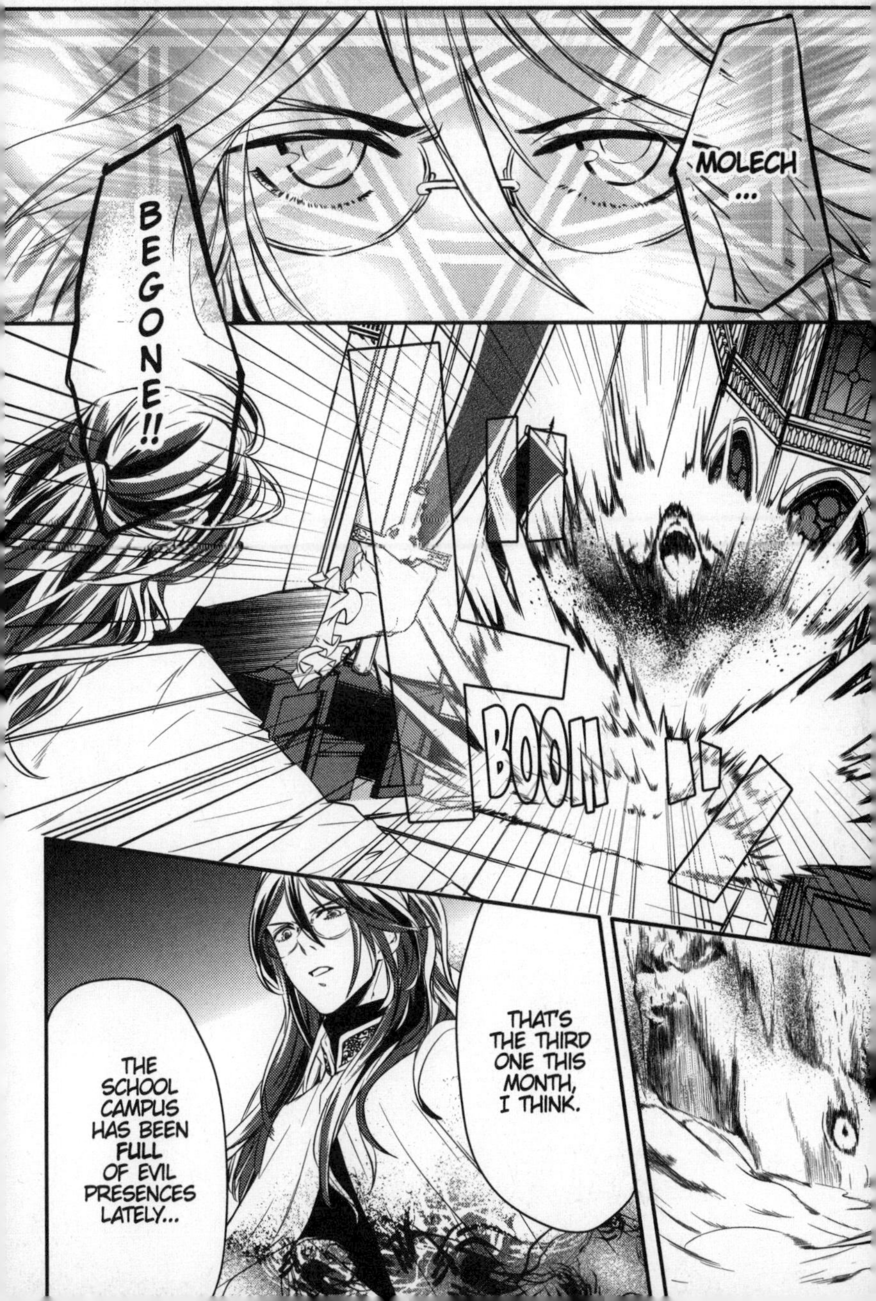
MOLECH ...
BEGONE!!
BOOM
THAT'S THE THIRD ONE THIS MONTH, I THINK.
THE SCHOOL CAMPUS HAS BEEN FULL OF EVIL PRESENCES LATELY...

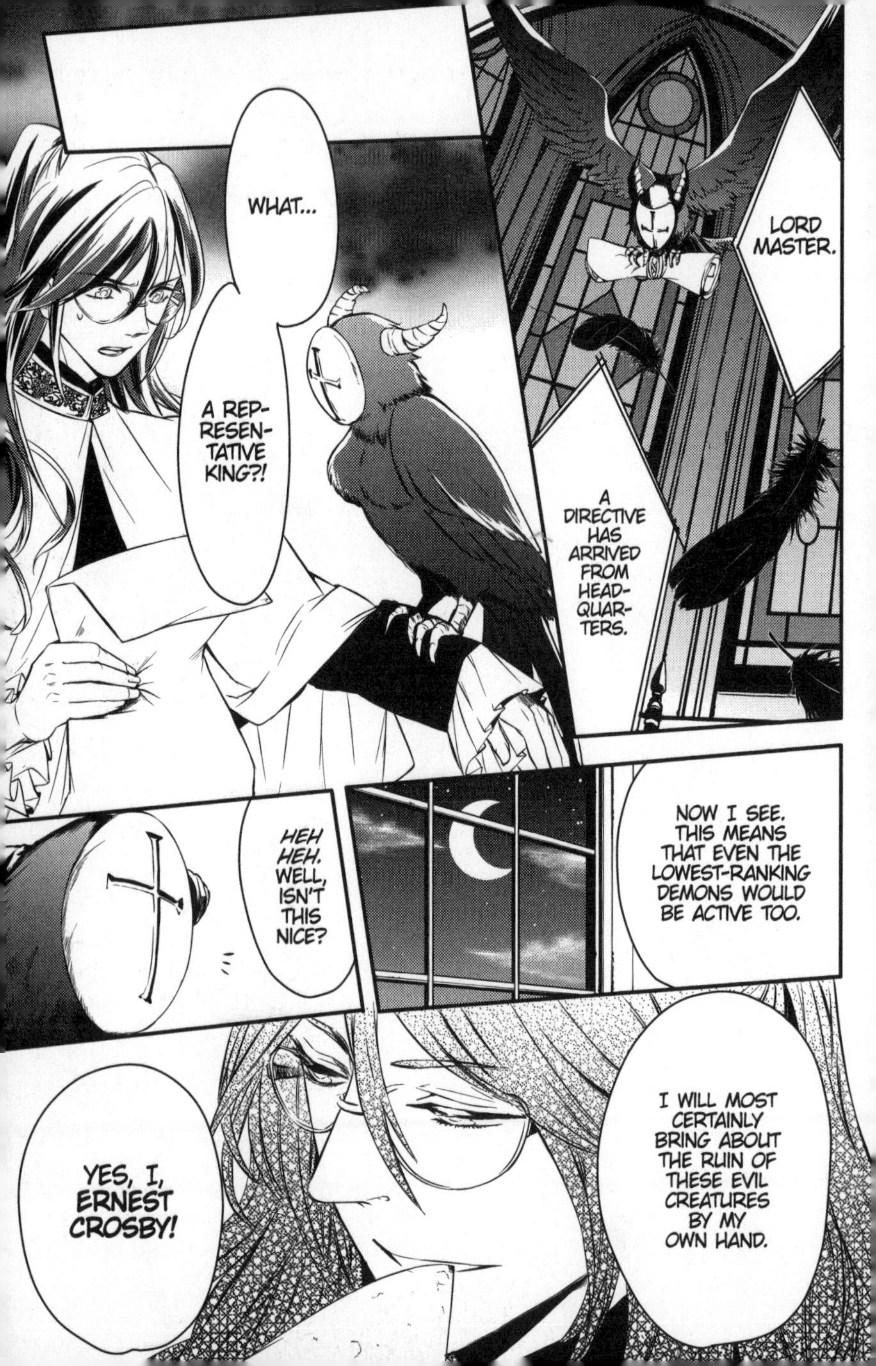
LORD MASTER.
A DIRECTIVE HAS ARRIVED FROM HEADQUARTERS.
WHAT...
A REPRESENTATIVE KING?!
NOW I SEE. THIS MEANS THAT EVEN THE LOWEST-RANKING DEMONS WOULD BE ACTIVE TOO.
HEH HEH. WELL, ISN'T THIS NICE?
I WILL MOST CERTAINLY BRING ABOUT THE RUIN OF THESE EVIL CREATURES BY MY OWN HAND.
YES, I, ERNEST CROSBY!

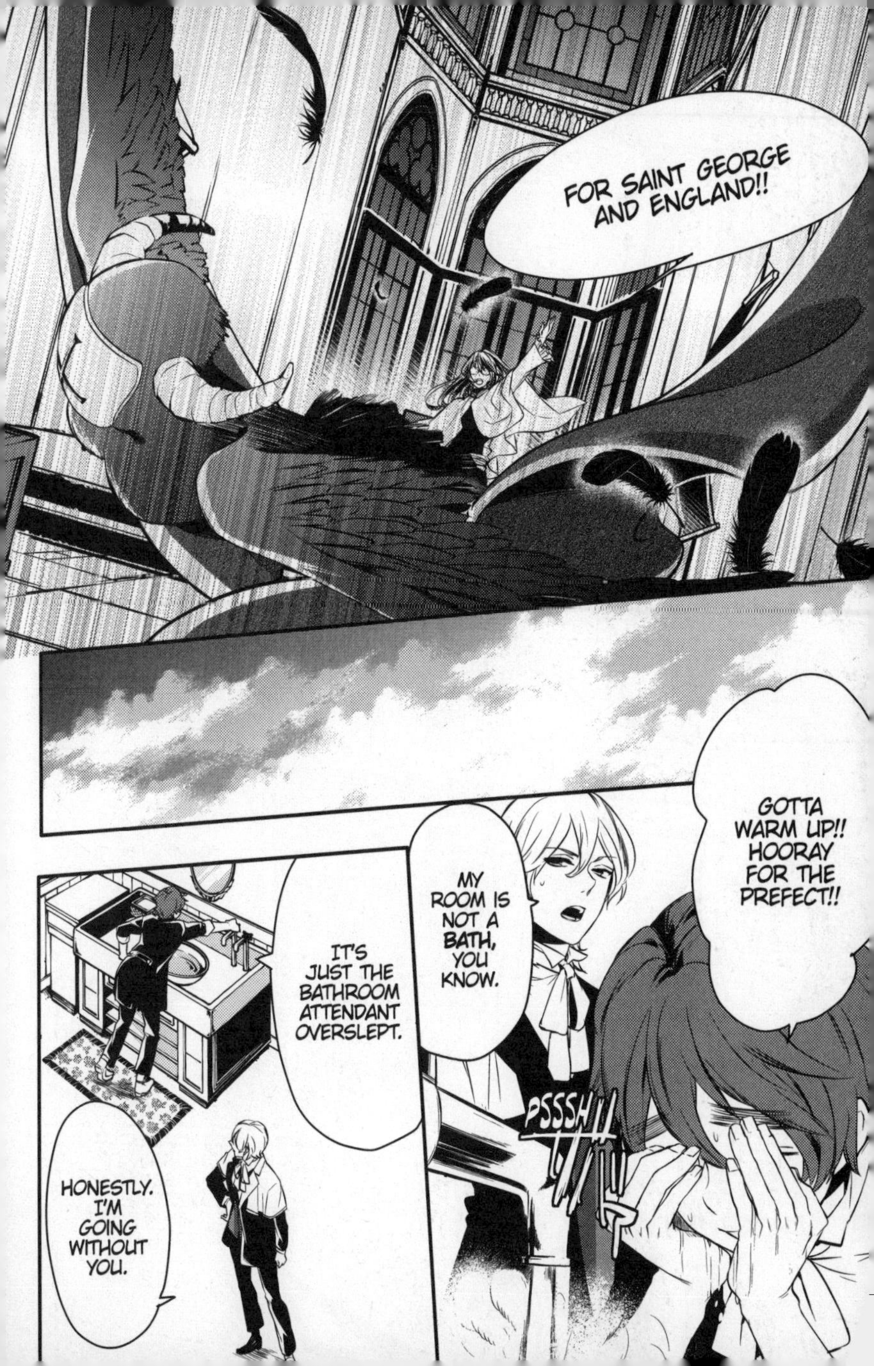
FOR SAINT GEORGE AND ENGLAND!!
GOTTA WARM UP!! HOORAY FOR THE PREFECT!!
MY ROOM IS NOT A BATH, YOU KNOW.
PSSSH
IT'S JUST THE BATHROOM ATTENDANT OVERSLEPT.
HONESTLY. I'M GOING WITHOUT YOU.

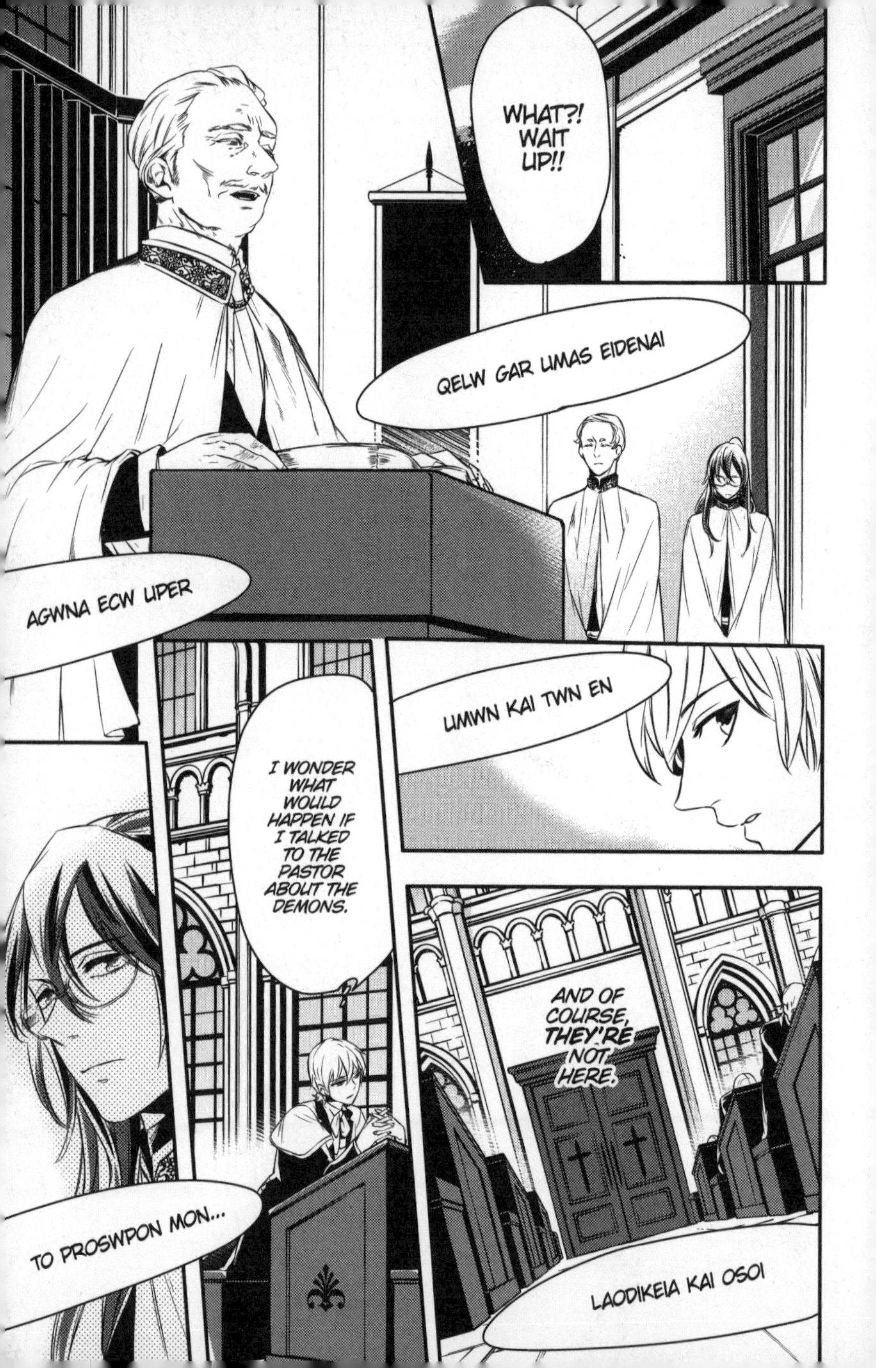
WHAT?! WAIT UP!!
QELW GAR UMAS EIDENAI
AGWNA ECW UPER
UMWN KAI TWN EN
AND OF COURSE, THEY'RE NOT HERE.
LAODIKEIA KAI OSOI
I WONDER WHAT WOULD HAPPEN IF I TALKED TO THE PASTOR ABOUT THE DEMONS.
TO PROSWPON MON...

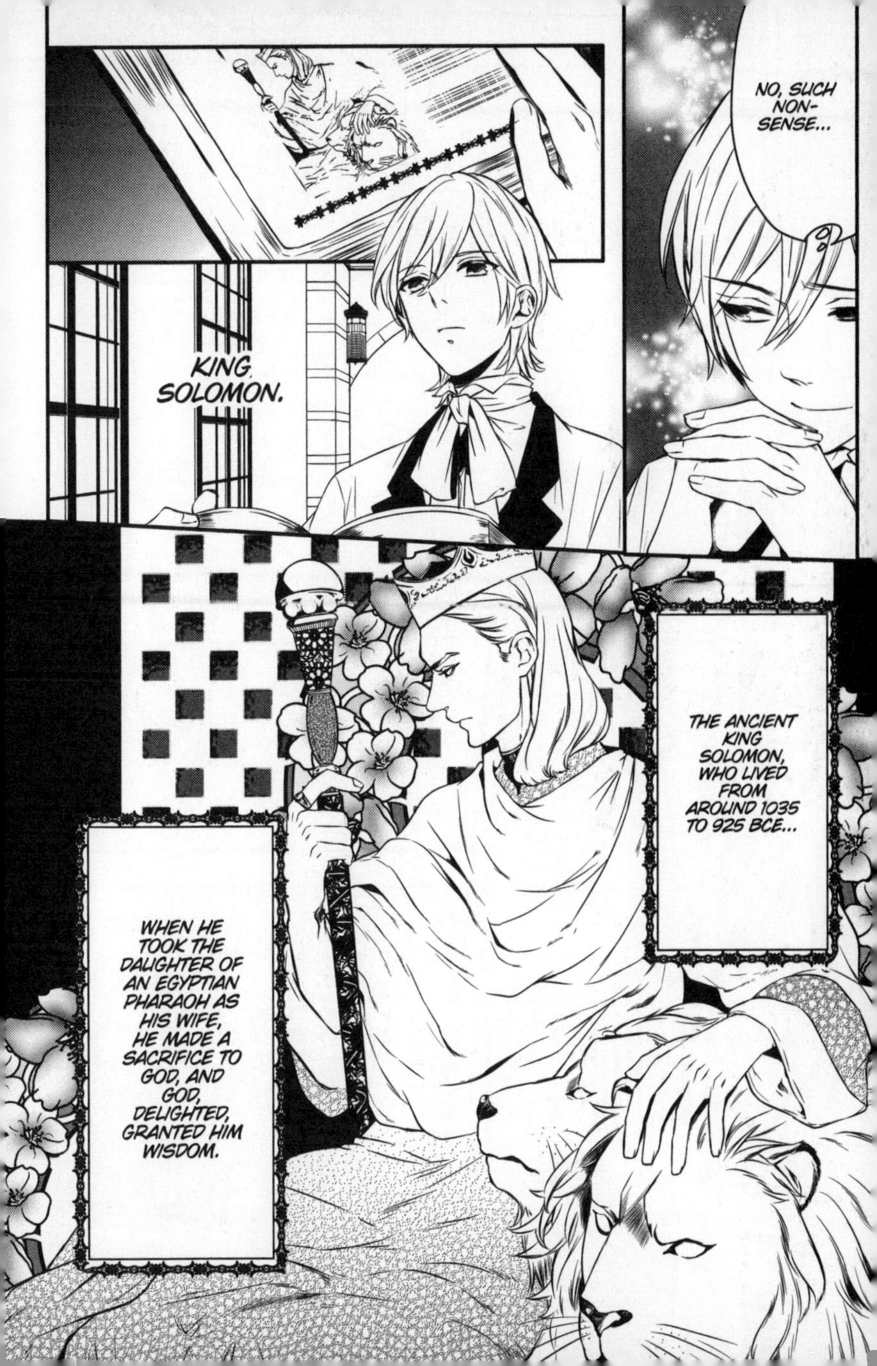
NO, SUCH NON-SENSE...
KING SOLOMON.
THE ANCIENT KING SOLOMON, WHO LIVED FROM AROUND 1035 TO 925 BCE...
WHEN HE TOOK THE DAUGHTER OF AN EGYPTIAN PHARAOH AS HIS WIFE, HE MADE A SACRIFICE TO GOD, AND GOD, DELIGHTED, GRANTED HIM WISDOM.

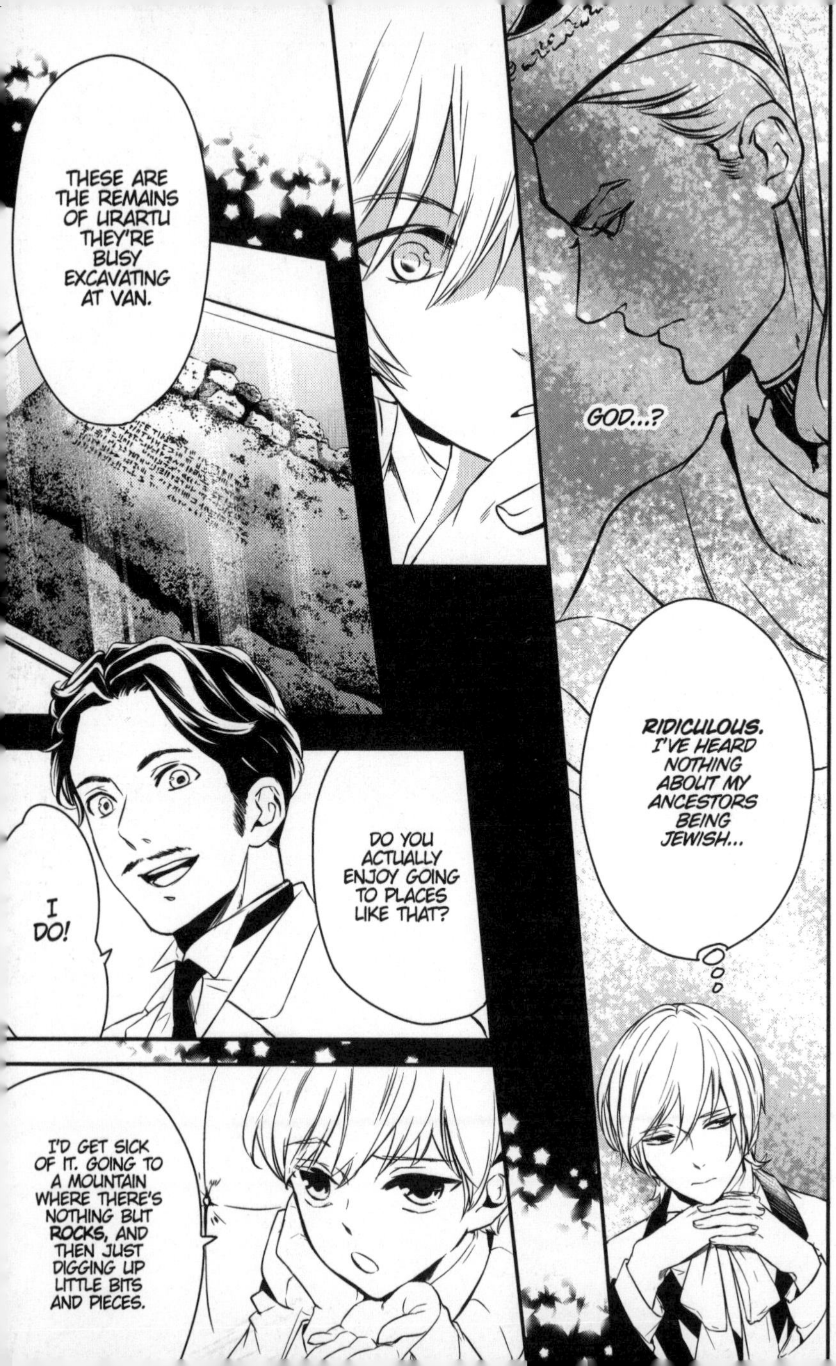
GOD...?
RIDICULOUS. I'VE HEARD NOTHING ABOUT MY ANCESTORS BEING JEWISH...
THESE ARE THE REMAINS OF URARTU THEY'RE BUSY EXCAVATING AT VAN.
DO YOU ACTUALLY ENJOY GOING TO PLACES LIKE THAT?
I DO!
I'D GET SICK OF IT. GOING TO A MOUNTAIN WHERE THERE'S NOTHING BUT ROCKS, AND THEN JUST DIGGING UP LITTLE BITS AND PIECES.

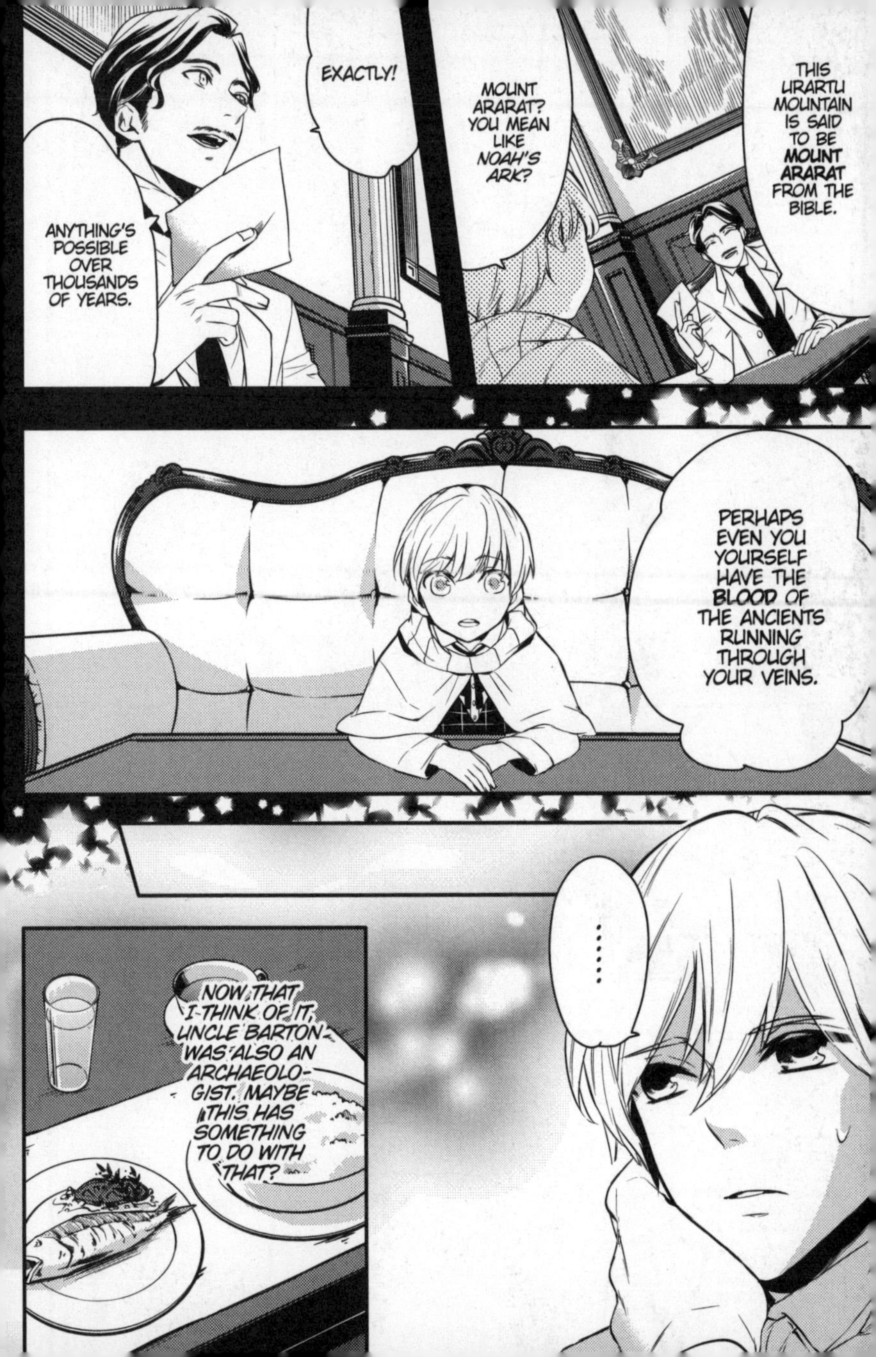
THIS URARTU MOUNTAIN IS SAID TO BE **MOUNT ARARAT** FROM THE BIBLE.
MOUNT ARARAT? YOU MEAN LIKE *NOAH'S ARK?*
EXACTLY!
ANYTHING'S POSSIBLE OVER THOUSANDS OF YEARS.
PERHAPS EVEN YOU YOURSELF HAVE THE **BLOOD** OF THE ANCIENTS RUNNING THROUGH YOUR VEINS.
......
NOW THAT I THINK OF IT, UNCLE BARTON WAS ALSO AN ARCHAEOLOGIST. MAYBE THIS HAS SOMETHING TO DO WITH THAT?

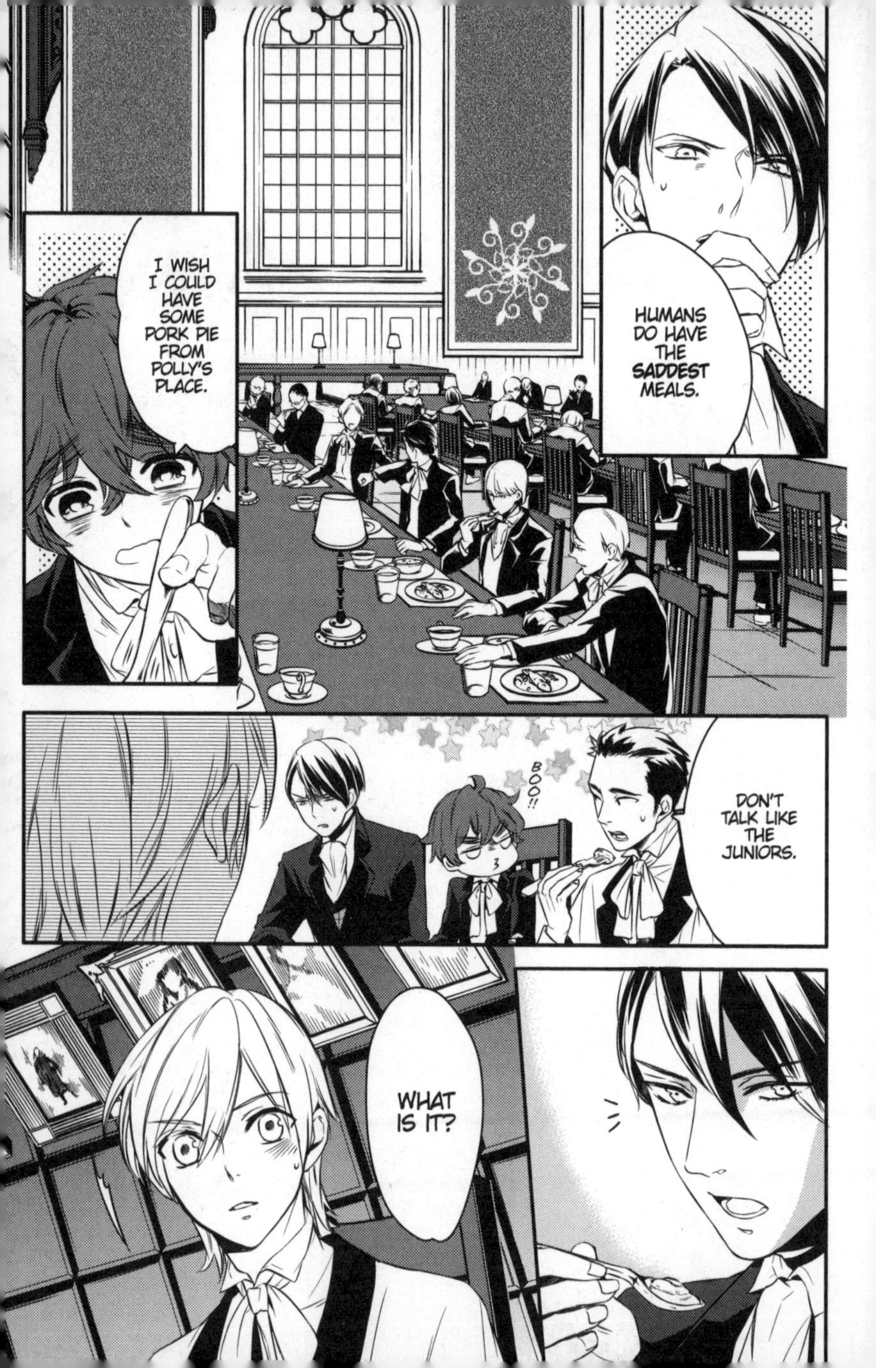
HUMANS DO HAVE THE SADDEST MEALS.
I WISH I COULD HAVE SOME PORK PIE FROM POLLY'S PLACE.
DON'T TALK LIKE THE JUNIORS.
BOO!!
WHAT IS IT?

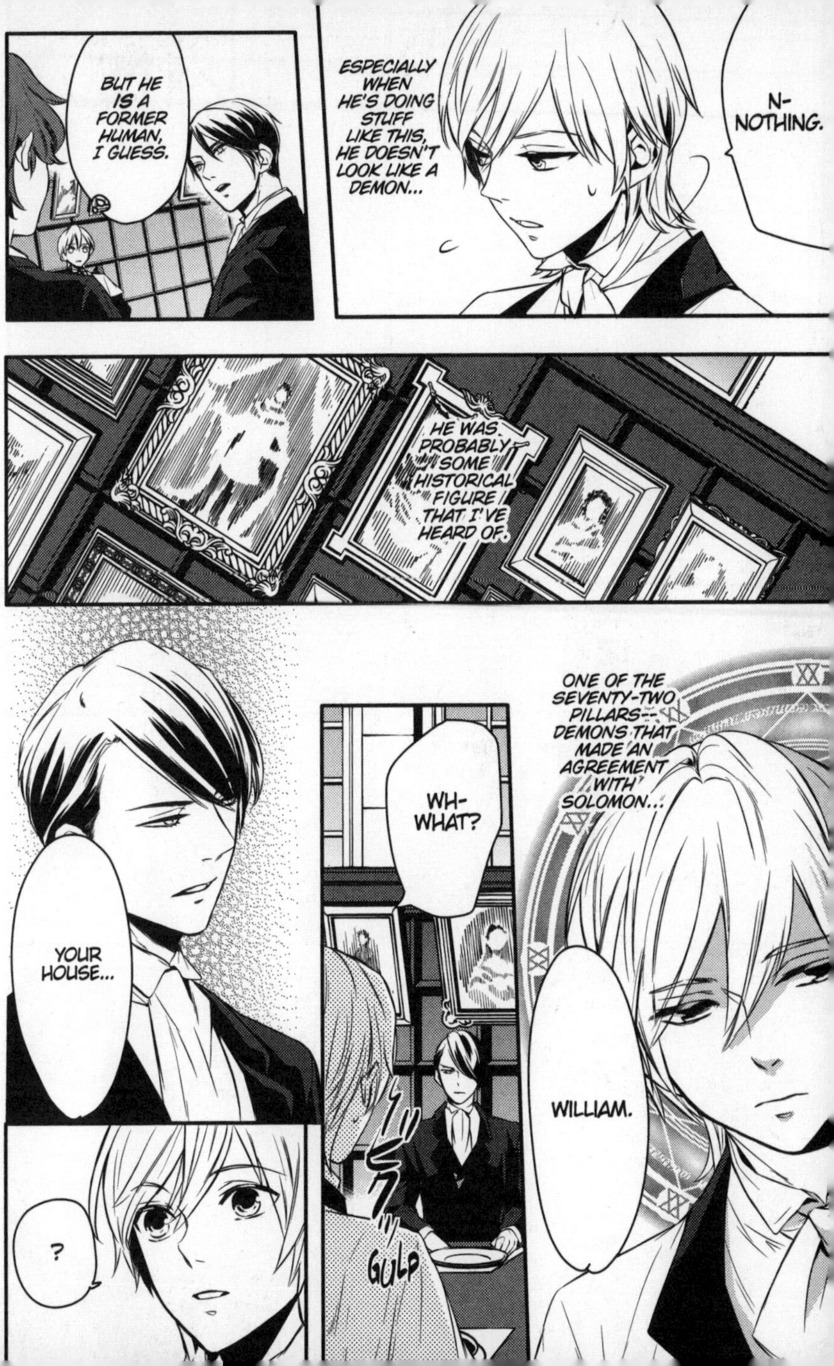
N-NOTHING.
ESPECIALLY WHEN HE'S DOING STUFF LIKE THIS, HE DOESN'T LOOK LIKE A DEMON...
BUT HE IS A FORMER HUMAN, I GUESS.
HE WAS PROBABLY SOME HISTORICAL FIGURE THAT I'VE HEARD OF.
ONE OF THE SEVENTY-TWO PILLARS-- DEMONS THAT MADE AN AGREEMENT WITH SOLOMON...
WILLIAM.
WH-WHAT?
GULP
YOUR HOUSE...
?

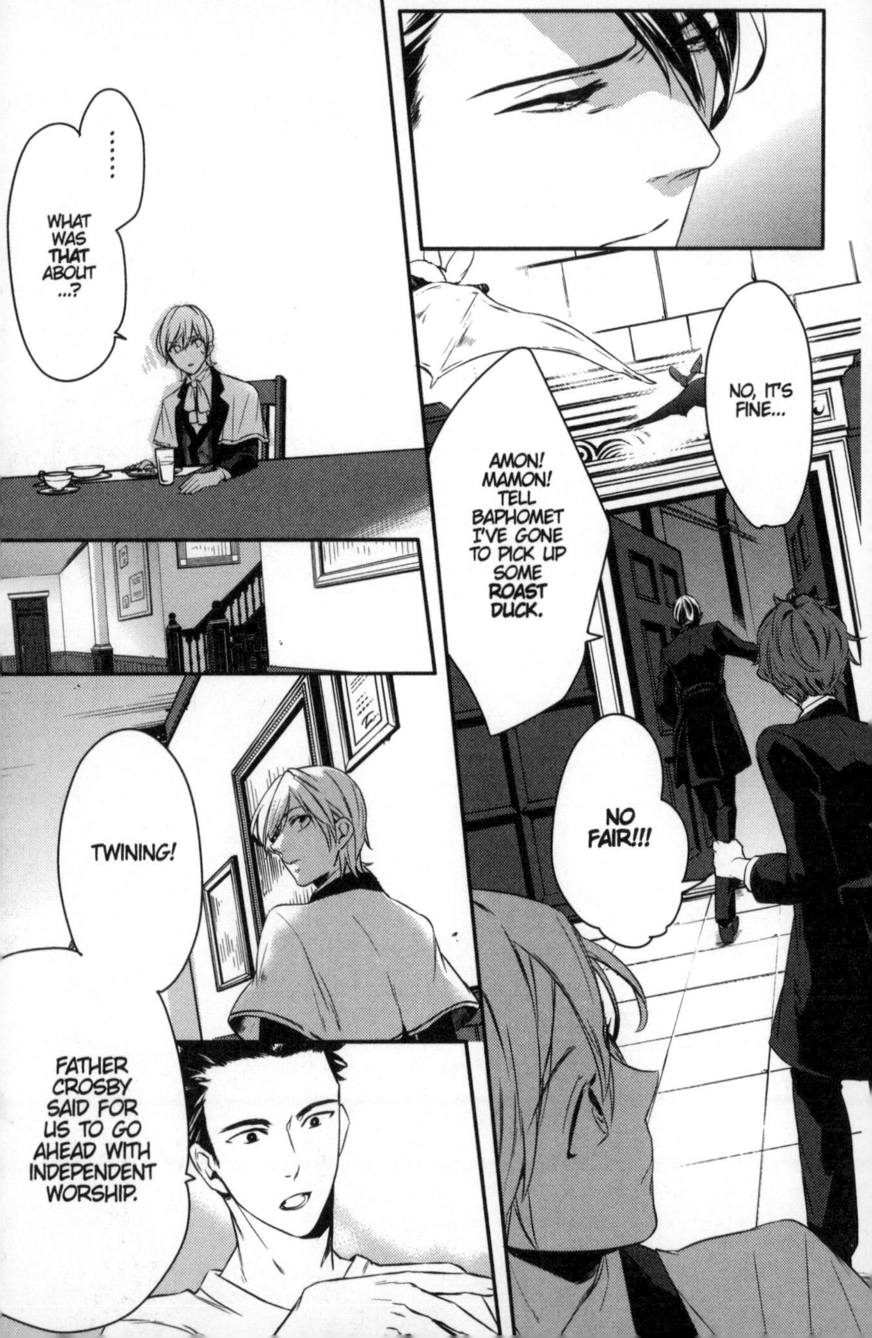
NO, IT'S FINE...
AMON! MAMON! TELL BAPHOMET I'VE GONE TO PICK UP SOME ROAST DUCK.
NO FAIR!!!
......
WHAT WAS THAT ABOUT ...?
TWINING!
FATHER CROSBY SAID FOR US TO GO AHEAD WITH INDEPENDENT WORSHIP.

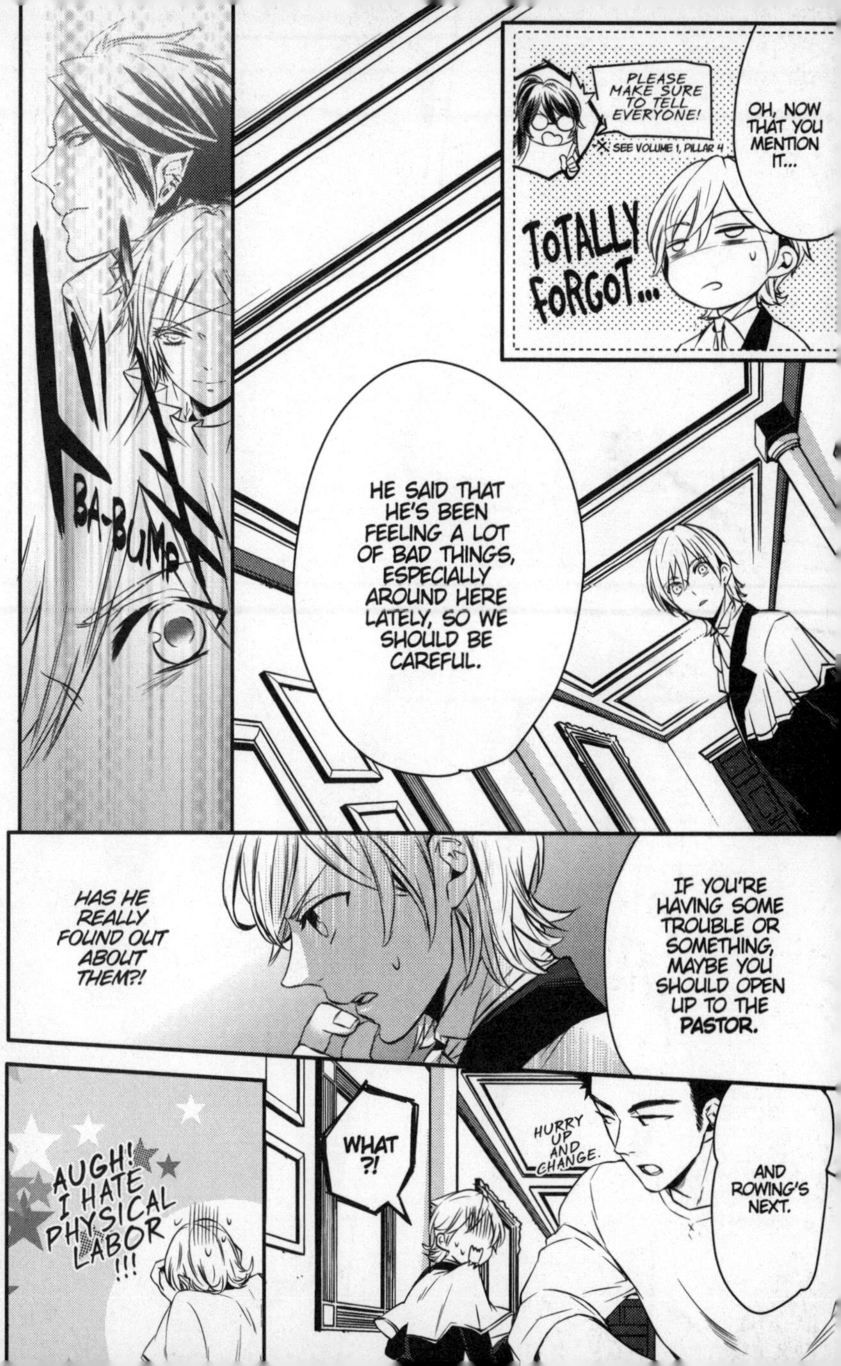
OH, NOW THAT YOU MENTION IT...
PLEASE MAKE SURE TO TELL EVERYONE!
※SEE VOLUME 1, PILLAR 4
TOTALLY FORGOT...
HE SAID THAT HE'S BEEN FEELING A LOT OF BAD THINGS, ESPECIALLY AROUND HERE LATELY, SO WE SHOULD BE CAREFUL.
BA-BUMP
IF YOU'RE HAVING SOME TROUBLE OR SOMETHING, MAYBE YOU SHOULD OPEN UP TO THE PASTOR.
HAS HE REALLY FOUND OUT ABOUT THEM?!
AND ROWING'S NEXT.
HURRY UP AND CHANGE.
WHAT?!
AUGH! I HATE PHYSICAL LABOR!!!

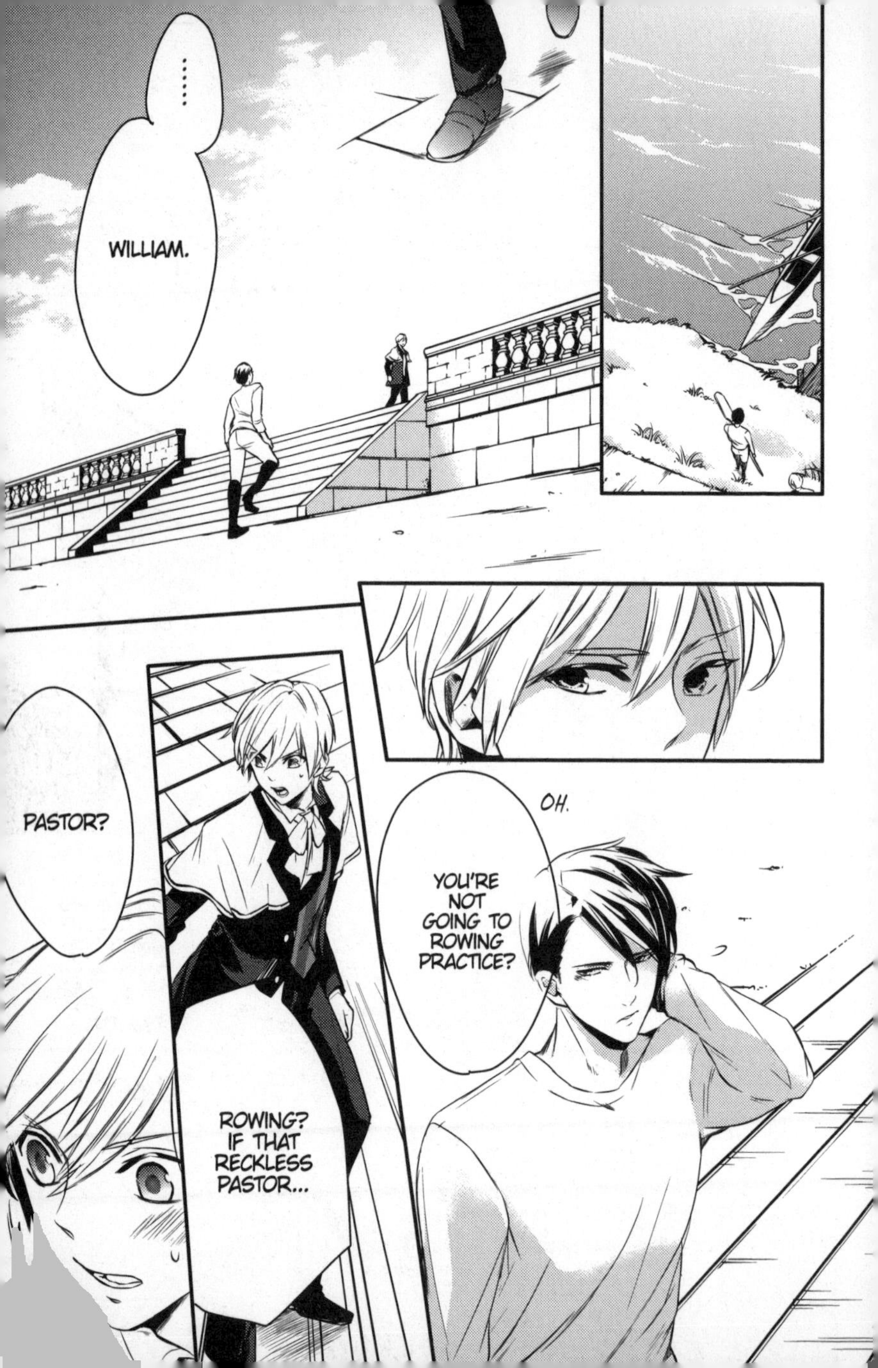
......
WILLIAM.
OH.
YOU'RE NOT GOING TO ROWING PRACTICE?
ROWING? IF THAT RECKLESS PASTOR...
PASTOR?

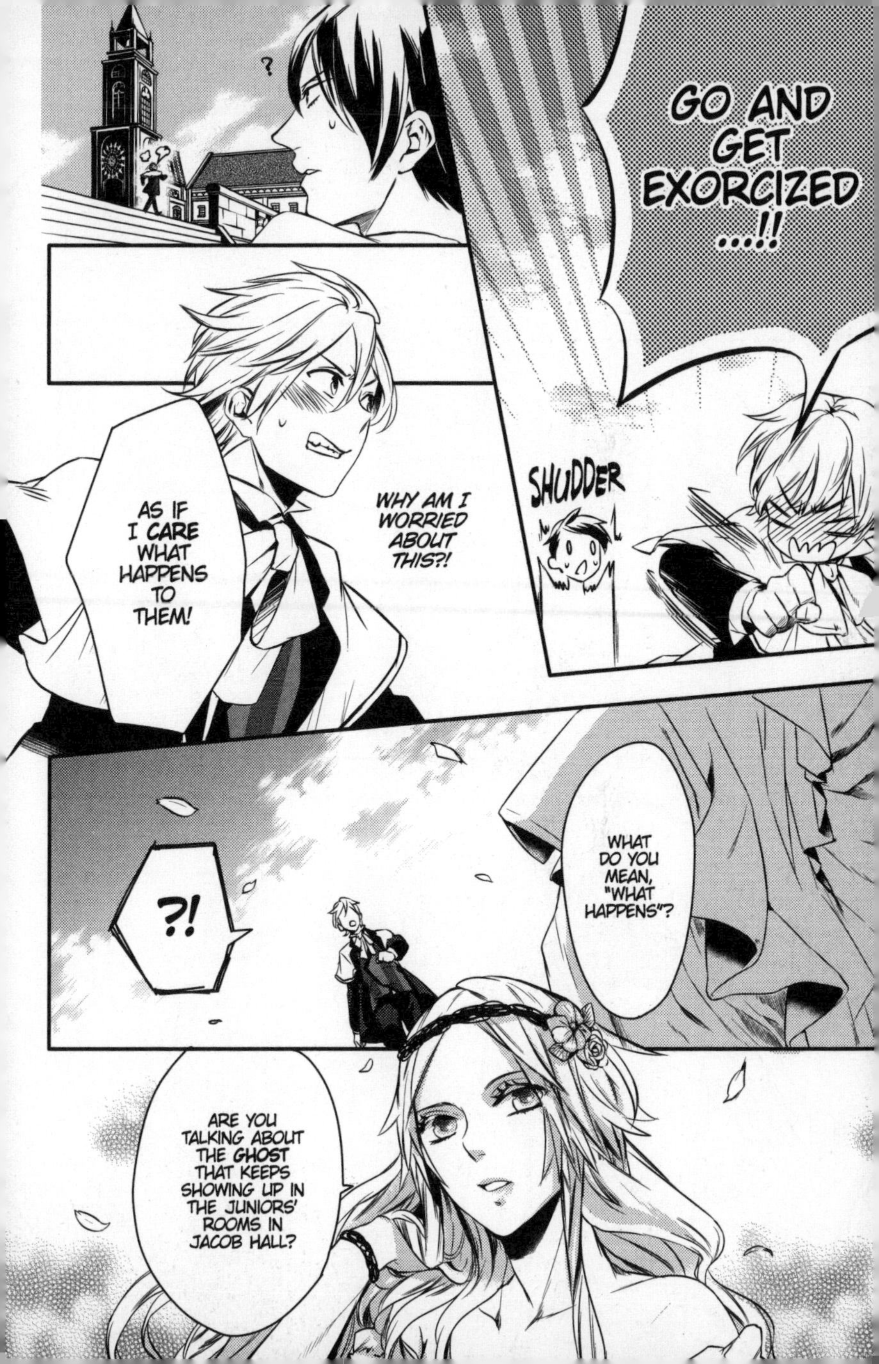
GO AND GET EXORCIZED ...!!
SHUDDER
?
WHY AM I WORRIED ABOUT THIS?!
AS IF I CARE WHAT HAPPENS TO THEM!
WHAT DO YOU MEAN, "WHAT HAPPENS"?
?!
ARE YOU TALKING ABOUT THE GHOST THAT KEEPS SHOWING UP IN THE JUNIORS' ROOMS IN JACOB HALL?

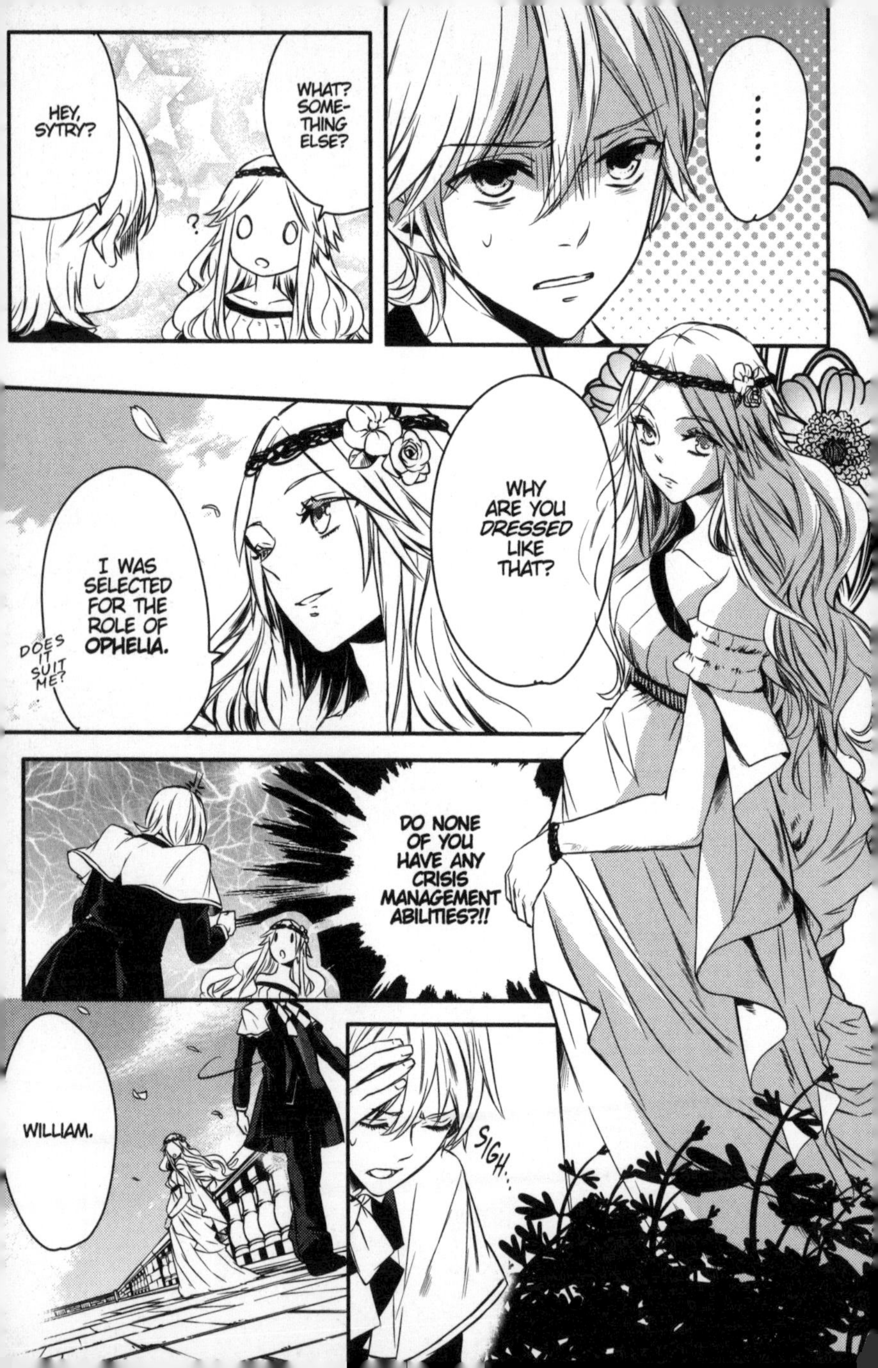
……
WHAT? SOMETHING ELSE?
HEY, SYTRY?
?
WHY ARE YOU DRESSED LIKE THAT?
I WAS SELECTED FOR THE ROLE OF OPHELIA.
DOES IT SUIT ME?
DO NONE OF YOU HAVE ANY CRISIS MANAGEMENT ABILITIES?!!
SIGH...
WILLIAM.

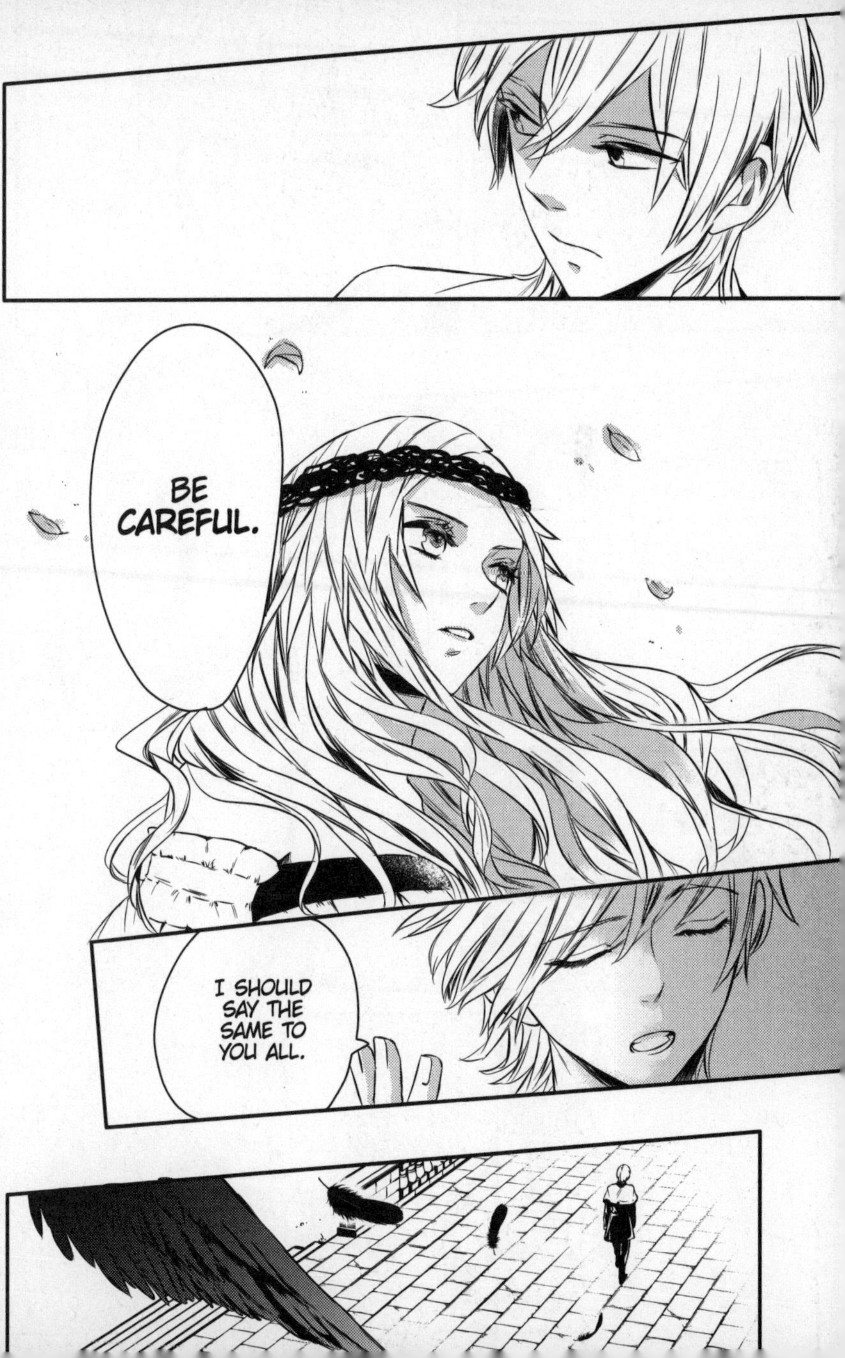
BE CAREFUL.
I SHOULD SAY THE SAME TO YOU ALL.

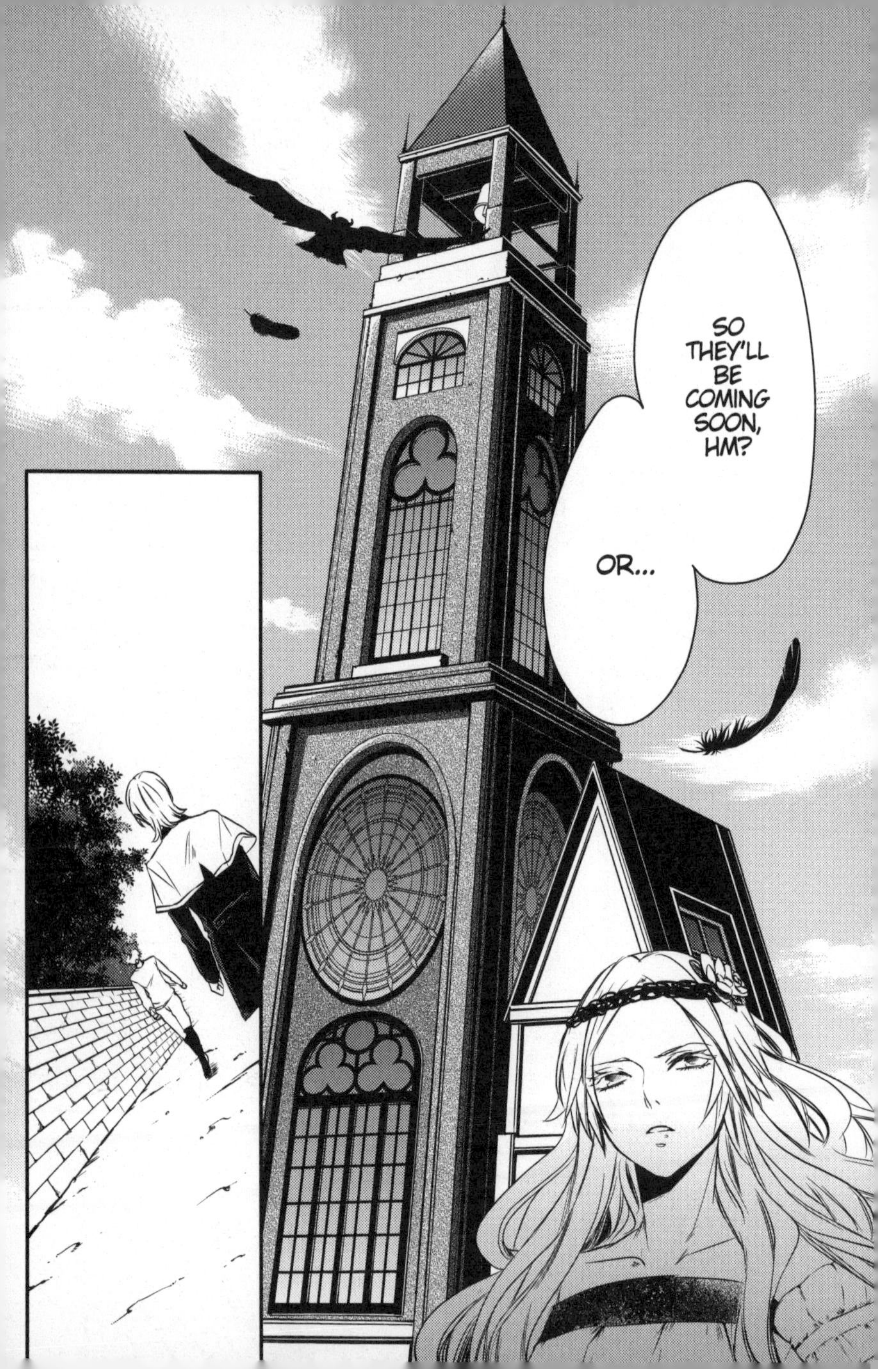
SO THEY'LL BE COMING SOON, HM?
OR...

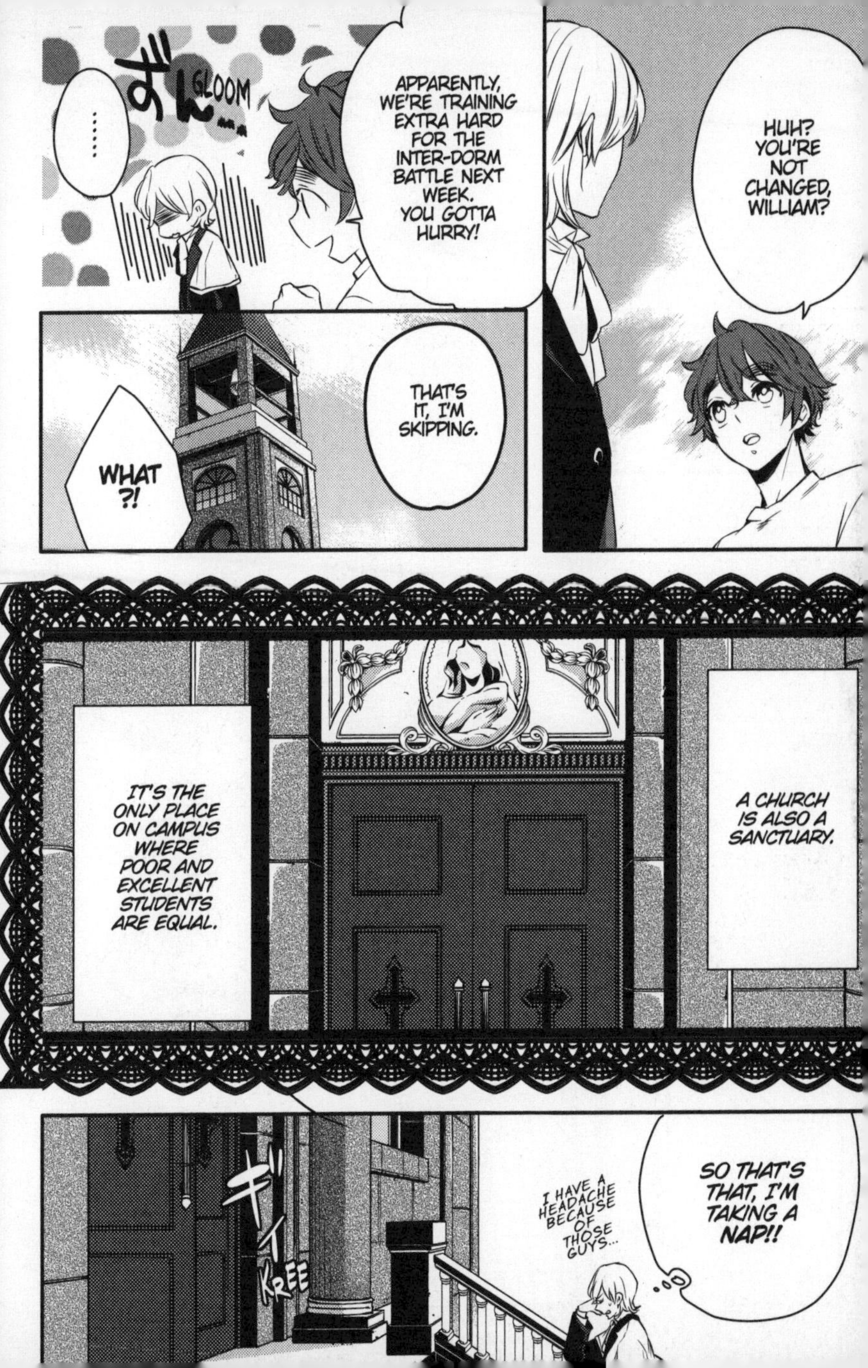
HUH? YOU'RE NOT CHANGED, WILLIAM?
APPARENTLY, WE'RE TRAINING EXTRA HARD FOR THE INTER-DORM BATTLE NEXT WEEK. YOU GOTTA HURRY!
ずん GLOOM
......
THAT'S IT, I'M SKIPPING.
WHAT?!
A CHURCH IS ALSO A SANCTUARY.
IT'S THE ONLY PLACE ON CAMPUS WHERE POOR AND EXCELLENT STUDENTS ARE EQUAL.
SO THAT'S THAT, I'M TAKING A NAP!!
I HAVE A HEADACHE BECAUSE OF THOSE GUYS...
ギィ KREE

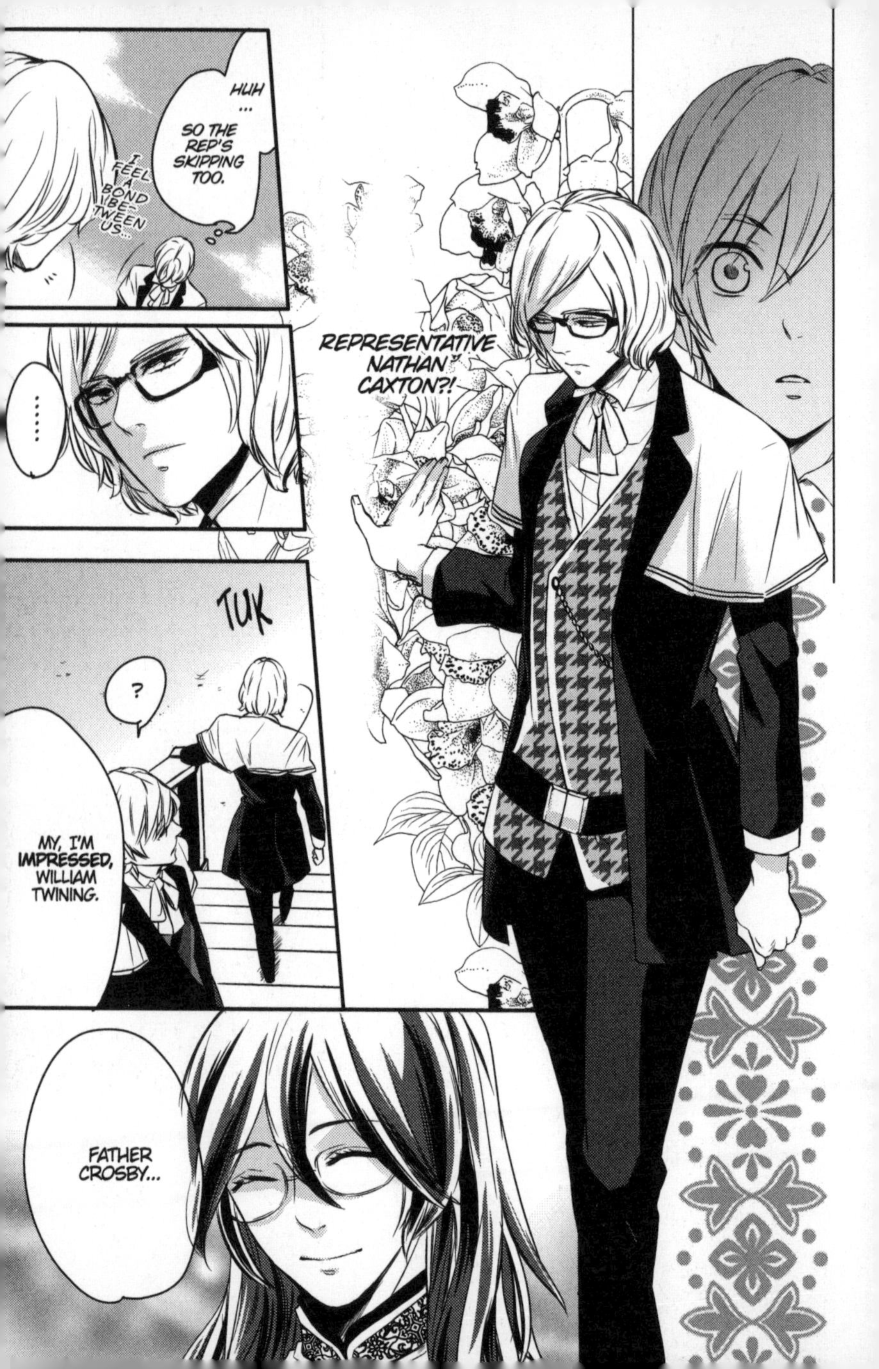
REPRESENTATIVE NATHAN CAXTON?!
HUH ... SO THE REP'S SKIPPING TOO.
I FEEL A BOND BE-TWEEN US...
...
......
TUK
?
MY, I'M IMPRESSED, WILLIAM TWINING.
FATHER CROSBY...

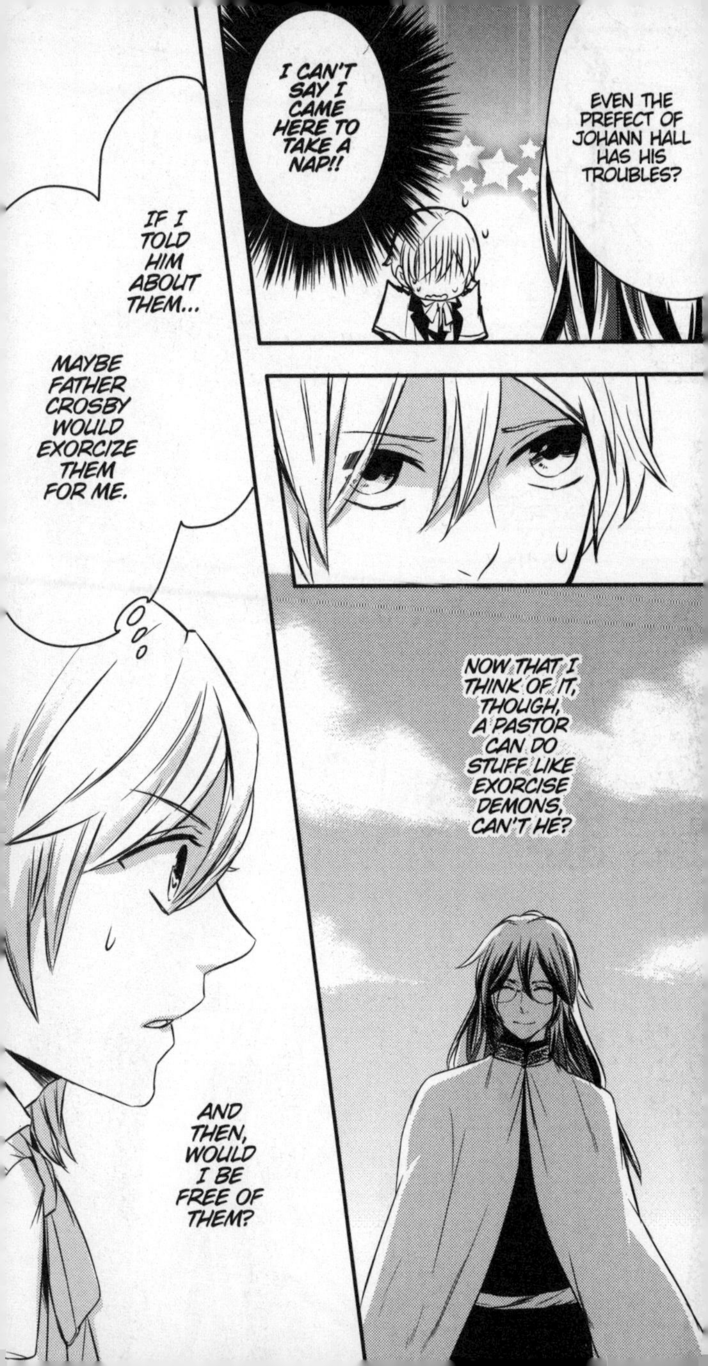
EVEN THE PREFECT OF JOHANN HALL HAS HIS TROUBLES?
I CAN'T SAY I CAME HERE TO TAKE A NAP!!
NOW THAT I THINK OF IT, THOUGH, A PASTOR CAN DO STUFF LIKE EXORCISE DEMONS, CAN'T HE?
IF I TOLD HIM ABOUT THEM...
MAYBE FATHER CROSBY WOULD EXORCIZE THEM FOR ME.
AND THEN, WOULD I BE FREE OF THEM?

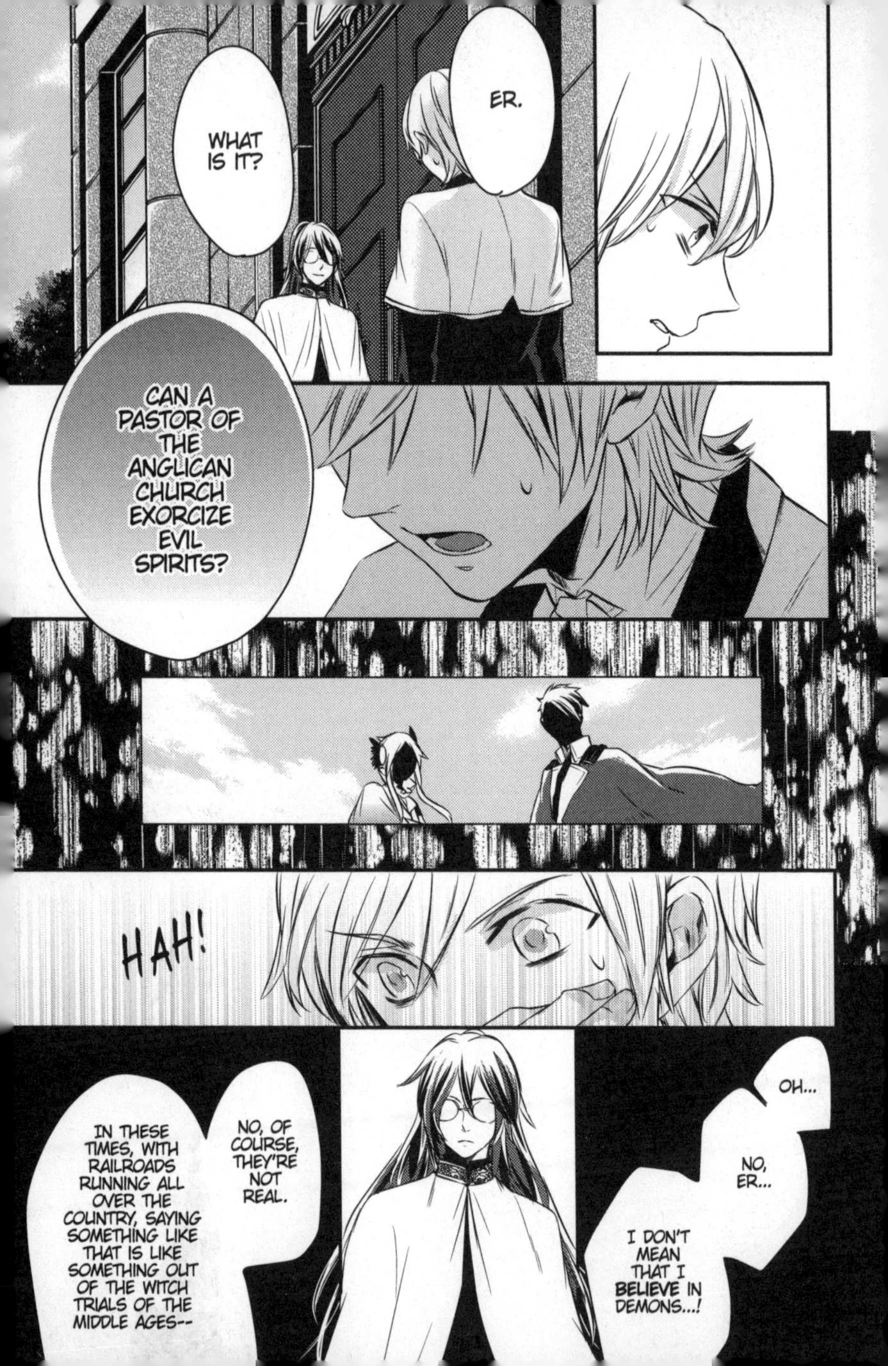
ER.
WHAT IS IT?
CAN A PASTOR OF THE ANGLICAN CHURCH EXORCIZE EVIL SPIRITS?
HAH!
OH...
NO, ER...
I DON'T MEAN THAT I **BELIEVE** IN DEMONS...!
NO, OF COURSE, THEY'RE NOT REAL.
IN THESE TIMES, WITH RAILROADS RUNNING ALL OVER THE COUNTRY, SAYING SOMETHING LIKE THAT IS LIKE SOMETHING OUT OF THE WITCH TRIALS OF THE MIDDLE AGES--

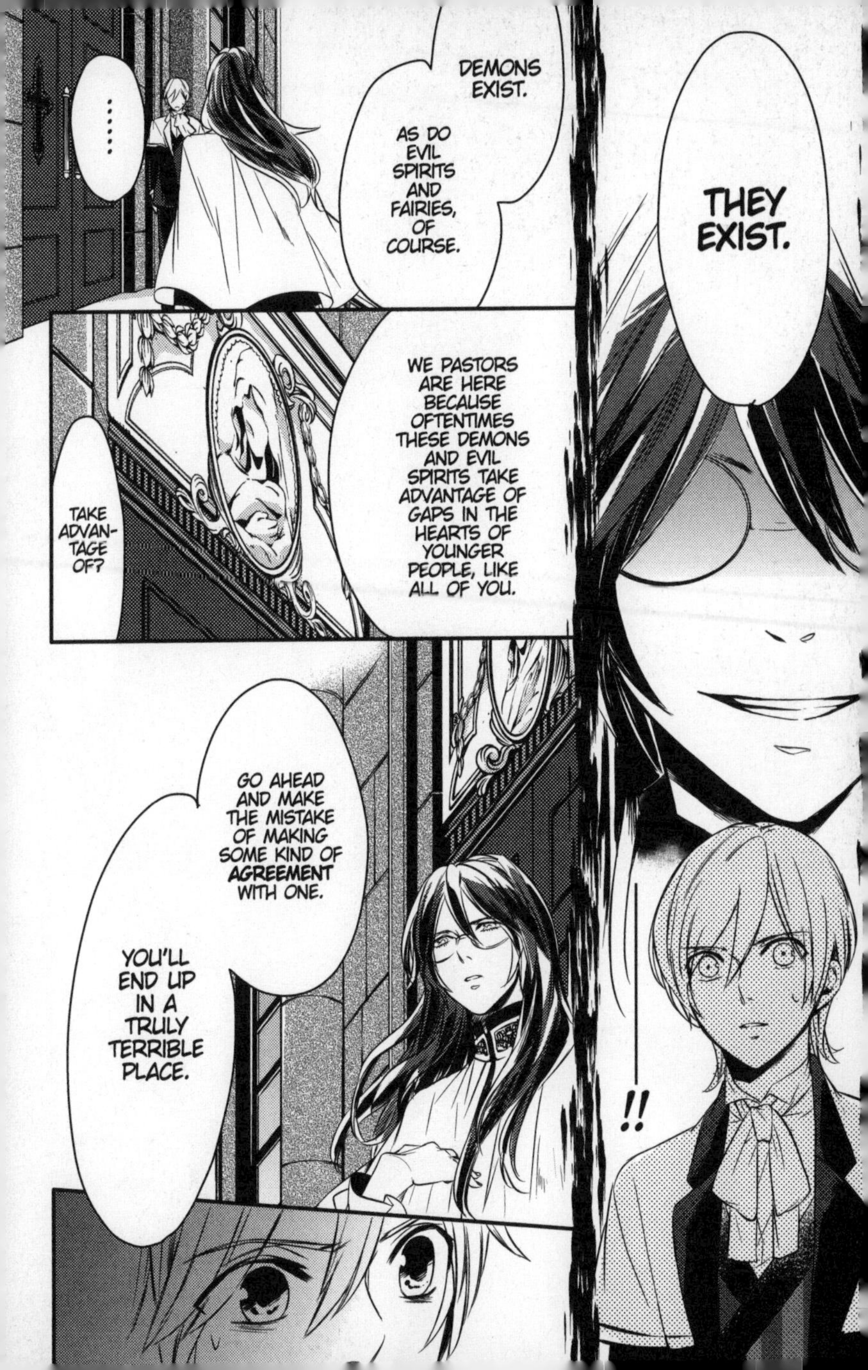
THEY EXIST.
!!
DEMONS EXIST.
AS DO EVIL SPIRITS AND FAIRIES, OF COURSE.
......
WE PASTORS ARE HERE BECAUSE OFTENTIMES THESE DEMONS AND EVIL SPIRITS TAKE ADVANTAGE OF GAPS IN THE HEARTS OF YOUNGER PEOPLE, LIKE ALL OF YOU.
TAKE ADVANTAGE OF?
GO AHEAD AND MAKE THE MISTAKE OF MAKING SOME KIND OF **AGREEMENT** WITH ONE.
YOU'LL END UP IN A TRULY TERRIBLE PLACE.

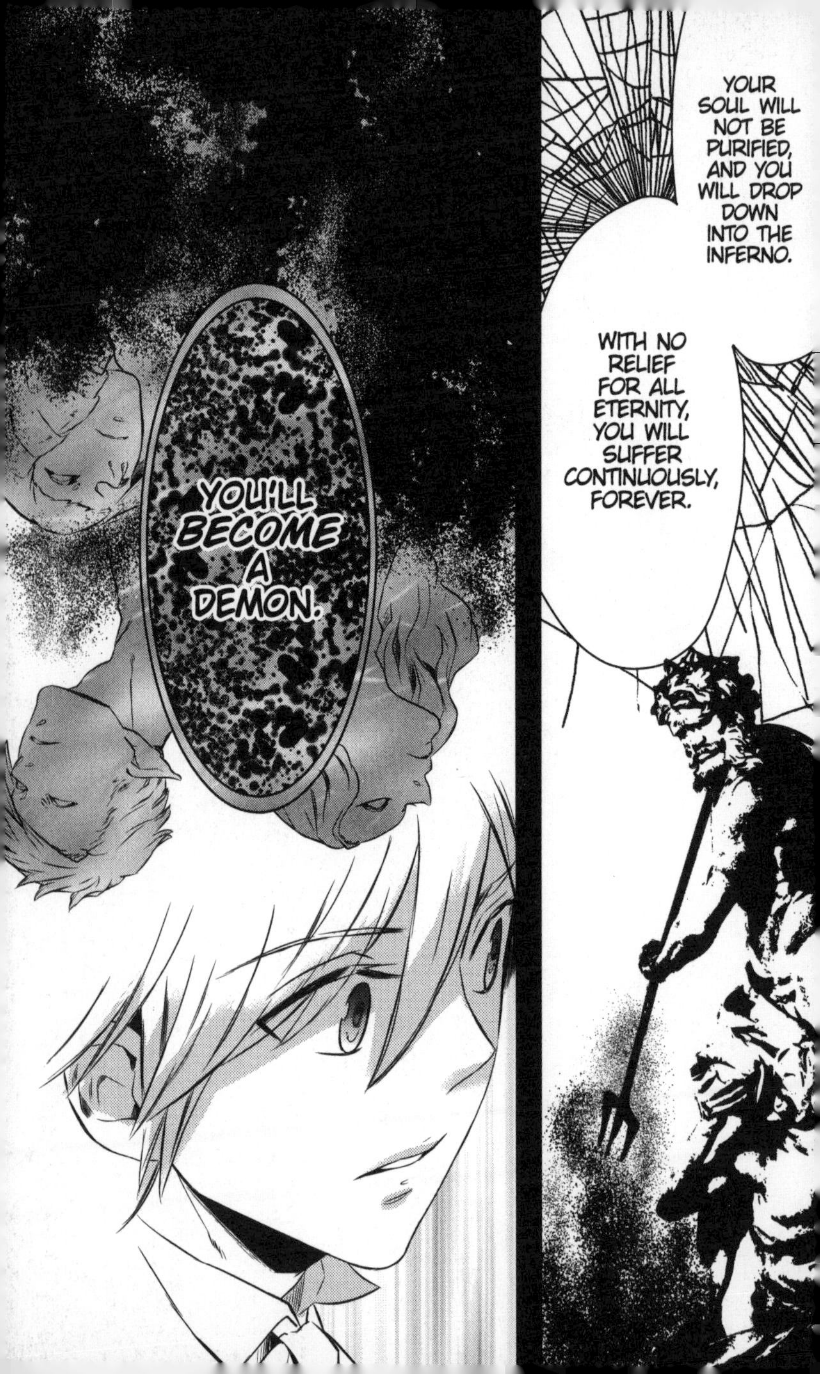
YOUR SOUL WILL NOT BE PURIFIED, AND YOU WILL DROP DOWN INTO THE INFERNO.
WITH NO RELIEF FOR ALL ETERNITY, YOU WILL SUFFER CONTINUOUSLY, FOREVER.
YOU'LL BECOME A DEMON.

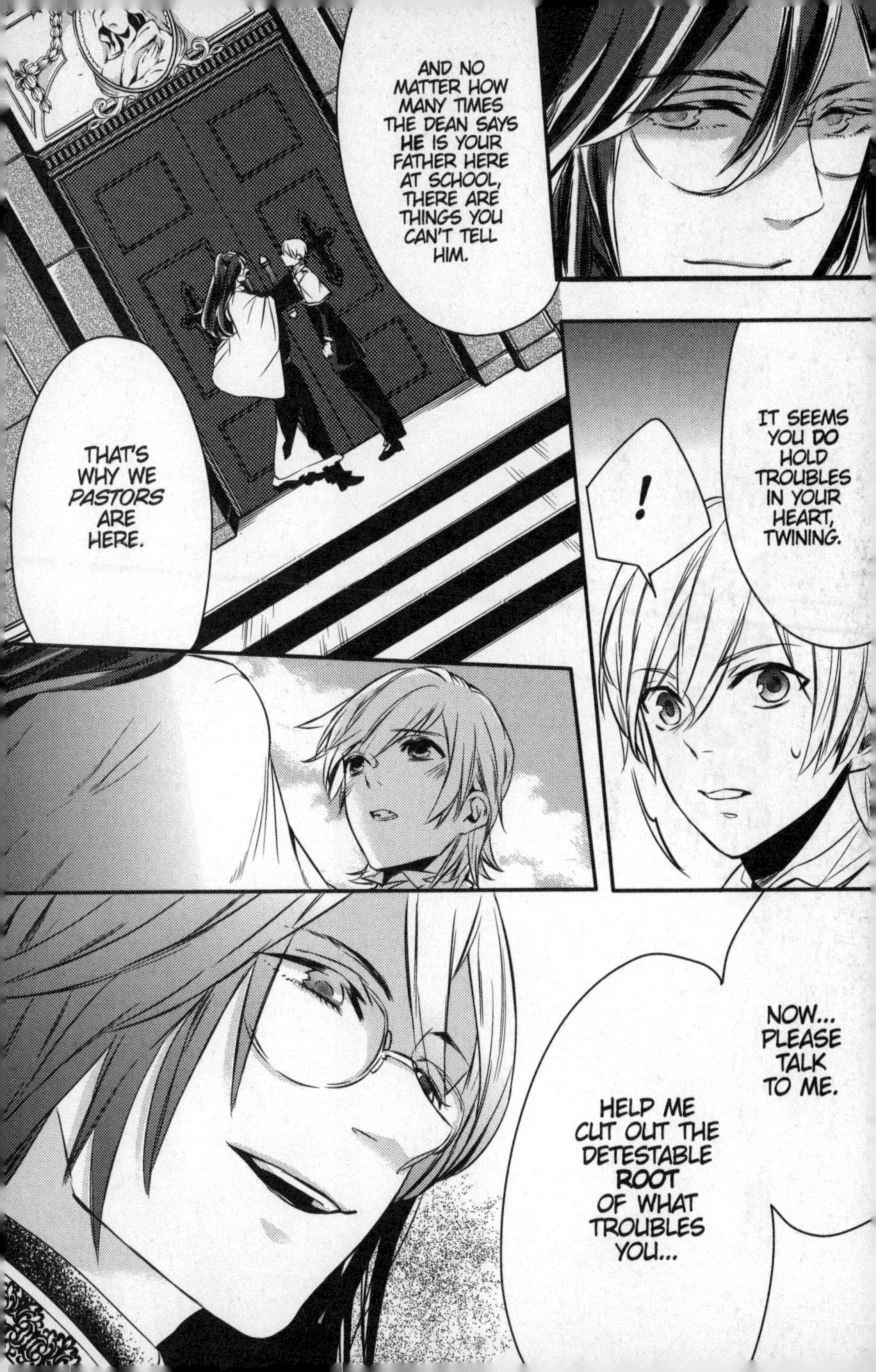
AND NO MATTER HOW MANY TIMES THE DEAN SAYS HE IS YOUR FATHER HERE AT SCHOOL, THERE ARE THINGS YOU CAN'T TELL HIM.
THAT'S WHY WE PASTORS ARE HERE.
IT SEEMS YOU DO HOLD TROUBLES IN YOUR HEART, TWINING.
!
NOW... PLEASE TALK TO ME.
HELP ME CUT OUT THE DETESTABLE ROOT OF WHAT TROUBLES YOU...

Pillar 11

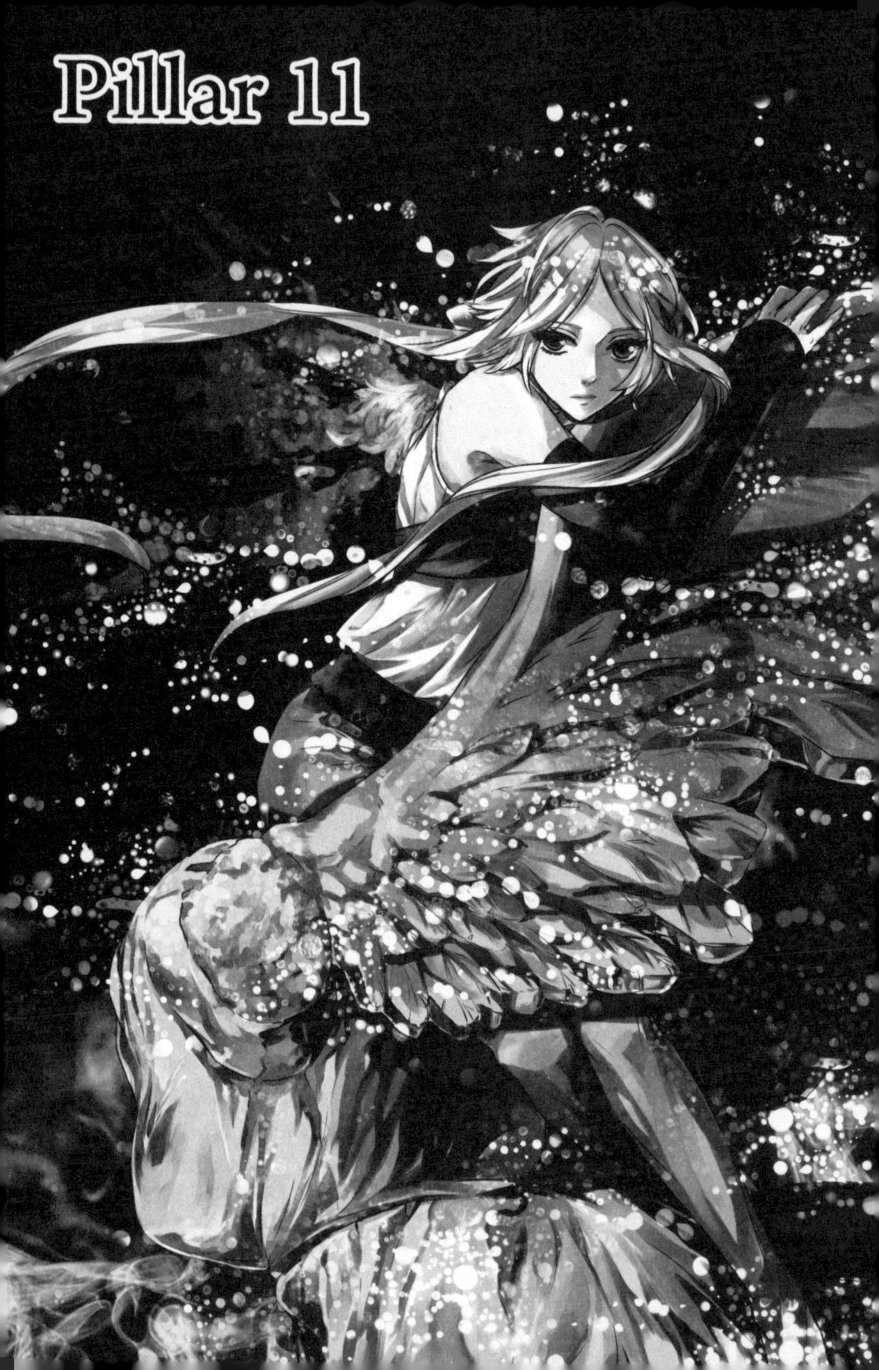

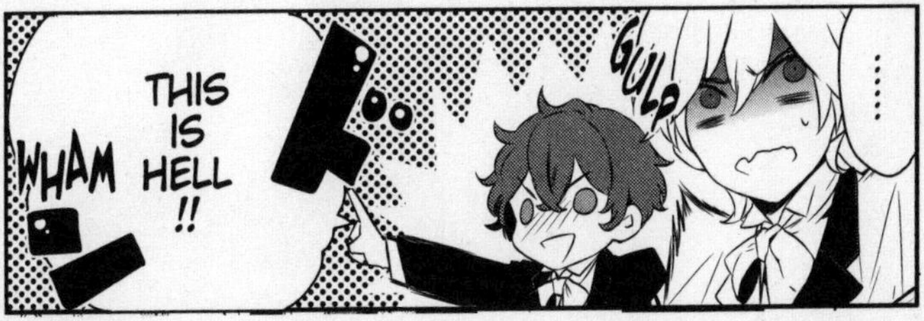

……
GULP
THIS IS HELL!!
WHAM

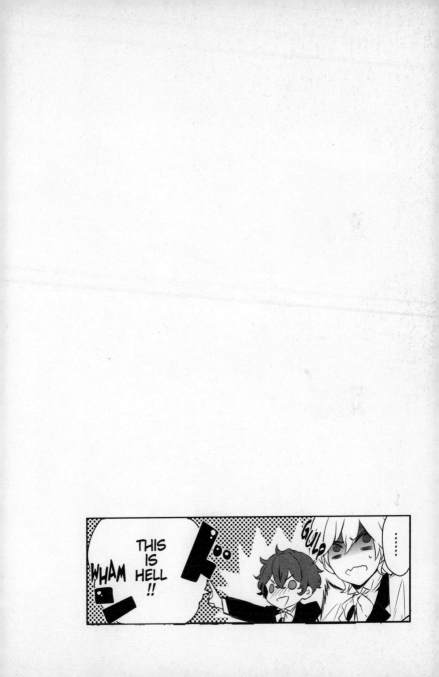

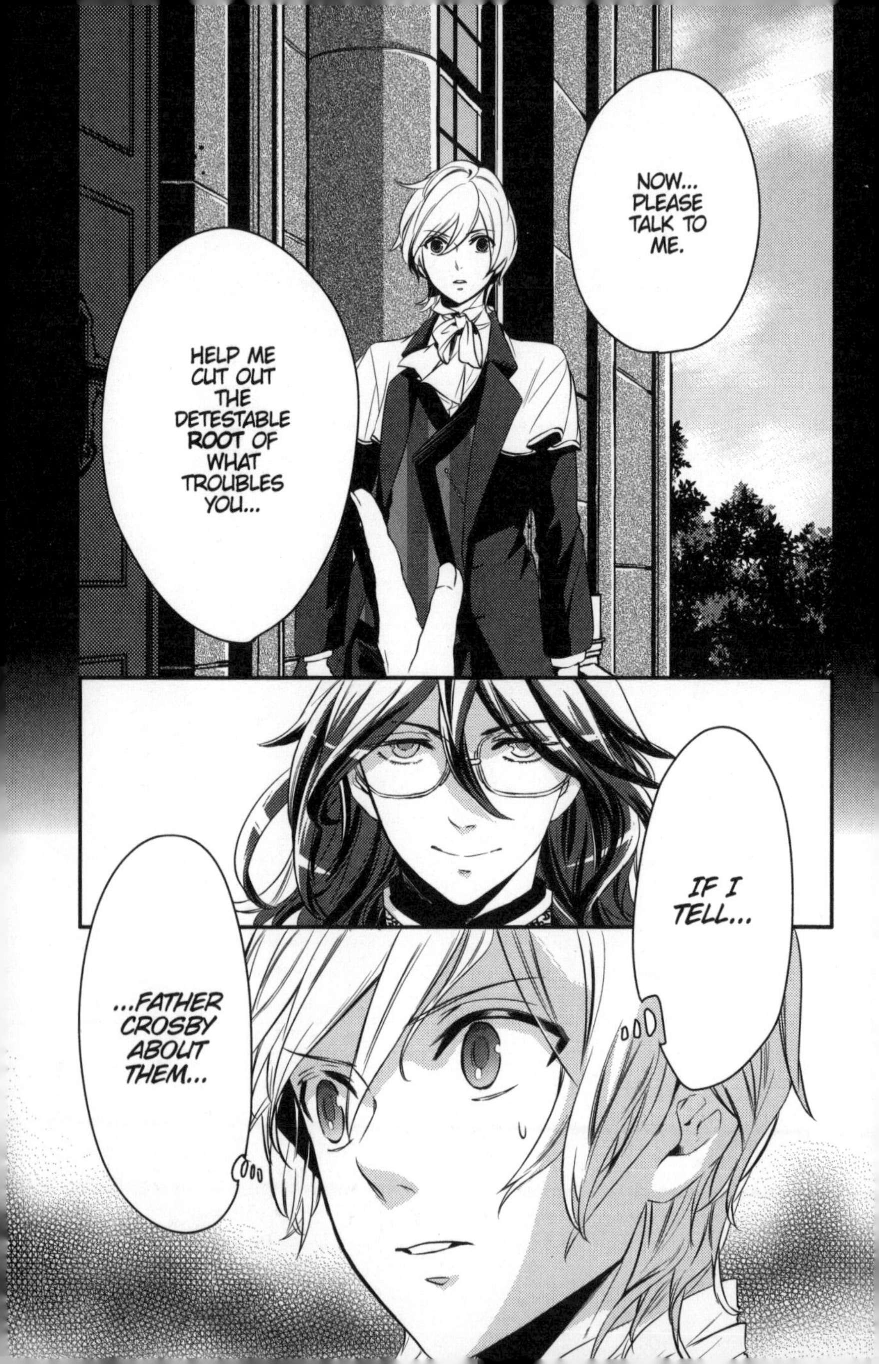
NOW... PLEASE TALK TO ME.
HELP ME CUT OUT THE DETESTABLE ROOT OF WHAT TROUBLES YOU...
IF I TELL...
...FATHER CROSBY ABOUT THEM...

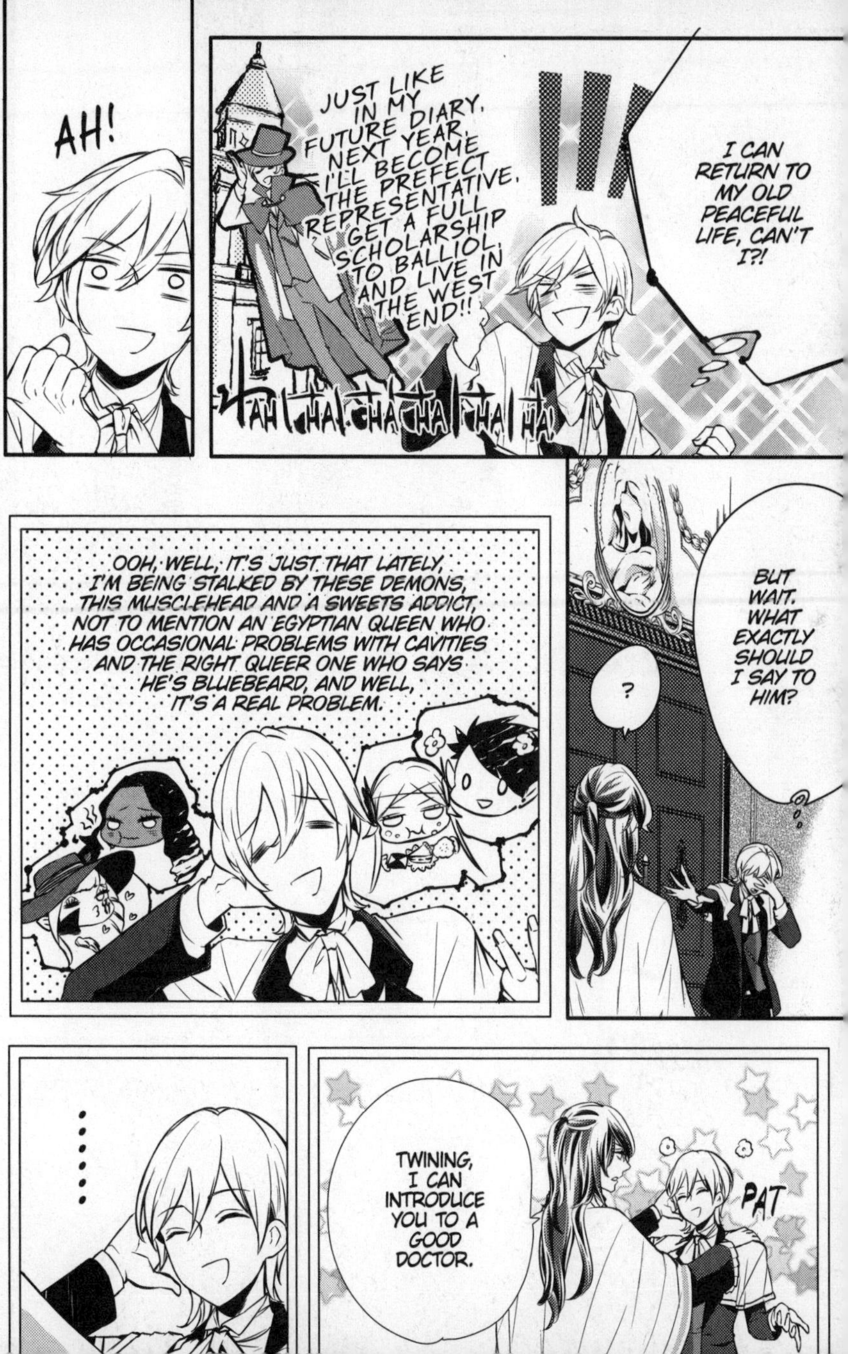
JUST LIKE IN MY FUTURE DIARY, NEXT YEAR, I'LL BECOME THE PREFECT REPRESENTATIVE, GET A FULL SCHOLARSHIP TO BALLIOL, AND LIVE IN THE WEST END!!
I CAN RETURN TO MY OLD PEACEFUL LIFE, CAN'T I?!
HAH HA HA HA HA HA HA!
AH!
BUT WAIT. WHAT EXACTLY SHOULD I SAY TO HIM?
?
OOH, WELL, IT'S JUST THAT LATELY, I'M BEING STALKED BY THESE DEMONS, THIS MUSCLEHEAD AND A SWEETS ADDICT, NOT TO MENTION AN EGYPTIAN QUEEN WHO HAS OCCASIONAL PROBLEMS WITH CAVITIES AND THE RIGHT QUEER ONE WHO SAYS HE'S BLUEBEARD, AND WELL, IT'S A REAL PROBLEM.
TWINING, I CAN INTRODUCE YOU TO A GOOD DOCTOR.
PAT
......

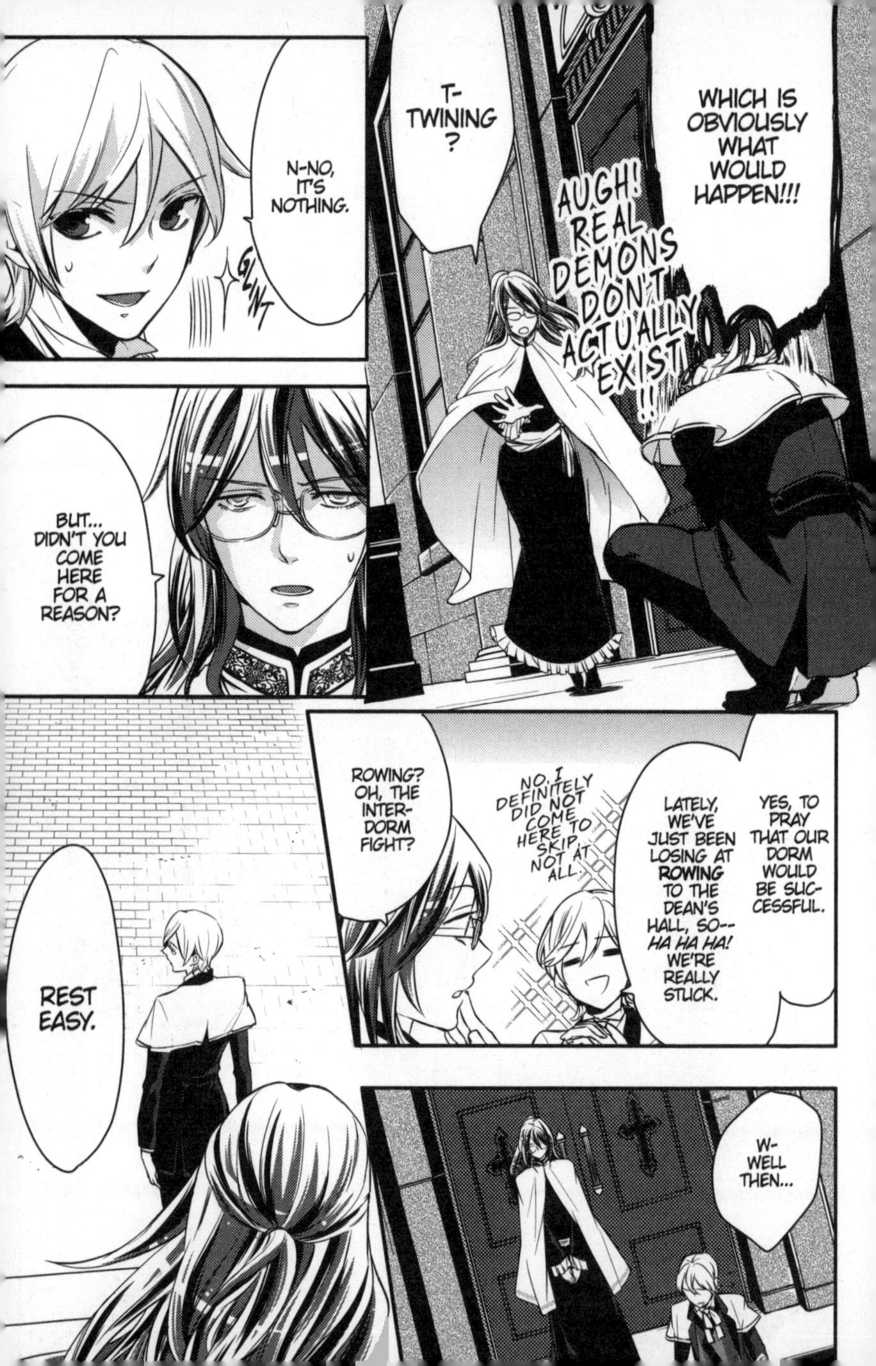
WHICH IS OBVIOUSLY WHAT WOULD HAPPEN!!!
AUGH! REAL DEMONS DON'T ACTUALLY EXIST!!
T-TWINING?
N-NO, IT'S NOTHING.
GLINT
BUT... DIDN'T YOU COME HERE FOR A REASON?
YES, TO PRAY THAT OUR DORM WOULD BE SUCCESSFUL.
LATELY, WE'VE JUST BEEN LOSING AT ROWING TO THE DEAN'S HALL, SO-- HA HA HA! WE'RE REALLY STUCK.
NO, I DEFINITELY DID NOT COME HERE TO SKIP, NOT AT ALL.
ROWING? OH, THE INTER-DORM FIGHT?
W-WELL THEN...
REST EASY.

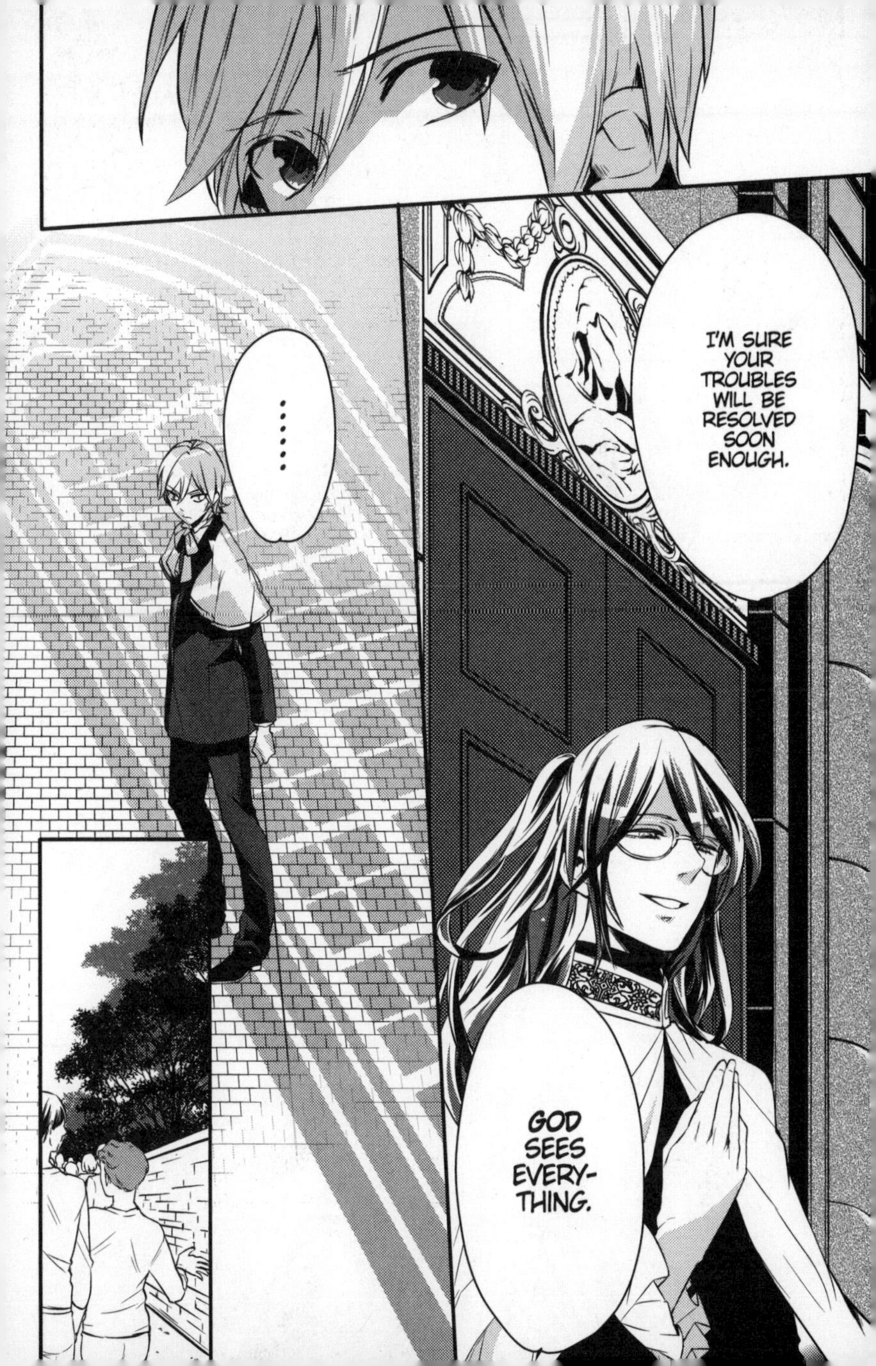
I'M SURE YOUR TROUBLES WILL BE RESOLVED SOON ENOUGH.
GOD SEES EVERY-THING.
......

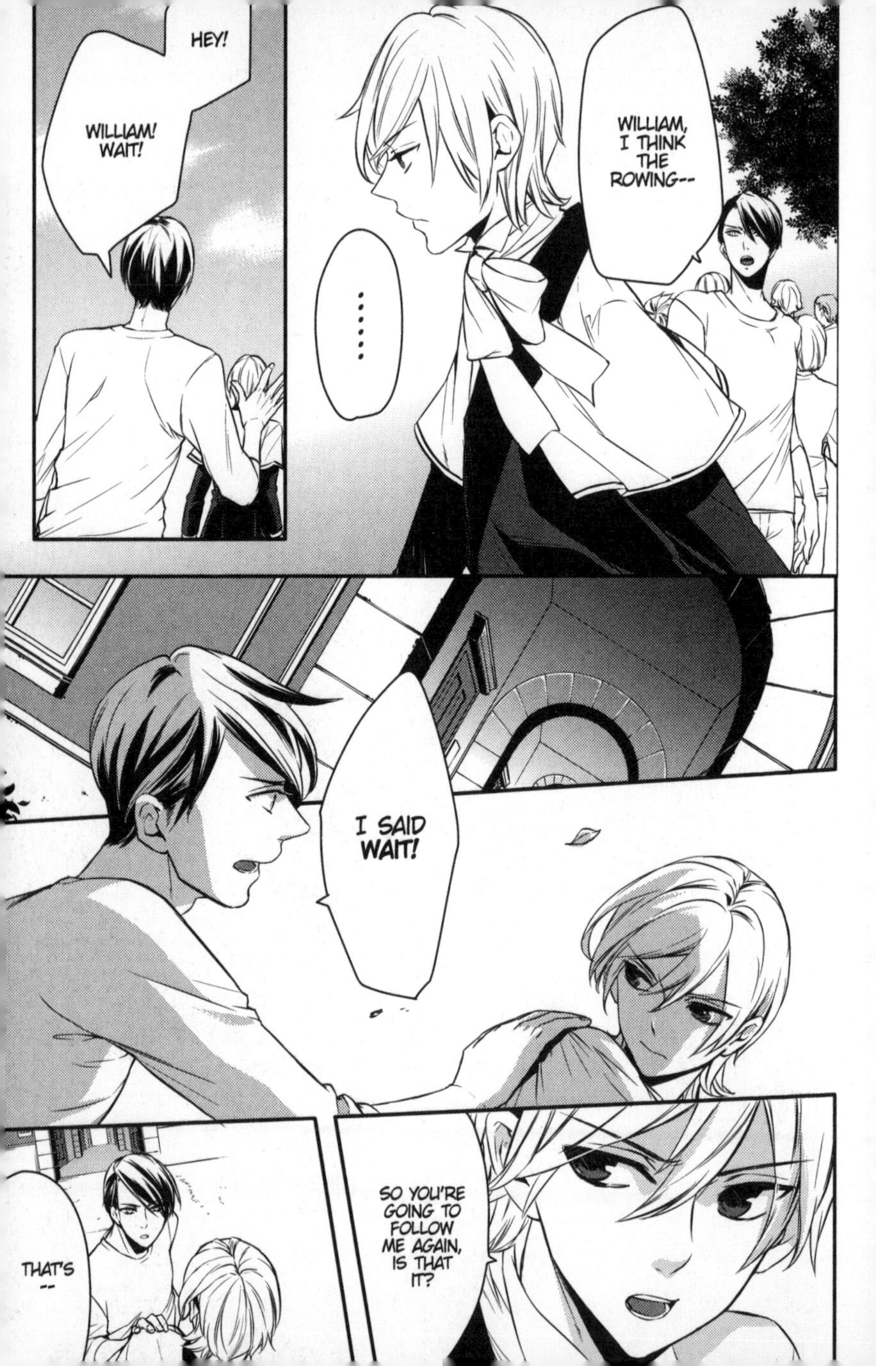
WILLIAM, I THINK THE ROWING--
......
HEY!
WILLIAM! WAIT!
I SAID WAIT!
SO YOU'RE GOING TO FOLLOW ME AGAIN, IS THAT IT?
THAT'S --

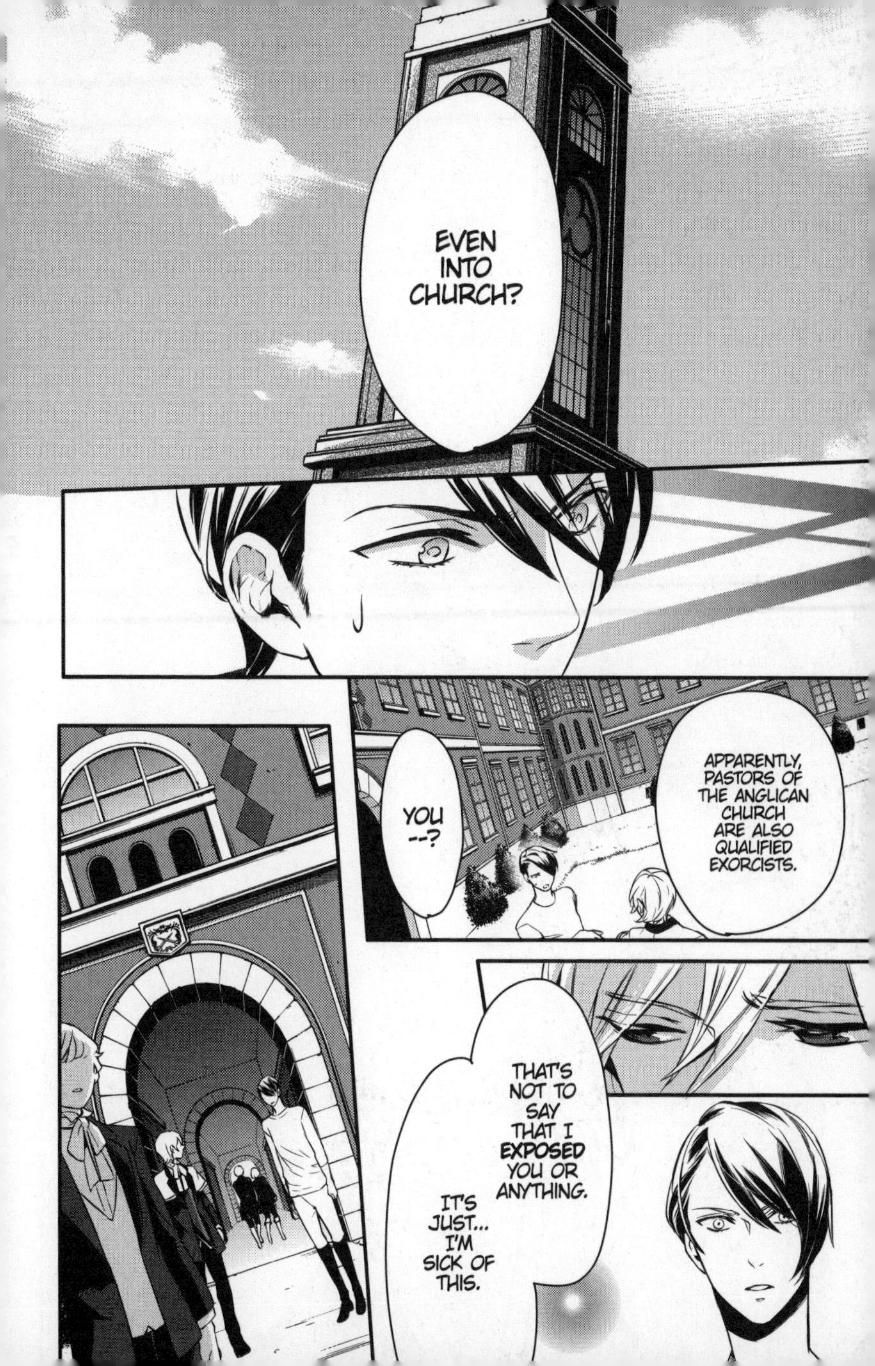
EVEN INTO CHURCH?
APPARENTLY, PASTORS OF THE ANGLICAN CHURCH ARE ALSO QUALIFIED EXORCISTS.
YOU --?
THAT'S NOT TO SAY THAT I **EXPOSED** YOU OR ANYTHING.
IT'S JUST... I'M SICK OF THIS.

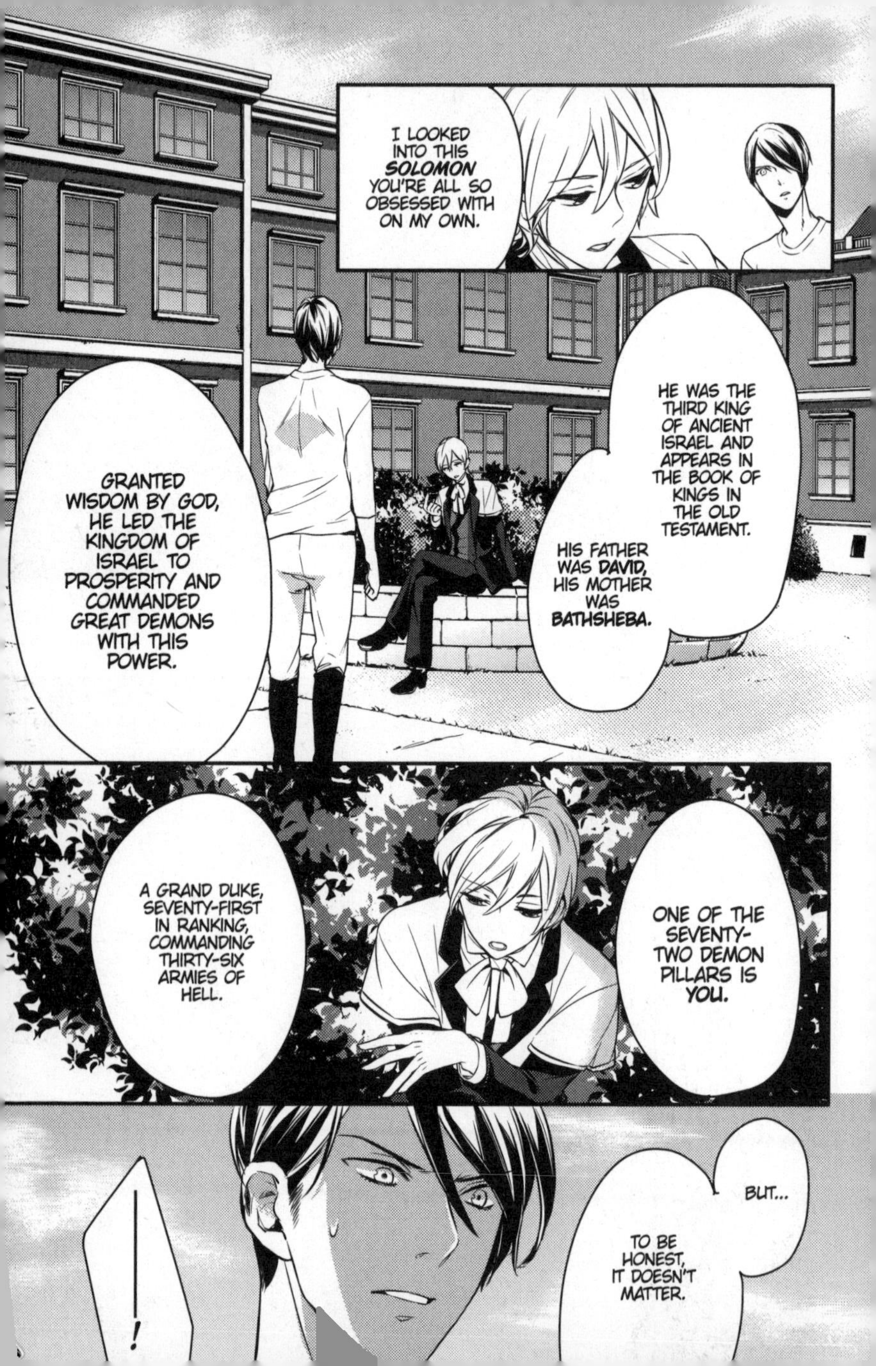
I LOOKED INTO THIS SOLOMON YOU'RE ALL SO OBSESSED WITH ON MY OWN.
HE WAS THE THIRD KING OF ANCIENT ISRAEL AND APPEARS IN THE BOOK OF KINGS IN THE OLD TESTAMENT.
HIS FATHER WAS DAVID, HIS MOTHER WAS BATHSHEBA.
GRANTED WISDOM BY GOD, HE LED THE KINGDOM OF ISRAEL TO PROSPERITY AND COMMANDED GREAT DEMONS WITH THIS POWER.
ONE OF THE SEVENTY-TWO DEMON PILLARS IS YOU.
A GRAND DUKE, SEVENTY-FIRST IN RANKING, COMMANDING THIRTY-SIX ARMIES OF HELL.
BUT...
TO BE HONEST, IT DOESN'T MATTER.
--- !

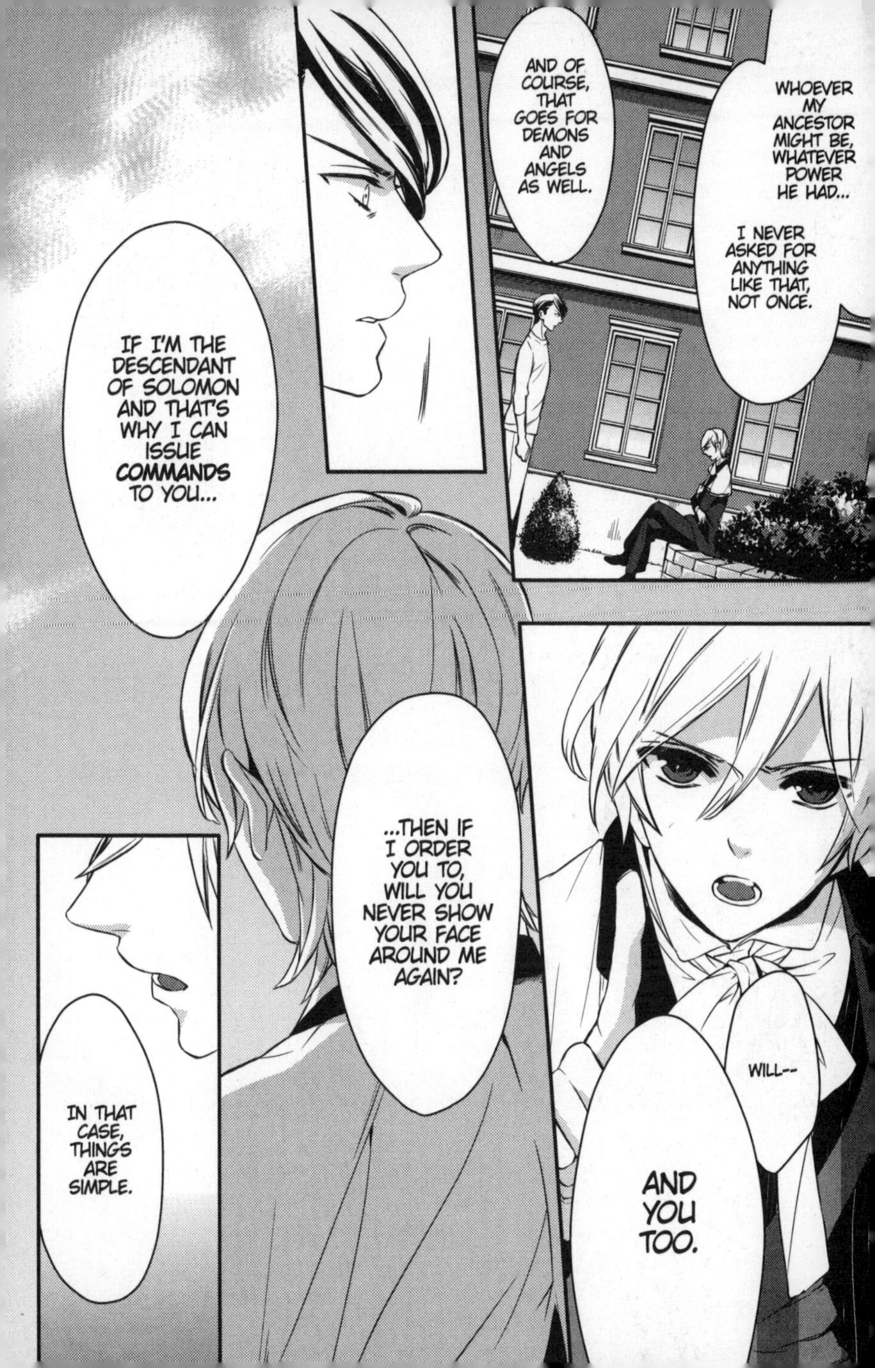
WHOEVER MY ANCESTOR MIGHT BE, WHATEVER POWER HE HAD...
I NEVER ASKED FOR ANYTHING LIKE THAT, NOT ONCE.
AND OF COURSE, THAT GOES FOR DEMONS AND ANGELS AS WELL.
IF I'M THE DESCENDANT OF SOLOMON AND THAT'S WHY I CAN ISSUE COMMANDS TO YOU...
...THEN IF I ORDER YOU TO, WILL YOU NEVER SHOW YOUR FACE AROUND ME AGAIN?
WILL--
AND YOU TOO.
IN THAT CASE, THINGS ARE SIMPLE.

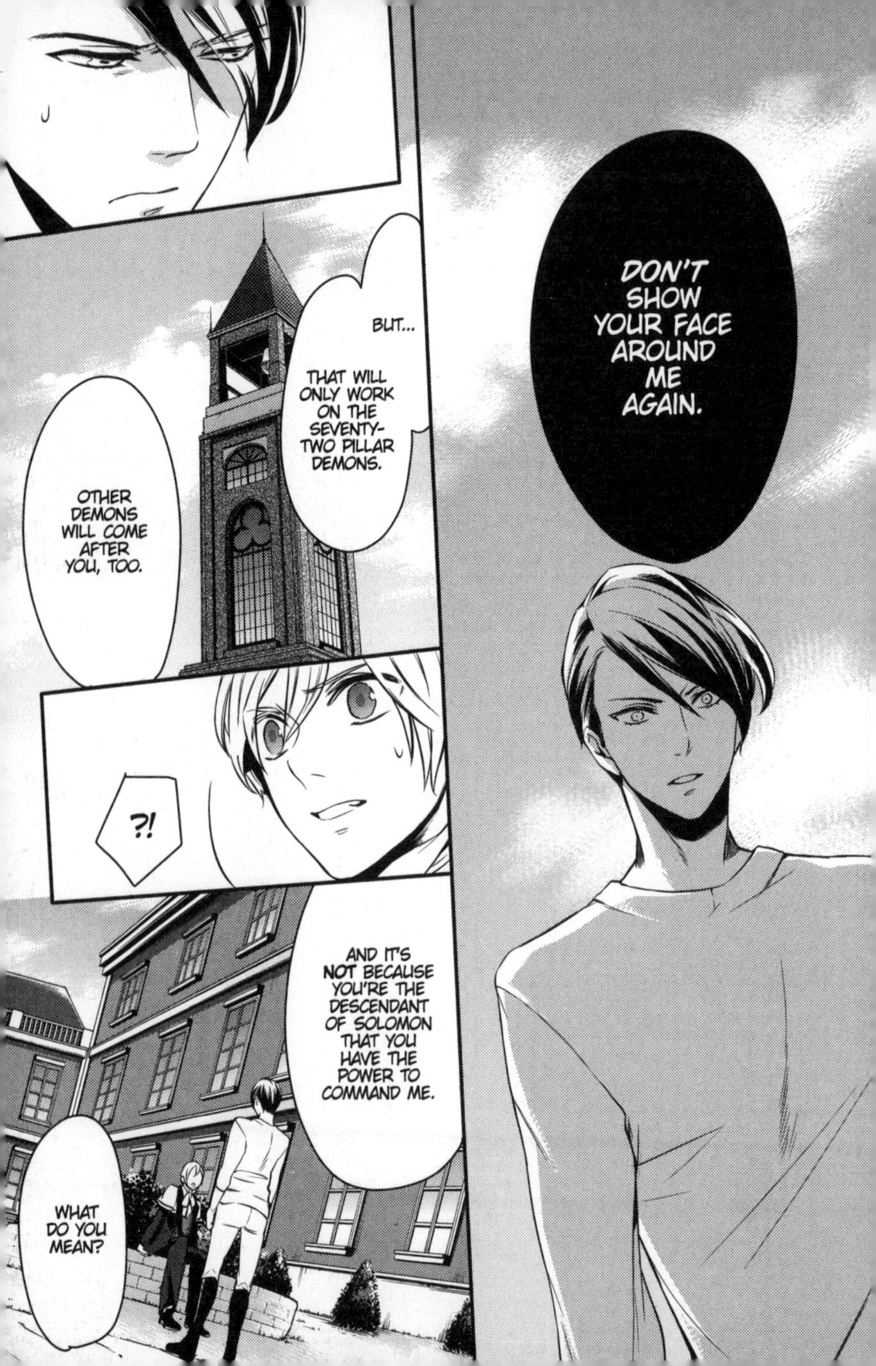
DON'T SHOW YOUR FACE AROUND ME AGAIN.
BUT...
THAT WILL ONLY WORK ON THE SEVENTY-TWO PILLAR DEMONS.
OTHER DEMONS WILL COME AFTER YOU, TOO.
?!
AND IT'S NOT BECAUSE YOU'RE THE DESCENDANT OF SOLOMON THAT YOU HAVE THE POWER TO COMMAND ME.
WHAT DO YOU MEAN?

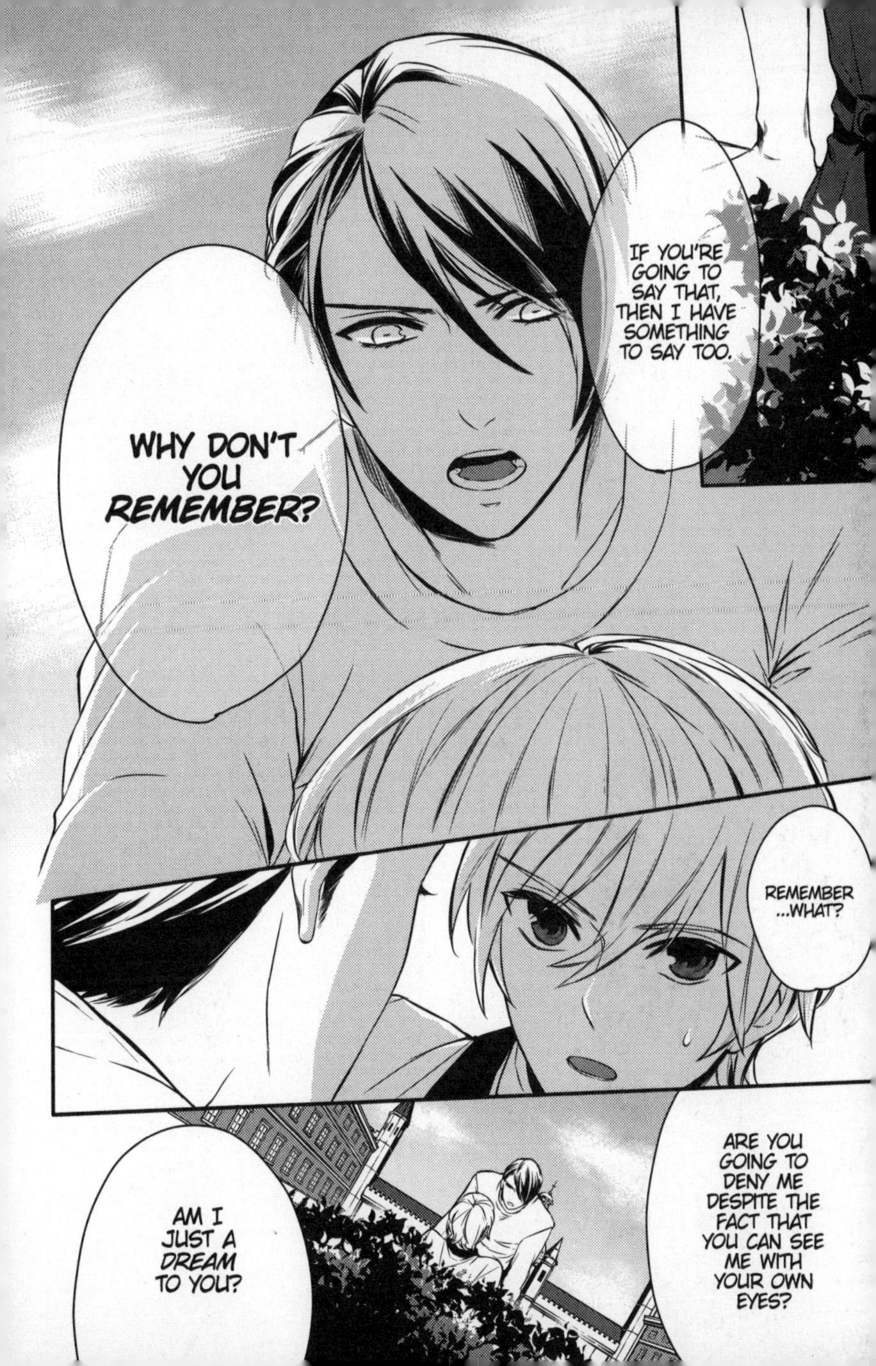
IF YOU'RE GOING TO SAY THAT, THEN I HAVE SOMETHING TO SAY TOO.
WHY DON'T YOU *REMEMBER?*
REMEMBER ...WHAT?
ARE YOU GOING TO DENY ME DESPITE THE FACT THAT YOU CAN SEE ME WITH YOUR OWN EYES?
AM I JUST A *DREAM* TO YOU?

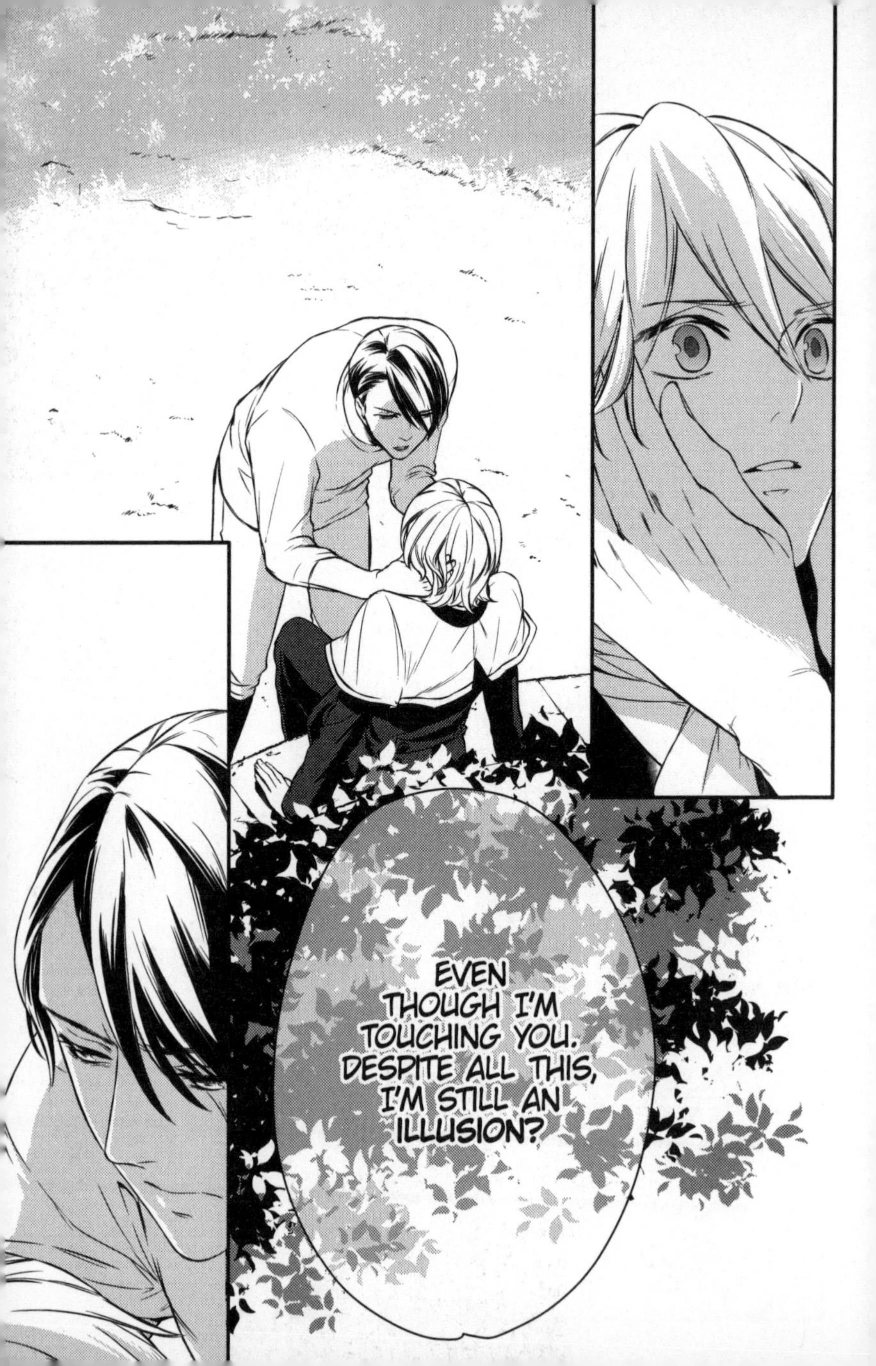
EVEN THOUGH I'M TOUCHING YOU. DESPITE ALL THIS, I'M STILL AN ILLUSION?

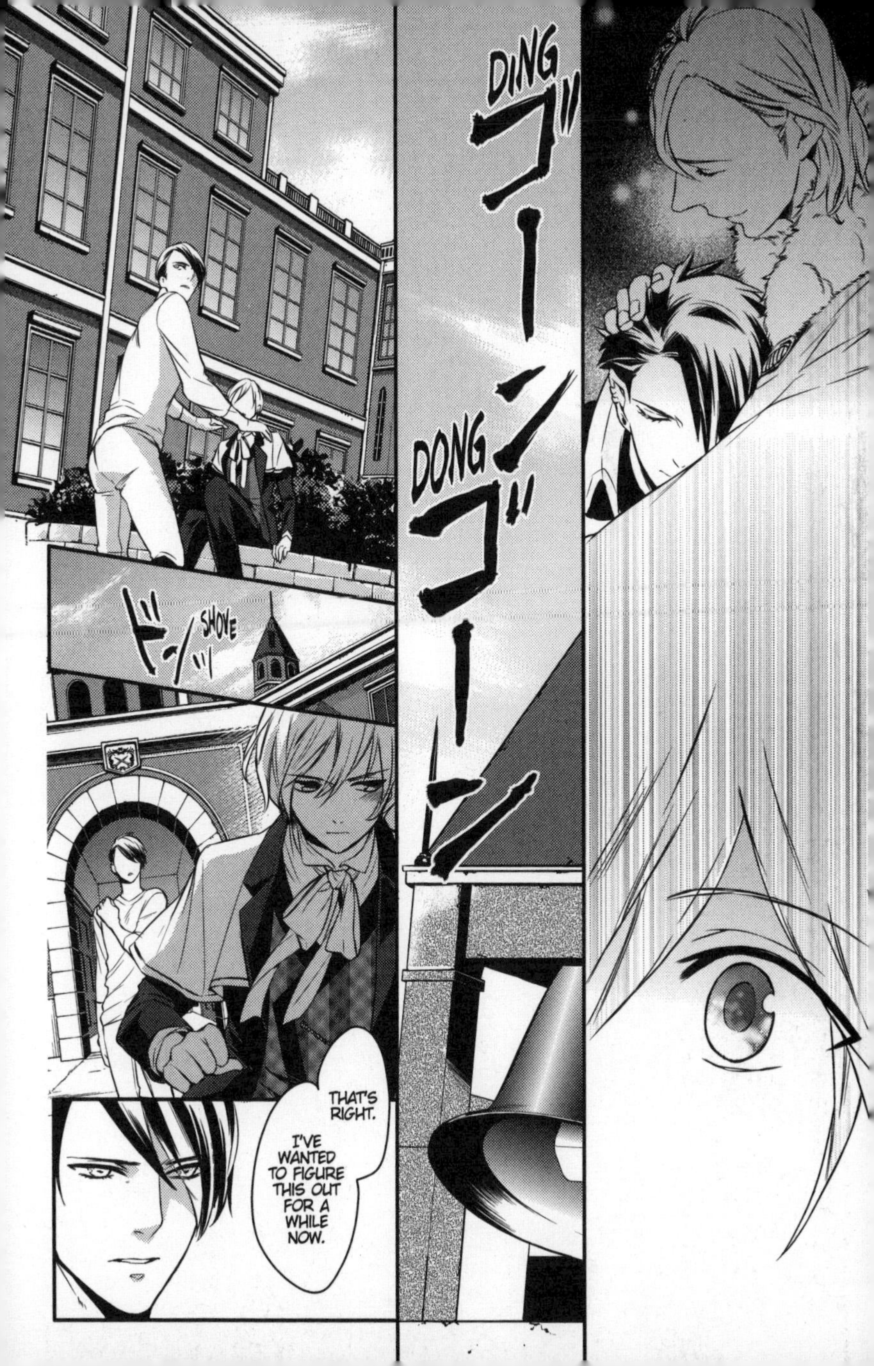
DING
ゴーン
DONG
ゴーン
ドンッ
SHOVE
THAT'S RIGHT.
I'VE WANTED TO FIGURE THIS OUT FOR A WHILE NOW.

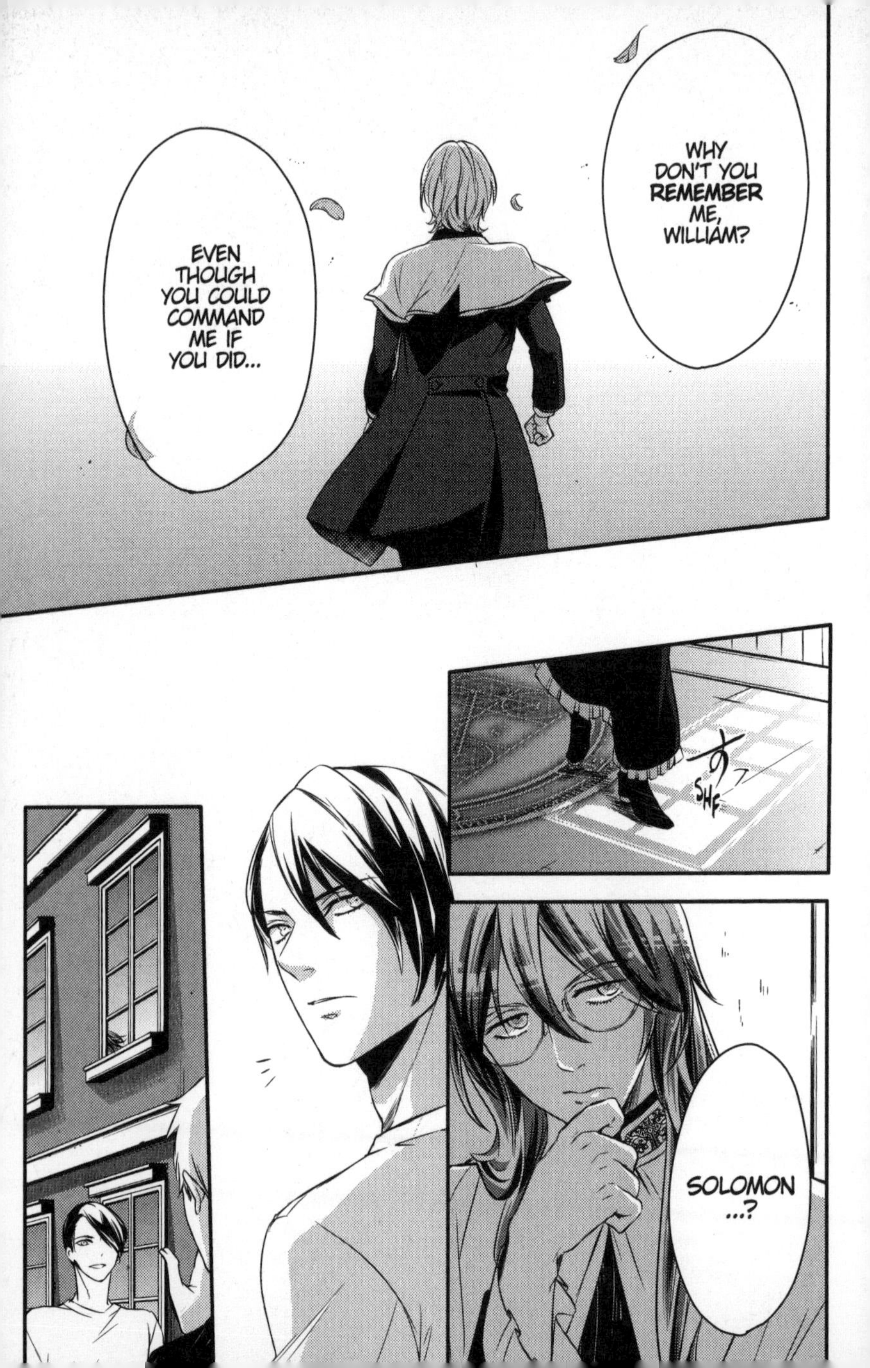
WHY DON'T YOU REMEMBER ME, WILLIAM?
EVEN THOUGH YOU COULD COMMAND ME IF YOU DID...
すっ
SHF
SOLOMON ...?

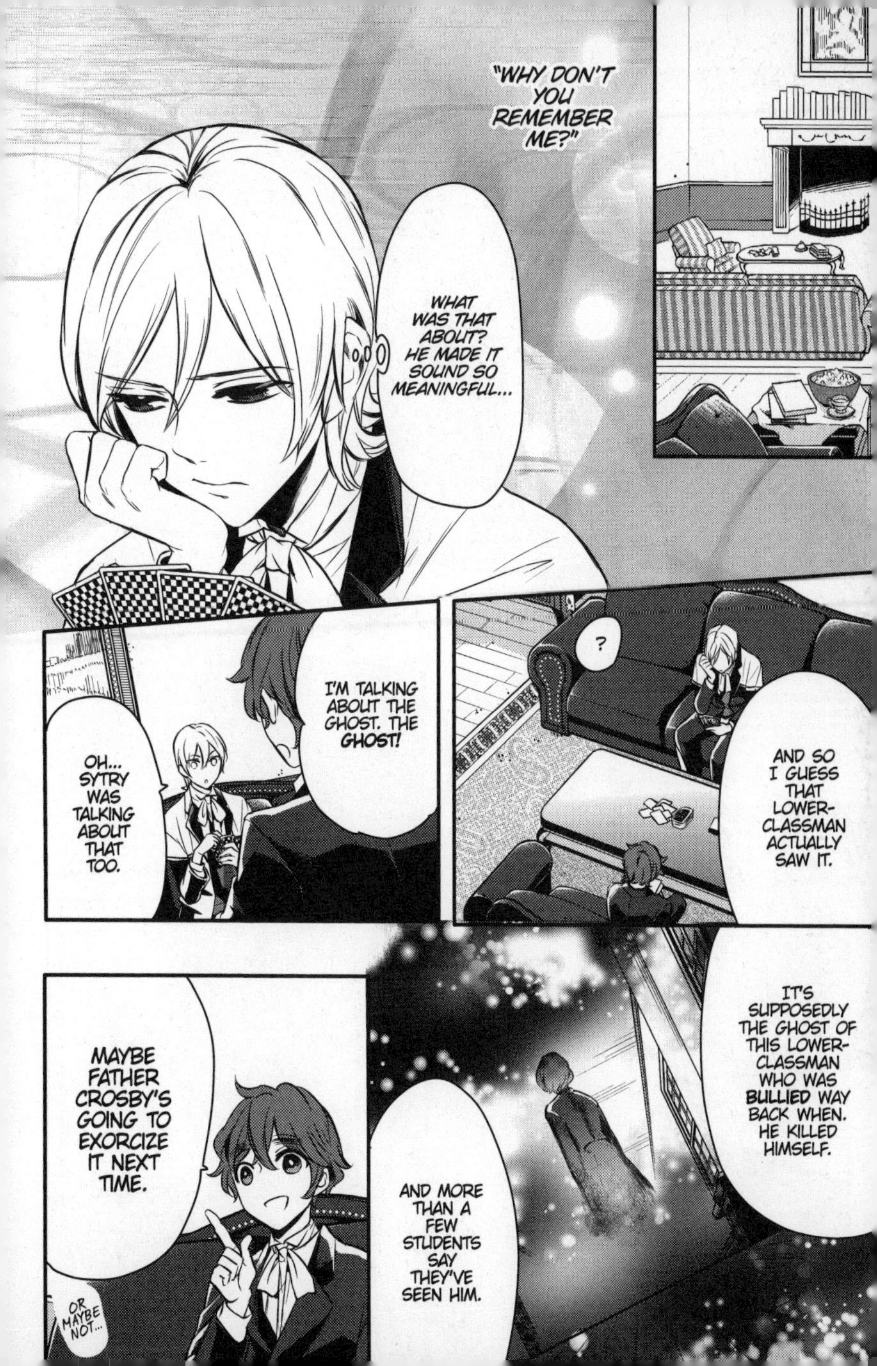
"WHY DON'T YOU REMEMBER ME?"
WHAT WAS THAT ABOUT? HE MADE IT SOUND SO MEANINGFUL...
?
AND SO I GUESS THAT LOWER-CLASSMAN ACTUALLY SAW IT.
I'M TALKING ABOUT THE GHOST. THE GHOST!
OH... SYTRY WAS TALKING ABOUT THAT TOO.
IT'S SUPPOSEDLY THE GHOST OF THIS LOWER-CLASSMAN WHO WAS BULLIED WAY BACK WHEN. HE KILLED HIMSELF.
AND MORE THAN A FEW STUDENTS SAY THEY'VE SEEN HIM.
MAYBE FATHER CROSBY'S GOING TO EXORCIZE IT NEXT TIME.
OR MAYBE NOT...

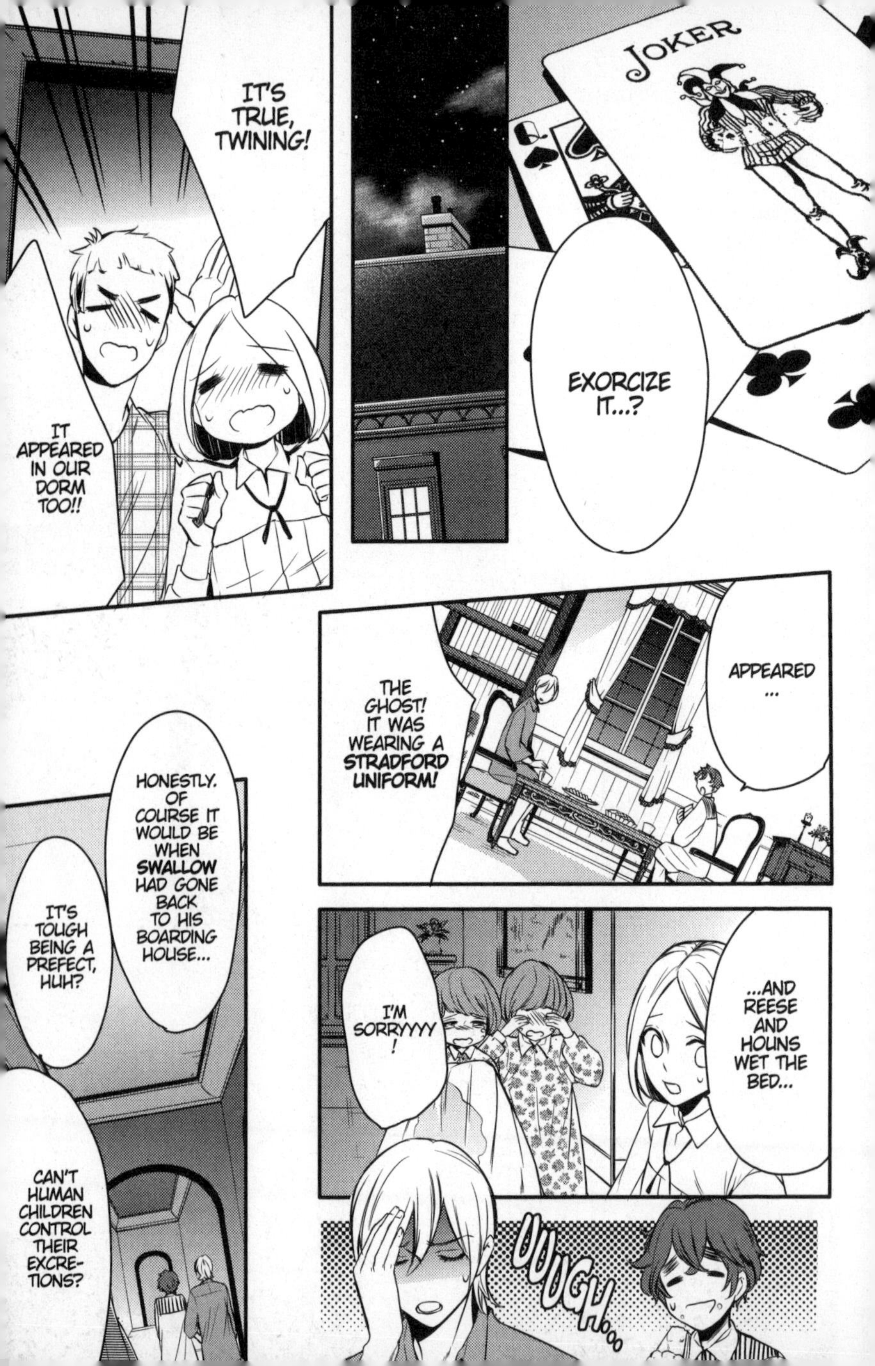
EXORCIZE IT...?
IT'S TRUE, TWINING!
IT APPEARED IN OUR DORM TOO!!
APPEARED ...
THE GHOST! IT WAS WEARING A STRADFORD UNIFORM!
...AND REESE AND HOUNS WET THE BED...
I'M SORRYYYY!
UUUGH...
HONESTLY. OF COURSE IT WOULD BE WHEN SWALLOW HAD GONE BACK TO HIS BOARDING HOUSE...
IT'S TOUGH BEING A PREFECT, HUH?
CAN'T HUMAN CHILDREN CONTROL THEIR EXCRETIONS?

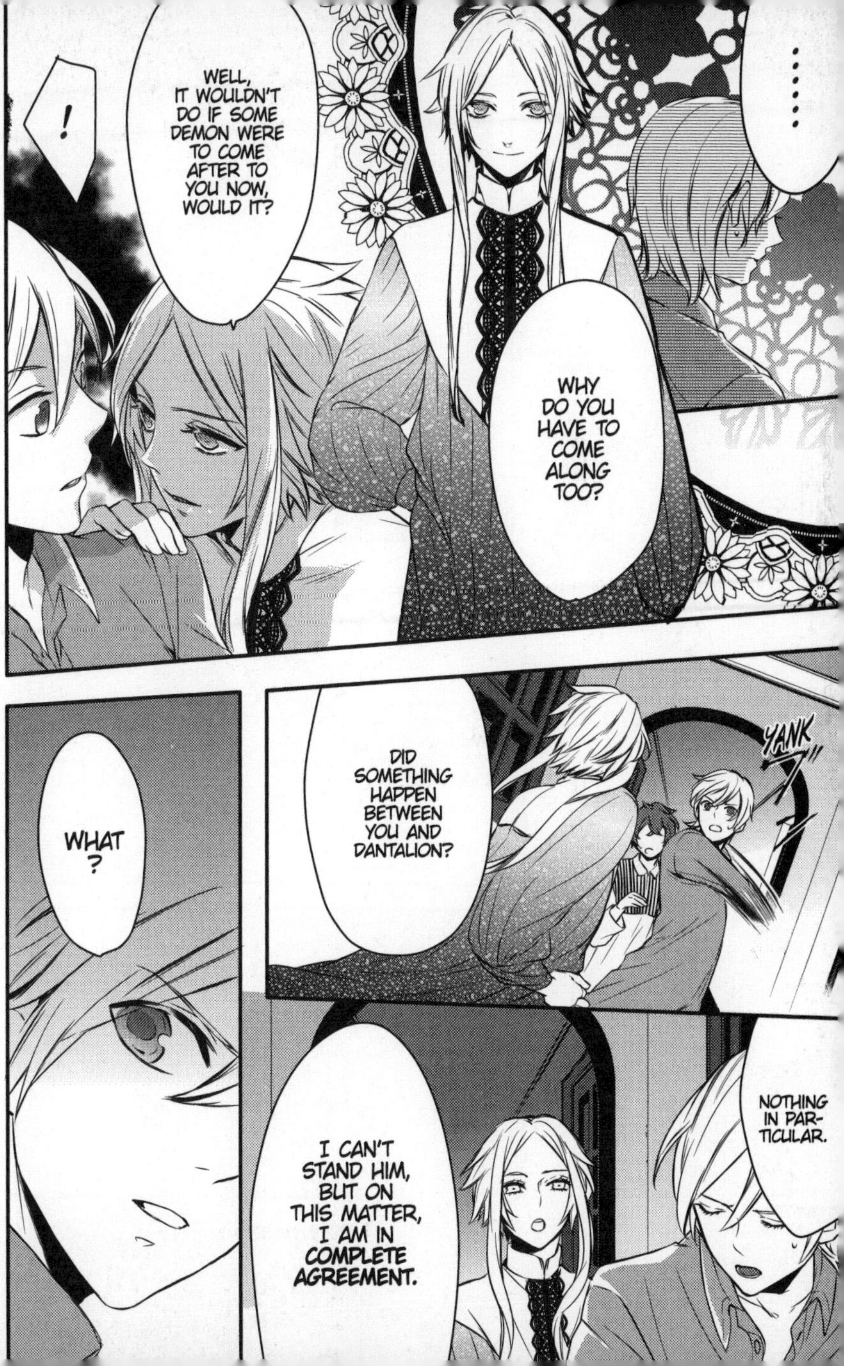
......
WHY DO YOU HAVE TO COME ALONG TOO?
WELL, IT WOULDN'T DO IF SOME DEMON WERE TO COME AFTER TO YOU NOW, WOULD IT?
!
YANK
DID SOMETHING HAPPEN BETWEEN YOU AND DANTALION?
NOTHING IN PAR-TICULAR.
I CAN'T STAND HIM, BUT ON THIS MATTER, I AM IN COMPLETE AGREEMENT.
WHAT?

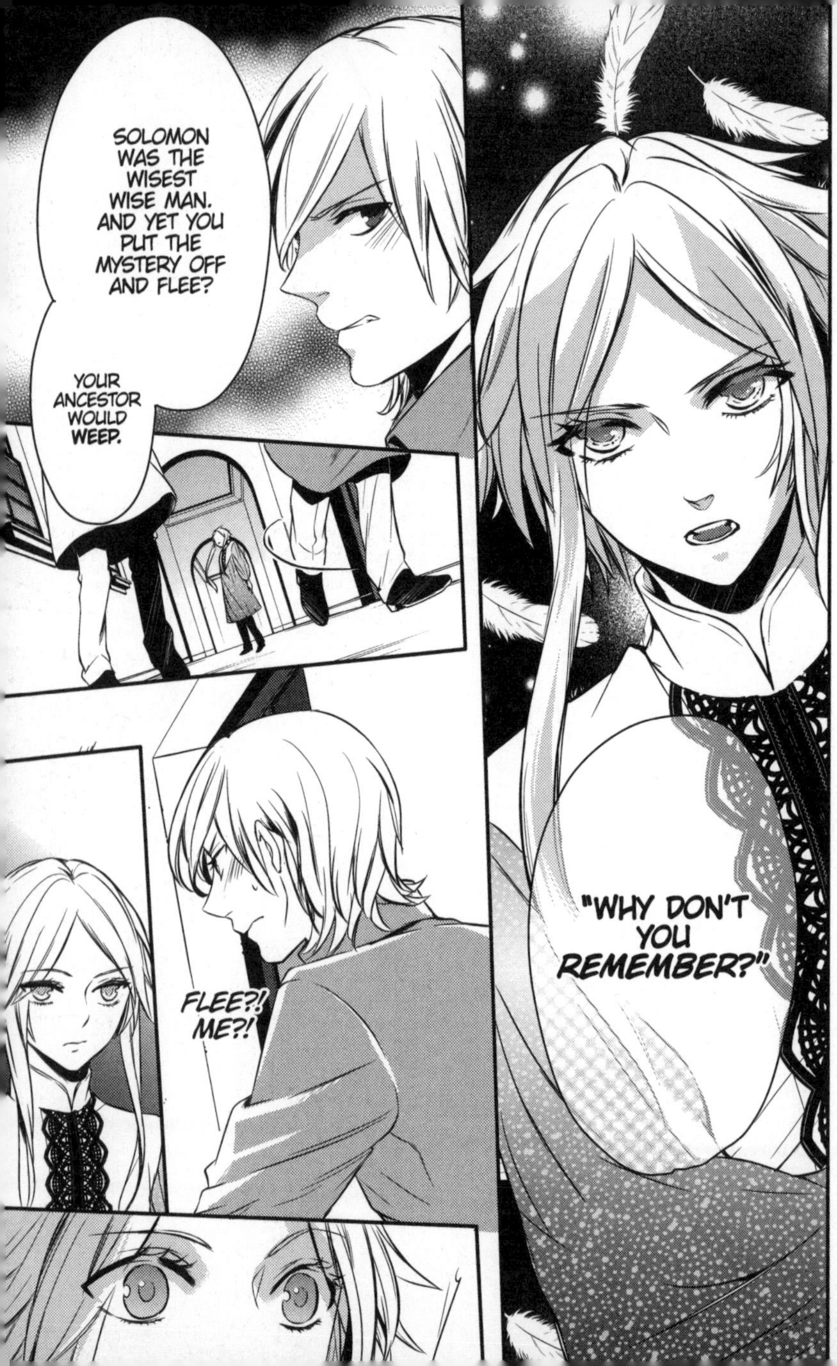
"WHY DON'T YOU REMEMBER?"
SOLOMON WAS THE WISEST WISE MAN. AND YET YOU PUT THE MYSTERY OFF AND FLEE?
YOUR ANCESTOR WOULD WEEP.
FLEE?! ME?!

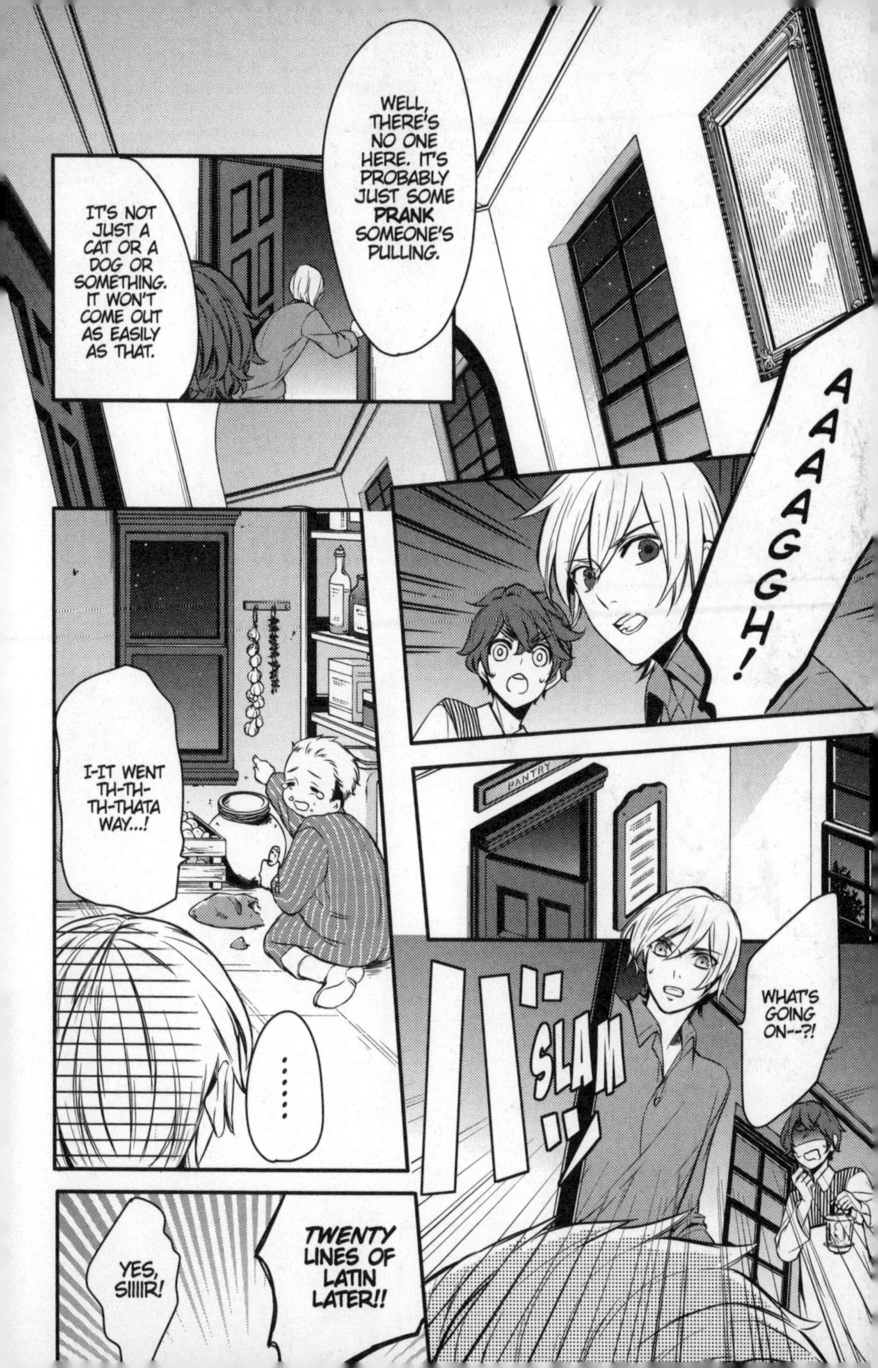
WELL, THERE'S NO ONE HERE. IT'S PROBABLY JUST SOME PRANK SOMEONE'S PULLING.
IT'S NOT JUST A CAT OR A DOG OR SOMETHING. IT WON'T COME OUT AS EASILY AS THAT.
AAAAAGGH!
PANTRY
WHAT'S GOING ON--?!
SLAM
I-IT WENT TH-TH-TH-THATA WAY...!
......
TWENTY LINES OF LATIN LATER!!
YES, SIIIR!

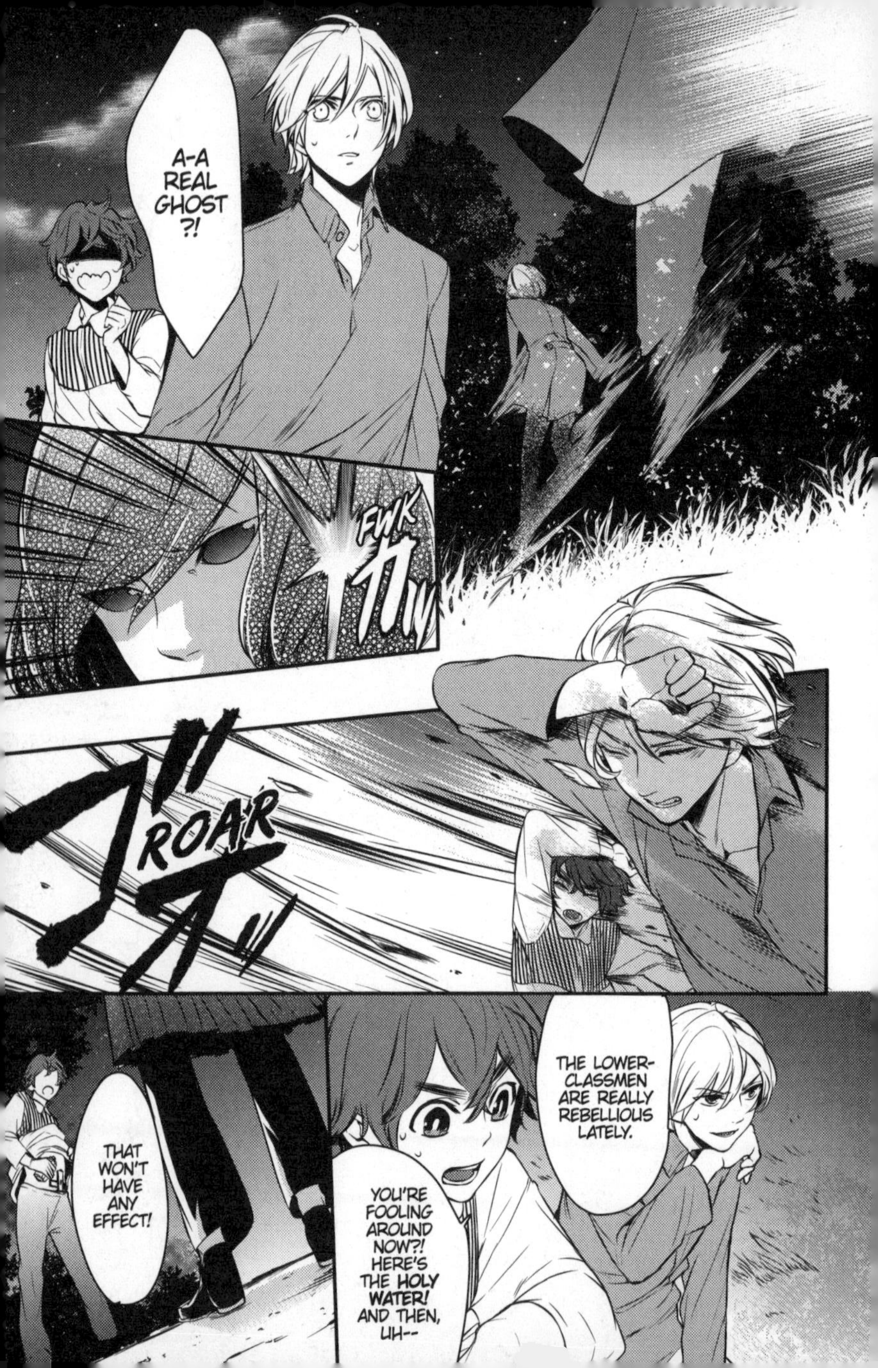
A-A REAL GHOST ?!
FWK カッ
ROAR ゴォッ
THE LOWER-CLASSMEN ARE REALLY REBELLIOUS LATELY.
YOU'RE FOOLING AROUND NOW?! HERE'S THE HOLY WATER! AND THEN, UH--
THAT WON'T HAVE ANY EFFECT!

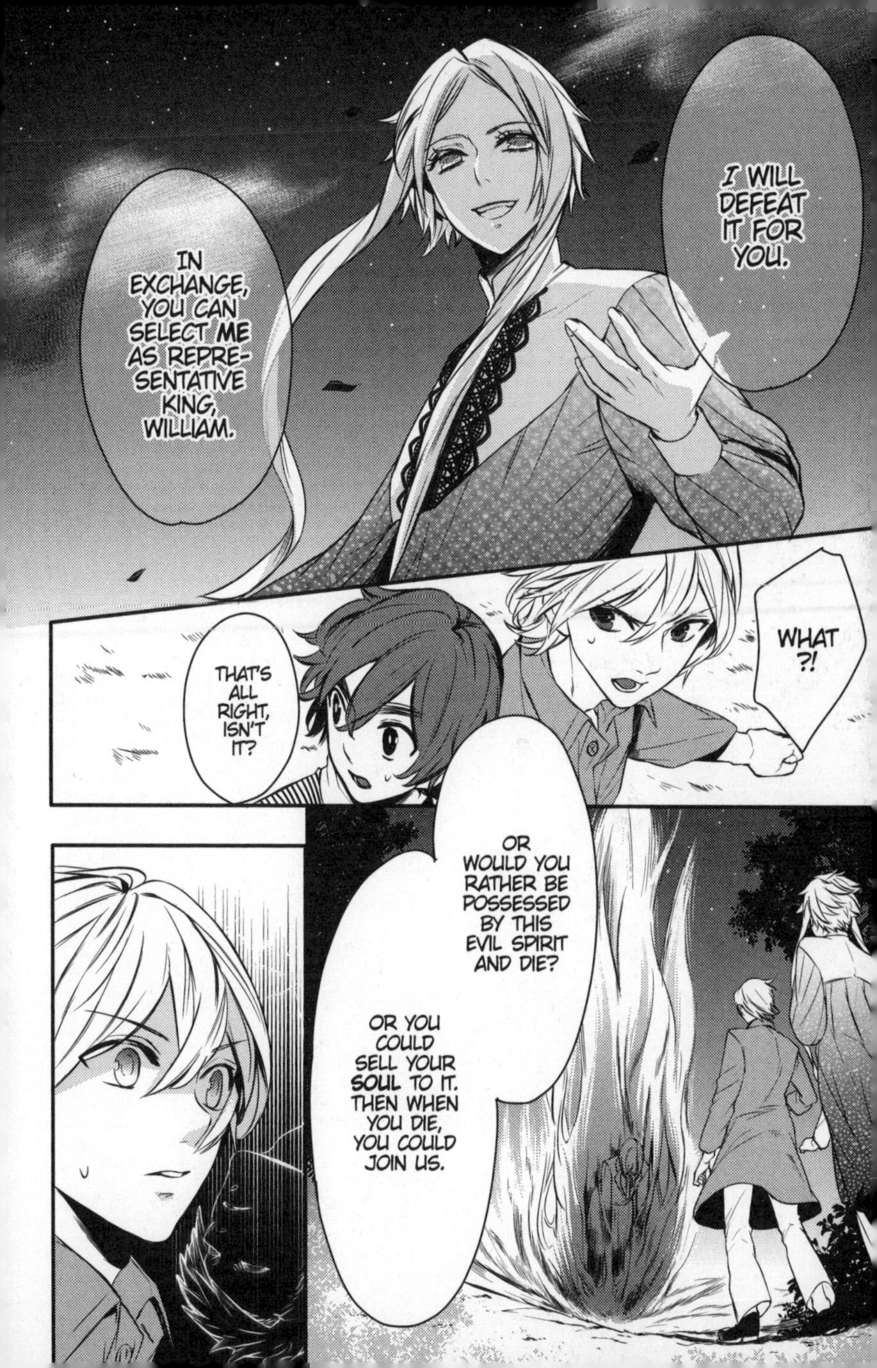
I WILL DEFEAT IT FOR YOU.
IN EXCHANGE, YOU CAN SELECT ME AS REPRE-SENTATIVE KING, WILLIAM.
WHAT?!
THAT'S ALL RIGHT, ISN'T IT?
OR WOULD YOU RATHER BE POSSESSED BY THIS EVIL SPIRIT AND DIE?
OR YOU COULD SELL YOUR SOUL TO IT. THEN WHEN YOU DIE, YOU COULD JOIN US.

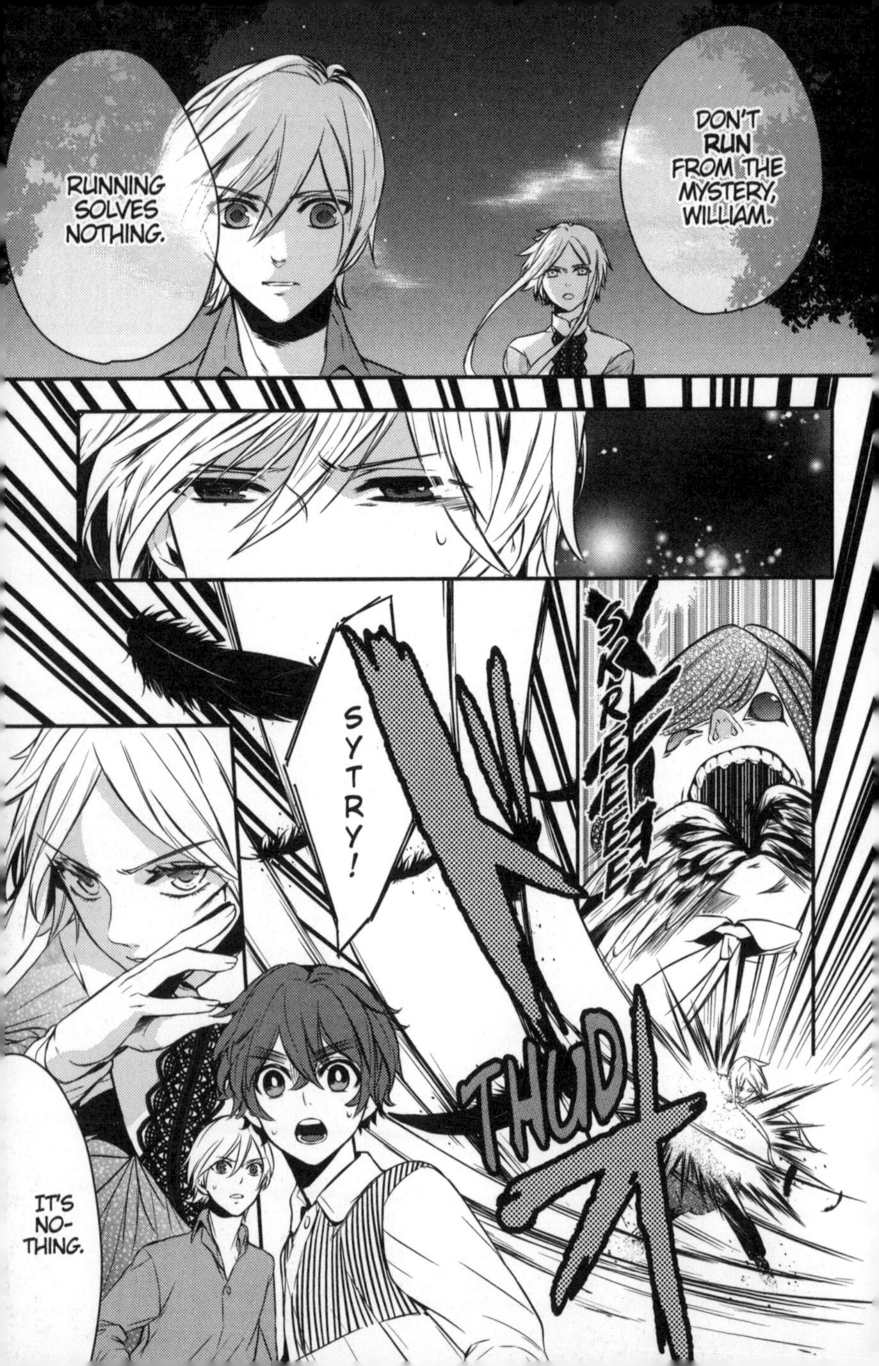
DON'T RUN FROM THE MYSTERY, WILLIAM.
RUNNING SOLVES NOTHING.
SKREEEEE
SYTRY!
THUD
IT'S NO-THING.

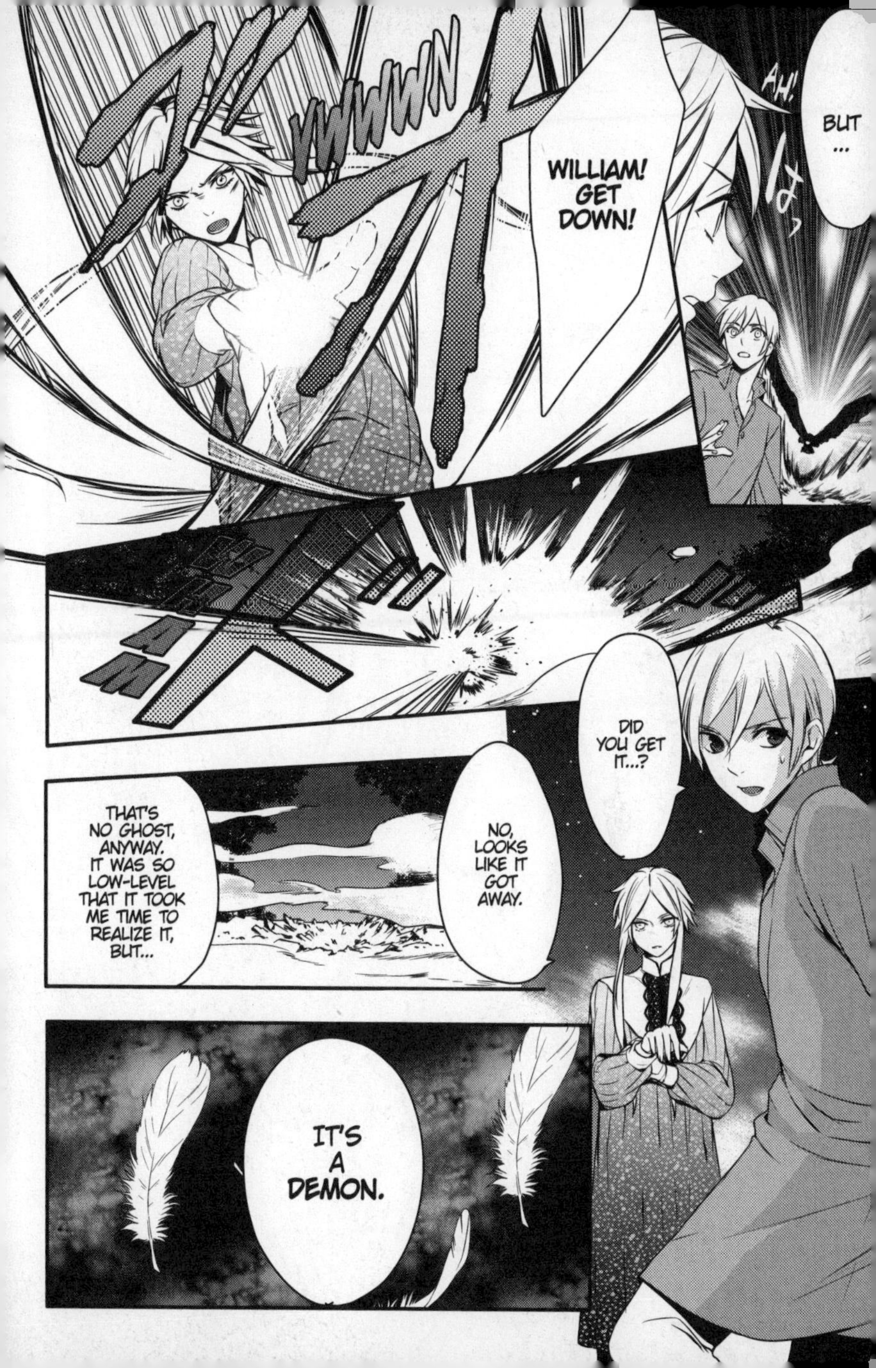
BUT ...
AH!
はっ
WILLIAM! GET DOWN!
DID YOU GET IT...?
NO, LOOKS LIKE IT GOT AWAY.
THAT'S NO GHOST, ANYWAY. IT WAS SO LOW-LEVEL THAT IT TOOK ME TIME TO REALIZE IT, BUT...
IT'S A DEMON.

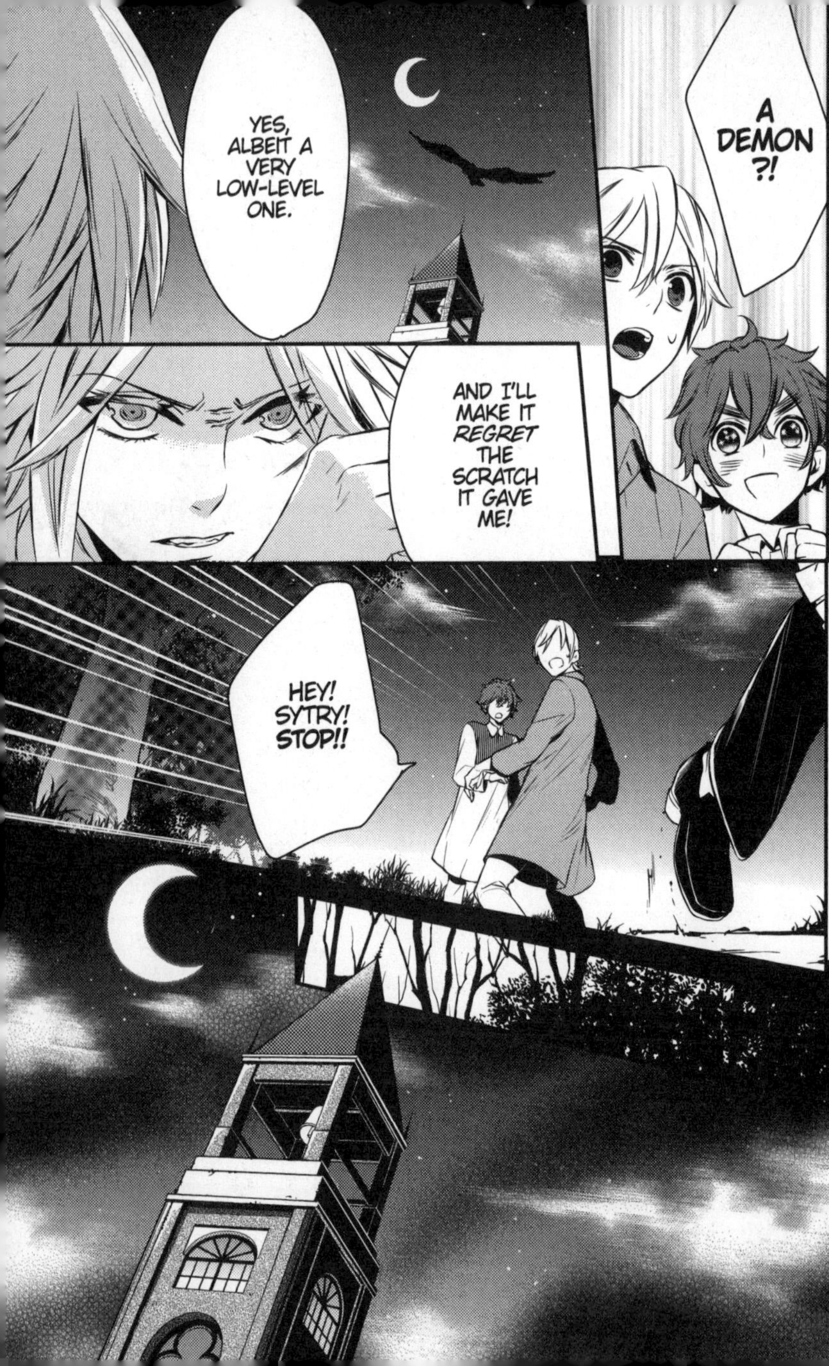
A DEMON?!
YES, ALBEIT A VERY LOW-LEVEL ONE.
AND I'LL MAKE IT *REGRET* THE SCRATCH IT GAVE ME!
HEY! SYTRY! STOP!!

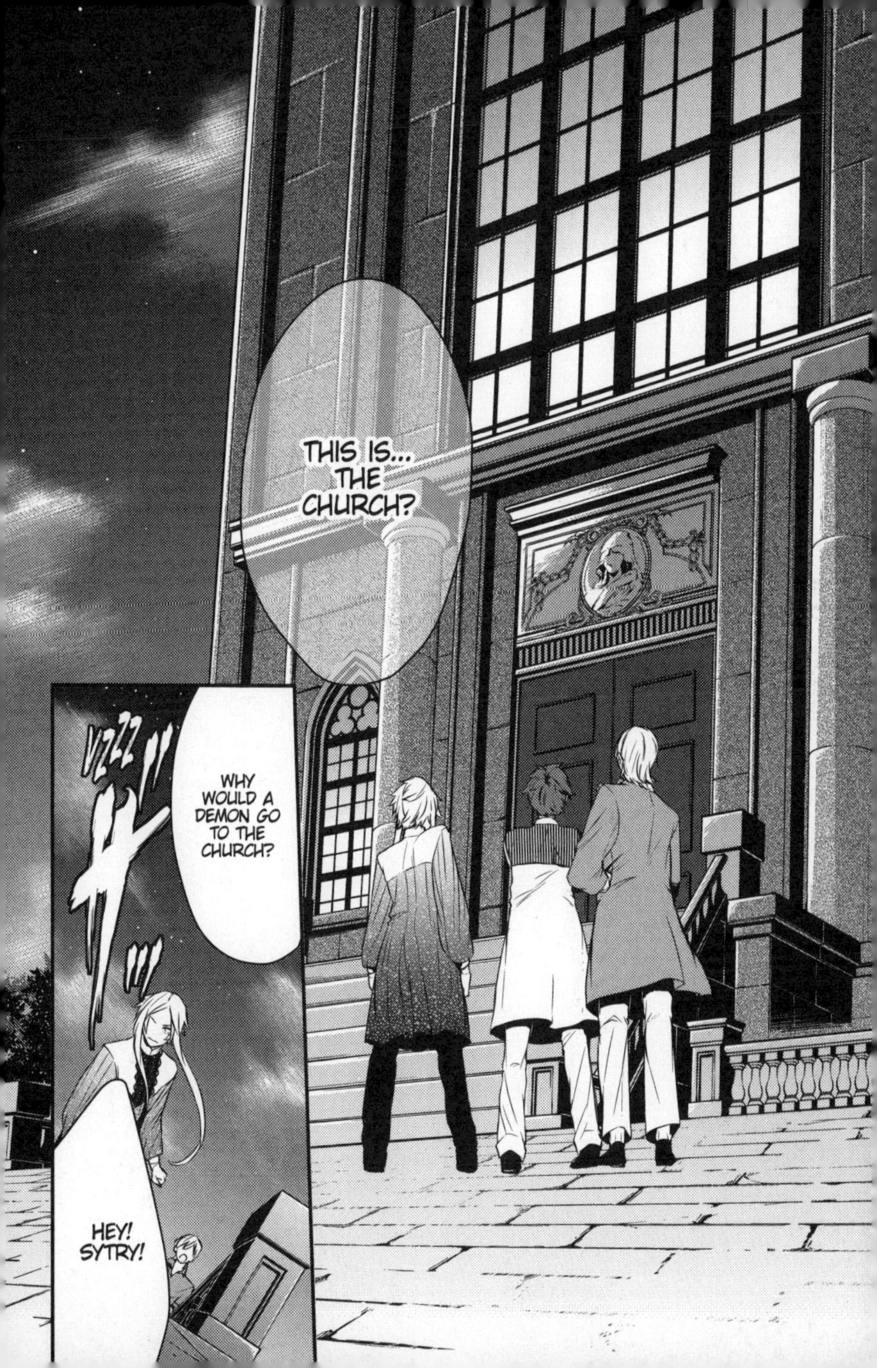
THIS IS... THE CHURCH?
WHY WOULD A DEMON GO TO THE CHURCH?
VZZZ
HEY! SYTRY!

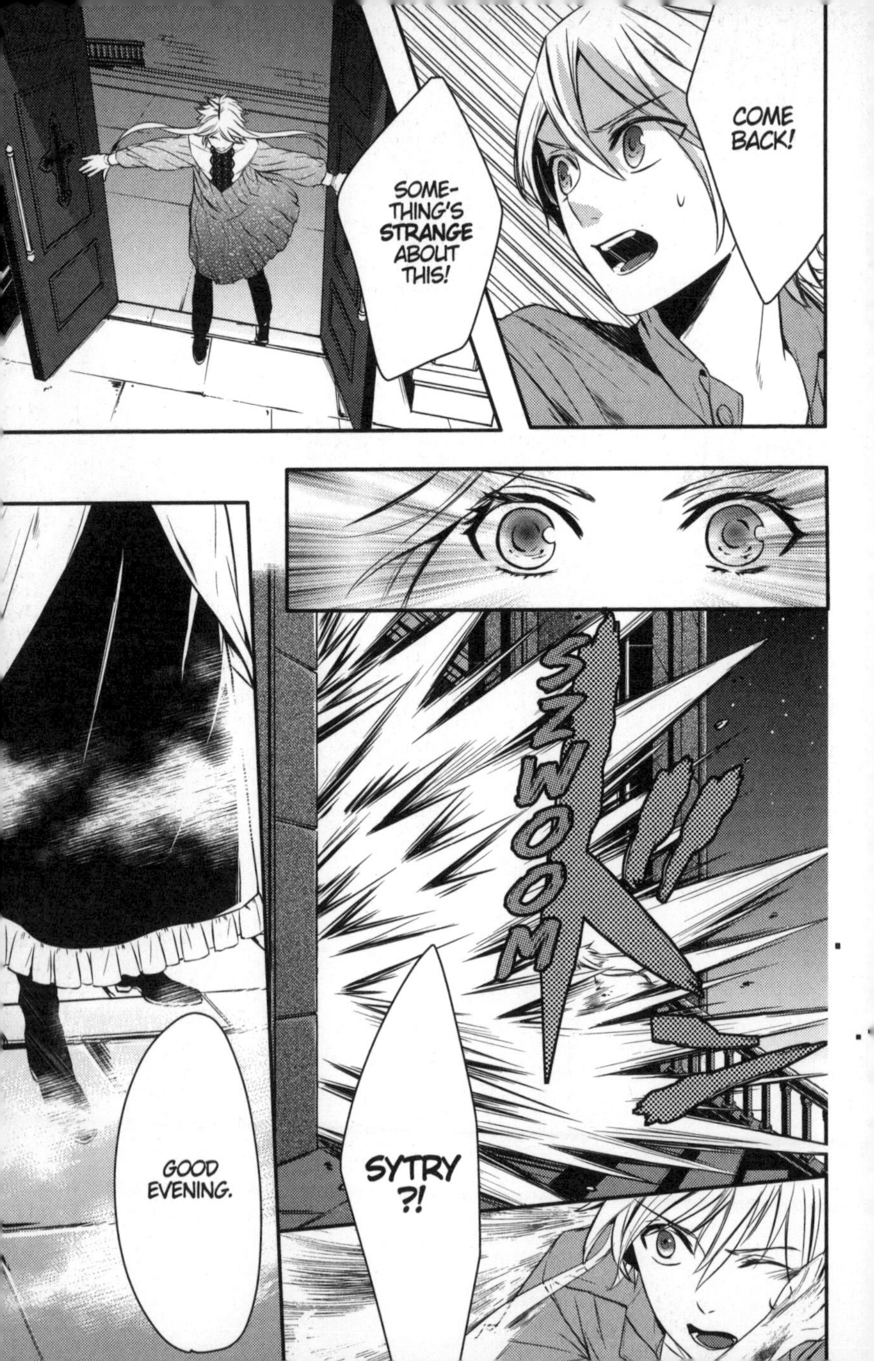
COME BACK!
SOME-THING'S STRANGE ABOUT THIS!
SZWOOM
SYTRY ?!
GOOD EVENING.

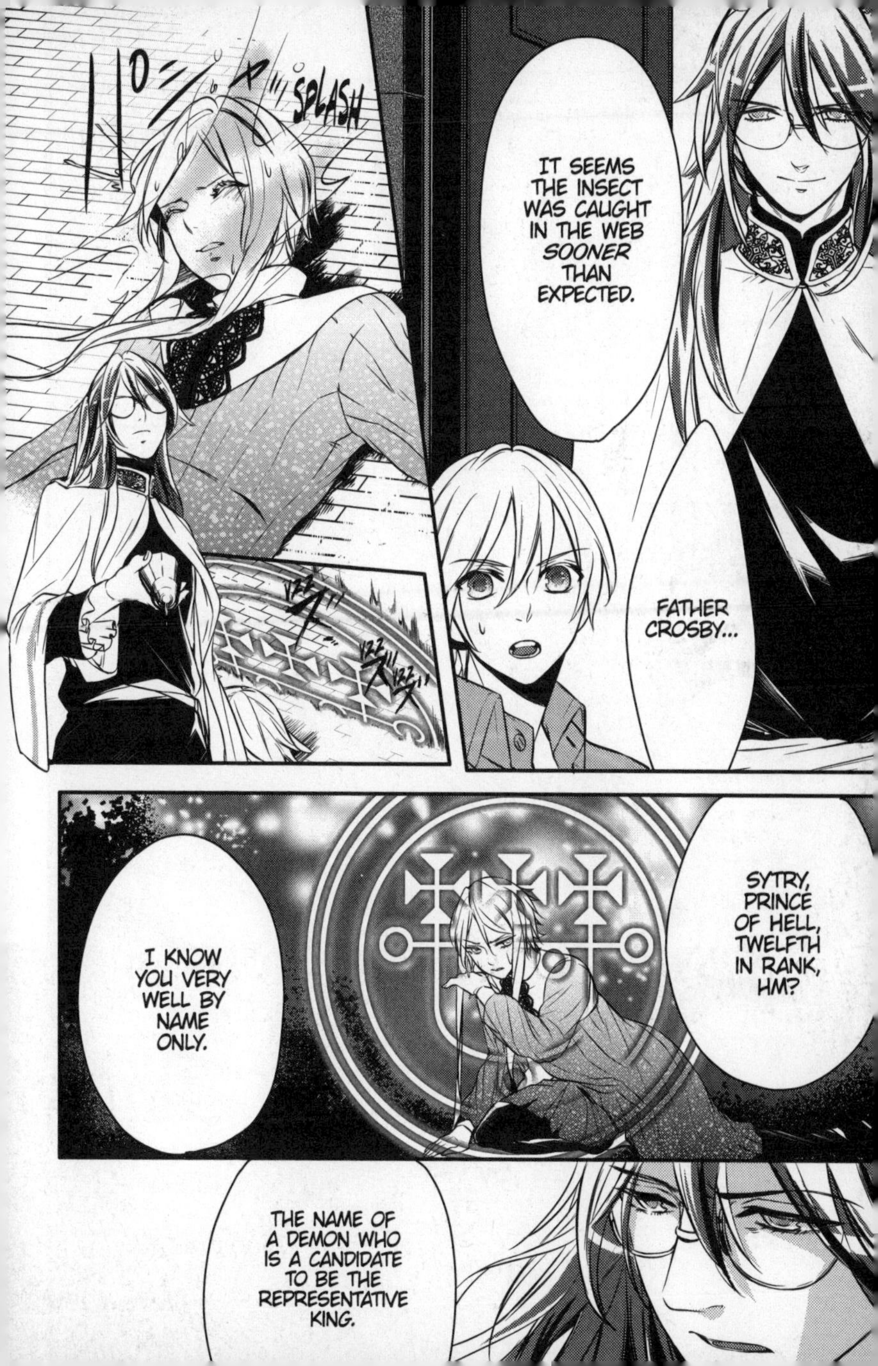
IT SEEMS THE INSECT WAS CAUGHT IN THE WEB *SOONER* THAN EXPECTED.
FATHER CROSBY...
SPLASH
SYTRY, PRINCE OF HELL, TWELFTH IN RANK, HM?
I KNOW YOU VERY WELL BY NAME ONLY.
THE NAME OF A DEMON WHO IS A CANDIDATE TO BE THE REPRESENTATIVE KING.

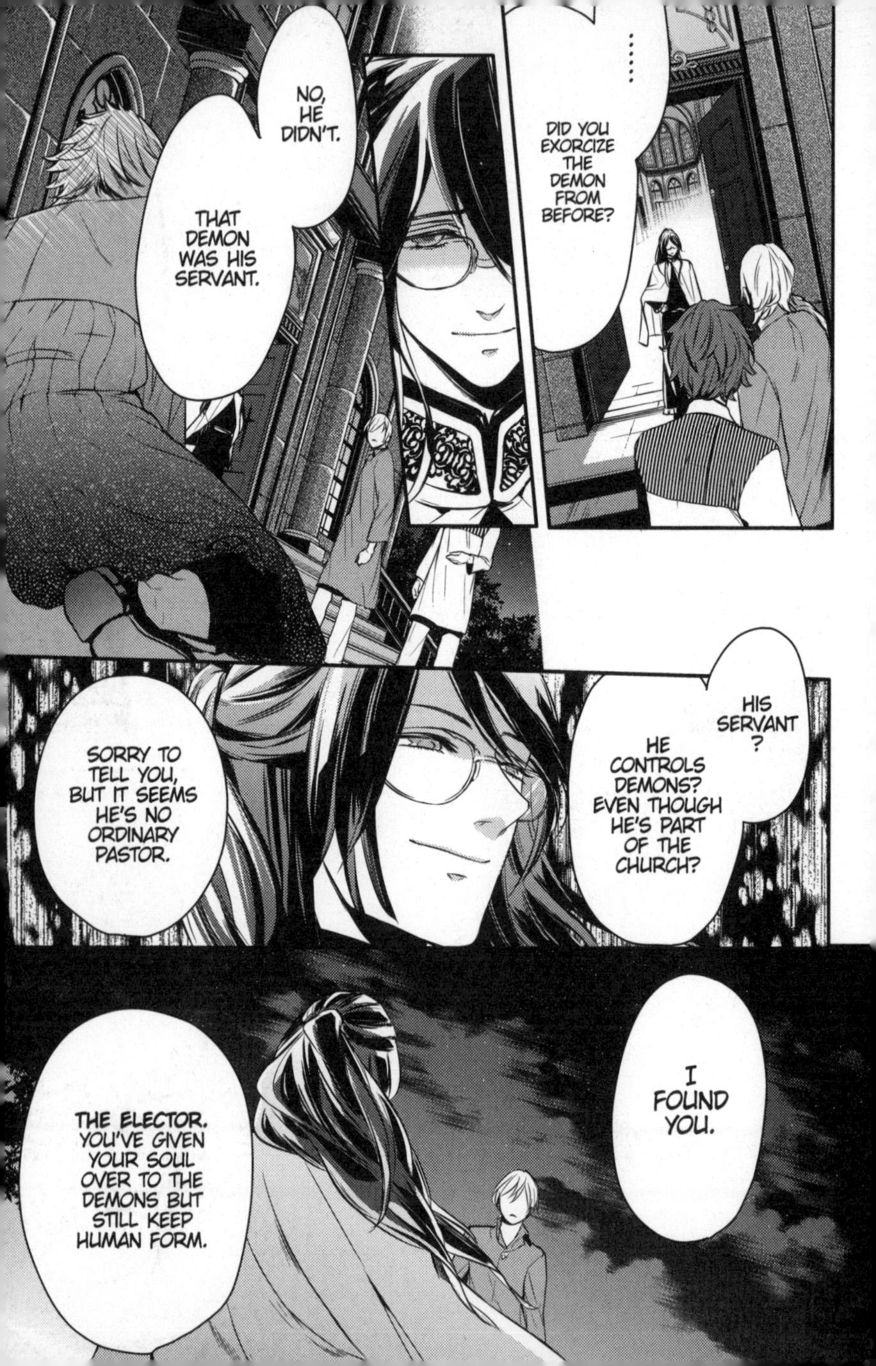
......
DID YOU EXORCIZE THE DEMON FROM BEFORE?
NO, HE DIDN'T.
THAT DEMON WAS HIS SERVANT.
HIS SERVANT?
HE CONTROLS DEMONS? EVEN THOUGH HE'S PART OF THE CHURCH?
SORRY TO TELL YOU, BUT IT SEEMS HE'S NO ORDINARY PASTOR.
I FOUND YOU.
THE ELECTOR. YOU'VE GIVEN YOUR SOUL OVER TO THE DEMONS BUT STILL KEEP HUMAN FORM.

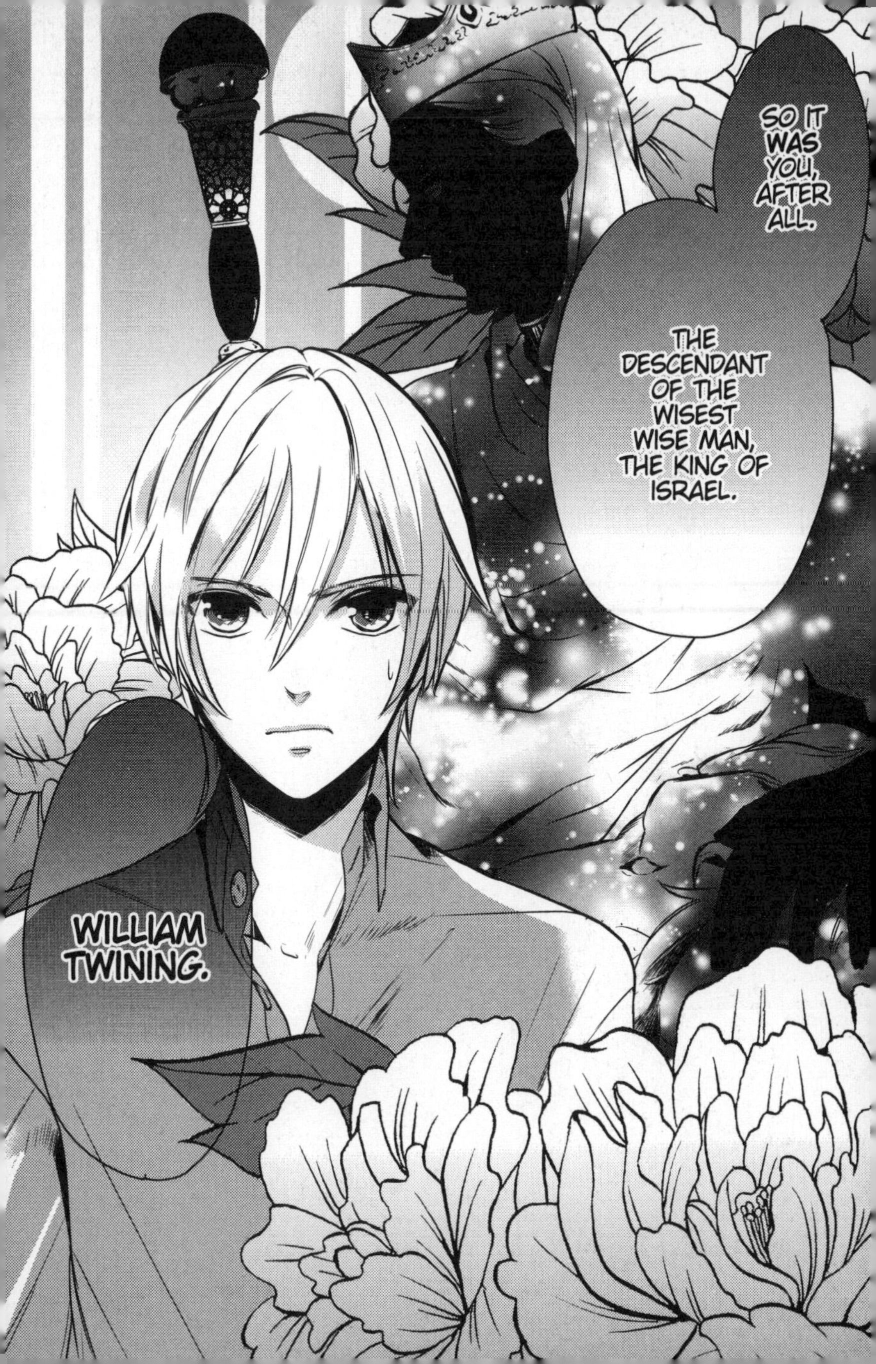
SO IT WAS YOU, AFTER ALL.
THE DESCENDANT OF THE WISEST WISE MAN, THE KING OF ISRAEL.
WILLIAM TWINING.

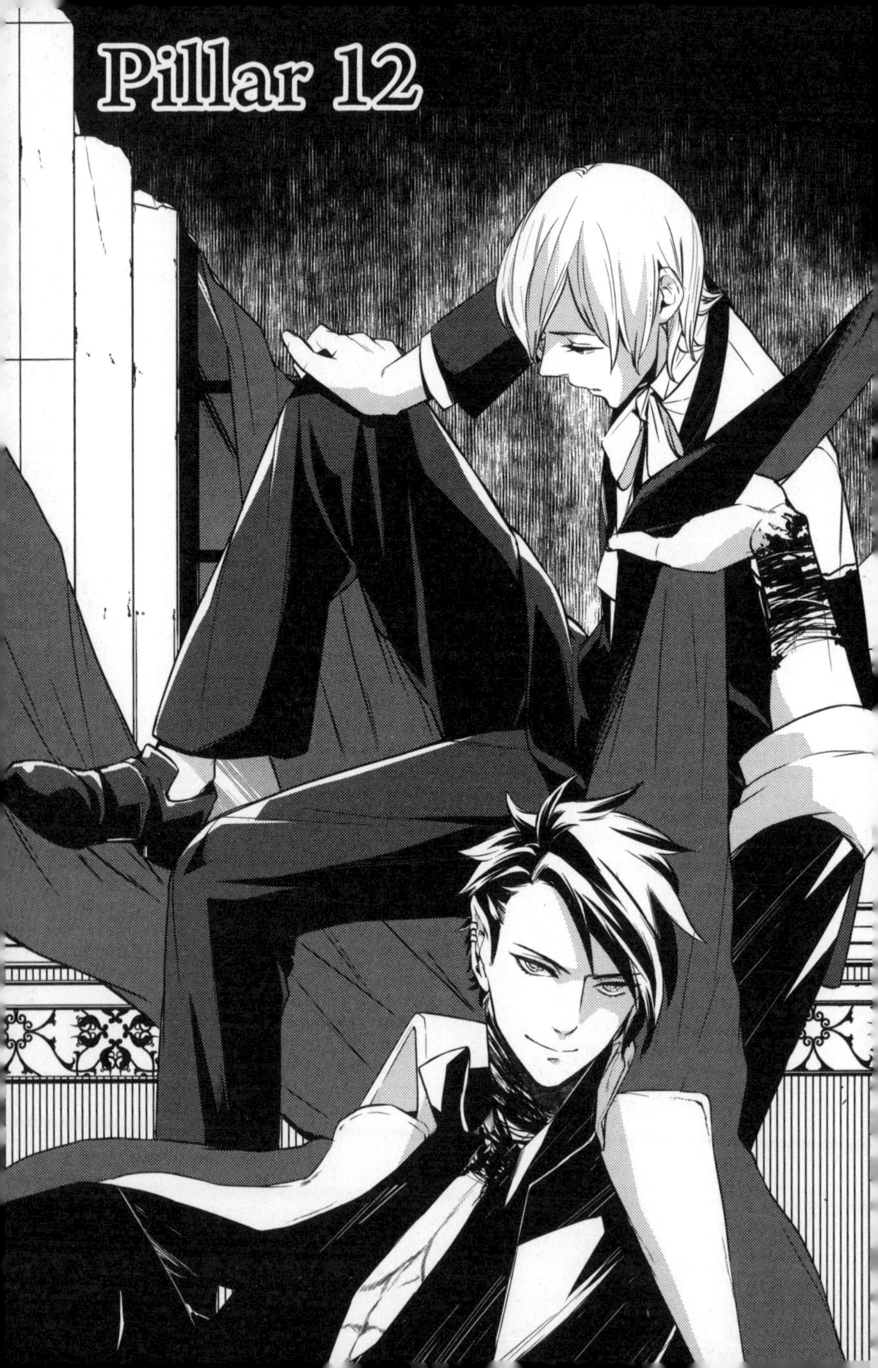
Pillar 12

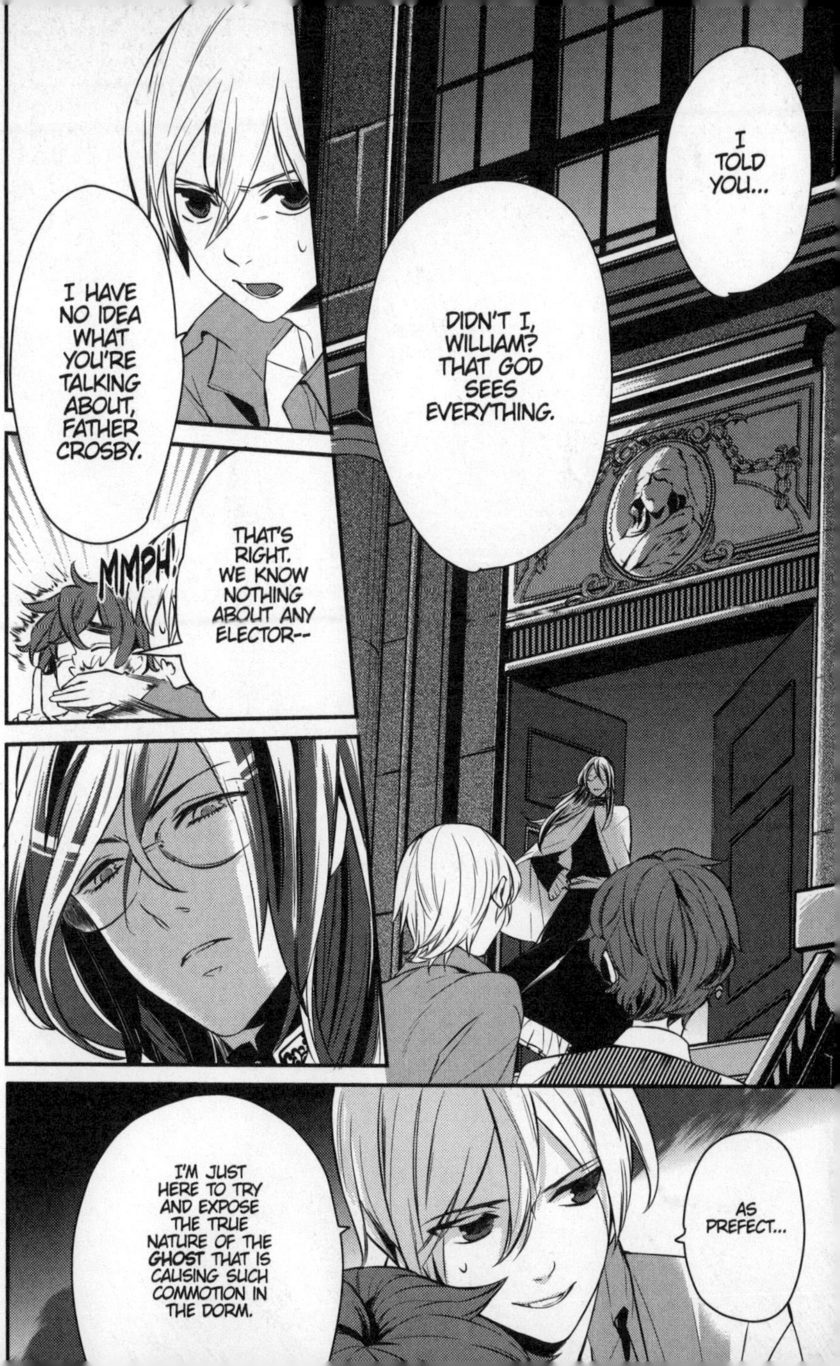
I TOLD YOU...
DIDN'T I, WILLIAM? THAT GOD SEES EVERYTHING.
I HAVE NO IDEA WHAT YOU'RE TALKING ABOUT, FATHER CROSBY.
MMPH!
THAT'S RIGHT. WE KNOW NOTHING ABOUT ANY ELECTOR--
AS PREFECT...
I'M JUST HERE TO TRY AND EXPOSE THE TRUE NATURE OF THE GHOST THAT IS CAUSING SUCH COMMOTION IN THE DORM.

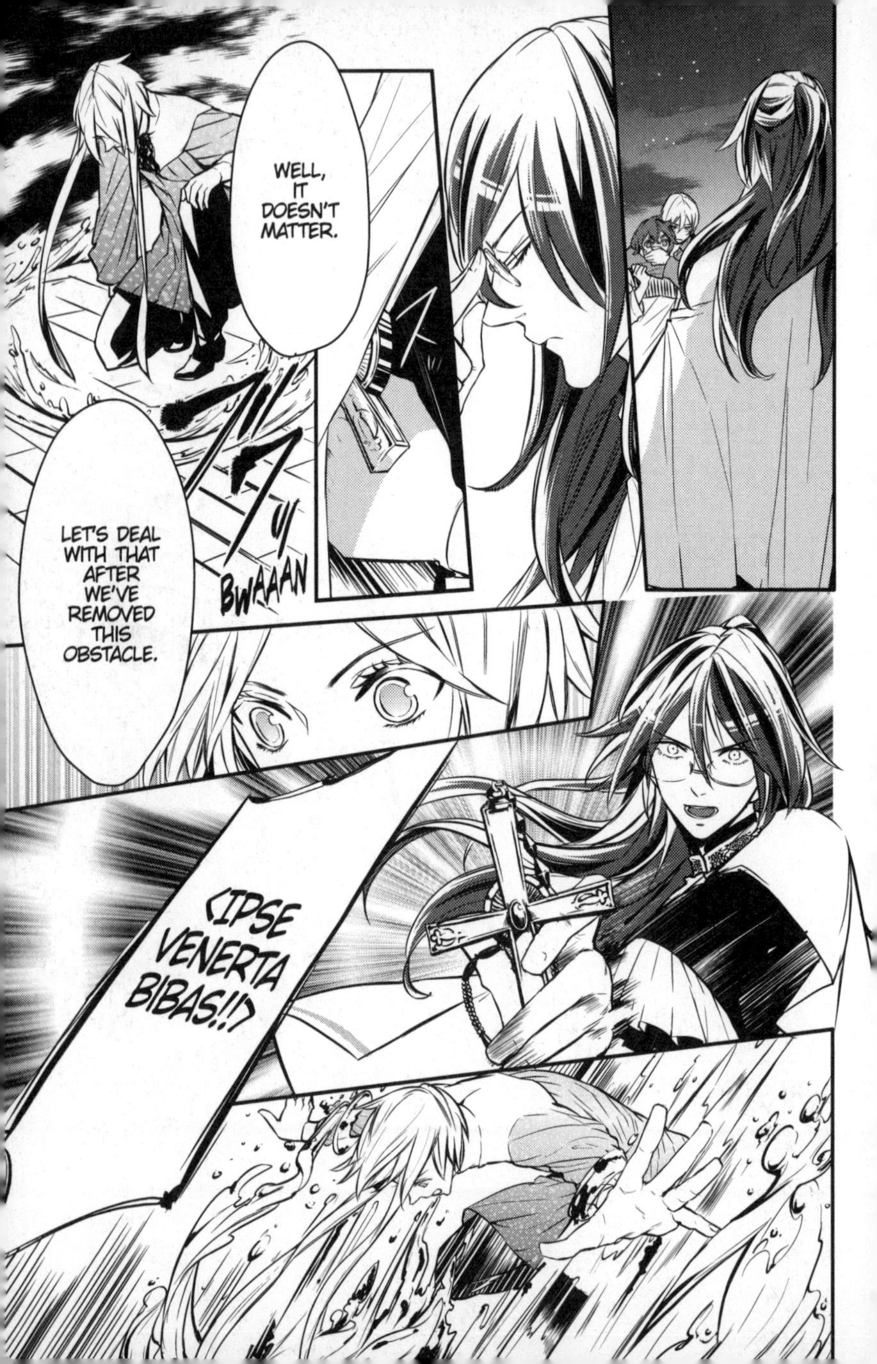
WELL, IT DOESN'T MATTER.
LET'S DEAL WITH THAT AFTER WE'VE REMOVED THIS OBSTACLE.
BWAAAN
<IPSE VENERTA BIBAS!!>

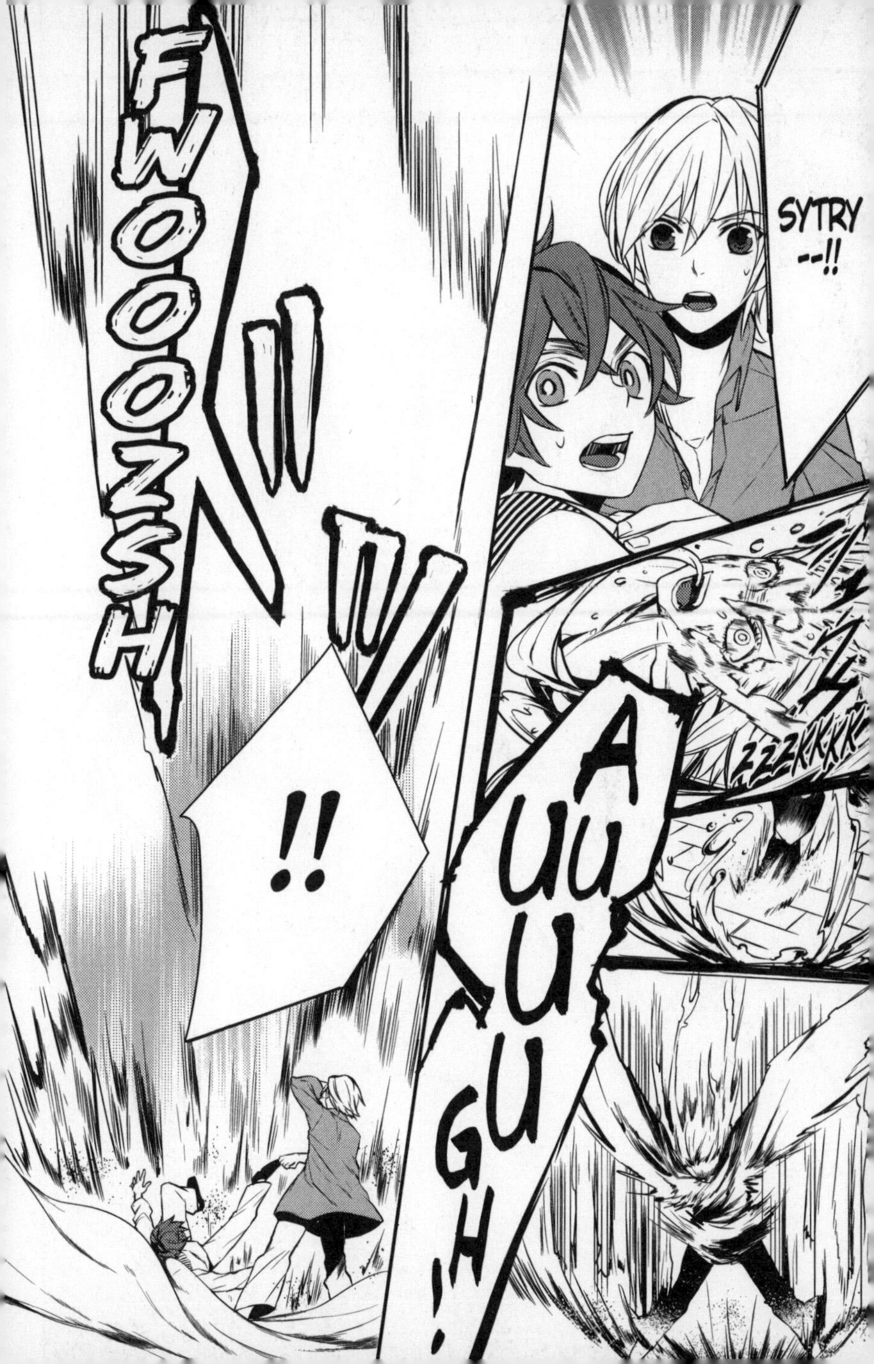
SYTRY --!!
ZZZKKKK
AUUUUGUGH!
FWOOOOZSH
!!

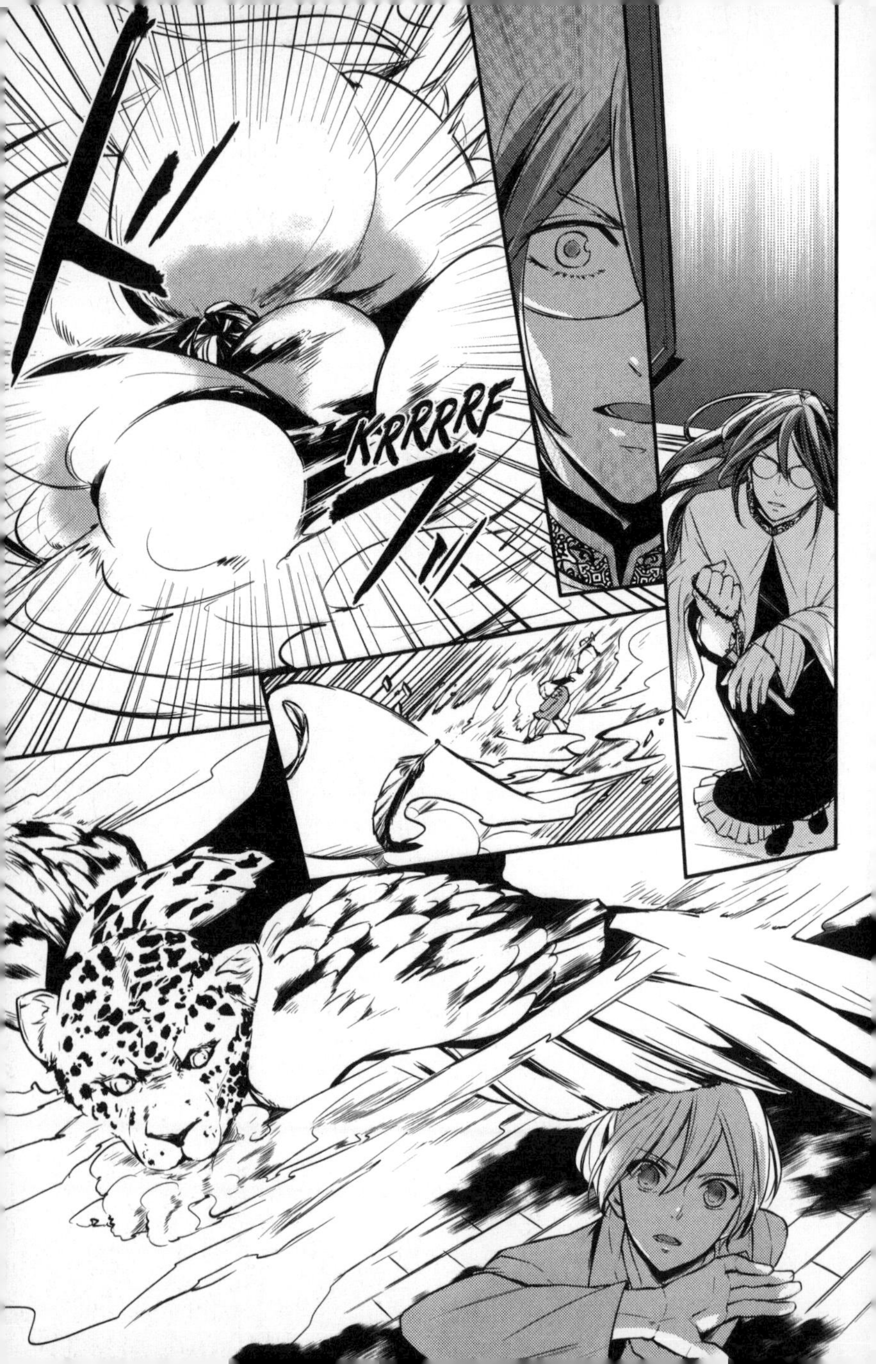
KRRRRF

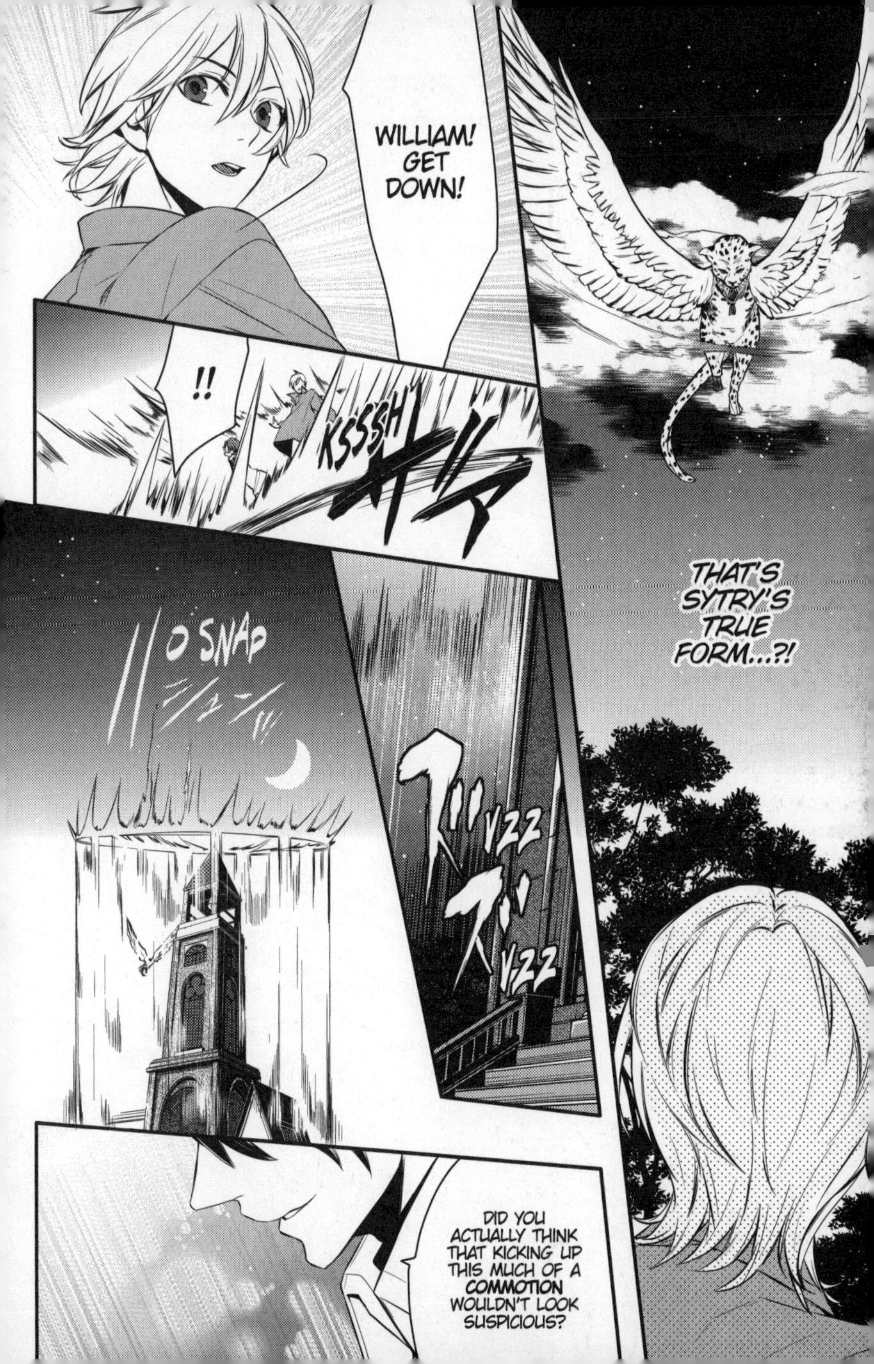
THAT'S SYTRY'S TRUE FORM...?!
WILLIAM! GET DOWN!
!!
KSSSH
VZZ
VZZ
SNAP
DID YOU ACTUALLY THINK THAT KICKING UP THIS MUCH OF A COMMOTION WOULDN'T LOOK SUSPICIOUS?

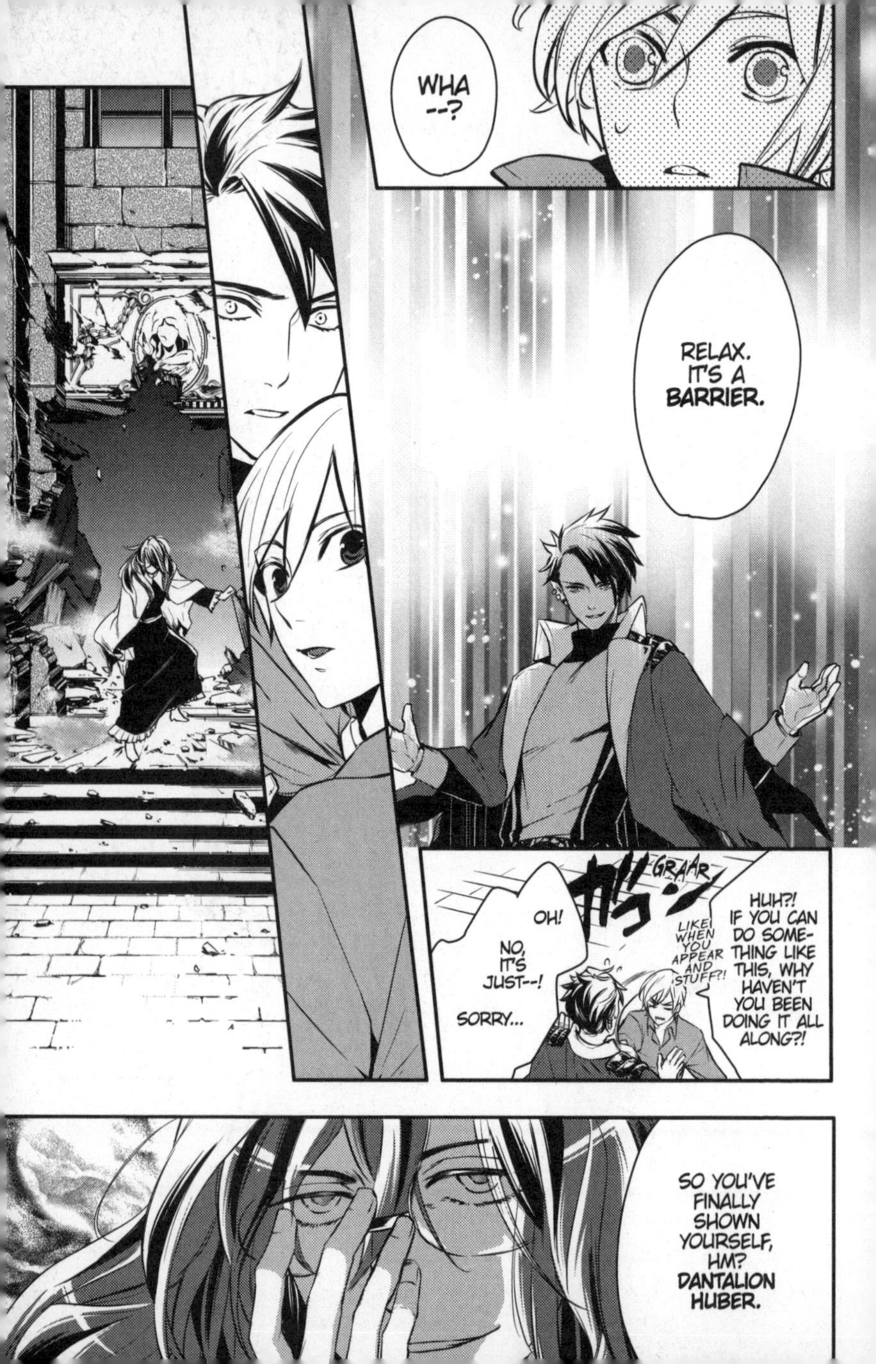
WHA--?
RELAX. IT'S A BARRIER.
GRAAR
HUH?! IF YOU CAN DO SOME-THING LIKE THIS, WHY HAVEN'T YOU BEEN DOING IT ALL ALONG?!
LIKE WHEN YOU APPEAR AND STUFF?!
OH!
NO, IT'S JUST--!
SORRY...
SO YOU'VE FINALLY SHOWN YOURSELF, HM? DANTALION HUBER.

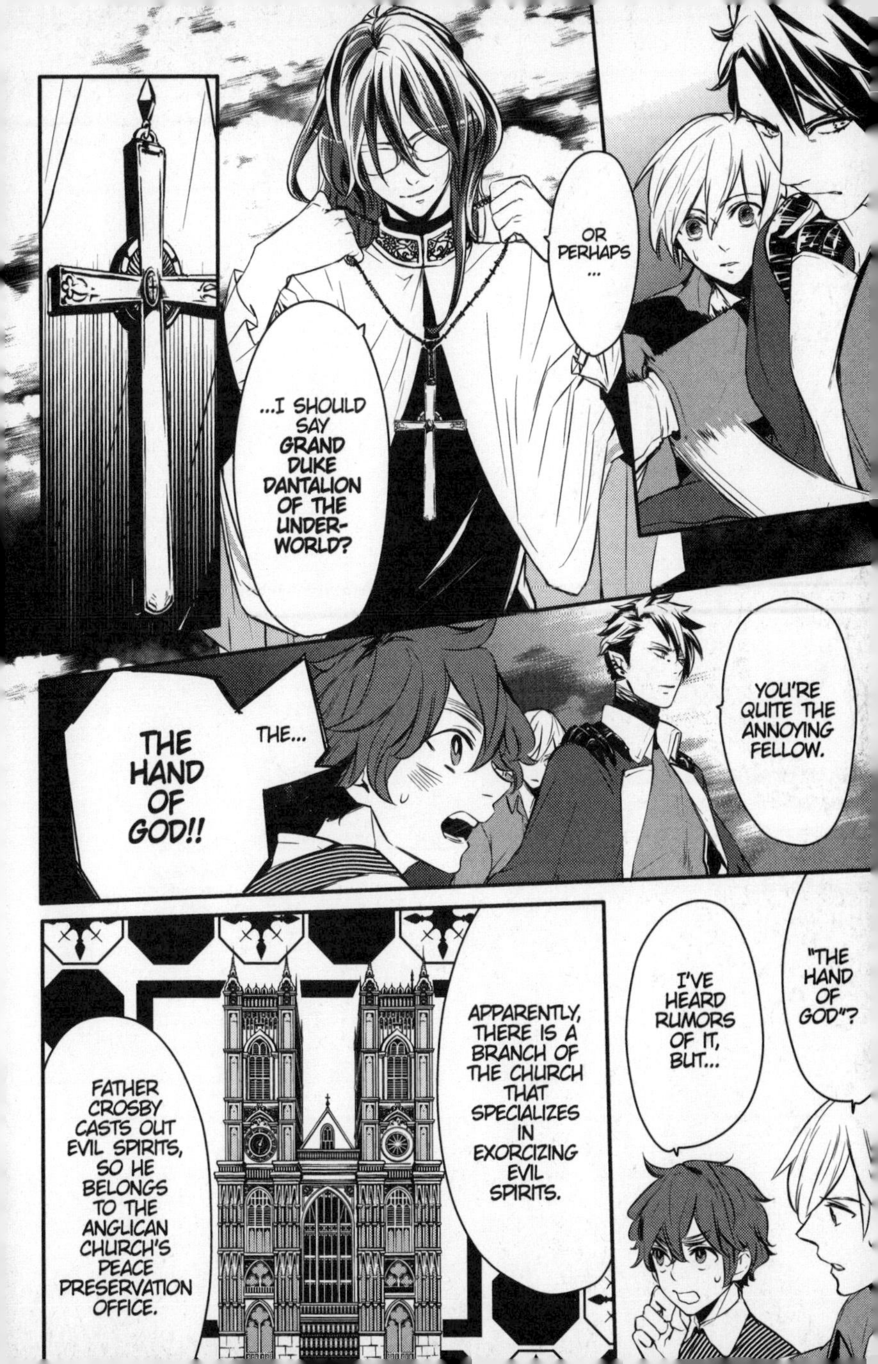
OR PERHAPS ...
...I SHOULD SAY GRAND DUKE DANTALION OF THE UNDER-WORLD?
YOU'RE QUITE THE ANNOYING FELLOW.
THE...
THE HAND OF GOD!!
"THE HAND OF GOD"?
I'VE HEARD RUMORS OF IT, BUT...
APPARENTLY, THERE IS A BRANCH OF THE CHURCH THAT SPECIALIZES IN EXORCIZING EVIL SPIRITS.
FATHER CROSBY CASTS OUT EVIL SPIRITS, SO HE BELONGS TO THE ANGLICAN CHURCH'S PEACE PRESERVATION OFFICE.

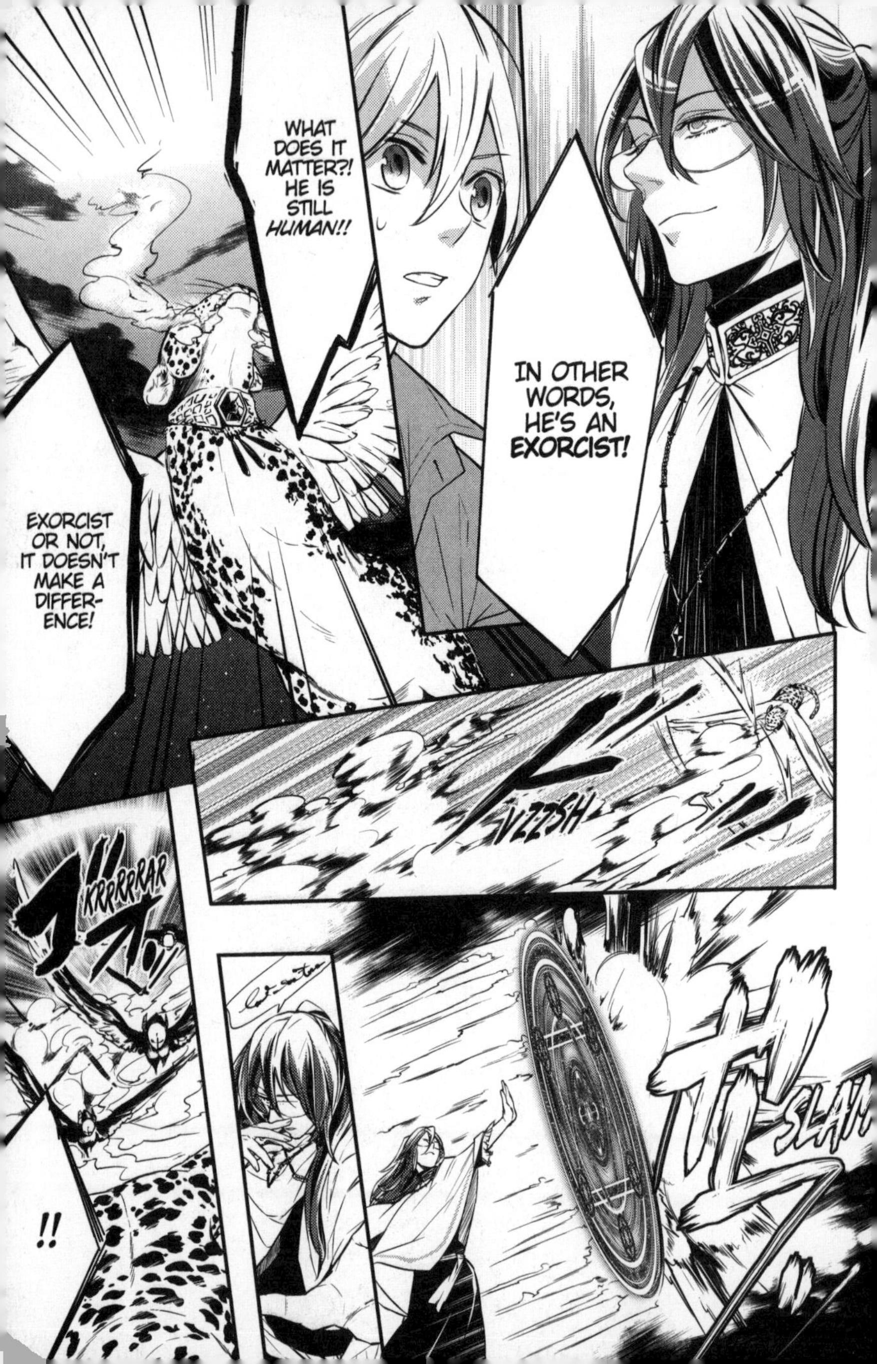
IN OTHER WORDS, HE'S AN EXORCIST!
WHAT DOES IT MATTER?! HE IS STILL HUMAN!!
EXORCIST OR NOT, IT DOESN'T MAKE A DIFFER-ENCE!
VZZSH
KRRRRRAR
SLAM
!!

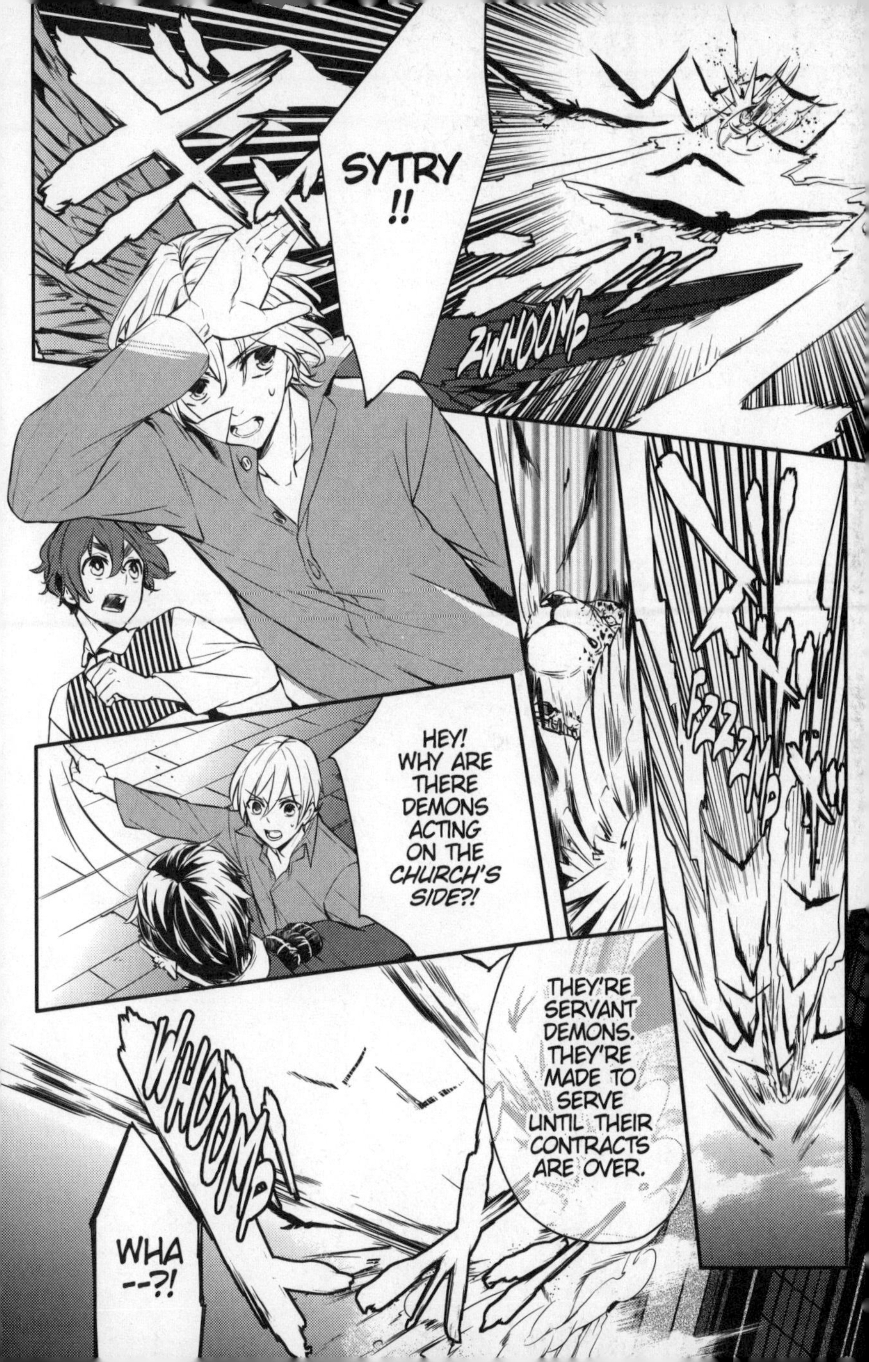
SYTRY !!
ZWHOOM
FZZZM
HEY! WHY ARE THERE DEMONS ACTING ON THE CHURCH'S SIDE?!
THEY'RE SERVANT DEMONS. THEY'RE MADE TO SERVE UNTIL THEIR CONTRACTS ARE OVER.
WHOOM
WHA --?!

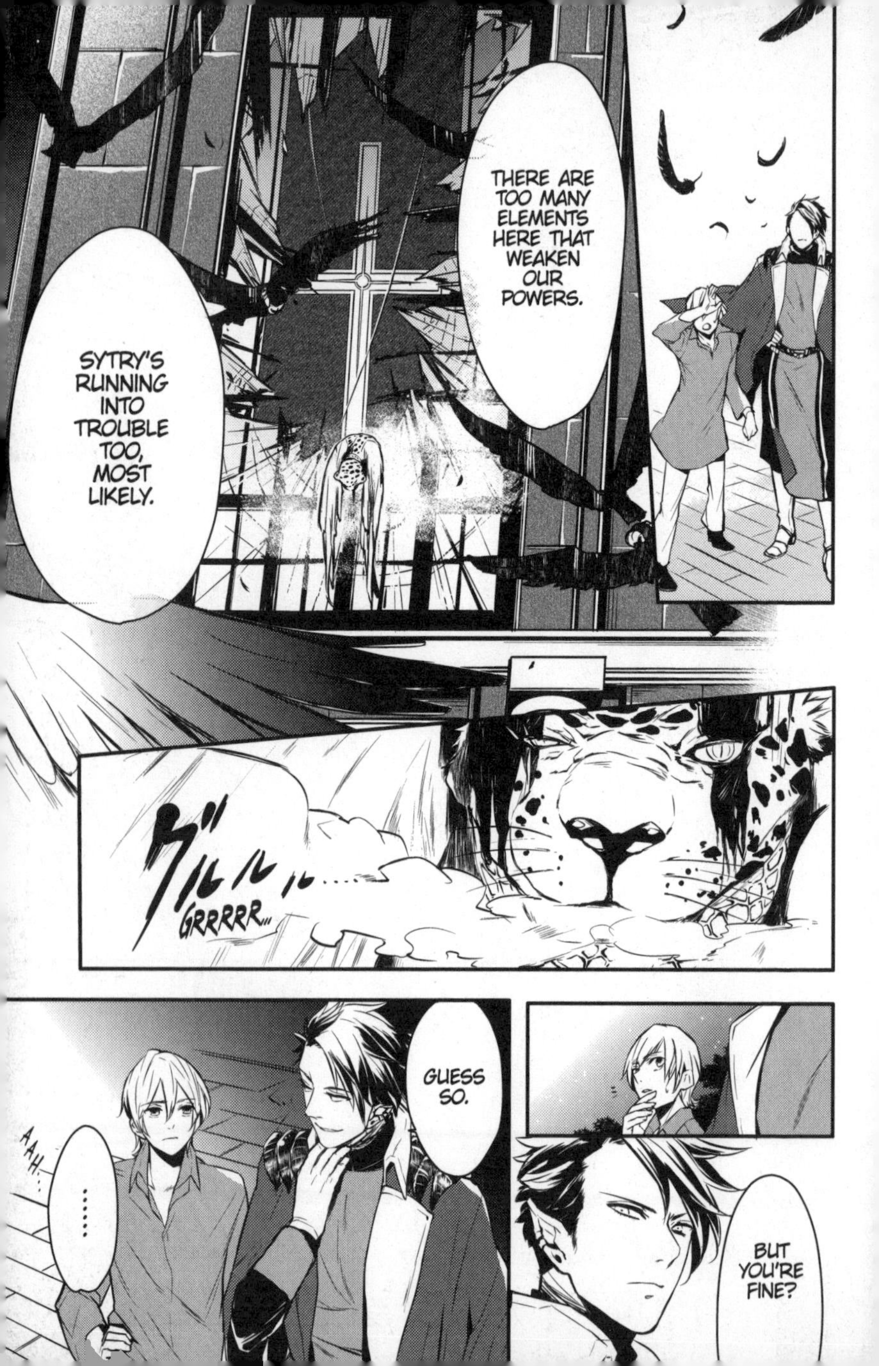
THERE ARE TOO MANY ELEMENTS HERE THAT WEAKEN OUR POWERS.
SYTRY'S RUNNING INTO TROUBLE TOO, MOST LIKELY.
ヴルル....
GRRRRR...
BUT YOU'RE FINE?
GUESS SO.
......
AAH...

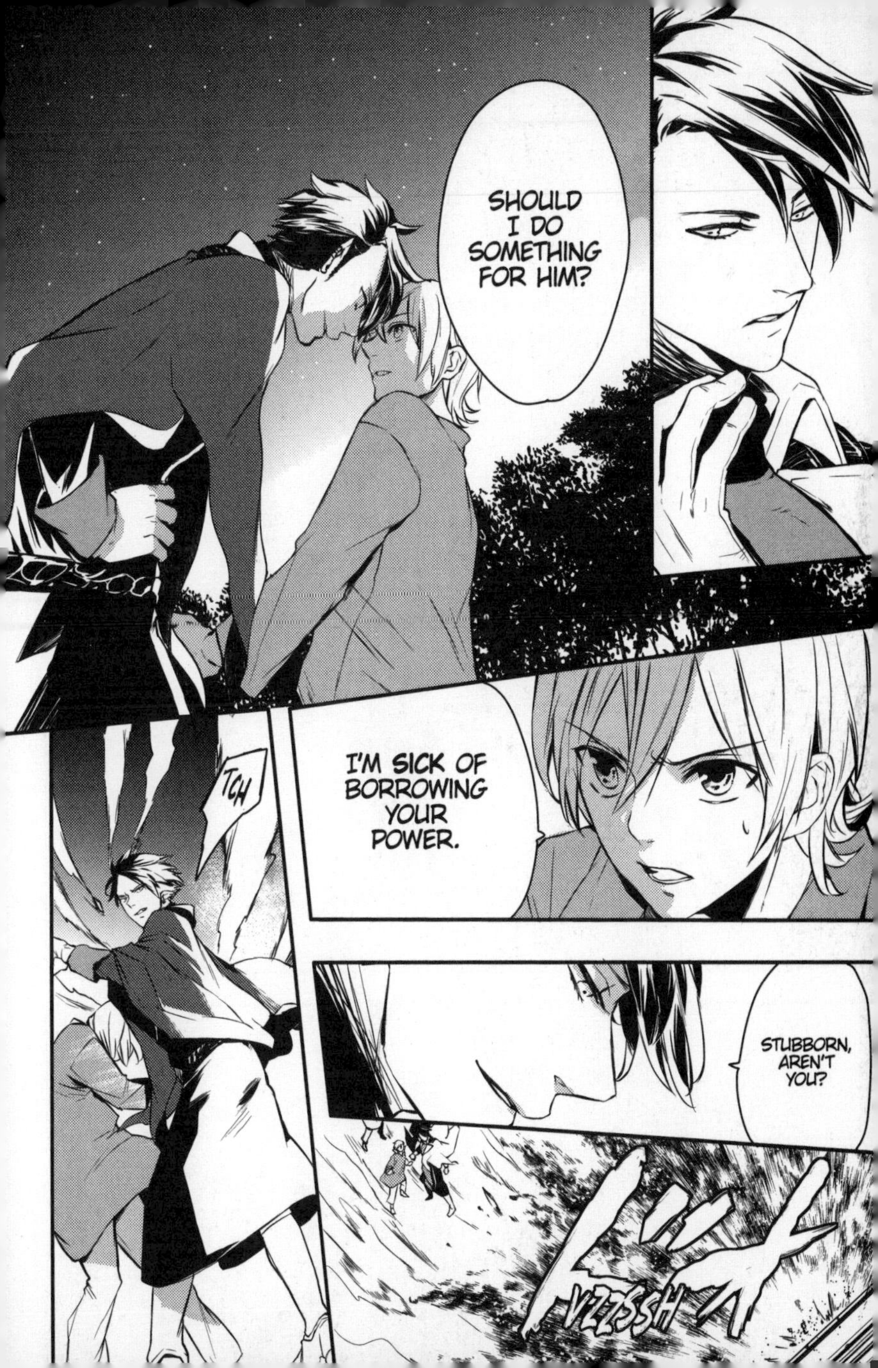
SHOULD I DO SOMETHING FOR HIM?
I'M SICK OF BORROWING YOUR POWER.
STUBBORN, AREN'T YOU?
VZZSSH
TCH

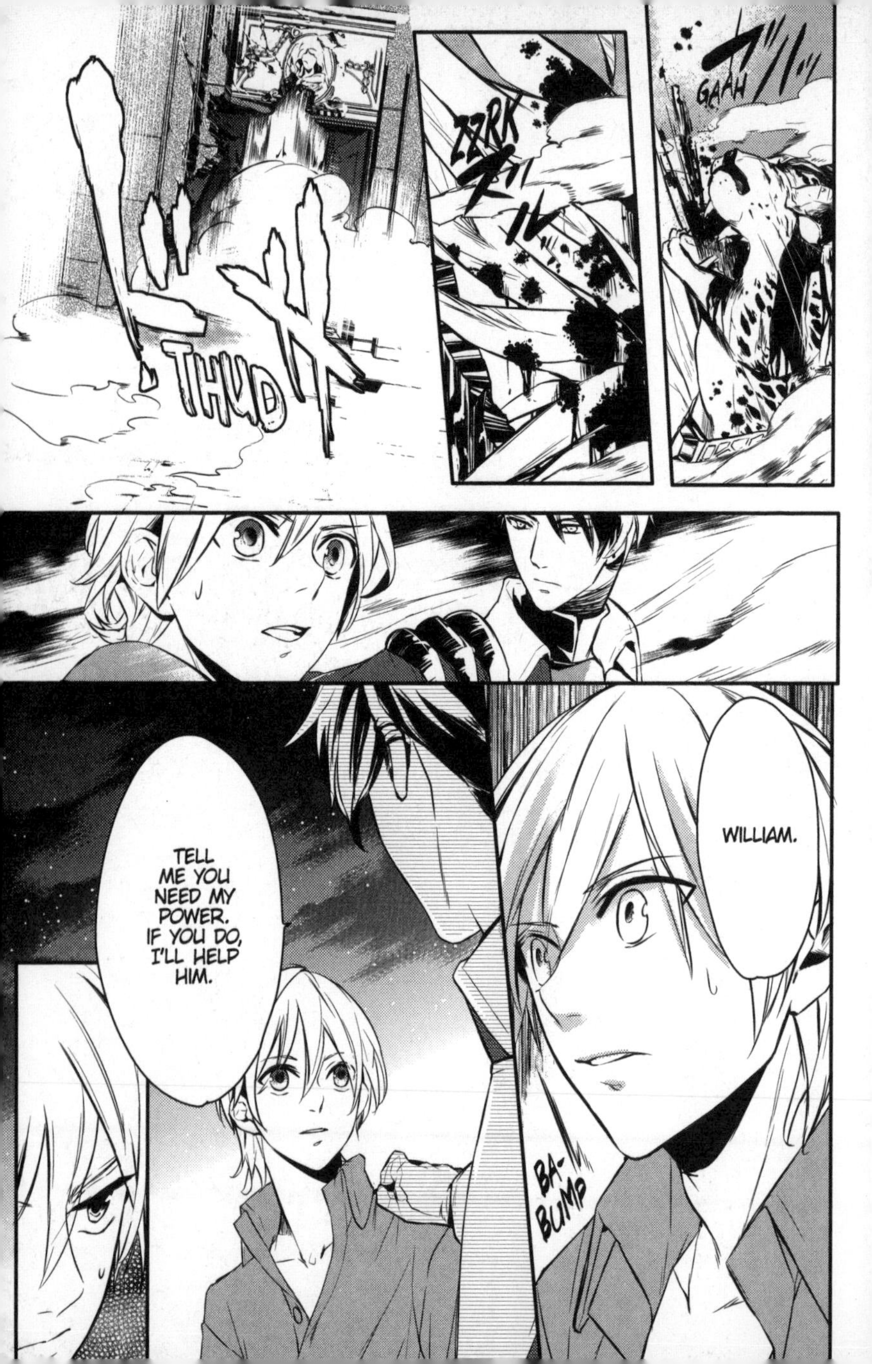
GAAH
ZZRK
THUD
WILLIAM.
BA-BUMP
TELL ME YOU NEED MY POWER. IF YOU DO, I'LL HELP HIM.

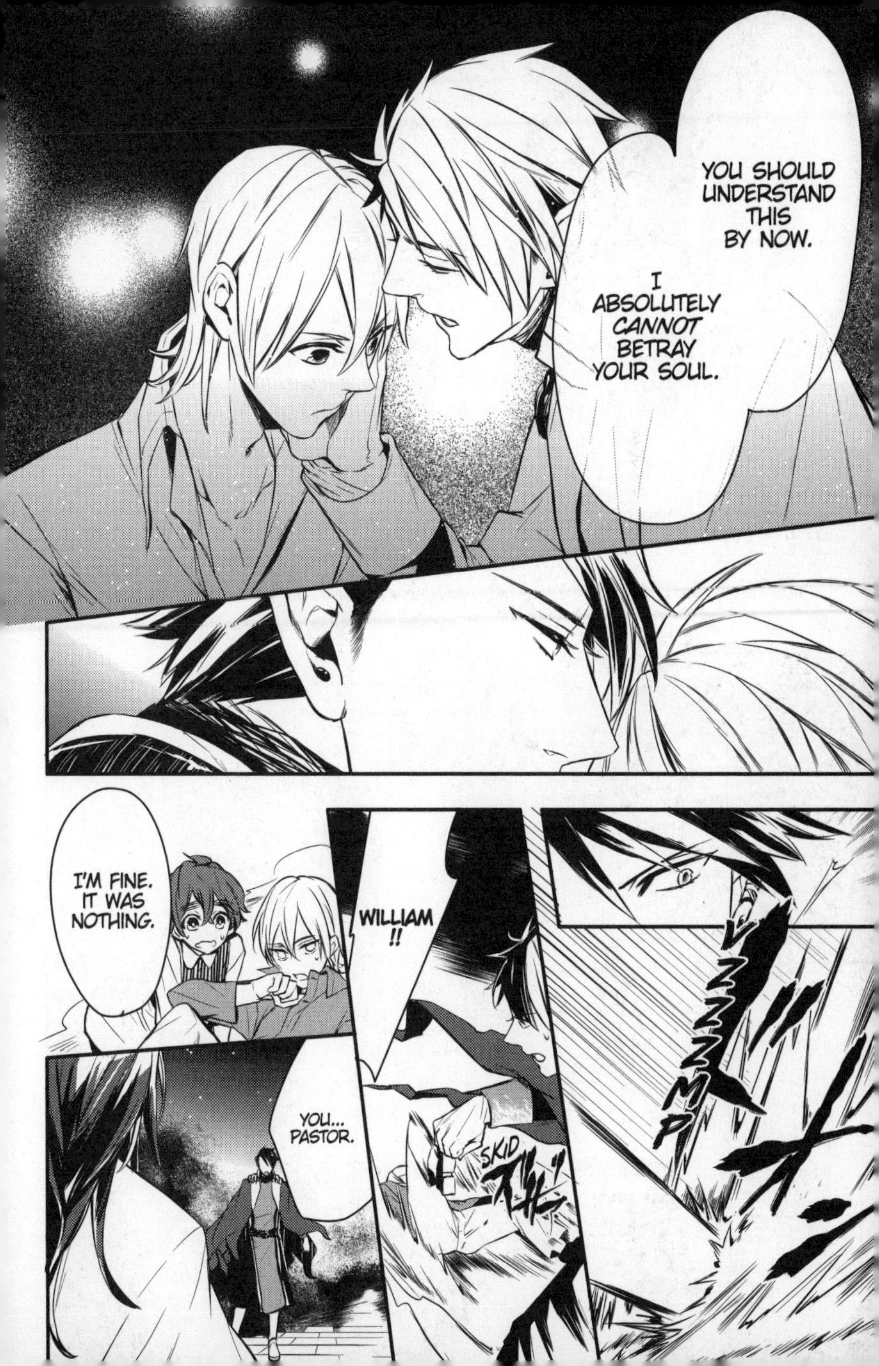
YOU SHOULD UNDERSTAND THIS BY NOW.
I ABSOLUTELY *CANNOT* BETRAY YOUR SOUL.
VZZZZMP
SKID
WILLIAM!!
I'M FINE. IT WAS NOTHING.
YOU... PASTOR.

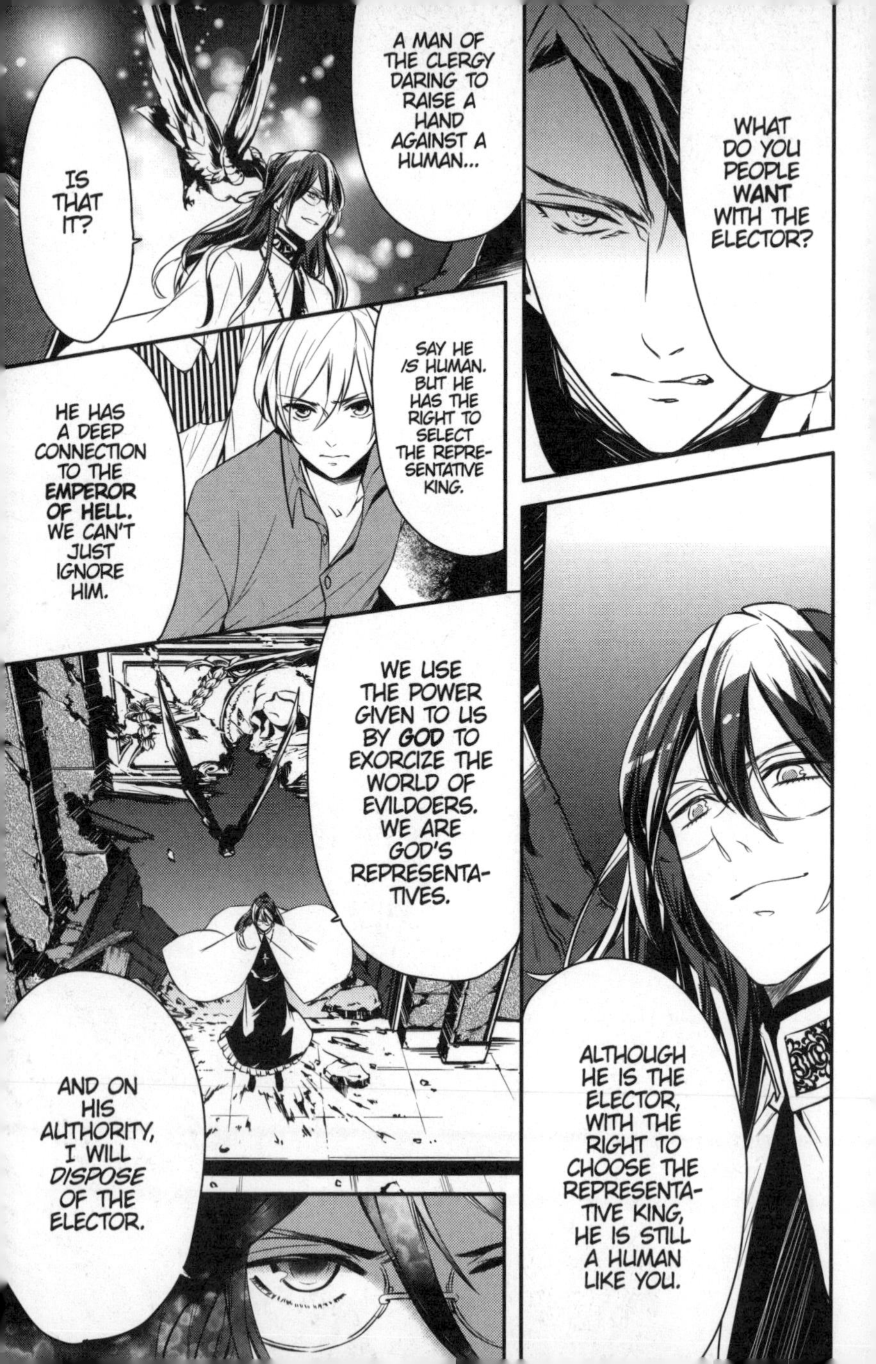
WHAT DO YOU PEOPLE **WANT** WITH THE ELECTOR?
A MAN OF THE CLERGY DARING TO RAISE A HAND AGAINST A HUMAN...
IS THAT IT?
SAY HE *IS* HUMAN. BUT HE HAS THE RIGHT TO SELECT THE REPRE-SENTATIVE KING.
HE HAS A DEEP CONNECTION TO THE **EMPEROR OF HELL.** WE CAN'T JUST IGNORE HIM.
ALTHOUGH HE IS THE ELECTOR, WITH THE RIGHT TO CHOOSE THE REPRESENTA-TIVE KING, HE IS STILL A HUMAN LIKE YOU.
WE USE THE POWER GIVEN TO US BY **GOD** TO EXORCIZE THE WORLD OF EVILDOERS. WE ARE GOD'S REPRESENTA-TIVES.
AND ON HIS AUTHORITY, I WILL *DISPOSE* OF THE ELECTOR.

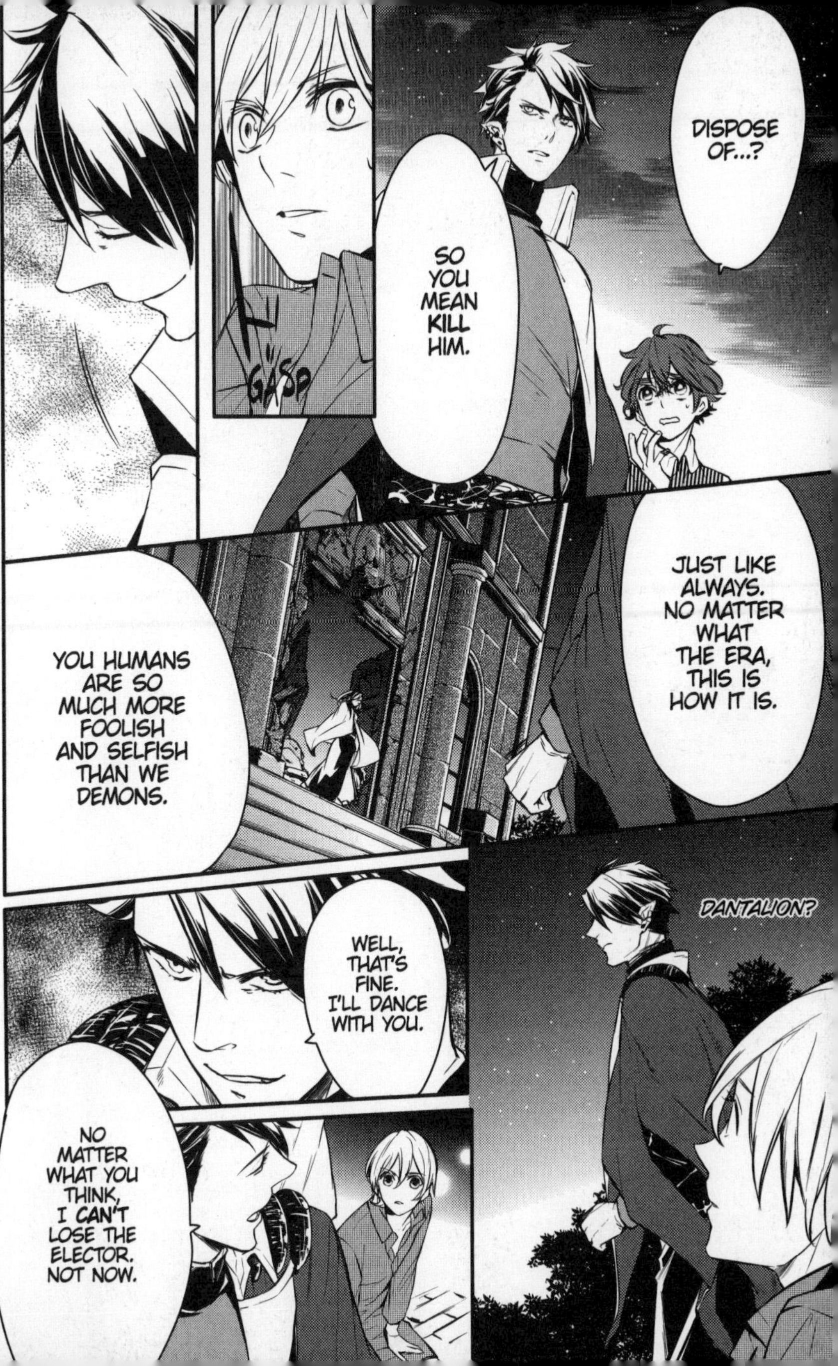
DISPOSE OF...?
SO YOU MEAN KILL HIM.
GASP
JUST LIKE ALWAYS. NO MATTER WHAT THE ERA, THIS IS HOW IT IS.
YOU HUMANS ARE SO MUCH MORE FOOLISH AND SELFISH THAN WE DEMONS.
DANTALION?
WELL, THAT'S FINE. I'LL DANCE WITH YOU.
NO MATTER WHAT YOU THINK, I CAN'T LOSE THE ELECTOR. NOT NOW.

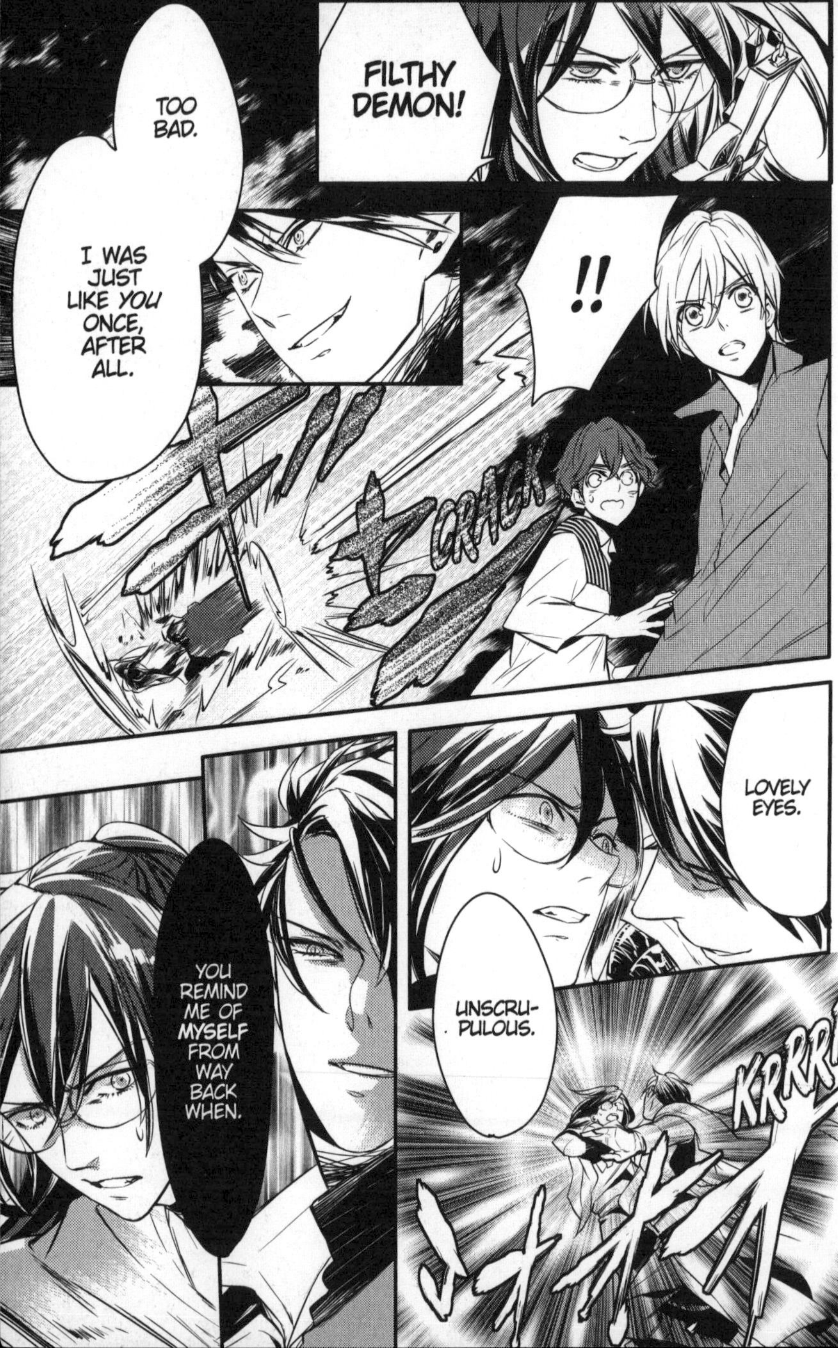
FILTHY DEMON!
TOO BAD.
I WAS JUST LIKE *YOU* ONCE, AFTER ALL.
!!
CRACK
LOVELY EYES.
UNSCRU-PULOUS.
KRRRR
YOU REMIND ME OF MYSELF FROM WAY BACK WHEN.

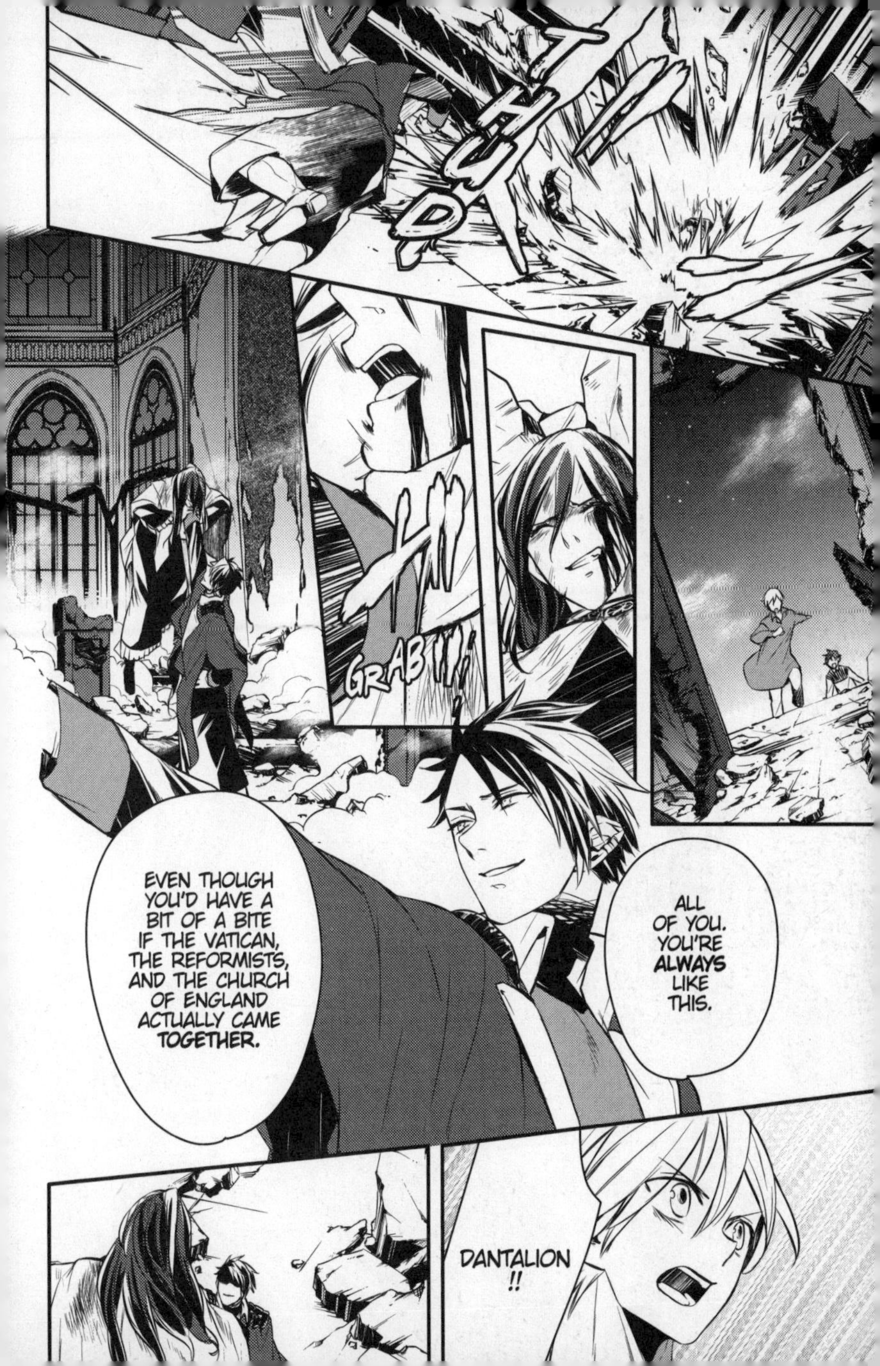
THUD
GRAB!!
ALL OF YOU. YOU'RE **ALWAYS** LIKE THIS.
EVEN THOUGH YOU'D HAVE A BIT OF A BITE IF THE VATICAN, THE REFORMISTS, AND THE CHURCH OF ENGLAND ACTUALLY CAME **TOGETHER.**
DANTALION !!

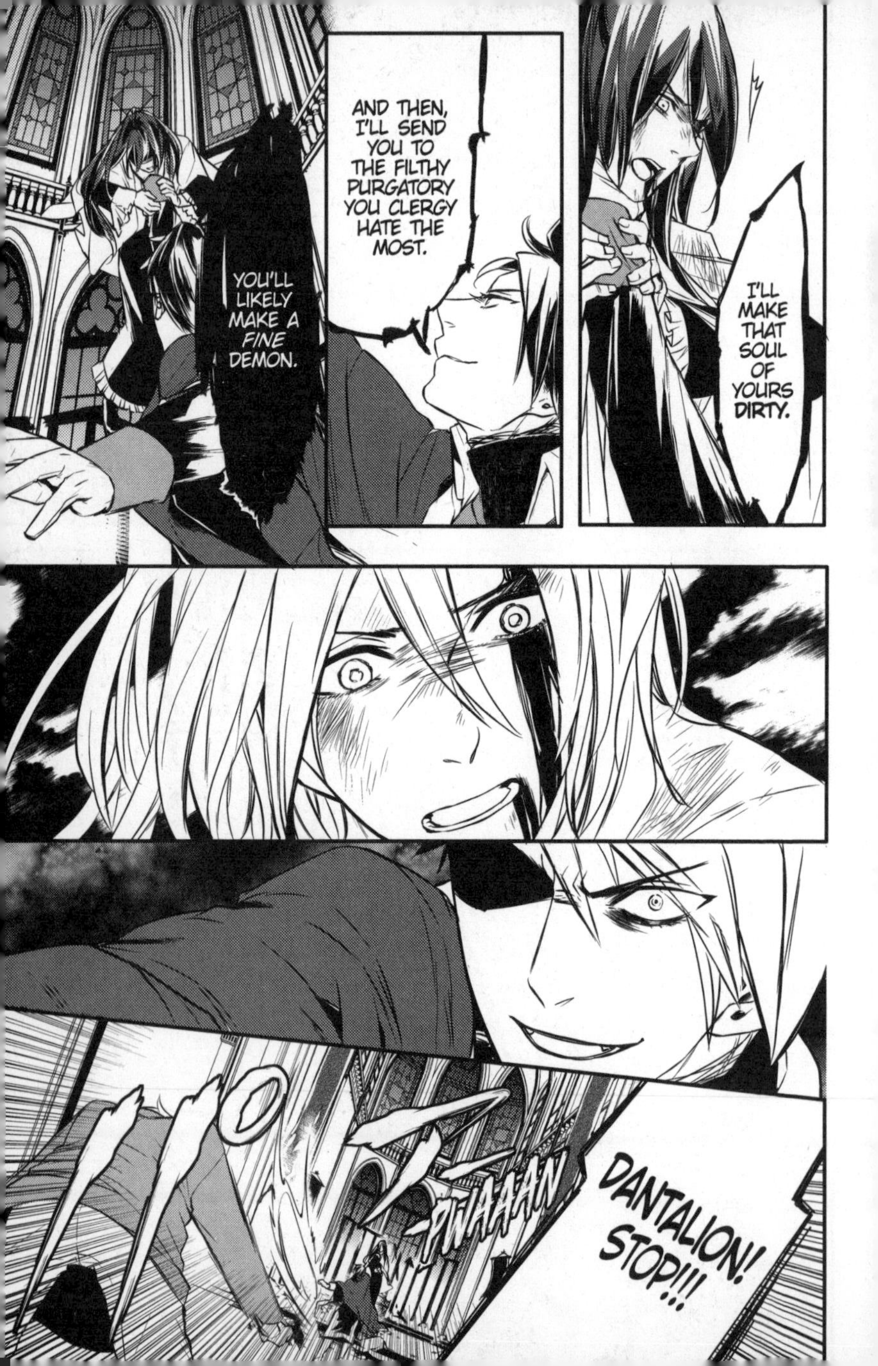
I'LL MAKE THAT SOUL OF YOURS DIRTY.
AND THEN, I'LL SEND YOU TO THE FILTHY PURGATORY YOU CLERGY HATE THE MOST.
YOU'LL LIKELY MAKE A *FINE* DEMON.
DANTALION! STOP!!!
PWAAAAN

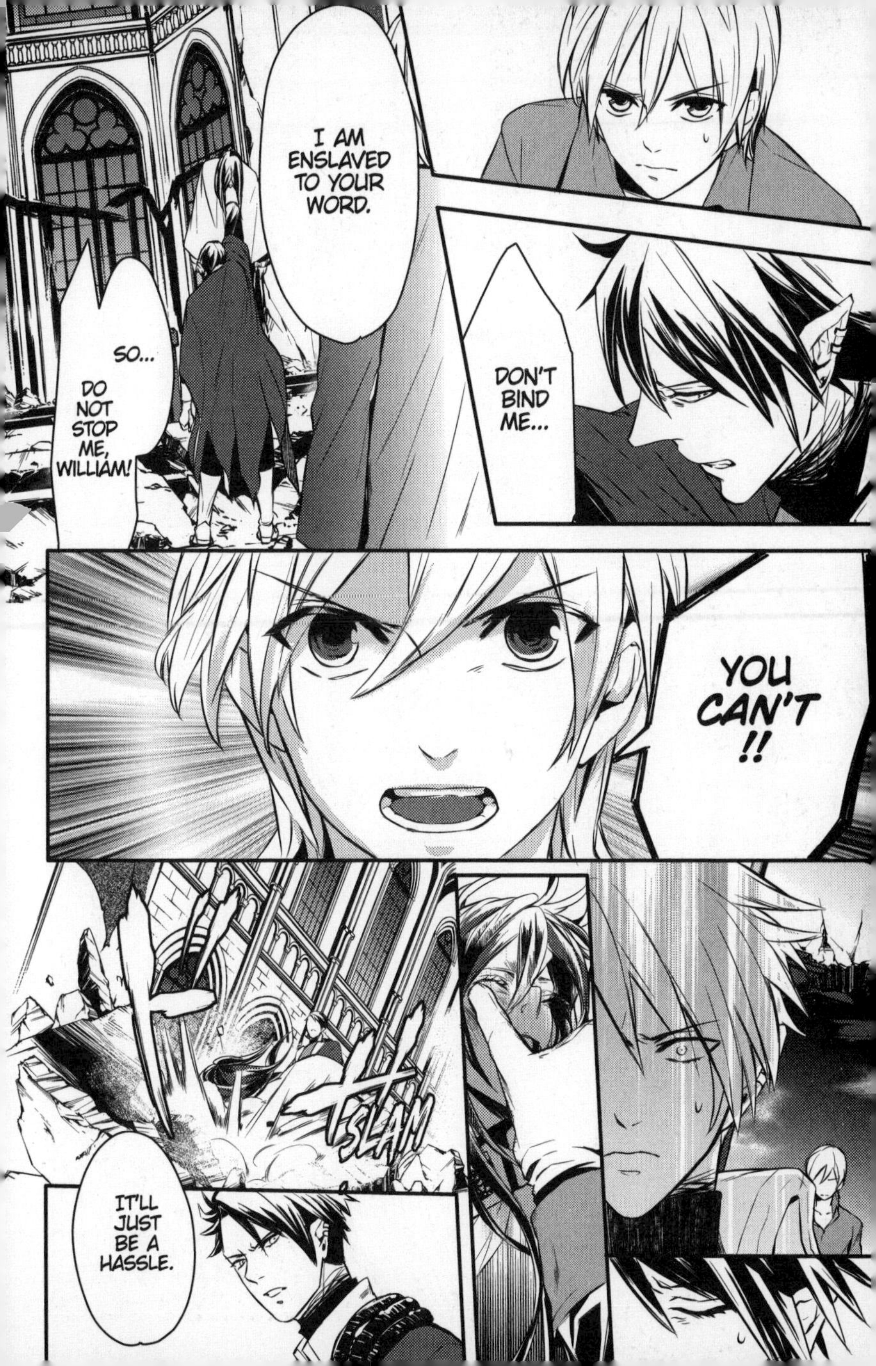
DON'T BIND ME...
I AM ENSLAVED TO YOUR WORD.
SO... DO NOT STOP ME, WILLIAM!
YOU CAN'T!!
SLAM
IT'LL JUST BE A HASSLE.

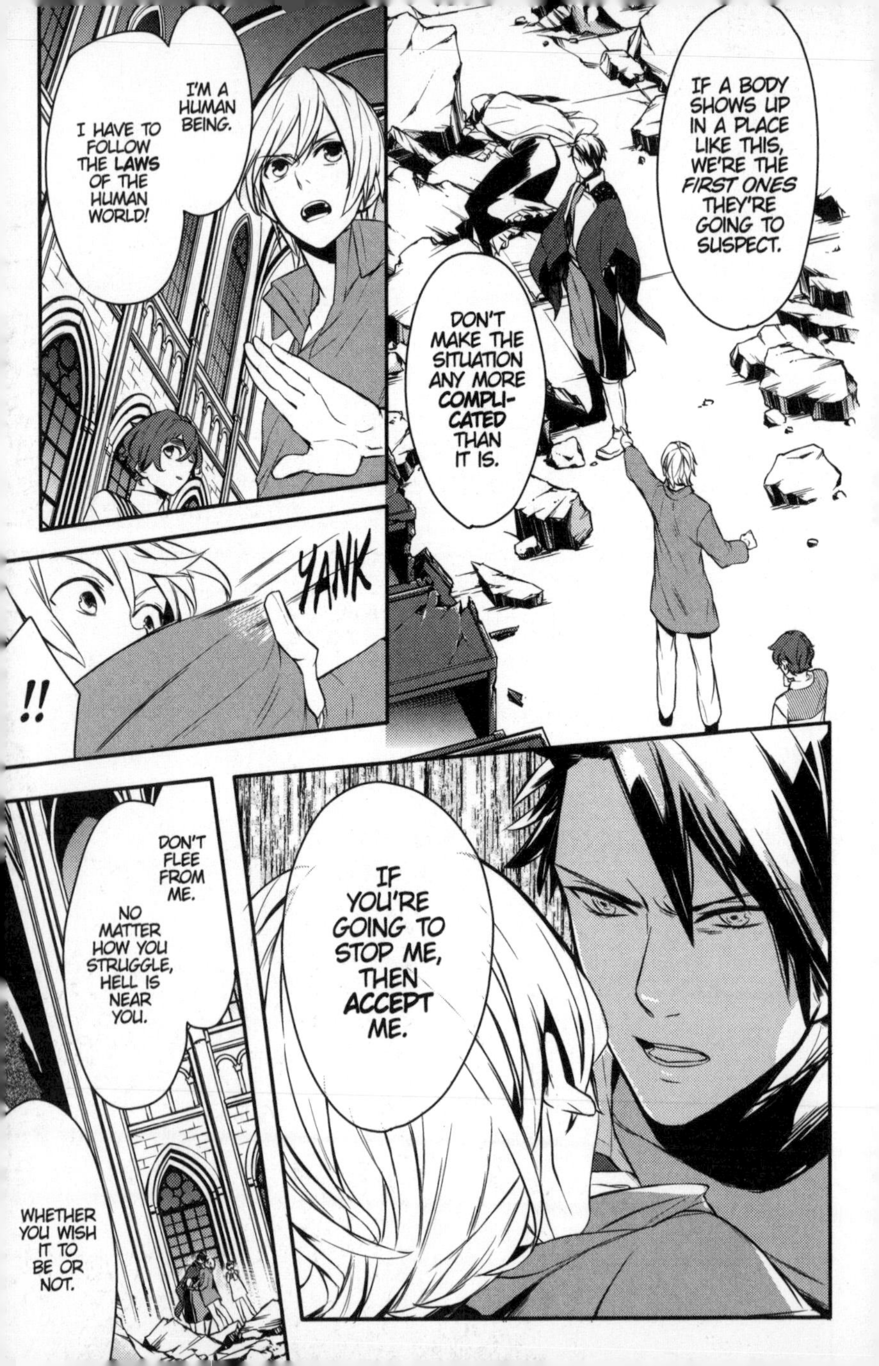
IF A BODY SHOWS UP IN A PLACE LIKE THIS, WE'RE THE *FIRST ONES* THEY'RE GOING TO SUSPECT.
DON'T MAKE THE SITUATION ANY MORE **COMPLICATED** THAN IT IS.
I'M A HUMAN BEING.
I HAVE TO FOLLOW THE **LAWS** OF THE HUMAN WORLD!
YANK
!!
IF YOU'RE GOING TO STOP ME, THEN **ACCEPT** ME.
DON'T FLEE FROM ME.
NO MATTER HOW YOU STRUGGLE, HELL IS NEAR YOU.
WHETHER YOU WISH IT TO BE OR NOT.

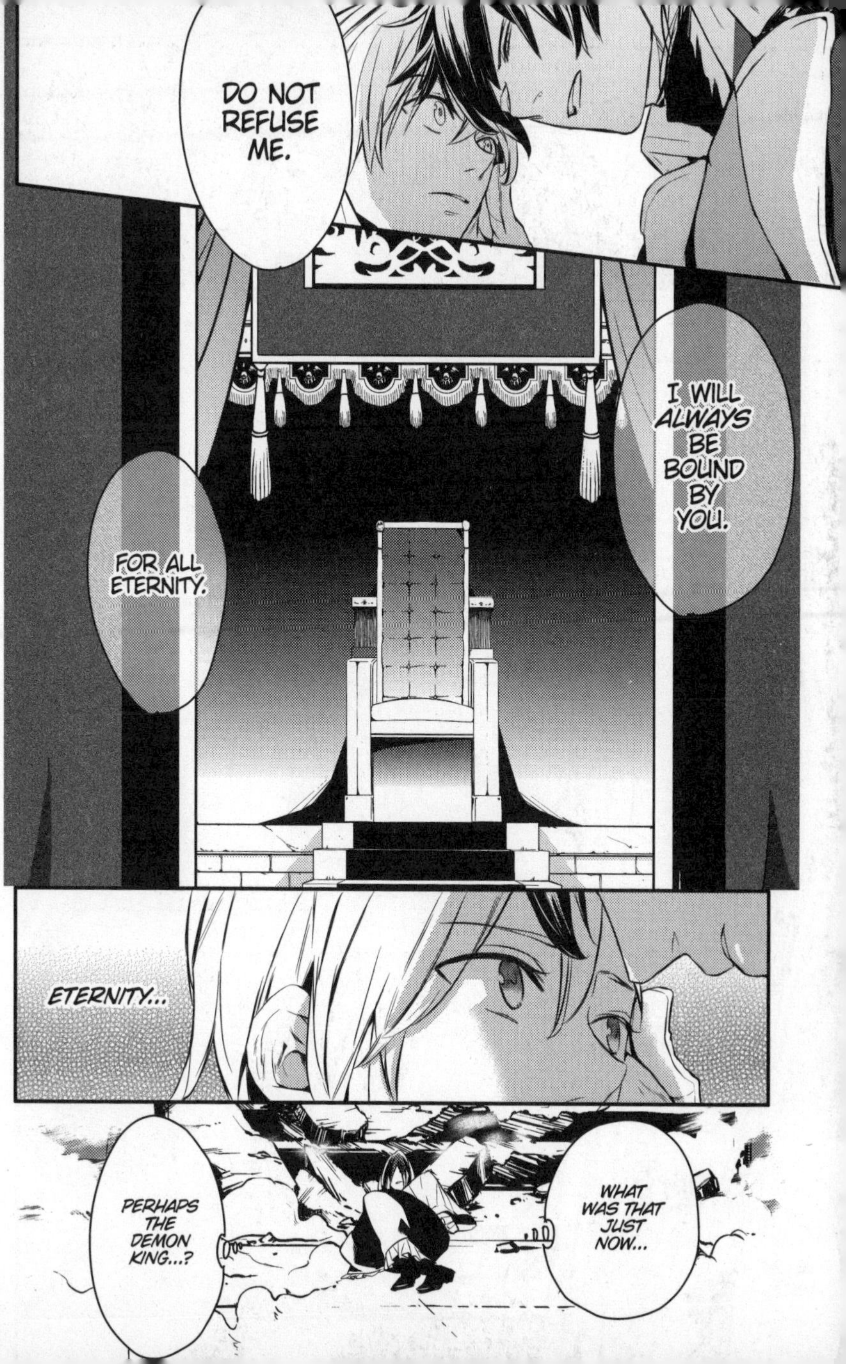
DO NOT REFUSE ME.
I WILL ALWAYS BE BOUND BY YOU.
FOR ALL ETERNITY.
ETERNITY...
WHAT WAS THAT JUST NOW...
PERHAPS THE DEMON KING...?

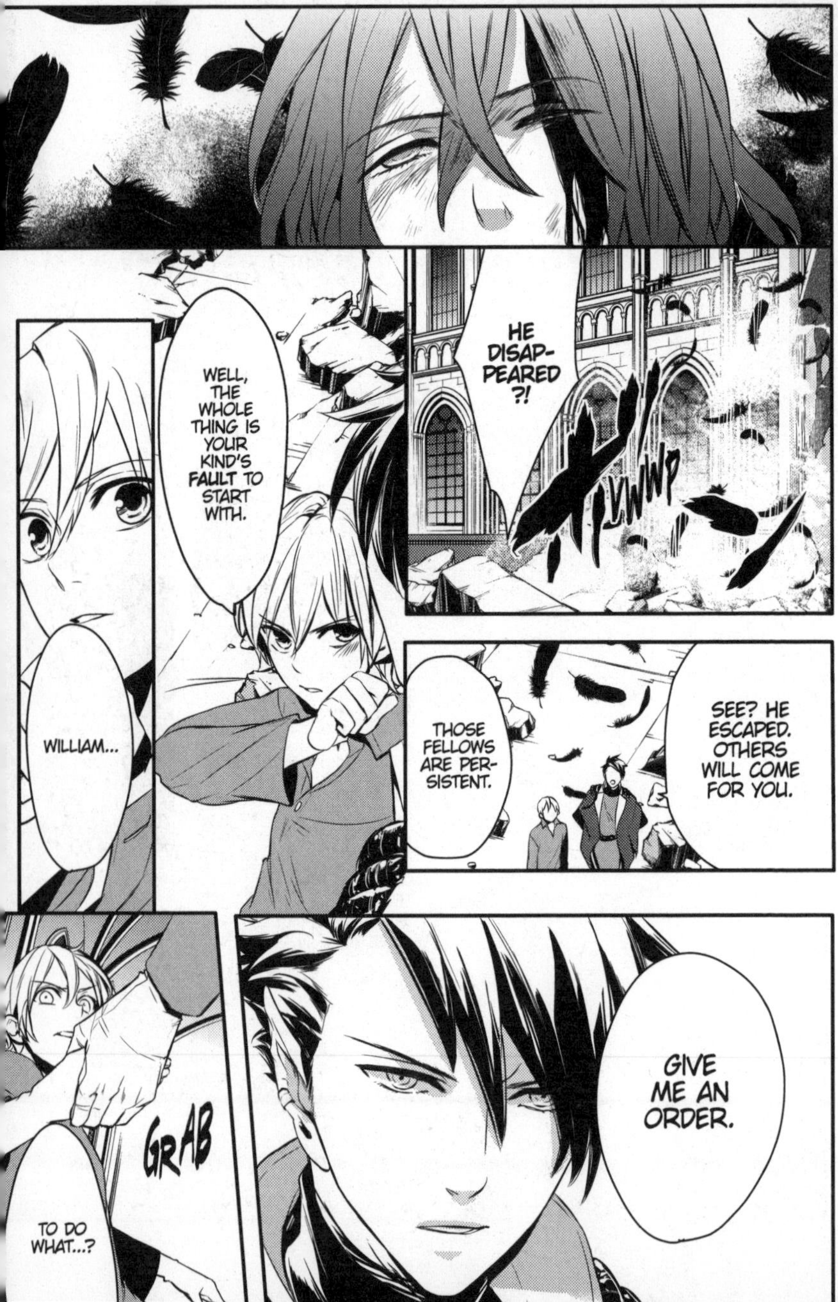
HE DISAPPEARED?!
VWWP
SEE? HE ESCAPED. OTHERS WILL COME FOR YOU.
THOSE FELLOWS ARE PERSISTENT.
WELL, THE WHOLE THING IS YOUR KIND'S FAULT TO START WITH.
WILLIAM...
GIVE ME AN ORDER.
GRAB
TO DO WHAT...?

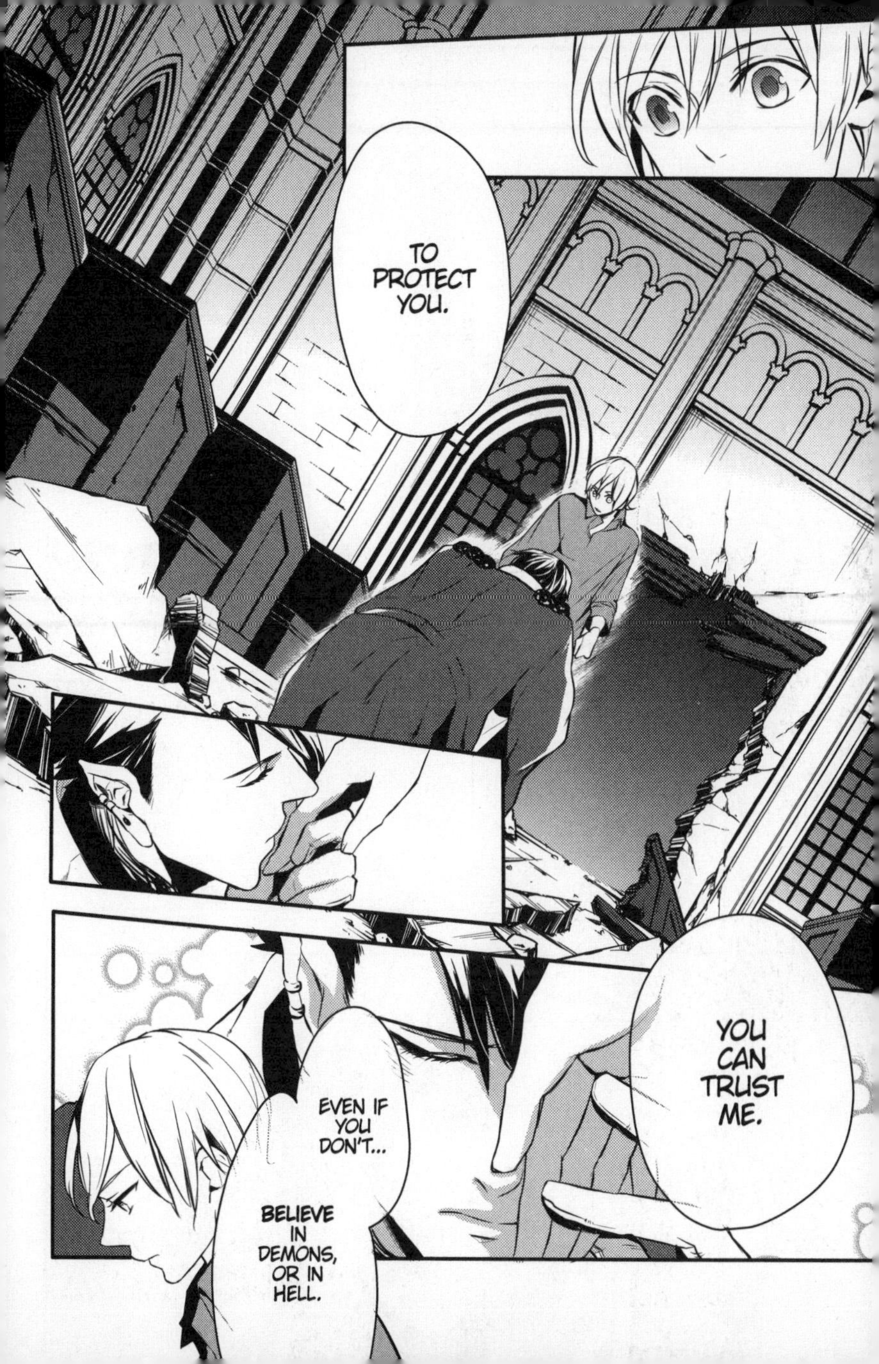
TO PROTECT YOU.
YOU CAN TRUST ME.
EVEN IF YOU DON'T...
BELIEVE IN DEMONS, OR IN HELL.

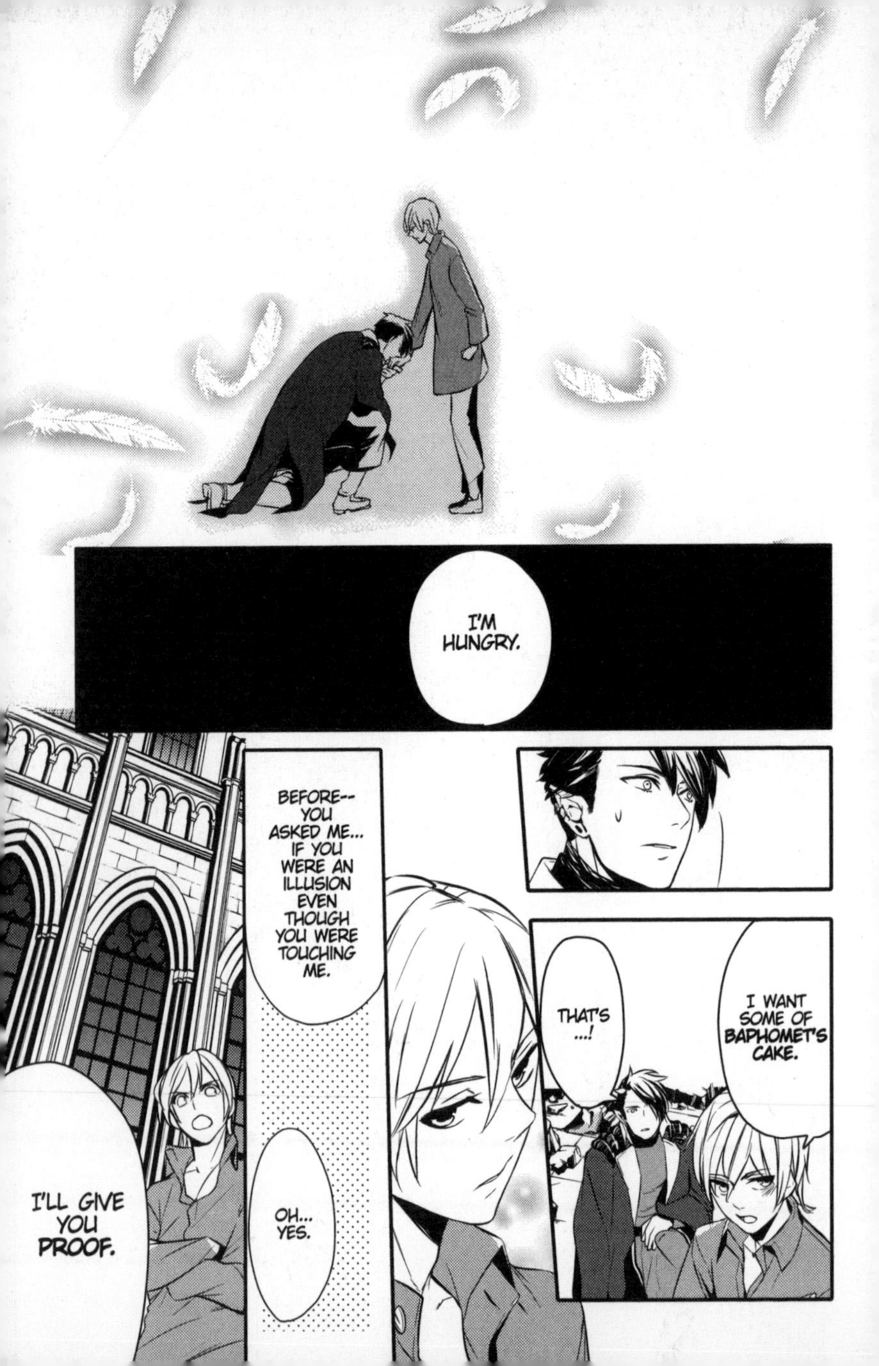
I'M HUNGRY.
I WANT SOME OF BAPHOMET'S CAKE.
THAT'S ...!
BEFORE-- YOU ASKED ME... IF YOU WERE AN ILLUSION EVEN THOUGH YOU WERE TOUCHING ME.
OH... YES.
I'LL GIVE YOU PROOF.

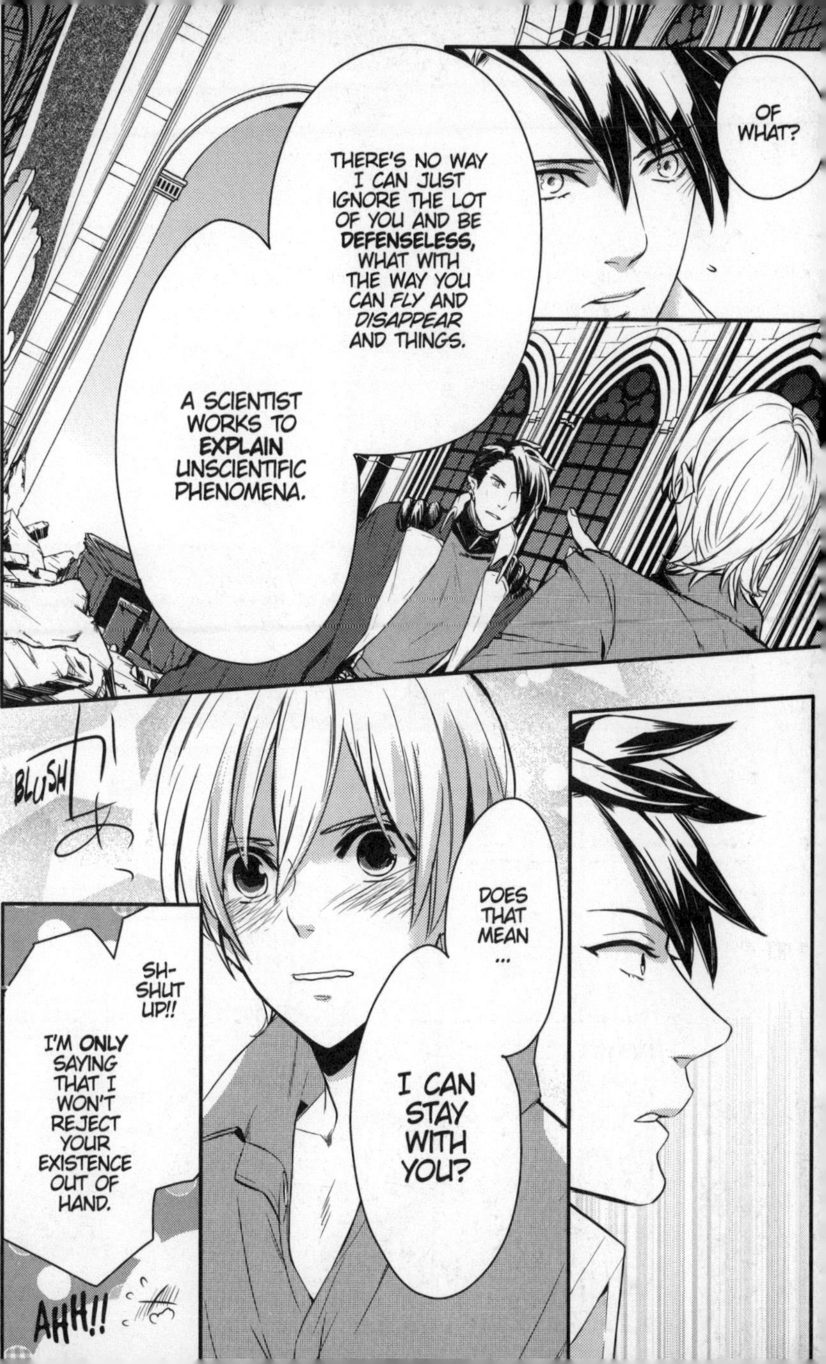
OF WHAT?
THERE'S NO WAY I CAN JUST IGNORE THE LOT OF YOU AND BE DEFENSELESS, WHAT WITH THE WAY YOU CAN FLY AND DISAPPEAR AND THINGS.
A SCIENTIST WORKS TO EXPLAIN UNSCIENTIFIC PHENOMENA.
DOES THAT MEAN...
I CAN STAY WITH YOU?
BLUSH
SH-SHUT UP!!
I'M ONLY SAYING THAT I WON'T REJECT YOUR EXISTENCE OUT OF HAND.
AHH!!

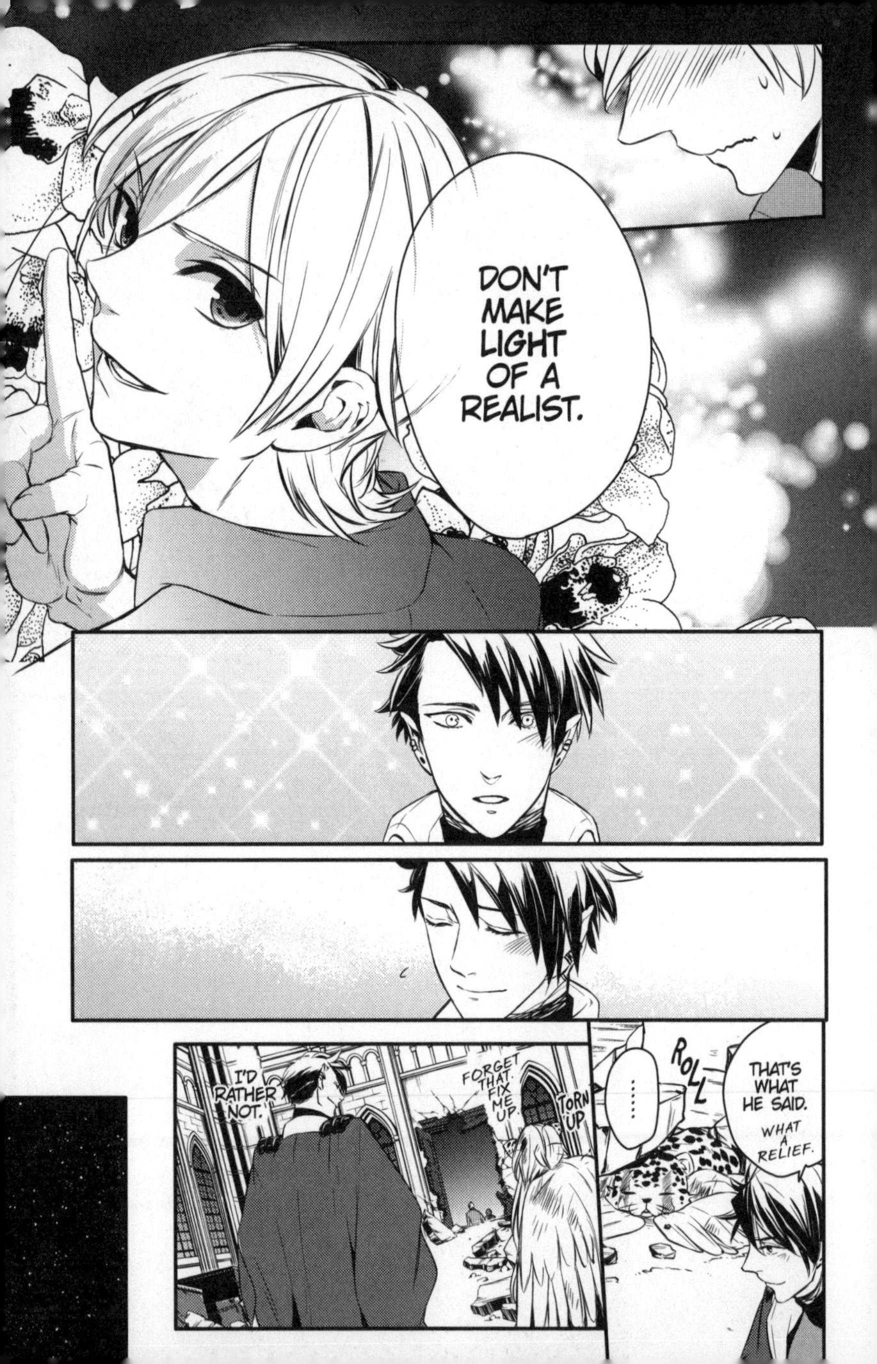
DON'T MAKE LIGHT OF A REALIST.
THAT'S WHAT HE SAID.
WHAT A RELIEF.
ROLL
......
FORGET THAT. FIX ME UP.
TORN UP
I'D RATHER NOT.

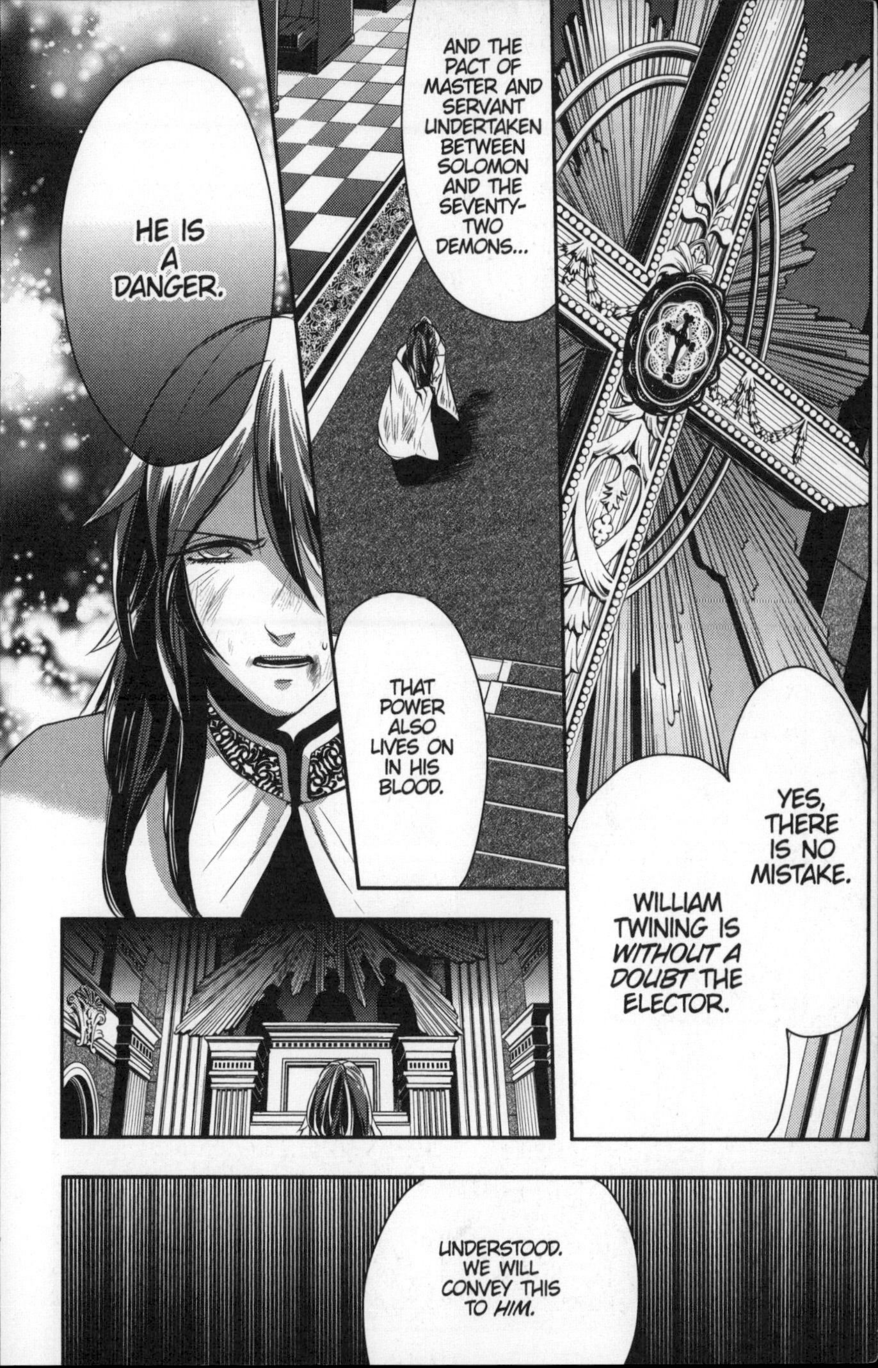
AND THE PACT OF MASTER AND SERVANT UNDERTAKEN BETWEEN SOLOMON AND THE SEVENTY-TWO DEMONS...
THAT POWER ALSO LIVES ON IN HIS BLOOD.
HE IS A DANGER.
YES, THERE IS NO MISTAKE.
WILLIAM TWINING IS *WITHOUT A DOUBT* THE ELECTOR.
UNDERSTOOD. WE WILL CONVEY THIS TO *HIM*.

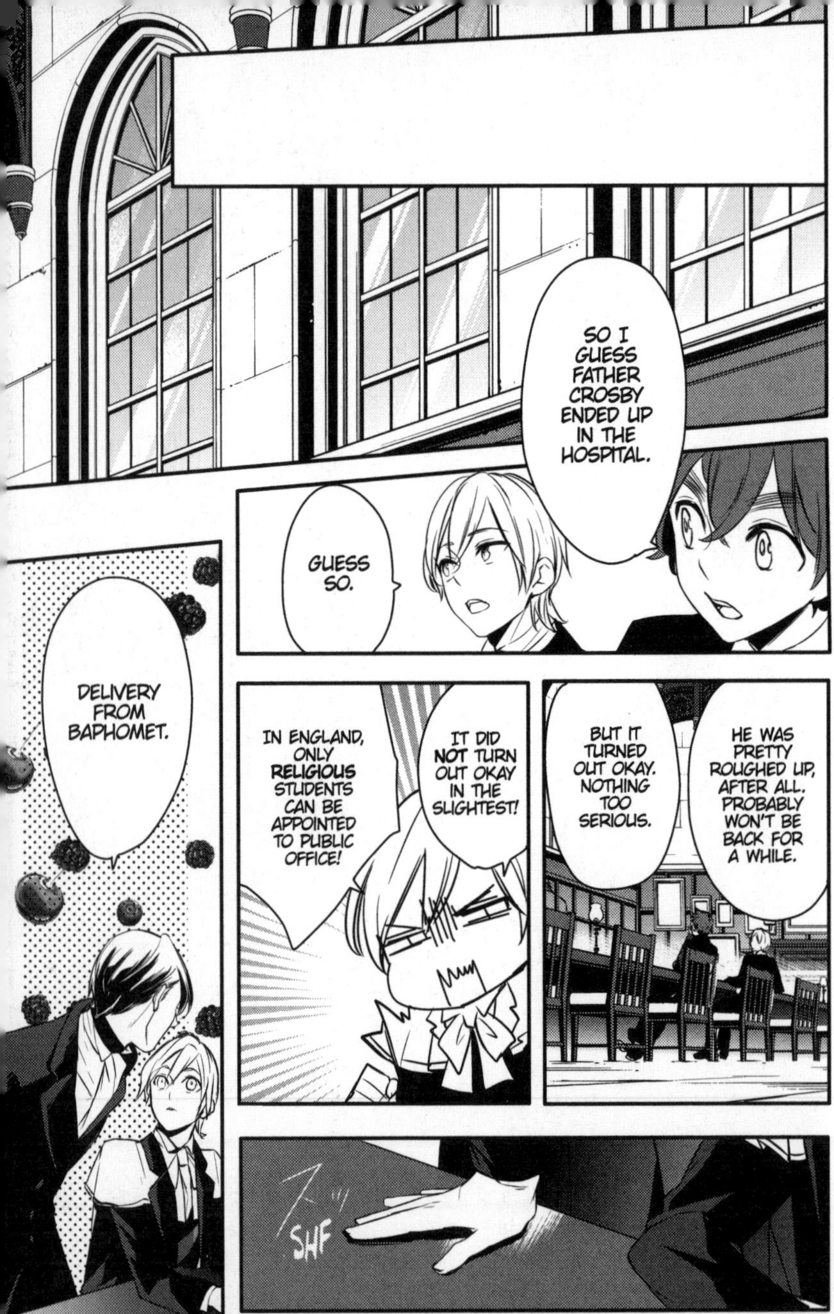
SO I GUESS FATHER CROSBY ENDED UP IN THE HOSPITAL.
GUESS SO.
HE WAS PRETTY ROUGHED UP, AFTER ALL. PROBABLY WON'T BE BACK FOR A WHILE.
BUT IT TURNED OUT OKAY. NOTHING TOO SERIOUS.
IT DID **NOT** TURN OUT OKAY IN THE SLIGHTEST!
IN ENGLAND, ONLY **RELIGIOUS** STUDENTS CAN BE APPOINTED TO PUBLIC OFFICE!
SHF
DELIVERY FROM BAPHOMET.

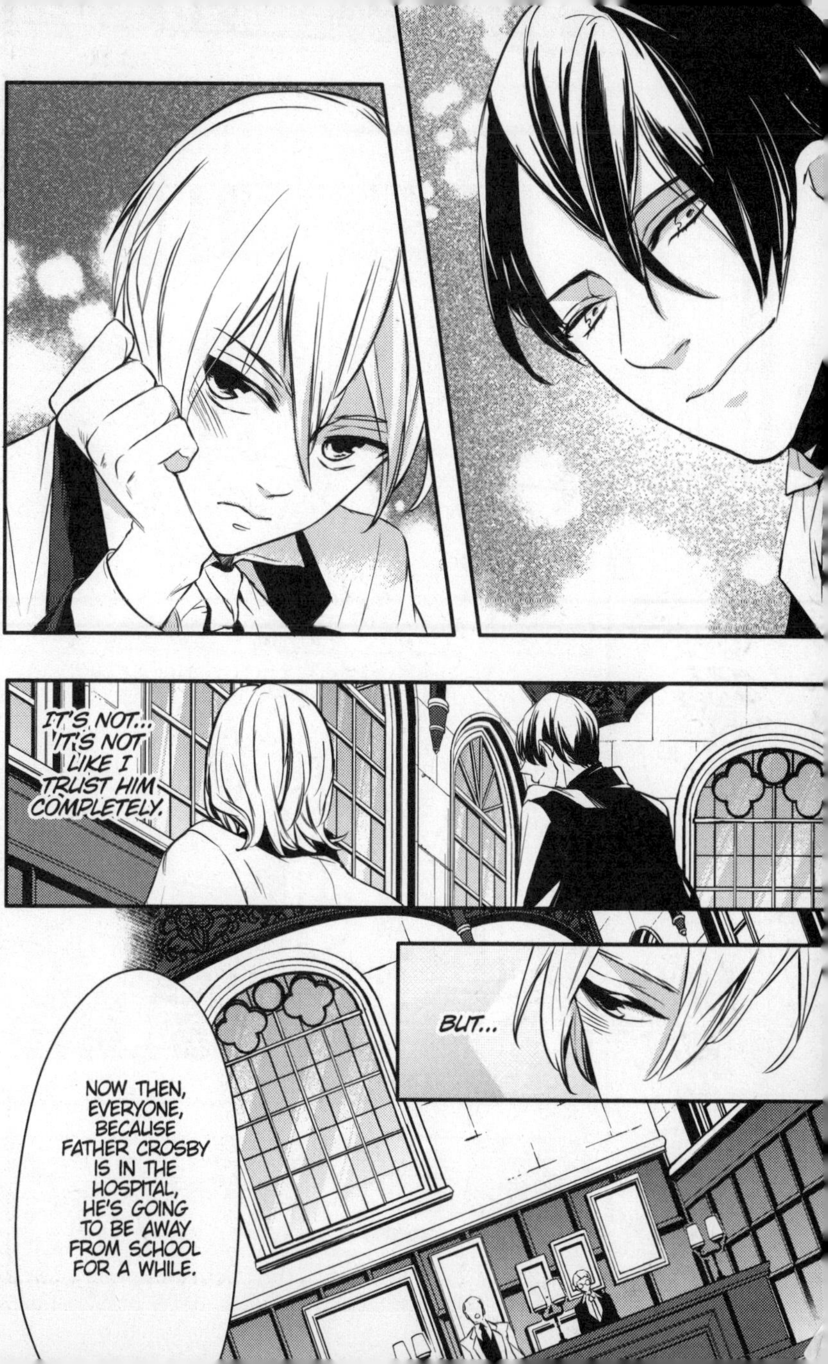
IT'S NOT... IT'S NOT LIKE I TRUST HIM COMPLETELY.
BUT...
NOW THEN, EVERYONE, BECAUSE FATHER CROSBY IS IN THE HOSPITAL, HE'S GOING TO BE AWAY FROM SCHOOL FOR A WHILE.

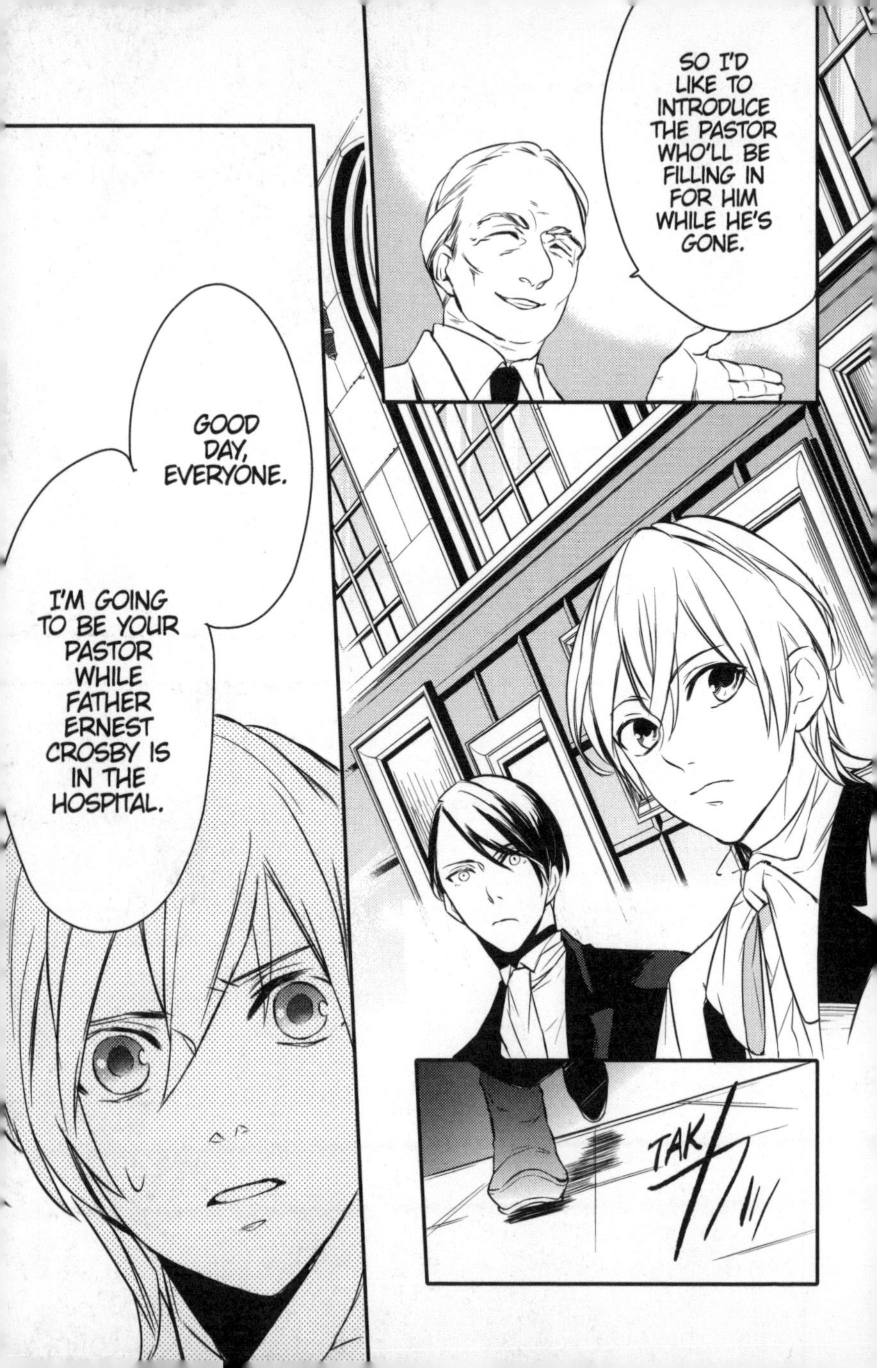
SO I'D LIKE TO INTRODUCE THE PASTOR WHO'LL BE FILLING IN FOR HIM WHILE HE'S GONE.
TAK
GOOD DAY, EVERYONE.
I'M GOING TO BE YOUR PASTOR WHILE FATHER ERNEST CROSBY IS IN THE HOSPITAL.

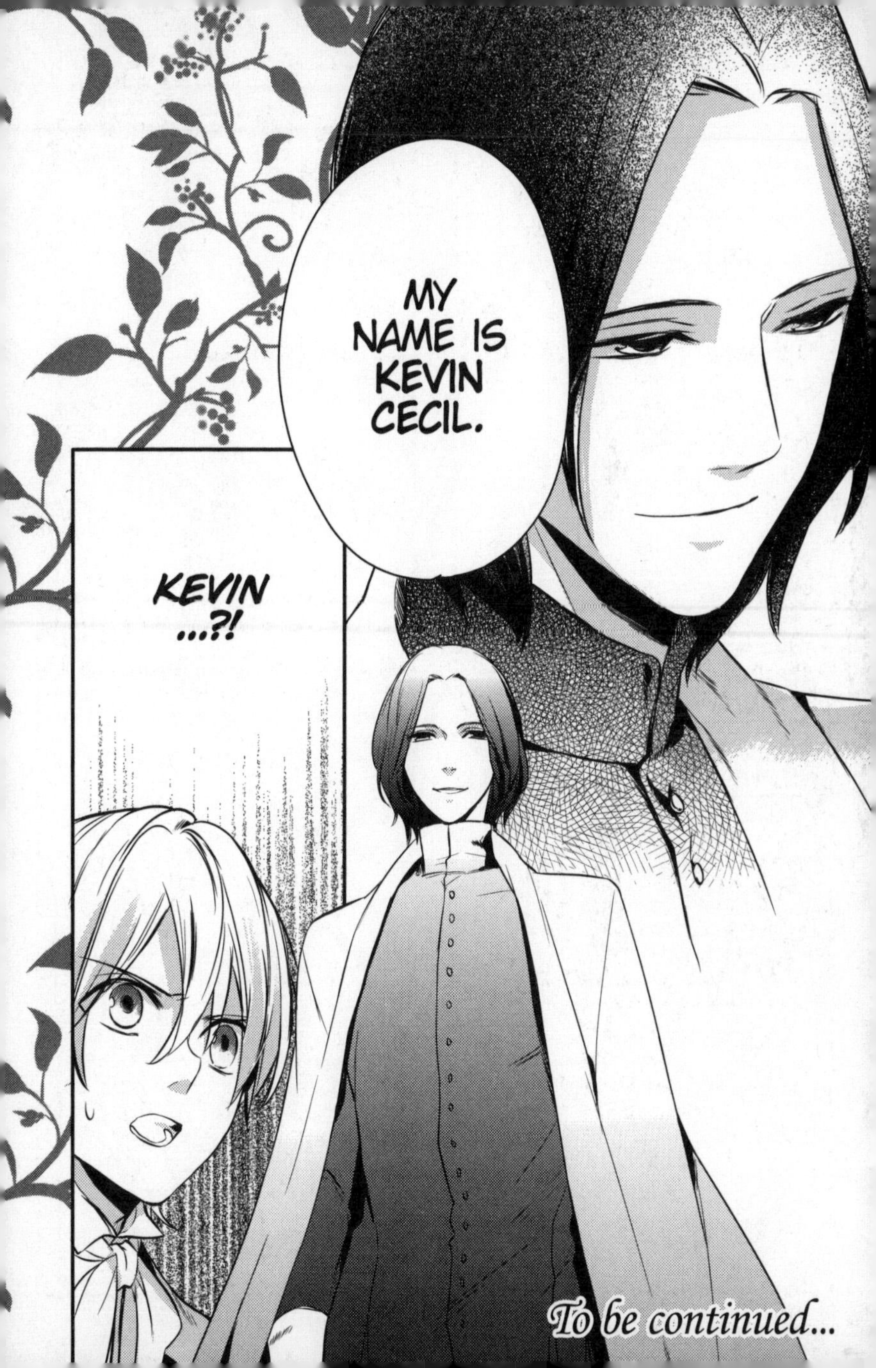
MY NAME IS KEVIN CECIL.
KEVIN ...?!
To be continued...

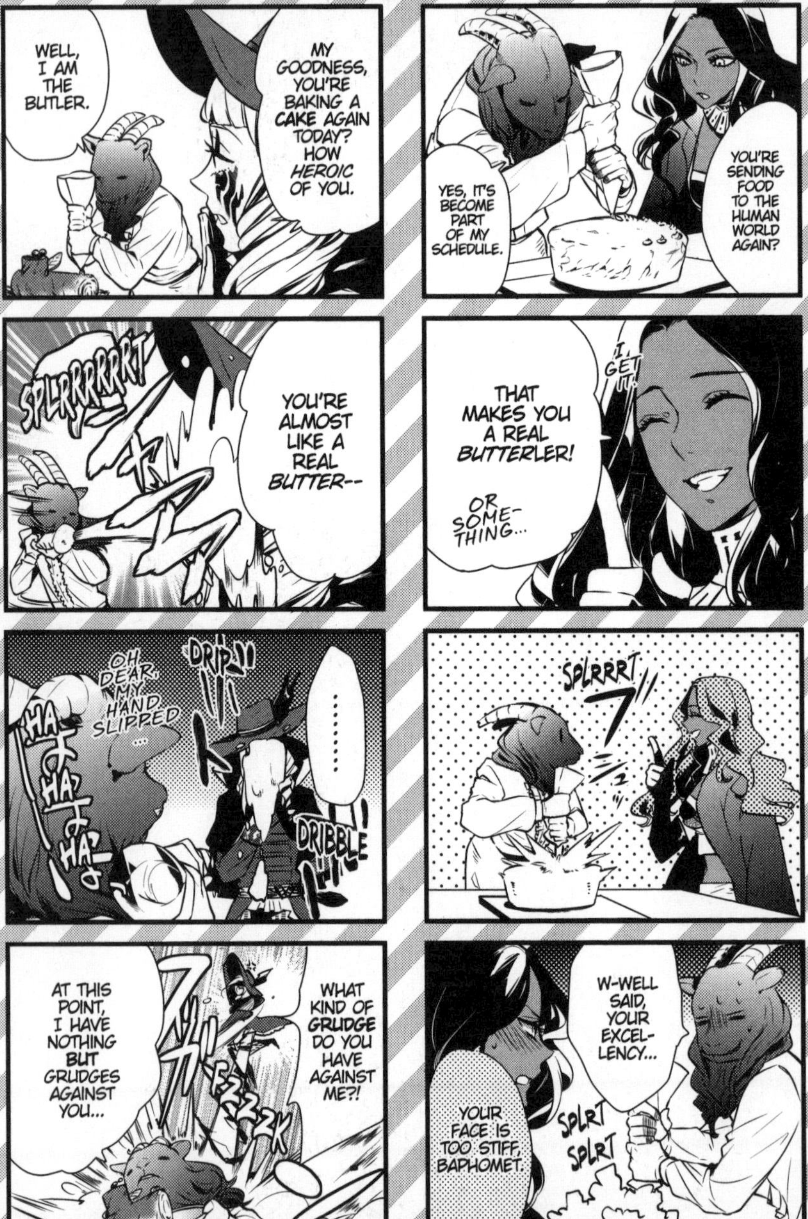
YOU'RE SENDING FOOD TO THE HUMAN WORLD AGAIN?
YES, IT'S BECOME PART OF MY SCHEDULE.
I GET IT.
THAT MAKES YOU A REAL BUTTERLER!
OR SOMETHING...
SPLRRRT
W-WELL SAID, YOUR EXCELLENCY...
YOUR FACE IS TOO STIFF, BAPHOMET.
SPLRT SPLRT
MY GOODNESS, YOU'RE BAKING A CAKE AGAIN TODAY? HOW HEROIC OF YOU.
WELL, I AM THE BUTLER.
YOU'RE ALMOST LIKE A REAL BUTTER--
SPLRRRRRRT
......
DRIP
DRIBBLE
OH DEAR, MY HAND SLIPPED...
HA HA HA
WHAT KIND OF GRUDGE DO YOU HAVE AGAINST ME?!
AT THIS POINT, I HAVE NOTHING BUT GRUDGES AGAINST YOU...
FZZZZK

END

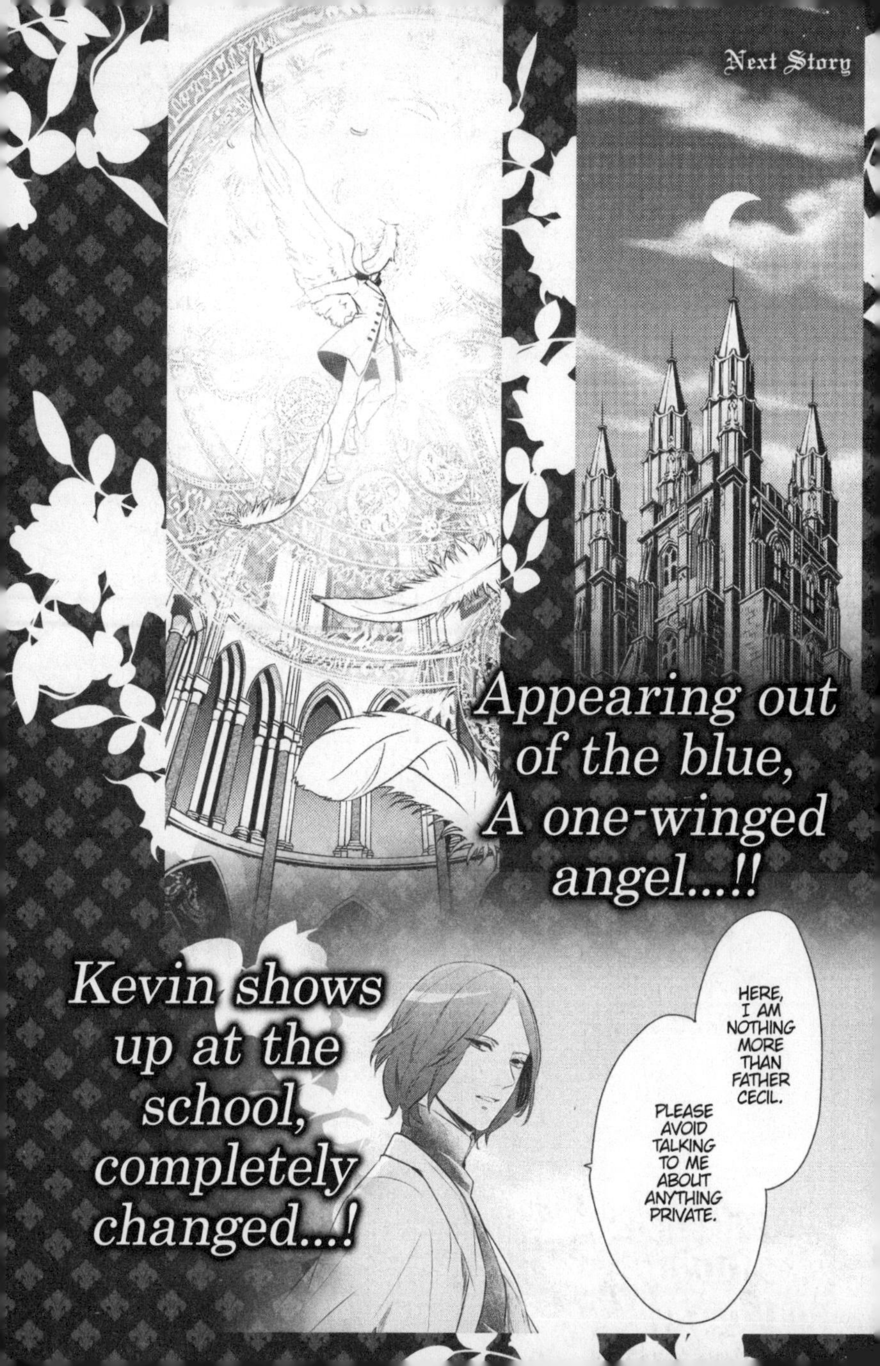

Next Story
Appearing out of the blue, A one-winged angel...!!
HERE, I AM NOTHING MORE THAN FATHER CECIL.
PLEASE AVOID TALKING TO ME ABOUT ANYTHING PRIVATE.
Kevin shows up at the school, completely changed...!

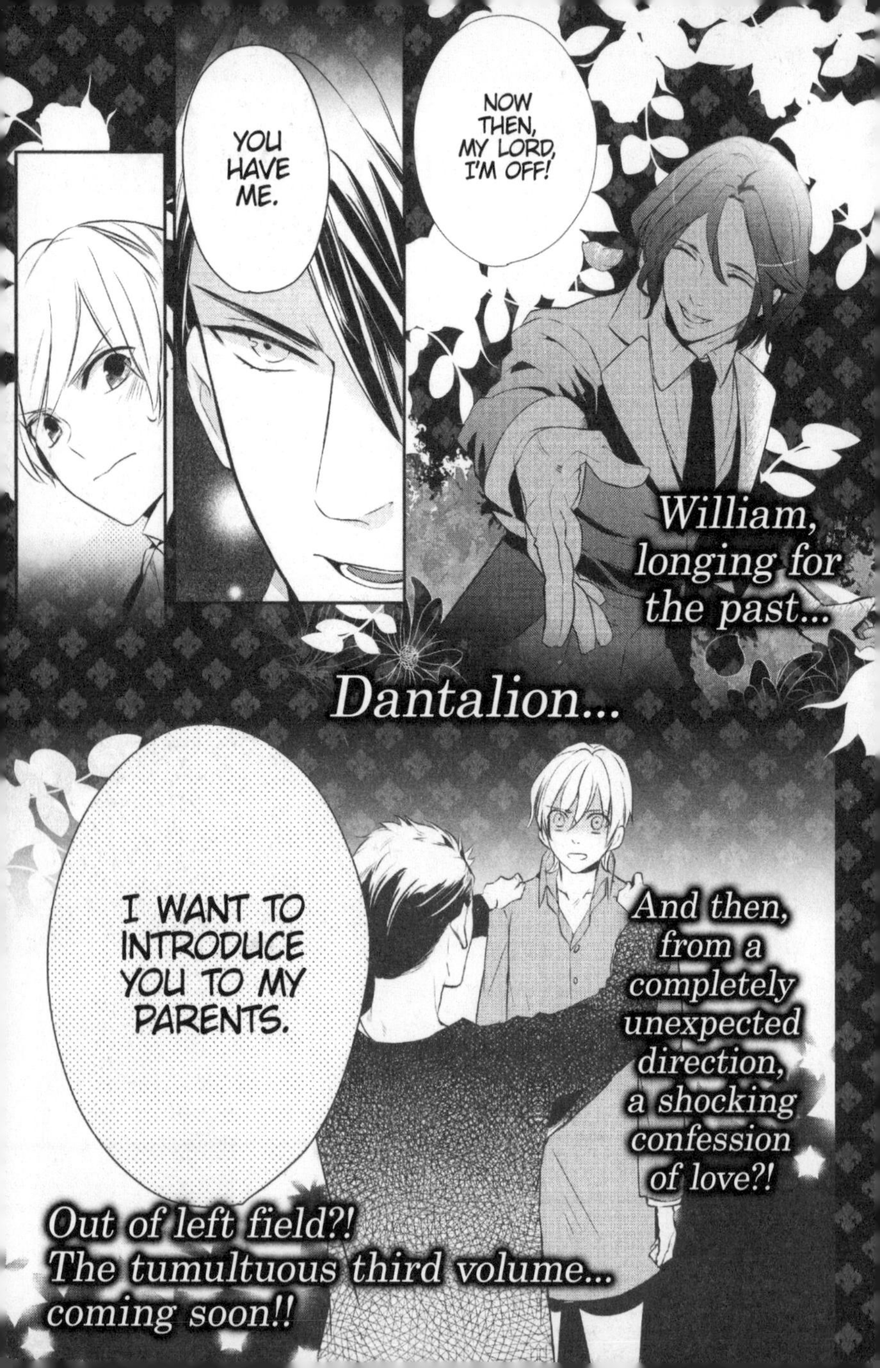
NOW THEN, MY LORD, I'M OFF!
YOU HAVE ME.
William, longing for the past...
Dantalion...
And then, from a completely unexpected direction, a shocking confession of love?!
I WANT TO INTRODUCE YOU TO MY PARENTS.
Out of left field?! The tumultuous third volume... coming soon!!

SEVEN SEAS ENTERTAINMENT PRESENTS

Devils a...

art by UTAKO YUKIHIRO / story by ...

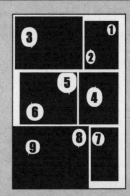

TRANSLATION
Jocelyne Allen

ADAPTATION
Danielle King

LETTERING
Roland Amago

LAYOUT
Bambi Eloriaga-Amago

COVER DESIGN
Nicky Lim

PROOFREADER
Lee Otter

MANAGING EDITOR
Adam Arnold

PUBLISHER
Jason DeAngelis

MAKAI OUJI: DEVILS AND REALIST VOL. 2
© Utako Yukihiro/Madoka Takadono 2010
First published in Japan in 2010 by ICHIJINSHA Inc., Tokyo.
English translation rights arranged with ICHIJINSHA Inc., Tokyo, Japan.

Seven Seas books may be purchased in bulk for educational, business, or
promotional use. For information on bulk purchases, please contact Macmillan
Corporate & Premium Sales Department at 1-800-221-7945 (ext 5442)
or write specialmarkets@macmillan.com.

Seven Seas and the Seven Seas logo are trademarks of
Seven Seas Entertainment, LLC. All rights reserved.

ISBN: 978-1-626920-42-2

Printed in the USA

First Printing: July 2014

10 9 8 7 6 5 4 3 2 1

FOLLOW US ONLINE: www.gomanga.com

READING DIRECTIONS

This book reads from *right to left*, Japanese style.
If this is your first time reading manga, you start
reading from the top right panel on each page and
take it from there. If you get lost, just follow the
numbered diagram here. It may seem backwards at
first, but you'll get the hang of it! Have fun!!